PAPA S

JIMMY BURNS is a prize-winning aut[hor] ... previous books are *The Land That Lost Its Heroes* (Somerset Maugham non-fiction prize, 1987), *Hand of God: The Life of Diego Maradona* and *Barça: A People's Passion*. He lives in London.

PAPA SPY

A true story of love, wartime espionage in Madrid, and the treachery of the Cambridge spies

JIMMY BURNS

BLOOMSBURY
LONDON · BERLIN · NEW YORK

First published in Great Britain 2009
This paperback edition published 2010

Bloomsbury Publishing Plc
36 Soho Square
London W1D 3QY

www.bloomsbury.com

Bloomsbury Publishing, London, New York and Berlin

A CIP catalogue record for this book is available from the British Library

ISBN 978 1 4088 0309 7

10 9 8 7 6 5 4 3 2 1

Typeset by Hewer Text UK Ltd, Edinburgh
Printed in Great Britain by Clays Ltd, St Ives plc

To K

CONTENTS

Preface

In my study where I write this now, there is a somewhat faded photograph of my late father, Tom Burns, and me, his youngest son, when I was a young boy growing up between Spain and England. He is painting a sea landscape from a cliff's edge somewhere, I believe, in the Basque country where we used to spend family holidays. I am sitting on the grass behind him, craning my neck up as if trying to discover what is on his canvas.

The photograph was taken in the mid-1950s when my father had established a reputation as a leading publisher with an extraordinary network of friends and professional associates he had built since the 1930s. They included writers like Evelyn Waugh and Graham Greene, whose early works he had helped publish or promote, senior figures at the BBC, and within the intelligence community, and, as I would belatedly discover, a member of the British royal family.

Publishing, including later editing the influential Catholic weekly *The Tablet*, was a job he devoted much of his public life to until his retirement, and one for which he was recognised in the obituaries published extensively in national newspapers following his death from cancer in 1995.

And yet through my own experiences of my father, from sharing his interest in the works of Ian Fleming, Len Deighton and John Le Carré, to introductions to some of his less public friends in London's club land, I had encountered other aspects of his life that seemed to point to a dedicated service to some secret government department or other, but which remained shrouded in mystery, if not mythology.

During the 1970s, when I was still sharing a flat with him, he came in one day from a reception at the Soviet embassy, clutching a bottle of vodka. Days later he seemed overjoyed that a Russian attaché he had befriended had been expelled from the UK for alleged spying activities. He showed even greater passion the day that Kim Philby, the MI6 officer who betrayed his country, died in Moscow. 'He was a traitor responsible for betraying many of my friends,' he raged over his whiskey.

Some of the 'friends' he introduced me to once I had begun my career as a journalist included senior figures in the Foreign Office and Ministry of Defence, as well as important figures in MI6, MI5, and the wartime Special Operations Executive who, while as helpful to me as they could possibly be, remained loyally protective of my father's past and present.

My father has taken some secrets with him to his grave, and much of his work during the Cold War years is still shrouded in official secrecy, apparently to protect agents, operations, and even family members that have outlived him, but he left me with some tantalising clues, sufficient for me to set out on a journey of discovery.

In our family home in London, few items fascinated me more as a child than the German-made handgun and a Minox miniature camera my father kept in his private study. The pistol, he told me once I was old enough to understand, had been taken as a small trophy from the German embassy in Madrid. The Minox, he spoke of as a useful work 'tool' in taking pictures of documents. I would later read that it had been standard issue to spies and their agents in the 1940s and 1950s.

I grew up knowing very little about what my father had got up to during the Second World War. All I knew was that he had not fought as a soldier like most of my friends' fathers, but had been on 'government service' in Spain, a country better known for its Civil War and a bloody dictator called Franco. Only much later would I discover the extent to which his work straddled the world of propaganda and espionage, and the controversial contribution he and others in the British embassy in Madrid made to Churchill's war effort, bolstering the Allied influence on Southern Europe and preventing the Germans from occupying Spain and North Africa, with Franco's help.

The *Generalísimo* Francisco Franco had been in power only five months when the Nazi panzer divisions rolled into Poland in September 1939. Franco had emerged triumphant from a bloody civil war that had left one million dead, an economy in tatters, and the majority of Spaniards in no mood to engage in another conflict. When the Allies declared war on Germany, Franco announced that his country would adopt the strictest neutrality. But the announcement barely hinted at the critical role Spain was to play in determining the outcome of the Second World War.

Germany's support for Franco during the Spanish Civil War had given Hitler a foothold south of the Pyrenees which the Fuhrer was determined to exploit. Franco, for his part, was surrounded by veterans of the Civil War who felt strongly identified with the Axis powers. With the German army sweeping across Northern Europe and poised to take France, by May 1940 Franco seemed certain of a German victory and considered forging a formal military alliance with Hitler and Mussolini. The potential consequences were only too clear to Churchill: German troops in large number crossing the Pyrenees, taking Gibraltar and the Spanish and Mediterranean ports, and delivering a potentially crippling blow to the Allied Cause.

It was at this juncture that Churchill appointed one of his most senior politicians and experienced ministers, Sir Samuel Hoare, as Britain's new ambassador to Spain. His task was to try to head off the growing German encroachment on the Iberian Peninsula, to maintain Spanish neutrality, and by so doing buy time so that the Allies could prepare their counter-offensive after the fall of France.

Hoare was not the only new arrival in the Spanish capital. Following close behind, and with none of the public and well documented fanfare surrounding Sir Samuel's entry into Spain, was the British embassy in Madrid's new first secretary and press attaché, Tom Burns.

While officially employed by the powerful MoI in running Allied propaganda across the Iberian Peninsula and in North Africa, Burns's covert role in the embassy included liaising with and reporting to the naval attaché, Captain Alan Hillgarth. Hillgarth had been Churchill's personal adviser on Iberian affairs since the Spanish Civil War, and oversaw special operations, POW escape routes, and – critically – secret intelligence activities headquartered in Madrid, including the bribing of Franco's general and officials.

In his own memoirs, published in 1946, my father's wartime ambassador – never known for his generosity of spirit towards his fellow peers, still less his own staff – commented in just a few lines that Tom Burns's assignment in Madrid was not without impact. He remarked that under Burns's 'vigorous direction, an insignificant section of the Embassy had developed into a great and imposing organisation'.

But the detail of this organisation has remained unknown until now largely because the war in Spain has been viewed from the perspective of official diplomacy, those who made a career of it, and other more public protagonists – and because my father trod in areas that the spies thought better kept secret, until at least they were ready to write their own official version of events.

It is many years since the boy who once gazed up at his father's painting grew up to work as a journalist with a special interest in Spain, and a fascination with the world of espionage. I count myself fortunate that in adulthood I forged a strong personal bond with my father that allowed me a unique access to a world whose doors have for far too long been closed to more widespread scrutiny by the general public.

These conversations and his own brief and selective memoirs, written in the fading light of his life – necessarily incomplete because they were written in a hurry by a dying man – provided some intriguing pointers and revelations about a life partly lived out in shadow. But it was only after his death in 1995 that I began to conceive of using my father's experiences as a way of drawing a broader picture of how propaganda, and secret intelligence in the Second World War played such a central role in Spain and neighbouring Portugal, with Madrid a key centre of special operations both for the Allies and the Nazis.

My initial task involved trying to locate the few survivors of a rapidly disappearing generation of men and women who had known my father from the 1930s, and even earlier. It proved a challenging assignment.

The trail took me from an old people's home in Wiltshire to a mountain village outside Madrid, and involved a trip across the Atlantic. Along the way I interviewed an eclectic group of retired characters, from one-time English secretaries who had handled secret codes to Spanish countesses who had once worked as spies; from one-time Spanish Civil War urchins who had run secret errands for the British embassy, to former ambassadors. Not only were several of the individuals I was interested in beginning to suffer from memory loss, but there were others who despite admitting to working for or alongside my father, claimed they were still covered by the Official Secrets Act.

Nevertheless I managed to find a sufficient number of witnesses in reasonably good shape among my father's network of friends and former colleagues, who were happy to co-operate despite knowing that I intended to write about my father 'warts and all'. Sons and daughters filled in some of the gaps left by those who had long since died.

I was given the full co-operation of my own family members both in Spain and in England, led by my late mother Mabel Marañón, who generously shared her own memories before these sadly faded with the advent of dementia. This book is in part her story too, for it was in wartime Spain that my parents met and married in a wedding that became an event in the history of Anglo-Spanish relations.

I should point out that while providing a great deal of detail about a crucial period in my father's life, this is not in any sense a biography, still less an official one. I have focused on my father as a controversial player in the secret war in Spain, as a way of shedding new light on the ideological and personal tensions behind the Spanish Civil War, and some of the dramatic episodes of the Second World War.

For context and background, I have benefited from a growing bibliography emerging both on the history of Franco's Spain and the no-less-extensive outpouring of books on the intelligence world that have been published over the years on both sides of the Atlantic. But while I am also conscious of the popularity of certain novels fictionalising wartime Spain, my intention has been to deal with facts and only occasionally to speculate on the balance of reasonable probability. The period I cover is so rich in real personalities and incidents that it makes invention redundant.

This book took shape and substance during a five-year investigation that led me, in addition to numerous interviews, to hundreds of documents buried in family and government archives, and university libraries in the UK, Spain, and the US.

Half-way through my researches, I was given rare access to Franco's personal archive, which confirmed the *Generalísimo's* grip on power, while providing a fascinating insight into the extent to which the Spanish secret police – often in co-operation with the Germans – monitored the activities of the British embassy, and considered my father a key player in an intelligence game that was more often tolerated than obstructed by the Spanish authorities.

On a more personal front, I also discovered hundreds of wartime love letters which had been written to the late Ann Bowes-Lyon by my father, during a tempestuous affair conducted prior to his marriage, and which Ann – the Queen's mother's cousin – had kept secret until her death. The letters were hidden in an outhouse of her country home and their existence was kindly brought to my attention by Anton D'Abreu, her son.

Ann shared several male friends with Tom Burns, her controversial suitor, although not all of his Catholic friends approved. Auberon Waugh, Evelyn's son, claimed that my father had approached his father once to seek his advice on what to wear in Ann's aristocratic family presence. 'A gentleman would probably wear tweeds, but you, Burns, should wear high-heeled boots and carnations behind the ears,' quipped Evelyn.

Thankfully my father secured a more stable relationship with my mother, one that allowed him to develop professionally and deepen his love of Spain and its people, even if this clouded his judgement of the Franco regime in a way that led some of his detractors to consider him a German agent.

One certainty that emerges from my research is that my father was not – as he was suspected by Franco, and named as such in Stephen Dorrill's history of the service – the head of MI6 in wartime Spain. He was much too controversial and strident in fighting his own corner to subject himself to control by any organisation. He did recruit agents, gather and report secret information, and was involved with other spies in some of the more high-risk propaganda and covert operations of wartime Spain.

The extent to which my father made as many enemies as friends in the intelligence world in the Second World War was made clear to me in February 2008, while I was in the midst of writing the first draft chapters of this book. Quite unexpectedly, I received word through a friendly source that files secretly held by the security service MI5 on my father for sixty-seven years had been approved for release and that I would be able to look at them first. They were and I did.

The files – a rather more generous offering than the disparate secret papers that I had so far obtained from a variety of sources, were among the latest batch of Second World War files transferred for public scrutiny at the National Archive by the intelligence world, with official historians being appointed to be part of the selection process.

The files that were handed to me covered the years my father was in Madrid, 1941–46, and were packed with an assortment of reports by double agents, internal exchanges between MI5 and MI6 officers, memos written by my father and others he considered to be his friends.

Information ranged from the seemingly incontrovertible – my father writing in support of Spanish journalists who were later suspected of being German spies – to flippant observations and tawdry gossip, such as the fact that my father was not British born, and was suspected of speaking with a slight foreign accent, or that he liked dancing and had a reputation as a womaniser.

In the end one of the most striking aspects of the files was that they were largely written and complied by individuals who were later exposed or suspected of being Soviet agents, such as Kim Philby, Anthony Blunt, and Tomas Harris. They showed a strongly subjective bias against my father because of his support for Franco during the Spanish Civil War, and his opposition to any attempt by the Allies and the left to force the overthrow of the Spanish regime during the Second World War, although they were written at a time when paranoia about fifth-column activity by German agents was at its height.

The files, however, make it clear that this view of Burns as fascist and potential traitor was not by any means shared by other sectors of the intelligence community, still less the Foreign Office, who valued highly Burns's sources and the reporting that ensued from them. While never trained as a spy, and considered a potential Walter Mitty by some of his colleagues because of his 'foreign' blood and fervent Catholic faith, Burns impressed key figures in his embassy and the Churchill government with the quality of his sources and the accuracy of reporting out of Madrid, Lisbon, and Tangier. The last volume of the file I was handed ends in 1948, just as the Cold War was getting under way. Within a few years Philby and the other Cambridge spies had been exposed and defected. By then my father was on the side of the angels.

As for me, the true father I set out to discover remains elusive if only because his mixed background and Catholicism account for his contradictions in wartime as in peace. He fell in love with two very different women, had a network of friends that crossed ideological, cultural, and theological boundaries, enjoyed his Garrick Club as much as his bullfights, was theologically liberal and politically conservative, in work and play a hard-nosed pragmatist and inveterate romantic, and in the end was considered both a good spy and a bad one, both morally and professionally.

I have woven his story into the bigger picture of life in London, Spain, Portugal, and North Africa during those defining years of the Second World War. The broader canvas is a story of personal courage, intrigue, passion, betrayal and enduring faith.

I remain indebted to the late Tom Ferrier Burns, and the late Mabel Marañón Moya, without whose existence I would not have the story, nor be here to write it. In their lifetime they were always hugely supportive of me as a journalist and author, and were the most loving parents I could have hoped for. While they may not have approved of some of the material that I have uncovered, they always encouraged my reverence for truth and it is in that spirit that I have written this book.

The seed for this book was planted by *The Use of Memory*, my father's memoir published in 1993, two years before his death. The memoirs are not so much an autobiography as an elegant work of letters, composed of several different strands, and largely focused on his Catholicism, from his schooldays with the Jesuits to his campaigning period as an editor passionately defending the reforms of Vatican 11. The book was praised for the deft and perceptive characterisation of the fascinating friendships that enriched his life, but it left its mainly Catholic reviewers arguing over his interpretation of the faith.

*   *   *

While sympathetic to the view that my father's conscience would require him to focus on his relationship with his God in his dying days, I was not alone in viewing his memoirs as an opportunity missed to write more about his wartime years which he covered as a series of impressionistic sketches. Nonetheless one reviewer described his short account of his time in Madrid as a 'scintillating tragi-comedy like some pages from Greeneland'. The chapter ends with my father remarking enigmatically that during his 'parenthetical appointment nothing was quite what it seemed to be, and nobody was quite himself'.

The idea that such a world of intrigue might be worth exploring was initially shared with and accepted by my then agent, Caroline Dawnay at Peters, Fraser & Dunlop, and by my then editor at Bloomsbury, Mike Jones. Both subsequently moved to new organisations, but their generosity of spirit was such that they did all they could to ensure that the project remained on track.

My researches into the correspondence between my father and some of his friends and a widening list of useful contacts within the retired intelligence community in the United States was hugely assisted by Nicholas Scheetz at Georgetown University. The staff and residents of John J. Burns Library and Fr Philip Kiley at St Mary's in Boston College provided further assistance in tracing relevant material.

During an extended sabbatical in the US, Jackie Quillen generously provided hospitality in Georgetown, Washington DC, as did my nephews James and Peter Parker, and their respective wives Kristen and Susie, in Boston and New York. In Massachusetts Nigel and Katherine Adam provided additional company and accommodation. Special thanks for an informative lunch, exchange of emails, and a book, go to a long-term friend of my Spanish family, Mrs Archibald Roosevelt.

The curator of the CIA's Historical Intelligence Collection, Hayden B. Peake, offered some useful insights into Kim Philby one evening at the Special Forces Club, while Katherine Gresham helped me order and make sense of the private papers of her uncle-in-law, the late intelligence officer Walter Bell, as did his widow Tatti, since deceased. There were others who helped on both sides of the Atlantic who asked not be identified and I have respected that.

In the UK, some of the experts in the field came to my rescue on the frustrating occasions I hit a brick wall of official secrecy and Whitehall bureaucracy. I was particularly fortunate in counting on the guidance of Whitehall expert Professor Peter Hennessy, of Professor Keith Jeffery, official historian of MI6, and, in even greater measure, of Professor Christopher Andrew and Dr Peter Martland, official historians of MI5.

Thanks to Chris and Peter I was able not only to draw on their insights, but also to engage in a fruitful exchange of information with their inspired and hardworking postgraduate students and fellows at Cambridge University, of whom I would like to make special mention of Calder Walton, Owen Ryan, and Tony Craig.

On certain aspects of signals intelligence and special operations, thanks go to my helper at GCHQ and to Duncan Stuart and Professor Michael Foot, who provided me with relevant documents and other useful information. Antony Beevor generously pitched in with some useful additional insights and clarifications in the later stages of research.

In Spain and Germany, José de Pascual Antonio Luca de Tena proved a diligent researcher, and Ana Momplet a good insurance against losing meanings in translation. In the Basque country, Juan Carlos Jiménez de Aberasturi encouraged me to look at escape routes and hidden connections.

In Portugal, the Municipality of Cascais, Ana Vicente and Michael Stowe were as always both welcoming and supportive, as were the descendants of Roy Campbell, led by Frances Cavero.

Others who have helped along the way include Professor Paul Preston, Professor Hugh Thomas, Professor Luis Suárez, Dr Collado Seidel (in Germany and Spain), Javier Juárez, Pablo Kessler, Antonio Lopera, Victor and Philip Mallet, Mary Uzzell Edwards, Magdalene Goffin, Jonathan Stordy, the late Peter Laing, the late Marquesa de Santa Cruz, the Countess of Romanones, Mary Keen, Bernard Dru, Mary Walsh, Septimus Waugh, Ian Thomson, Tessa Frank, Michael Walsh, Philip Vickers, Alma Starkie, Alan Hunt, Carlos Sentís, José Luis García Fernández, Patricia Martínez Vicente, Tristan Hillgarth, Dolores Jaraquemada, Pepe Maestre, the Haynes and Gómez-Beare families, Rafael Gómez Jordana – father and son, Philip Wright OBE, Frank Porral, Julia Stonor, Patrick Buckley, Julia Holland, Hallam and John Murray, Jaime Carvajal de Urquijo, Piru Urquijo, Michael Richey, Denis McShane, Iñaki Goiogana, Vincent O'Doherty, Sir Raymond Carr, Pat Davies, José Antonio Muñoz Rojas, Paul Burns, John Cumming, Juan Fernández Armesto, Felipe Fernández Armesto, Rafa Gandarios, Iñigo Gurruchaga, Jaime Salas, Colin Cresswell, the late Barbara Wall, Olive Stirling, Helen Oliver, Begoña Cortina, Tom Catan, Mark Mulligan, Leslie Crawford, Isa Gutiérrez de la Cámara.

Thanks too to the library staff at the *Financial Times* – Peter Cheek, Bhavna Patel, and Neil McDonald, and those who showed me where to look at the National Archives in Kew, the London Library, the Fundación Francisco Franco, the Hemeroteca Municipal del Ayuntamiento de Madrid, the Museo de Historia de Madrid, the library of Municipal History in Madrid, the Spanish Ministry of Foreign Affairs, Archivo de Nacionalismo Vasco – Fundación Sabino Arana, Cambridge University Library, the British embassy in Madrid, and the Garrick Club.

My former editor Lionel Barber and colleagues at the FT, not least George Parker, Alex Barker, and Jim Pickard, gave me time, and space, and much necessary humour in the early stages of researching this book, before I left the newspaper. Special thanks to Ben Fenton and Fred Studermann who provided advice, translation, and logistical support, as did Richard Norton-Taylor and Alan Travis of the *Guardian*.

Early drafts took shape thanks to meticulous reading by Robert Graham, Peter Martland, Hugh Thomas, my brother Tom Burns, and Anton D'Abreu.

My brother David Burns and sister Lady Parker showed their support by allowing me – the youngest of the family – to draw on the family archive, and raised no objections to the project.

Thanks to Annabel Merullo and Tom Williams at PFD and Bill Swainson and Anna Simpson at Bloomsbury the project came to life again. And the biggest, biggest thanks of all go to Kidge, Julia, and Miriam who endured the book from gestation to birth.

London/Madrid, May 2009

1

CATHOLIC ROOTS

When his Majesty's ambassador to Madrid Sir Samuel Hoare first saw Tom Burns striding purposefully towards him across the room, we do not know what he thought but we can surmise that he wondered whether Burns was suited to the competing demands for delicate diplomacy, propaganda, and secret intelligence in the Spain of the Second World War. Prior to taking up residence in the Spanish capital, Hoare had been an MI6 station chief in pre-Revolutionary Russia and a senior diplomat in Rome before going on to serve as Foreign Secretary, First Lord of the Admiralty, Lord Privy Seal, Home Secretary, Secretary of State for India and Secretary of State for Air.

Forty years of public service had given Hoare an instinctive wariness of outsiders. With his dark hair, suave looks and impeccable manners, the wartime embassy's latest recruit appeared to Hoare to be someone playing the role of an Englishman without actually being one. His name, his light green-grey eyes, and fair skin suggested Celtic blood, but he also had a Latin swagger about him. The fact that Burns had been born in Chile and was a fervent Catholic further fuelled his suspicion.

Hoare, at sixty years old, was nearly twice Burns's age. Unmistakably Anglo-Saxon in appearance and from a staunchly Anglican background, he was cut from quite a different cloth. In his own memoirs, Hoare described himself as 'very English, very respectable, and very traditional'. According to the experts in the College of Arms, there were few families with a longer all-English descent than the Hoares. The ambassador was also well read in British military and colonial history.

When addressing the challenge facing his special wartime mission – that of stopping the Germans from marching into neutral Spain – Hoare was fond of quoting a memorandum from one of his heroes, the Duke of Wellington, to Viscount Castlereagh in the aftermath of the Napoleonic Wars. 'There is no country in Europe in the affairs of which foreigners can interfere with so little advantage as Spain. There is no country in which foreigners are more disliked, and even despised, and whose manners and habits are so little congenial with those of other nations in Europe.'

Be that as it may, Sir Samuel Hoare's responsibility was to keep Franco's Spain neutral, and yet this passionate English Catholic was the man he had been sent to run his press office and win the propaganda war.

Tom Burns was born in the Chilean seaside resort of Viña del Mar in 1906, the seventh child of David Burns, a Scotsman who had gone to South America from his home in Brechin to seek a livelihood as a bank manager. His mother, Clara Swinburne, while descended from English North Country stock as well as of Basque blood, was Chilean-born and bred. The Burnses left for London after a devastating earthquake nearly killed the baby of the family before destroying the family home. My father was only six months old when the roof collapsed over him, leaving his nanny partly buried under the rubble and himself miraculously alive with his only injury a cut lip. A permanent scar left an enduring reminder of survival in the midst of disaster. Tom Burns was a cradle Catholic, owing his early spiritual nourishment to his mother, Clara.

In fact her influence in the family was so great that on her arrival in England it drew her husband away from his Scottish Presbyterianism and towards induction into a Catholic Church that was undergoing a revival across Europe, and nowhere more than in Britain. By the early twentieth century, the influence of Cardinal Newman in drawing Anglicans closer to Rome, and the literary cache of Catholic writers like Hilaire Belloc and G.K. Chesterton, brought in their wake a new generation of young intellectuals who saw in their religion the only valid alternative to chaos.

Burns's father was austere and dedicated to his life in the City at a time when a banker was trusted as a counsellor by his customers.

He was also enormously appreciative of books. He had returned from Chile with a huge library: Conrad, Dickens, Henry James, George Eliot, as well as the French classics bound in handsome editions. He was fond of making Shakespeare his main point of reference during his rare intrusions into family life. Hearing his daughters arguing in the playroom, he would murmur to himself, '*Her voice was ever sweet, gentle and low – an excellent thing in a woman.*' Keats would occasionally come to the rescue, as when he once trod in a dog mess on the front porch and lamented, '*I cannot see what flowers are at my feet*'. Such eccentricities would mark his youngest son, turning him into something of a maverick in later life. And yet it was the mother's deeply ingrained religion that prevailed. Like his three older brothers, Burns was educated by the Jesuits. 'Give me a boy at seven, and he is mine for life,' goes the old Jesuit saying. At seven Burns was sent to Wimbledon College, a Jesuit school in west London, where he began to be formally instructed in the basics of Catholic dogma as laid down in the Catechism.

Burns found himself absorbing the mysteries of a faith that had at its core the doctrine of the Real Presence. He munched on his first Communion wafer, and sipped at the chalice, fully believing that this was the Body and Blood of Jesus Christ, as recited by the priest, and that the words were part of the same kind of mystification as that experienced by the apostles at the Last Supper.

Burns's second year of Catholic schooling coincided with the outbreak of the First World War. It was a time, he would later recall, that brought him closer to his father, as the only son left at home. They played a lot of chess and pored over a large map of the Western Front, moving little flags as the fortunes of war fluctuated. Only later would the personal agonies behind such symbols touch the Burns household with brutal suddenness.

Burns, his parents, four sisters (he was followed now by Alice, two years younger) and two brothers (a third, George, was studying for the priesthood) were on holiday by the sea in Felixstowe, Suffolk, on 4 August 1914, when the life as he and his siblings had enjoyed it together – treasure hunts in the garden, tea dances, tennis parties – died. The front page of the *Daily Mirror* on that day was wholly taken up with a photograph of the Kaiser with his waxed moustache and wearing the helmet of the Death's Head Hussars. By that afternoon British soldiers were already digging trenches in the garden which overlooked the sea. Burns's two older brothers – Charles and David – enlisted in the army, while his oldest sister Dorothy left her convent school and volunteered as a nurse in a military hospital.

Charles survived, invalided out after being injured, and returned to his medical studies, but David, an officer in the Black Watch, was killed in Flanders during the third Battle of Ypres, on 1 October, 1 day short of his twentieth birthday and six weeks before the Armistice of 1918.

The Burnses were enthusiastic letter writers from an early age. During the last weeks of his life, David wrote regularly to his youngest sister, Alice, who was a nine-year-old schoolgirl at the time, writing letters home that barely hinted at the horrors of the sodden trenches and the killing fields beyond. In early September 1918, he wrote with darkening humour: 'Thank you very much for your interesting letter and the drawing of me in a gas mask. I will do my best to gratify your desires for a *Hun* helmet but at present I'm afraid the nearest I've been to the wily *Bosche* is when he comes over and bombs us like he did last night.'

Burns (then aged twelve) was with his sister Alice and their mother when the telegram bearing the news of David's death arrived. After opening it, Clara sat stunned in the hall, with the paper in her hands, silenced by shock, and waiting for her husband to return from his job in the City. She told her children to restrain their tears and to mourn silently. 'There was no more plotting of little flags on the map,' recalled Burns many years later. 'Our war was over. Quite soon it was for everyone and they went mad with joy so that an awful irony was added to our empty world.'

Days later a Roman Catholic chaplain wrote to say that David had taken Holy Communion a few days before being first wounded in the leg and then shot in the head by a German machine-gunner. His regimental commander commended him for his skills as a runner and his bravery in the line of fire. Then David's adjutant, Tim Milroy, returned from the front and married Burns's second sister Clarita. Later Tim introduced his younger brother Bill to Alice, and they too eventually married. Burns's faith in God was rekindled, and he would long treasure, with a mixture of worship and trepidation, the enduring memory of his beloved and heroic brother, an awkward role model of selfless sacrifice in the line of duty, cut off in the flower of youth.

Burns was fourteen when, two years after the end of the Great War, he went to Stonyhurst College, a leading Catholic boarding school in the north of England also run by Jesuits. Stonyhurst considered itself unique, with a history of its early founders beginning in exile during the Elizabethan persecution of Catholics, the first boys drawn from recusant homes near Blackburn, Lancashire. While firm in its Catholicism, it was a school that also drew its identity from its loyalty to the British state. Thus, near a centuries-old room full of original portraits dedicated to the Stuart royal lineage the Reformation had interrupted, was a memorial to more than a thousand old boys who had died for King and Country, six of them decorated with the Victoria Cross.

Burns's best school friend Henry John, a son of the painter Augustus, was a soldier of sorts, but not in any traditional sense. John was infused with an adventurous and polemical spirit that flourished in the spirit of enquiry that some Jesuits teachers encouraged among their students, most notably a sage called Fr Martin D'Arcy. Under his tutelage the two boys developed a fondness for theology and a belief that in their faith lay the key to confronting the materialism of the prevailing culture. They chose to become militant evangelisers.

With the encouragement of their teachers, Burns and John spent their holiday time at Speaker's Corner in Hyde Park. There, mounted on soap boxes, the young crusaders expounded various 'truths' of their Catholic doctrine amidst much heckling from the largely agnostic crowd.

With the end of schooldays came a sense of a bigger world and an even greater longing to be part of a universal Church capable of transforming the experience of it. John was persuaded by his Jesuit mentors to further his religious studies in Rome as a step towards joining the order himself. He was about to make his final vows when Burns suggested they take a journey together, away from the rigours of life near the Vatican. By boat, train and camel, the two friends travelled to Libya and Tunisia in search of the troglodytes who lived below ground level, and of the Ouled Nail, belly dancers of legendary sensuality. They discovered remnants of the troglodytes in countless caves dug into the sides of vast craters near Togourt, and shades and phrases of St Augustine amidst the stones of Carthage.

For the two friends, the journey proved to be the parting of the ways. John returned to England where he embarked on the final stages of his training for the priesthood. Despite securing the necessary academic qualifications, Burns decided against applying for Oxford or Cambridge, believing that it would mean a financial strain on his parents and a postponement of a more challenging world beyond British shores that he was anxious to discover.

Thus, with 'an open mind and a small purse', he decided to pursue his studies in France, and one day in 1924 caught a train to Paris to seek out the vibrant intellectual life of French Catholicism that was then flourishing on the Left Bank. He had just turned eighteen. In Paris, Burns rented a room in a 'sleazy hotel' in Montparnasse before immersing himself in the writings of French Catholic philosophers who boldly proclaimed the dawn of a new era of social and spiritual transformation. They ranged from the neo-fascism of Charles Maurras's Action Française to the neo-Thomist theology of Jacques Maritain, politically on the left if still opposed to its agnosticism, and proclaiming instead the imminence and immediacy of God in all things.

It was in Paris that Burns dabbled in the bohemianism of the Left Bank bookshop Shakespeare & Company, the meeting place for aspirant American writers, and shared a mutual if platonic infatuation with Gwen John, sister of Augustus, mistress of Rodin and lesbian lover of Maritain's sister-in-law. Burns and the much older Gwen – his best friend's aunt – spent much of their time maintaining their tense relationship in intimate conversations, when not writing letters to each other about their common faith.

On his return to London a year later, Burns revived his public-speaking assignments proclaiming the revival of pan-European Catholicism; he would later compare proselytising to the work of a 'secret agent in a foreign land, carried out with a mixture of excitement and dread of self-betrayal'. Enlisted by the Catholic Evidence Guild, an organisation of lay volunteers, Burns campaigned with the missionary zeal he had learnt from the Jesuits, convinced of the truth of his faith, and happy to take on hecklers.

They included equivalent fanatics from the Protestant Alliance and the Rationalist Association. 'With their bowler hats and mackintoshes and loud rasping voices, I imagined them as KGB men,' Burns later recalled. The Guild had been founded in 1918, the year after the Russian Revolution.

It was through the Guild that Burns met his first employers, an Australian called Frank Sheed and his English wife, Maisie Ward. The couple were not only street-corner evangelists, but also ran a successful family publishing firm. Burns carried publishing in his blood. His great uncle James was a Catholic convert who had published the works of Newman under the imprint Burns & Oates.

While there was no family succession to the firm because James Burns's son became a priest, Tom Burns had always revered the memory of his great uncle and dreamed of one day bringing the Burns family back into the business. Burns cut his own literary teeth as a commissioning editor before a prompt promotion to manager with Sheed & Ward, whose owners had identified the commercial potential of the growing Catholic revival and its engagement with the mainstream of literary and political debate.

Soon after joining the publishing house, Burns pulled off a coup, securing the rights in 1926 to Belloc's *A Companion to H.G. Wells' Outline of History*. The book formed part of a heated debate between Belloc – one of the literary icons and father figures of the Catholic revival – and Wells, the atheist who gave utopian visions precedence over spiritual realities.

Burns had first met Belloc when he was still a schoolboy. He had read Belloc's *The Path to Rome* and then written to the author for advice on how to cross the Pyrenees on foot, the subject of another book in which he combined a Catholic instinct for pilgrimage with an explorer's love for adventure through travel. Belloc had responded to the young man's enquiry by inviting him to a meeting at the Reform Club. There he drew sketch maps of mountain paths and recommended an inn on the Spanish–French border for accommodation.

Within minutes of entering Spain, Burns found himself hopelessly lost in the mountains. He lacked a compass, and Belloc's instructions proved an inadequate reference point for the plethora of paths which seemed to straggle in all directions. Burns followed a path that ran parallel to a stream and eventually came across what he took to be a guardian angel – a woman leading a donkey laden with firewood, on her way to the nearby village. There, as the sun dipped behind the mountains, Burns found a religious procession forming, led by a priest wrapped in a golden chasuble and protected by a canopy under which he held a large communion host in a monstrance.

Burns picked up a candle and accompanied the other men of the village as they walked slowly behind the priest through the cobbled streets, in a murmured litany of hymns and prayer. It was the feast of Corpus Christi, one of the great events of the Catholic calendar. And on this, his first visit to Spain, Burns was enthralled by the folklore and the strong undercurrent of mysticism which he had felt was blended as nowhere else.

He spent the rest of his time in the Pyrenees travelling through nearby villages with a troupe of performing dogs and their owners. Their most popular act had a terrier dressed up as a priest witnessing a wedding between two other dogs dressed as bride and groom. The central joke had the 'bride' repeatedly straying from the marriage service and collapsing on a nuptial bed with her hind legs in the air, before being pulled back to the ceremony by the 'priest'. Thus did Spain unravel itself with its unique blend of piety, sensuality and anarchic irreverence. Reflecting on that period in his memoirs, Burns identified a foreshadowing of critical moments in his life by intimations that were not recognised as such at the time, but which came to find a place in a pattern as the years went by. He called his schoolboy Pyrenean adventure the first Spanish prologue.

After Belloc came other 'names' which Burns attracted to his growing publisher's list. The Catholic literary icon G.K. Chesterton offered Burns a book of verses, *Our Lady of the Sorrows*, and later a book of essays. On the rare occasion that G.K. was neither on a ritual drinking binge with Belloc nor cloistered with his wife at their house in Beaconsfield, Chesterton invited Burns to take a taxi ride with him through central London. As the cab passed the Cenotaph, G.K. cut short their conversation and in silence raised his hat to salute the memorial to Britain's war dead. Like the portraits of the old Stonyhurst boys who had won the VC, the image of Chesterton's tribute would for ever remain in Burns's memory as an example of how English Catholics could both defend their faith *and* be loyal patriots at the same time. G.K. had been one of Burns's idols during his schooldays and was to remain so for decades, his writing – so it seemed to his young publisher – as light and dexterous and timeless as a coracle.

And yet perhaps the most innovative if controversial of Burns's early stable of authors was Eric Gill, the woodcutter and sculptor whose writings and works of art came to have a defining influence on numerous Catholics during the 1920s and 1930s. Burns was seventeen when he visited Gill for the first time, the sculptor's junior by twenty-four years, but the gap seemed to narrow as they found common ground on matters of faith and art. Gill and his family were living in a community of other artists and craftsmen first at Ditchling, in Sussex. They later moved to Pigotts, near High Wycombe in Buckinghamshire, where Burns became a frequent visitor as publisher and friend. 'Pigotts came to be a weekend home-from-home for me,' Burns later recalled. 'In those years one was alert to everything that life had to offer, negotiating a minefield of ideas and emotions in a no-man's-land between opposed trenches: those of my faith and those of the world outside. Pigotts seemed to me a safe billet if ever there was one.'

By the early 1930s Burns was living in Glebe Place, off the King's Road, Chelsea, near his friend Harman Grisewood, a BBC announcer who was destined to rise high in the Corporation. A contemporary of Evelyn Waugh at Oxford, Grisewood's cocktail parties were immortalised in Waugh's novel *Vile Bodies* as those given in 'basement flats by spotty announcers', although the author may have also been thinking, less generously, of John Heygate, a BBC news editor he held responsible for the break-up of his first marriage to Evelyn Gardner. A letter survives from this period giving a sense of how Burns enjoyed life outside his working hours. It is written by Grisewood to David Jones, the Welsh artist and writer whom Burns had befriended at Eric Gill's and added to his growing Catholic network. While the subject of the letter is the advice Grisewood wants to give Jones about book writing, the BBC man struggles to concentrate in the presence of Burns, who appears to be in a state of woman-induced euphoria: '. . . Tom is dancing a tremendous dance and his room strewn with rejected white ties, and enigmatically, fragments of a charming crystal necklace'.

By the early- to mid-1930s several of the generation that had celebrated a cult of youth in the 1920s as a band of pleasure-seeking bohemians had become increasingly dispersed. But if, as D.J. Taylor has put it, something of the 'original spark' had gone out of the *Bright Young Things*, turning the one-time fanatics of the party-going scene into jaded veterans, the Catholics among them still seemed to flourish in a network that managed to accommodate both success and spiritual anxiety.

While Burns pursued his publishing career, building up an impressive list of authors, his best school friend Henry John was thrown into emotional turmoil by the intense, if platonic, friendship he had formed with his mentor Fr D'Arcy and his struggle to cope with the obligations of celibacy imposed on his training to be a Jesuit priest. In 1934 John abandoned the Jesuit order and embarked on a series of doomed affairs with women. By the summer of 1935 John had fallen in love with Olivia Plunket Greene, one of the more enduring survivors of the *Bright Young Person* society.

A complex personality, Plunket Greene had left a trail of shattered loves behind her, including Evelyn Waugh, and continued to attract men like moths to a light. She mirrored the young John with her tortured mixture of repressed sexuality and religious faith. The girl who was happy to party, get drunk, and tease her suitors to the brink of intercourse was also the girl that claimed to have visions of the Virgin Mary urging her to a life of chastity.

That summer, Plunket Greene rejected John's plea that they should sleep together with a letter insisting that she could not enter an 'immoral' relationship with him. Soon after receiving it, John swam out to sea off the coast of Cornwall and drowned. His body was washed up two weeks later, having, as his father Augustus put it, 'suffered the attention of sea gulls'. Burns, one of Olivia's enduring male friends with whom he shared an unconsummated mutual attraction, refused to accept that he might have committed suicide as others believed.

While assuming a sense of guilt in the sorry affair – it was he who had introduced Henry John to Plunket Greene – Burns would later claim that by the mid-1930s his friendship with his best old school friend had cooled somewhat. 'Henry had given much more than joy to my youth, but his last years had disclosed a chasm between us and had filled me with foreboding,' Burns wrote in his memoirs.

These were halcyon years before there were even rumours of war, with a packed diary of cocktail parties, debutante balls and nightclubs. Burns discovered that he was on an informal hostess register, much in demand for his dashing looks, intelligence, manners and skills as a dancer. When not dressing up in white tie and tails and taking a debutante to her ball, Burns would drink several whiskies from his personal bottle at one or other of his habitual night dives the Gargoyle, Hell and the 43, where the lights were low, the music less controlled, the women looser.

It was on one such night that Tom Burns and Evelyn Waugh got to know each other in a nightclub of dubious repute. The fact that Burns had some foreign blood in him, and had not gone to Oxford, marked him out as different from the undergraduate friends Waugh had stuck with since public school. But they shared friends in common they had come to know independently from each other. Both men cultivated extensive contacts in the literary world and had learnt to comport themselves in patrician circles. Waugh and Burns shared a snobbism that attracted them to and filled them with admiration for the English upper-class. They were also both fascinated by matters of faith. According to Burns, when he met Waugh the author – then close to conversion to Catholicism – saw himself as a man who had joined a regiment 'with traditions and rules which he never questioned'. As someone who had taken to the soapbox in defence of the Catholic faith, Burns respected such loyalty.

Burns and his circle of Catholic friends contemplated the emergence of communism, and the spread of industrialism, and feared the erosion of the sacral in daily living, an alienating period in history which threatened to undermine civilisation itself. The challenge was to shake up the Catholic Church and its members in a way that might increase their relevance and their influence in modern society.

A key battleground for the reform movement was the media, so it was perhaps unsurprising that Burns should single out the *Tablet* as a target for a takeover. The *Tablet* was an intellectual Catholic weekly which, under the ownership of the Catholic Primate of Great Britain, the Archbishop of Westminster Cardinal Bourne, had adopted an editorial line that Burns regarded as 'sectarian and puritanical, pompous and parochial'. As Catholicism entered the 1930s, Burns coordinated a thinly veiled campaign of criticism of the magazine, attacking in particular the theologically conservative editor, Ernest Oldmeadow.

The conflict between Burns and Oldmeadow was a sparring match that needed a specific issue of major principle to develop into open warfare. The spark that lit the fuse was the publication in 1932 of Evelyn Waugh's novel *Black Mischief*. The book was widely acclaimed, but Oldmeadow found its comic treatment of African politics and social mores, particularly a thinly disguised parody of Roman Catholic teaching on birth control, morally reprehensible and unworthy of someone who had recently converted to the Catholic faith. On 7 January 1933 Oldmeadow wrote a review of *Black Mischief* in which he proclaimed the novel 'a disgrace to anybody professing the Catholic name'.

Two weeks later, on 21 January, Waugh was able to rely on a powerful counter-attack. Planned and executed by Burns, it drew on an alliance of prominent Catholic laymen and clergy who put their names to a letter to the *Tablet* accusing Oldmeadow of exceeding 'the bounds of legitimate criticism' with remarks that amounted to an 'imputation of bad faith'. Within three years, in January 1936, Burns had organised a buyout of the *Tablet*, putting it under secular Catholic ownership and replacing Oldmeadow as editor with Douglas Woodruff, an old Oxford friend of Waugh's and a leader writer at *The Times*.

It was partly under Burns's influence that Waugh followed up *Black Mischief* with a biography of the Catholic Elizabethan Jesuit martyr Edmund Campion, with the royalties going to the Oxford Jesuit college Campion Hall, whose then master was Burns's old schoolteacher Fr D'Arcy.

When the book was republished in 1961, Waugh reflected that 'we are nearer to Campion that when I wrote of him'. He drew an analogy between cruelty shown to Catholics in Tudor England, and the even greater 'savagery' committed by communist regimes of Eastern Europe against their Catholic subjects. To that extent Waugh's description of a Church forced underground and priests becoming martyrs foreshadowed the pro-Franco stance he, Burns and many other Catholics were to take during the Spanish Civil War.

Before its outbreak in July 1936, Burns had befriended another author, Graham Greene. The two had met for the first time in 1929. Burns had just finished reading *The Man Within*, Greene's third novel and the first to be published. Of that first encounter Burns would later write: 'Graham leapt into my landscape like a leprechaun, as it seemed to me: witty, evasive, nervous, and sardonic, by turns. He stood out in the company we both kept in those days, which was mainly of publishers and authors, joyfully joined in plans and projects. Nothing was stereotyped, nothing predictable, for the world as we knew it was free – little knowing of the bondage to come.'

It was at about this time that Greene remarked that his political progress thus far in his life had been 'rather curved'. That was perhaps an understatement for the shifting political loyalties he had shown during and since his university days. He had supported the Conservative Party at Oxford before toying with joining the Liberals, joined the Communist Party 'as a joke' in 1925, volunteered as a special constable to help break the General Strike of 1926, before in 1933 becoming a member of the Independent Labour Party, whose chairman had accused the Labour Party of being counter-revolutionary. At the time of Greene's joining, the ILP's newspaper the *New Leader* had begun printing letters by Leon Trotsky, a first step along a path that was to see it backing, along with George Orwell, the Trotskyite POUM (United Marxist Workers Party) in the Spanish Civil War. By 1938 Greene, who had converted to the Catholic faith in 1926, a year before his marriage to Vivien Dayrell-Browning, had been persuaded by his friend Burns to write his first article for the *Tablet*.

Three years earlier, in the summer of 1935, Burns had paid his second, and similarly providential, visit to Spain. He was answering an invitation from two of his best friends, the writer Barbara Lucas and her academic husband Bernard Wall, Stonyhurst old boy, to join them on their honeymoon in Pamplona for a small holiday of wine, *tapas* and a bullfight starring Juan Belmonte.

The bullfighter had already achieved some international notoriety thanks to Ernest Hemingway's popular novel *Fiesta*. In the 1930s Belmonte was already a veteran, close to the end of his career. He had come out of retirement to shore up his dwindling finances. The legend had returned. Hemingway had written that no real man had ever worked as close to a fighting bull as Belmonte, which is why the uninitiated were advised to see him as soon possible before he was killed. Burns had dreamt of meeting Belmonte, alive.

The opportunity came when he least expected it. Shortly after the Walls had left London for Spain, Burns received a telegram from Pamplona. It was from Barbara and it was a cry for help. Three days into their honeymoon, the young newly-weds were still struggling to consummate their union fully. Barbara beseeched Burns to come and join her and her husband as quickly as possible and act both as mediator and counsellor. Burns initially felt awkward, although his long-standing friendship and loyalty to both Barbara and Bernard prevailed. As he later recalled, 'To be a gooseberry to a loving couple was not my idea of fun or duty. But the summons was clearly heartfelt.'

Burns enlisted the support of his mutual friend, René Hague, Eric Gill's son-in-law. Taking first the ferry from Folkestone to Boulogne, and then a third-class train ride south, Burns and his companion crossed the Pyrenees. They had barely left the platform and begun to make their way from the station to the Walls' hotel, than they spotted a poster. It announced that Belmonte was bullfighting the following afternoon in the nearby town of Logroño.

Belmonte had killed more than a thousand bulls in his career, but as he grew older he insisted that his bulls should not be too large, and not too dangerously armed with horns. But that afternoon he ventured deep into the bull's space, his glittering suit touching the black hide, his prominent jaw jutting in defiance. There were moments when he drew away, and seemed, as Hemingway had seen him, 'utterly contemptuous and indifferent' to what the crowd expected of him. By this stage in

Belmonte's career many of his fans thought him 'past his sell-by date' – getting old, and losing his nerve. But Burns saw only an artist in the sand, confronting death head-on. Thus began a curiously un-English passion for bullfighting that would remain with him for the rest of his life.

It was while Burns was repairing the initially dysfunctional Wall union that news reached them of war in Abyssinia. The Italians had nursed a grievance against Ethiopia since their ignominious defeat there in 1896 by Emperor Memelik II, an alleged descendant of King Solomon and the Queen of Sheba. After a phoney war lasting several months comprising military skirmishes over waterholes and other disputed territories, and impotent diplomatic protests, Italian troops attacked in force in October 1935. With the fortieth anniversary of the earlier humiliation approaching, Benito Mussolini, *Il Duce*, had set his sights on a new Roman Empire in eastern Africa, joining Ethiopia with Eritrea and Italian Somaliland.

One witness to the Italian attack was George Steer, the South African-born correspondent for *The Times*. In an article for the *Spectator* Steer described Ethiopia as the 'last African Empire to be invaded by a white Power, when feeling against the colour bar is rising all over Africa'. He warned that the subjugation of Ethiopia risked lighting a fire 'throughout the African bush'. In his articles Steer painted a stark contrast between the poorly equipped but brave Ethiopians (they fought mainly with rifles, swords and spears) struggling against the brute, well-equipped force of a fascist military machine, using any means it thought necessary to achieve victory, including the deliberate bombing of civilians to demoralise the enemy.

Such a perception was not shared by the network of Catholics that Burns had gathered around him. Burns's first meeting with Waugh had taken place just after the writer had returned from his first visit to Abyssinia where he had reported on Haile Selassie's coronation for *The Times*. Waugh's accreditation with *The Times*, to file on spec, had been partly facilitated by Burns's close associate Douglas Woodruff after his approaches to several other newspapers has been turned down. It was the experience of that first trip to Abyssinia that helped forge

Waugh's friendship with Burns and led to their first joint publishing venture.

Returning from his latest journey to Spain, Burns got back in touch with Waugh. The novelist was at the time actively courting Laura Herbert while anxiously awaiting news of his petition to Rome for annulment from his first wife, Evelyn. The process was proving tortuously slow, and threw him into bouts of depression. The emotional quagmire which drew in the two friends still revolved round their shared involvement with the Herbert sisters. While Waugh was focused on marrying Laura, Burns had befriended Laura's more extrovert and garrulous sister, Gabriel.

It was against this background that Burns, then building up his list at Longman, seized on a commercial and political opportunity, and commissioned Waugh to write a book on the Abyssinian war which he felt was guaranteed to sell well and give the Catholic perspective on an Italian venture that appalled much of the British nation.

Mussolini's invasion had fuelled considerable media interest in the UK and elsewhere in Europe, and writers like Waugh, with a developing literary reputation and knowledge of the region, were at a premium. Burns signed up Waugh as part of a triangular deal with the *Daily Mail*, negotiated for the novelist by his sharp-witted agent Augustus Peters, under which Waugh would have his expenses covered and receive an equally generous payment for a series of dispatches from Abyssinia.

The journey produced the second of Waugh's non-fiction books on Abyssinia, *Waugh in Abyssinia*. Burns had decided on the title, thinking the pun on the author's name was clever, punchy and, most important, marketable. Waugh had wanted to call it *A Disappointing War*. So he told his friend and biographer Christopher Sykes: 'Tom [Burns] as a professional publisher knew that a title that suggested disappointment would unquestionably result in disappointing sales.' Waugh, strongly encouraged by his publisher, portrayed his experience of Abyssinia as a clash between civilisations, with the Italians representing the cause of socio-economic progress, and the locals, barbarism. Sykes saw in the book the influence of the Old Catholic lay patriarch Hilaire Belloc, who saw in Mussolini, like Napoleon, the personification of benevolent power and greatness.

When the book was published at the end of 1936, the British public and Europeans in general were taking sides once again – this time over Spain. While the context was one of a civil war, the arguments revolved around similar issues, with the British and French governments signing up to a policy of non-intervention, and Italy, Germany and Russia getting militarily involved on opposing sides. Catholics once again tried to influence the agenda, this time portraying General Franco as the force of Christian civilisation intervening to stop Spain sliding into the grasp of atheistic communism.

In the early hours of 11 July 1936, a light passenger aircraft took off from an airfield in Croydon as part of a covert operation that was to unravel into the start of the bloodiest civil war in modern history. On board the Dragon Rapide were Luis Bolín, the London correspondent for the right-wing monarchist Spanish newspaper *ABC*, and two glamorous nineteen-year-old English girls, Diana Pollard and her friend Dorothy Watson, posing as tourists on a flight to the Canary Islands.

Bolín was just one of several players in an elaborate conspiracy to draw into a military uprising General Francisco Franco, at the time military commander of the Canary Islands. To ensure his joining in the coup against Spain's civilian government, the main army conspirators and their civilian allies arranged for a small plane to fly from England, pick up Franco and then take him to Spanish Morocco where the rebel forces were gathered.

Money for the operation was put up by Juan March, a Spanish millionaire from Mallorca who had made his fortune in tobacco smuggling and arms deals during the First World War. March was a close friend of Franco. He had also established ties with British intelligence through Alan Hillgarth, the British consul in Palma, Mallorca's capital. It was March who helped transfer the necessary funds for the hire of the Dragon Rapide – £2000 – into an account held in the Fenchurch Street branch of Kleinwort Benson & Sons, a merchant bank in the heart of the City of London.

The plane was hired by Bolín with the backing of several London-based Spaniards led by the monarchist unofficial London ambassador of the nationalist forces, the Duke of Alba, and a group of English

Catholics, led by Douglas Jerrold, a right-wing Tory and publisher. While there is no evidence to suggest that Burns was directly involved in the plot, it is reasonable to assume that he was aware of it through his close friendship with Jerrold and chose to maintain its secrecy.

It was Jerrold who introduced Bolín to Hugh Pollard, a retired army officer and fellow Catholic, who was put in charge of organising the logistics of the operation, including the recruitment of an RAF pilot turned mercenary, Captain William Begg.

Of all the plotters it was Pollard who was the most intriguing; he was, according to one of his friends, 'one of those romantic Englishmen who specialise in other people's revolutions'. Educated at Westminster School and with a degree in engineering from London University, Pollard – whose favourite hobbies were hunting and shooting – enlisted as a trooper in the Northumberland Hussars.

Before volunteering his services to the British Army in the First World War, Pollard used his riding and shooting skills in the Mexican Revolution, helping organise the escape of the toppled dictator Porfirio Díaz in 1911. He subsequently took part in the pro-Spanish uprising in Morocco of 1913 which deposed the Sultan Abdul Aziz and placed Mulay Hafid on the throne. In North Africa, Pollard and March had a common bond, for it was thanks to the subsequent Spanish colonial presence in Morocco that the Spanish entrepreneur had added to his riches, developing a tobacco monopoly. Pollard's duties after the First World War included at one point working as a police staff adviser in Dublin Castle, where suspect Irish republicans were interrogated. After this, his career turns somewhat nebulous, almost certainly because he became embroiled in British intelligence. In 1940, the security service MI5 began to investigate Pollard as a suspected member of the British Union of Fascists and Nazi sympathiser, only to discover that he had been enlisted as an MI6 agent after serving, under cover as a journalist, in military intelligence and government propaganda operations. Fluent in several languages, he was also the author of several military books, most notably an expert's manual on small arms commissioned by the War Office.

Pollard was thus almost certainly a spy. Once he had been briefed on the Franco plot, he decided to give it his full support, convinced that he was serving the cause of the Roman Catholic faith. He agreed to volunteer his daughter Diana and her friend as cover. The two debutantes carried operational orders aboard the Dragon Rapide between the covers of *Vogue* magazine. Six days later, at 5 p.m. on 17 July, the first of a series of coordinated military risings took place in Morocco. The Spanish Civil War had begun.

The gathering storm of German territorial expansion and militarism during the 1930s, and the apparent slowness in British rearmament in the face of the threat, were the subject of passionate denunciation inside and outside Parliament by Winston Churchill. And yet when the Spanish Civil War broke out Churchill agreed with foreign secretary Anthony Eden that it was essential for Britain to maintain her neutrality in the struggle. Their shared principal motive was a strategic one and based solely in what they believed best served British interests: the wish to avoid the Spanish conflict becoming the principal battleground for a general European war.

It was just over thirty years since Churchill had last had any real interest in Spanish matters. In 1895 he had gone to Cuba in a semi-official capacity as a military observer, reporting as well for the *Daily Graphic*. Cuba at the time was one of the last remaining colonies of the Spanish Empire, and was in the throes of a rebellion by the islanders. He was shocked by the corruption of the colonial administration – 'on a scale almost Chinese' – but impressed by the professionalism and bravery of the Spanish troops and their commander General Valdez whose campaign he accompanied. The Spanish military for its part honoured Churchill – a Sandhurst-trained cavalry officer – with a medal for courage in the field.

In his dispatches, Churchill showed some understanding of the Cuban rebels' cause but he was shocked by their military tactics which he described as that of 'incendiarists and brigands – burning canefields, shooting from behind hedges, firing into sleeping camps, destroying property, wrecking trains, and throwing dynamite'. These, Churchill, concluded, were 'perfectly legitimate in war, no doubt, but they are not acts on which States are founded'. He would think on the lessons of Cuba when later, at the outbreak of the Second World War, he encouraged the formation of Special Operations Executive (SOE) with its orders to set Europe ablaze.

Perhaps there was a reason for Churchill to have forgotten Spain over the intervening years when his interests had ranged from military planning in the First World War to Home Rule in Ireland. And yet the Spanish Civil War prompted memories of Cuba, the nearest the old warrior had come to seeing Spaniards at war. From the outset Churchill was careful not to criticise the military uprising. By contrast, he showed little sympathy for the Republican government, which he regarded as revolutionary in character and tainted by its record of violent industrial and agrarian militancy and anti-clericalism.

On being presented to the newly appointed republican ambassador to London, Pablo de Azcárate, in October 1936, Churchill turned red with anger, muttered 'Blood, blood, blood', and refused the Spaniard's outstretched hand. The perception was fuelled by the partisan reports about the summary executions of Franco sympathisers which reached him from within the Foreign Office, influential English Catholics, and, most particularly, Hillgarth, the Naval Intelligence officer serving as British consul in Mallorca who was to remain a trusted contact on matters Spanish for over a decade.

The son of a Harley Street surgeon, Hillgarth had entered naval college as a young boy, before serving and getting wounded as a Royal Navy midshipman during the Dardanelles campaign of the First World War, when Churchill had served as First Lord of the Admiralty. During the 1920s Hillgarth became a military adviser to the Spanish Foreign Legion during its confrontation in Morocco with the uprising of the Rif's tribes. Among the Legion's officers and one of its founders was a young major named Francisco Franco.

Returning to London, Hillgarth became part of a social network that drew together the upper classes and emerging literary figures and in 1929 married Mary Gardner. 'A young man called Alan Hillgarth, very sure of himself, writes shockers, ex-sailor', Evelyn Waugh had noted in his diary two years earlier.

Hillgarth had planned to spend an extended honeymoon sailing round the world in a converted Dutch schooner, but the romantic idea collapsed along with the stock market. Less rich than they had been brought up to be, the Hillgarths sailed from England to Palma, Mallorca, and there sold the boat.

The proceeds from that eventually helped them purchase Son Torella, a run-down but palatial residence and estate whose widowed absentee owner – a member of the Spanish nobility – had left for the mainland to become a nun. When the Hillgarths settled there in 1932, the house was half occupied by cows, donkeys and mules. Contraband tobacco was stored in the galleries and the olive press had been stripped of its hydraulic equipment. It took two years to make the house habitable with the help of local master masons, Mary Hillgarth's private income and a fortunate lottery ticket in which the Hillgarths had 'gone halves' with a friendly Austrian barman called Joe.

Windows were glazed, bookcases carved and installed, the rooms retiled and repainted and filled with a mixture of local antique wooden furniture and portraits of the Gardner family. Apart from the attentive restoration of the house, Mary Hillgarth took special care in creating a garden that was a piece of England grafted on to the Mediterranean. The house had long-established cypresses, palms and lotus trees, planted by the previous owners to provide shelter and shade from the Mediterranean storms and hot summers. Mary planted herbaceous borders, and a thousand irises – Dutch Wedgewoods and Yellow Queens.

Son Torella was already something of an idyll when Winston Churchill and his wife Clementine visited it in the late autumn of 1935. It was a restful place – bursting with scents and colours – which contrasted with the dark shadow of German military expansion that threatened mainland Europe, and the frustration Churchill felt at having his political peers ignore his warnings. Churchill's hopes of being brought back into government after an extended period on the backbenches had been dashed when he was left out of Stanley Baldwin's cabinet despite an overwhelming election victory for the Conservatives to which he had contributed. Bruised and verging on despair, Churchill dealt with the resurgent 'black dog' of depression by taking a long working and painting holiday.

Hillgarth was by then serving as the British honorary vice-consul in Mallorca. Initially the job had mainly consisted of getting drunken

British seamen out of Spanish jails, but Hillgarth had soon manoeuvred it into a 'cover' posting, whereby he doubled up as a spy. He adeptly exploited his position to make influential friends among the local community, and gain useful political and military intelligence on an island that was not without strategic importance as a naval base in the Mediterranean. When Churchill came to visit him he played the perfect host, letting him paint and laying on large quantities of food and drink between discussions about worrying developments on the international front and the increasingly volatile state of Spanish politics.

Hillgarth's most immediate concern was less the threat of a war with Italy than the increasing disgruntlement many of his friends in Mallorca felt about the revolutionary politics of the Spanish left. In the traditionally deeply conservative and right-wing island, one of his key informants was the local businessman Juan March. The plot which was to involve March in financing Franco's involvement in the military uprising was only months away.

Years later, Tom Burns – by then a long-term friend of Captain Hillgarth – would reflect on the 1930s, not without a sense of guilt pricking his conscience over the sins of omission he had unwittingly contributed to: supporting Mussolini in Abyssinia with the pact formulated by the then foreign secretary Samuel Hoare, his future ambassador in Madrid; waking up belatedly to the real evil of Hitler; and passively acquiescing in the fiction of non-intervention in Spain. 'The rise of the dictatorships was reported in a muted and distorted fashion: an ugly development, better kept out of sight. Official compliance with broken treaties, near criminal efforts to satisfy Nazi expansionism, by offering to hand over territories that were not ours – such was the coin of our diplomacy. Rearmament, thought Mr Baldwin, would be electorally dangerous – a prospect which was apparently more alarming to him than any belligerent threat from abroad.'

By contrast, Burns reflected, only Winston Churchill had spoken out against government policy and apathy at 'every possible opportunity', ceaselessly exposing Britain's military vulnerability and Nazi Germany's growing power. And yet, despite Churchill's formidable eloquence, he was not taken seriously. It was not just Parliament that ignored him.

As Burns admitted: 'I remember thinking that he was aggravating great dangers in the very act of denouncing them. The prospect of peace receded with each new barrage of insults and accusations hurled against Hitler. Mine was a very widely shared view among many of my friends. We read *Mein Kampf*, published here in 1931, with incredulity; we distrusted the outpouring of the Left Book Club and were as ignorant of German concentration camps and the persecution of the Jews as of the Gulag Archipelago and the enslavement and "liquidation" of millions of political dissenters in the Soviet Union. Partly because the protagonists of protest against these horrors were, to me, suspect witnesses, partly because my life and work were at full stretch, I did not become involved in these matters.'

As Burns admitted, such omission was not due to a lack of witnesses. During the 1930s, he met and befriended Italian, German and Russian Catholics, all of whom had managed to escape from the political repression of their countries, and come to London as refugees. They included Don Luigi Sturzo, the founder of the Partito Popolare which Mussolini had banned, members of the German centre party whom Hitler had forced out of power, and the Russian Christian philosopher Berdyaev, who had fled Stalin. 'These solitary prophets and witnesses were welcomed with sympathy as if they had escaped from an earthquake, but an earthquake far removed from our island.'

And yet the Spanish Civil War brought the earthquake much nearer than Burns had believed possible at the time. It was a conflict that transcended ordinary politics, inflaming and dividing British public opinion as few other foreign questions had done since the Russian Revolution.

2

AUTHORS TAKE SIDES

The radicalisation of Spanish politics during the 1930s fuelled a growing alienation between some English Catholics and the secularist ascendancy in British literature represented by the Bloomsbury Group. 'There's something obscene in a living person sitting by the fire and believing in God,' the Bloomsbury icon Virginia Woolf had commented in 1928 on learning of T.S. Eliot's deepening involvement with the Christian faith. Seven years later Woolf was no less horrified on hearing that the South African-born poet Roy Campbell and his wife Mary had converted to Catholicism.

The Campbells had drifted into the Bloomsbury set during the late 1920s, she rather more wittingly than he. Campbell, who had studied at Oxford two years ahead of Evelyn Waugh, was taken on as a contributor to the *New Statesman* thanks in part to various leading Bloomsbury figures giving their seal of approval to his early poetry. But his deeply ingrained male chauvinism, political conservatism and religious devotion placed him at odds with the avowed socialism of Bloomsbury.

In 1928 Campbell left England for Provence after discovering his wife Mary's lesbian affair with Virginia Woolf's lover, Vita Sackville-West. For a while he lived among fishermen, and became a huge enthusiast of bullfighting, finding in the simplicity of the local people and the traditions of their culture a soothing contrast to the world of Bloomsbury.

After being reunited, the Campbells crossed into Spain in 1933, to avoid being sued by their neighbours. A goat they owned had escaped and gone on the rampage, destroying a number of young peach trees in the process. They stayed for a while in Barcelona where they witnessed an abortive revolution by a group of anarchists, one of several preludes to the civil war. They eventually settled in Toledo.

Surrounded by thick ancient walls, and perched on a hill overlooking the Tagus River, Toledo's surviving battlements served as a reminder of Spain's glorious past when the city had been the imperial capital and bastion of Christianity under the Holy Roman Emperor Charles V. It was filled still with convents, churches and seminaries.

When the left-wing Popular Front won the Spanish elections in February 1936, an ugly campaign of anti-clericalism shattered the Campbells' cultural idyll. In Toledo, which Campbell described as the 'whole embodiment of the crusade for Christianity against Communism', churches were burnt and nuns and priests attacked in the streets. To Campbell such deeds were the acts of barbarians bent on destroying the social fabric and soul of Spain. He reacted by staging a somewhat eccentric act of '*anti*-Red defiance', a month before the outbreak of the Spanish Civil War. It took place in the local bullring, for the passionate loyalty Campbell felt for the Catholic faith was surpassed only by his love of wine and bulls. Campbell got his wife to help him plait red and yellow, the colours of the old Monarchist flag, later usurped by Franco, (as opposed to the red, yellow, and purple of the Republican standard) into the manes and tails of a couple of horses and then got his young daughters, Teresa and Anna, to ride them across the ring before the start of the bullfight.

Four weeks later, Campbell was watering one of his horses when the peace of the day was shattered by the rattle of rifle fire, a signal that the civil war had begun. Within a month the Campbell family had fled Spain, having witnessed at first hand the horror of the looting and summary executions initially carried out in Toledo by the left-wing militias. It was at this point that Campbell began to see the conflict in Spain as something that transcended politics. In the words of his biographer Joseph Pearce, 'It was deeper than the struggle for temporary power. It was not a fight between fascism and communism, but between Christ and the anti-Christ – a fight to the death between good and evil, God and the Devil.'.

During his first days back in England, Campbell's bullfighting exploits, as well as his seemingly miraculous escape from the anarchist firing squads, were all over the British newspapers, drawing sympathy from fellow Catholics, among them Burns, whose own interest in Spain was developing into his primary concern as a publisher. As Burns later recalled, the civil war placed a barrier between him and the left-wing poets Wystan Auden and Stephen Spender, to whom he had been introduced when they were undergraduates at Oxford and who mixed in similar intellectual circles in London. By contrast, Roy Campbell now spoke 'more for my sympathies'.

The Catholic weekly the *Tablet*, which Burns now partly owned and managed, unhesitatingly took Franco's side in the civil war. It offered Campbell as much support as Burns could muster, beginning with a letter of accreditation as a war correspondent. Campbell spent much of what was left of the Spanish Civil War wielding the propagandist's cudgel, writing shrill poems, most of which were characterised by the kind of jingoistic triumphalism with which Franco personally stamped his military campaign.

Campbell later developed these into a five-thousand-word would-be epic, *The Spanish Civil War*, whose publication Burns oversaw at Longman, in 1939, the year after George Orwell published his *Homage to Catalonia*. While Orwell's book was a courageously objective essay on the hopes and shattered dreams of those who fought for the Spanish Republic, Campbell's poem, 'The Flowering Rifle', was an uncontrolled anti-communist and occasionally racist diatribe which even his sympathetic biographer found politically offensive and artistically flawed. 'It plods along with leaden boots firing scorn-blinded blanks at "bolshies", anarchists and Jews, offering only an occasional glimpse of the genius which its author possesses,' comments Pearce.

While in Spain, Campbell followed Burns's instructions and travelled by train to the Francoist-controlled university city of Salamanca. There he obtained a safe conduct from the chief of the Nationalist Press Office, Merry del Val, to the Madrid front, along with further letters of introduction to some of Franco's commanders. Campbell offered to enlist as a soldier with the anti-Republican monarchist *requetés* rather than with the Franco regulars, but he was told that it was as a writer and poet that he could best serve the Franco cause.

The regiment had weeks earlier happily accepted into its ranks another English Catholic friend of Burns's, the young Cambridge graduate Peter Kemp. Kemp's views as a student had been so right-wing that he had formed a splinter union of his own as a rival to the Conservative Association. He later claimed that his reasons for going to Spain were not entirely political – he had no idea what career he wanted to pursue and thought that he would spend a few months getting to know a 'strange country' and learn something about modern warfare. However, his politics determined the side he chose.

'Priests and nuns were shot simply because they were priests or nuns, ordinary people murdered just because they had a little money or property. It's to fight against that sort of thing that I am going to Spain,' Kemp told his friends.

Kemp's enlistment on Franco's side proved a rarity in contrast to the hundreds of his fellow countrymen who, with the encouragement of the Communist Party, joined the pro-Republic International Brigades. With the military assistance being offered by the Italians and the Germans, the Nationalist cause found it unnecessary to actively recruit further in Britain, particularly since to have done so would have further undermined the British government's policy of non-intervention.

Instead, Franco set up an agency in London to boost his propaganda efforts, enlisting the support of sectors of the media, and lobbying politicians and government officials. The agency, operating out of a suite in the Dorchester Hotel, was headed up by two Spanish aristocrats, the Marqués del Moral and the Duke of Alba, both of whom had been educated at Jesuit public schools in England, and had strong ties at the highest levels of London society.

Of the two, Alba was the most pivotal in terms of Anglo-Spanish relations. Spain's leading nobleman was descended from one of the oldest aristocratic lines in Europe. His full title was Jacobo María del Pilar Carlos Manuel Fitz-James Stuart y Falcó, the 17th Duke of Alba and 10th Duke of Berwick. As a descendant of an illegitimate son of King James II by Arabella Churchill, he was a cousin of Winston's, a tie that would give 'Jimmy' Alba a key diplomatic role as Franco's ambassador in London during the Second World War.

Nevertheless the challenge del Moral and Alba faced in winning over British intellectuals who felt ideologically stirred by the Spanish Civil War was underlined by a survey of British writers carried out in the spring of 1937. Of those questioned, 127 were in favour of the Republican government, while only five declared themselves against it. Campbell did not participate in the poll. He was already in Spain, feeling himself liberated from the Anglo-Saxon literary intrigues he found so claustrophobic and politically unconvincing.

Graham Greene could have participated but chose not to. Evelyn Waugh was the only Catholic to cast his vote, and he was one of the five who in effect voted in support of the military-led uprising. By now Burns had emerged as the common thread linking Campbell, Greene and Waugh – the three best-known Catholic authors at the time – for he had befriended each one of them separately, and managed to influence all of them in a way that benefited the Francoist cause.

Burns's takeover of the *Tablet* allowed him to extend his influence in the wider literary world. Into its pages he drew Greene in 1936 in what was to become an enduring relationship between the author and the international Catholic weekly. Greene was taken on as a regular reviewer, with the freedom to choose whatever book he liked for criticism. His *Tablet* journalism scorned the communism he had flirted with at university while holding back from the overtly pro-Francoist stance adopted by other contributors, led by the editor Douglas Woodruff.

When the pamphlet *Authors Take Sides on the Spanish Civil War*, based on the survey, was published in June 1937, Greene used the pages of the *Spectator* to mock the earnestness of those on the left, like Auden and Spender, who had engaged with the war in Spain initially with a self-consciously serious ideological intent. Greene contrasted the political rantings of the 1930s with the more easy-going attitudes of the Cambridge Apostles, among them Tennyson and his friend Henry Hallam, who in 1830 had undertaken secret missions in Spain in support of rebel activity, primarily for the thrill of it.

Years later, Greene told his official biographer Norman Sherry that one of the reasons he did not contribute to the *Authors Take Sides* survey was that, while he shared some sympathy for the Republican cause, he was horrified by the brutality sectors of the Spanish left had shown towards the religious orders and the clergy. The sympathy he felt for the Republic was principally focused on the Basque country, where a significant sector of the local population was both fervently Catholic and anti-Franco, fighting not for communism but for greater autonomy from the rest of Spain.

Greene's interest in the Basque country intensified in the light of what occurred in the region in a town called Gernika, where in medieval times the Catholic Kings of Spain had sworn before a totemic oak tree forever to respect the rights of the local people. It was there that on the afternoon of 26 April 1937 a force of Luftwaffe bombers and fighter planes carried out an attack of terrible destruction and human carnage – a scene Picasso later immortalised in one of the most famous of war paintings. From a military perspective, the bombing of Gernika was a brilliant success for the pilots of the Condor Legion. Estimates of fatalities among the 7,000 then inhabitants of the town have varied widely over the years. The Republican government estimated that at least 1,600 had been killed while Franco put the number of dead, somewhat absurdly, at twelve. More recently Basque investigators have opted for a figure of between 120 and 250 after studying the town records, and on the grounds that many of the children had been previously evacuated while adults managed to protect themselves in bomb shelters.

However, the physical devastation of Gernika caused by the German bombers provoked panic as well as impotent outrage throughout much of the Basque region at the time. The razing to the ground of much of the town with incendiary bombs signalled a new and terrifying development in modern warfare, targeting the civilian population in order to smash its morale. Only the arrival on the scene of a group of independently minded journalists, led by Christopher Home of Reuters news agency and George Steer, of *The Times*, made it a public relations disaster for Franco's side. Both men filed vivid reports of what they found, pointing the finger of blame for a callous act of inhumanity at the Germans and the Spanish general who had called on their assistance.

There then ensued a ferocious propaganda campaign, with claims and counter-claims about what exactly had gone on in Gernika. The first round began with a less than convincing denial from the Nationalists that the bombing had even taken place. On 28 April, the day Steer filed his report to *The Times* and the *New York Times*, another *Times* correspondent, James Holburn, filed from Salamanca, the Nationalist headquarters, reporting claims that Gernika had been set on fire by anti-Franco forces. Subsequently Nationalist press officers, under the management of Luis Bolín – the journalist who had helped organise the UK end of the Franco uprising – escorted visitors to Gernika on carefully controlled tours of the bombed town.

As part of a deliberate campaign of misinformation Bolín's co-conspirator, Captain Hugh Pollard (the Englishman who had flown on the plane that picked up Franco in the Canaries), penned a letter to *The Times* suggesting that even if the Nationalists had, after all, been responsible for the bombing, it was justified. Pollard alleged anti-Franco forces were supplying small arms to terrorists fighting British colonial interests in India and Egypt. It was a curious argument with an allegation based on flimsy evidence. It was nevertheless a typical exercise in misinformation by an expert in the black arts.

The propaganda pendulum continued to swing from one side to the other, underlining the extent to which Gernika had become much more than just another war story. It had become a symbol of each side's integrity, or lack of it. Basque Catholic priests were among those who remained at the forefront of denunciation of Nationalist brutality not just against Gernika but other towns bombed and then occupied by Franco forces. Twenty Basque priests, of whom one was an eyewitness of the bombing, and including the vicar-general of the diocese, wrote to Pope Pius XI telling him who had destroyed Gernika. Two of the priests acted as couriers and travelled to the Vatican, where their protests fell on deaf ears.

Meanwhile, Franco's spin doctor, Bolín, did not remain idle. He flew back to London and with his friends the Marqués del Moral and the Duke of Alba enlisted Burns's support in building up a body of influential opinion around a fundraising organisation called the Friends of Nationalist Spain. Among its keenest supporters was another of Bolín's British co-conspirators, the Catholic publisher Douglas Jerrold, who wrote a long article for the *Tablet* challenging Steer's version of events. A broader attack on the claims made by Basque Catholic priests and Steer, meanwhile, was contained in a letter that was circulated within the Jesuit community and the Vatican. It was written by Burns's older brother, George, who as a Jesuit priest had spent time during the Spanish Civil War officiating to Nationalist troops.

By June 1937, the Basque capital, Bilbao, was resisting a major offensive by Franco's army. The town had been supplied with additional ammunition, including new machine guns from Czechoslovakia, and its command reinforced with some of the best officers communist Russia could muster. But the 'ring of steel' – the elaborate system of defence positions which had been set up in the hills surrounding the town – had been undermined by the betrayal of a Basque officer, Major Goicoechea, who had defected to the Franco side, and the besieged town was suffering a pounding by sustained artillery fire supported by aerial bombing.

The dramatic events surrounding the civil war in the Basque country stirred the artistic imaginations of painters, poets and writers, among them Graham Greene. Ten years had passed since Greene had married Vivien, a committed Catholic, having himself converted a year earlier.

It was Franco's attack on the Republican-held Basque country that moved Greene initially, as he put it, to 'examine more closely the effect of faith on action'. But it was his continuing refusal to declare his political allegiance unequivocally and openly for one side or the other that probably saved him in literary terms even if it made him enemies on the left and the right. Divided loyalties and shifting political allegiances would come to provide the core tension in Greene's novels.

Looking back on the 1930s, Greene reflected that it was then that he had begun to see Catholicism as no longer primarily symbolic, 'a ceremony at an altar with the correct canonical number of candles, with the women in my Chelsea congregation wearing their best hats'. Nor was it a philosophical page in the Jesuit Fr D'Arcy's *Nature of Belief*, however much it might have impacted on his friend Burns's theological formation. It was, as Greene put it, 'closer now to death in the afternoon'. He went on: 'A restlessness set in which has never quite been allayed: a desire to be a spectator of history, history in which I found I was concerned myself.'

Beyond this, Greene's real motivation for choosing to go to Bilbao remains unclear. In his autobiography, he claimed that he travelled to Bilbao with a letter of recommendation from the Basque Delegation in London. The extensive archive which the Basque government preserved from that period contains no evidence of such a letter having existed – no copies, no exchange of correspondence or minuted meetings linked to it. The Delegation was not shy when it came to exploiting propaganda opportunities and yet Basques linked with that period have excluded any mention of recruiting Graham Greene to their cause in their accounts or those compiled by sympathetic historians. Nor have the BBC archives thrown up anything which might substantiate the claim made by Greene's official biographer Norman Sherry that the author's intention was to make a BBC broadcast about the besieged Basques.

According to Greene's account, 'they . . . [Sherry presumes that 'they' was the BBC]' sent him 'hurtling down to Toulouse', where the Frenchman who was supposed to take him across the border and into Bilbao in a two-seater plane got cold feet because Franco's guns were proving too accurate. But Sherry, drawing from a letter Greene wrote to his mother, offers a more mundane explanation – which is that the novelist wanted to return to London for the launch of a new magazine, *Night and Day*, to which he had been appointed literary editor the previous December, rather than waiting for an alternative way of getting to Spain.

No one was more pleased to see Greene cut short his trip to Bilbao than his friend Burns. Now that any thought of writing an anti-Franco novel based in Bilbao had effectively been scuppered, there emerged an alternative project with which Burns planned to tap Greene's literary talents in a less hesitant defence of the Catholic faith.

The idea had already been implanted in Greene's mind in embryonic form months before his aborted trip to Bilbao. On Burn's recommendation, Greene had read a book called *Mexican Martyrdom* which had been published in 1936. Written by an American Jesuit called Fr Parsons, the book was a graphic account of the persecution of the Catholic Church in Mexico following the Revolution. Here, far off on a distant continent, was a drama that appealed to Greene as an author and a Catholic, one that he could engage in without provoking the hostility of friends.

The original idea for a book by Greene on Mexico came from Frank Sheed, of the publishers Sheed & Ward, which Burns had joined in 1926. Initial negotiations through Greene's agent, David Higham, had led to an offer of an advance of £500. But progress towards a final contract was stalled with Greene initially diverted by the Basque situation in Spain, and subsequently by his taking up the literary editorship at *Night and Day*. The project was eventually dropped by Sheed, leaving it open for his former protégé Burns to make an alternative offer.

Burns was by now an experienced publisher with ideas of his own, and with a developed sense of the market and how it should be played. In early 1936 he had left Sheed & Ward and joined Longman, Green and Co., a long-established publishing firm that was looking to refresh its declining specialist list of Catholic and Anglican writing and to expand further its general list of authors, among them rising stars who preferred to call themselves writers and who were also Catholics.

Within months of securing Evelyn Waugh's travel book on Abyssinia, Burns had signed up Greene on Mexico, having convinced him that Longman was on its way to being, if it wasn't already, more that just a Catholic publishing house, with the greater market opportunities that that implied.

Burns and Greene had a friendship that drew strength from a similarity of character but contrasting circumstances. Both men stood out in the company they kept. They carried within them a radical strain which questioned orthodox assumptions in matters of faith as much as politics. Burns was still a bachelor, on the lookout for a woman with whom he could form a permanent relationship. He saw in Vivien, Greene's young wife, the ideal woman, constant and forgiving, an echo of his own (Burns's) mother, whom Burns had lived with briefly following his father's death in 1924.

Invited to dinner at the Greenes' home on Clapham Common, Burns was struck by how the 'gentle and beautiful' Vivien had 'it all arranged with such care'. This 'serenity in order in every detail' seemed to Burns to be so different from everything that he had been able to observe in Greene himself.

When Burns and Greene were alone together, Greene revealed another darker and more restless side to him, one that Burns sympathised with but struggled to suppress within himself thanks to his Jesuit upbringing. As Burns later recalled of that period, 'We were both too busy to see much of each other but there would come the occasional telephone call: "Let's go to Limehouse tonight – there's a ballet of Chinese nudes at the local theatre."' Even during his early days of sexual experimentation in Paris, Burns had drawn the line at brothels. Yet the topics of sex and religion, discussed over a bottle of whisky, produced a creative bond between the two men that was to last, off and on, till their dying days.

After one of their regular drinking sessions together, Greene wrote to his agent David Higham saying that he personally would much rather be published by Longman than Sheed & Ward as this would run much less of a risk of having him 'branded as a Catholic writer'.

The reality was that Burns could offer Greene as good if not better contacts and introductions to the world of Mexican Catholicism as Sheed had promised. Still Higham attempted to raise the stakes. He approached Greene's regular publisher, Heinemann, and suggested to Greene that he was on target for securing a satisfactory offer. Greene was unconvinced. He wrote back to Higham strongly expressing his view that it wasn't worth 'jockeying Heinemanns into a book which doesn't really interest them'.

Further haggling followed before Higham drew up Greene's contract with Burns, while refusing to contemplate a buyout of the option that Heinemann had on the author's entire fiction output. Nevertheless, it had become clear to Burns that neither Heinemann nor any other publisher shared his and Greene's interests. 'For them Mexico was far away and religion a hazy notion,' Burns later remarked. 'Graham and I saw it quite differently and were able to persuade my somewhat bovine board at Longman to accept my view and come up with £500 – quite a sum in those days for a writer untried in the field.' In fact the £500 was no more and no less than Sheed had offered Higham originally. Burns had got himself a bargain.

It was during the 1930s that Burns also developed a growing friendship with Evelyn Waugh. They courted the two Herbert sisters, forged ever closer links with the Jesuits and participated in joint publishing ventures. After publishing, with Burns's encouragement, a biography of Edmund Campion, the Jesuit martyr, Waugh followed in Greene's footsteps to Mexico on a writing commission funded by Clive Pearson, a younger son of the 1st Lord Cowdray, representing his family's powerful commercial interests in Central America.

The travel book that Waugh wrote on Mexico, *Robbery Under Law*, received lukewarm interest when it was published in 1939. It was the year of transition from the Spanish Civil War to the Second World War, when the dark implications of Hitler's ambition were finally beginning to dawn on the British public, and people had little time to get worked up over affairs in distant Mexico. Many writers on the left, like the journalist Tom Driberg, had been professionally engaged in the fight against Fascism for some time, while there were others – English socialites, like Unity and Diana Mitford – who held Hitler in awe, and supported Oswald Mosley's British Union of Fascists, as the party which could unite Britain and prevent the slide to world war. As late as September 1938, as part of his work for the Anglo-German Fellowship, Beverley Nichols entertained leaders of the Hitler Youth to lunch at the Garrick Club. *Robbery Under Law* includes a visceral attack on the world of left-wing British intellectuals as epitomised by Victor Gollancz's Left Book Club, which in Waugh's view had contributed only to romanticising the antics of revolutionaries in foreign lands, justifying actions that they could never have countered back in England.

Describing the different tourists he met in Mexico, Waugh raged against the ideologues: 'First in Moscow, then in Barcelona, now in Mexico, these credulous pilgrims pursue their quest for the Promised Land; constantly disappointed, never disillusioned, ever thirsty for the phrases in which they find refreshment.'

Waugh's friend and biographer Christopher Sykes considers *Robbery Under Law*, the novelist's most political book, a product of its time, when the ideological character of the Spanish Civil War incited numerous writers to proclaim their deepest beliefs. Neither Waugh nor Greene followed the example of authors like Laurie Lee, André Malraux, Orwell or Hemingway who took up arms in Spain. They chose instead their own idiosyncratic witness to European events, finding in Mexico a situation that allowed them to reconcile their faith with their political convictions.

Before going to Mexico, Waugh spent the first months of the Spanish Civil War initially in Abyssinia and then continuing his courtship in London of Laura Herbert, whom he married on 17 April 1937.

Laura was not the first of the Herbert sisters to have entered Waugh's circle. It was thanks to the encouragement and introduction of Fr D'Arcy that in the summer of 1933 Waugh had met Gabriel, Laura's oldest sister, while taking a Hellenic cruise with his Oxford acquaintance Alfred Duggan, the step-son of Lord Curzon, and a group of formidable Catholics. They included members of the Asquith family, and the Infanta Beatriz, the daughter of the Spanish King Alfonso XIII and Queen Victoria Eugenia, or 'Ena' as she came to be more popularly known, his consort.

Gabriel was a handsome, amusing and athletic twenty-two-year-old who had inherited her father Aubrey's half-brother Lord Carnavon's adventurous spirit. Waugh seems to have warmed to her particularly one night when she got drunk on too many gins.

Waugh kept no diaries from the summer of 1934 to the summer of 1936, but it was in this period leading up to the Spanish Civil War that he fell in love with Laura, while introducing Gabriel to his friend Burns, an introduction almost as fateful as that which had led the novelist to his first meeting with his future wife. While Waugh's courtship of Laura was complicated by the tortuously slow process of the annulment of his first marriage, Burns's romantic dalliance with Gabriel flourished, uncluttered by thoughts of marriage, or, as she perceived it in orthodox Catholic terms, carnal sin.

In July 1936, Waugh wrote a letter to Lady Mary Lygon, soon after his annulment had been granted by Rome, announcing that one of the reasons the marriage would not take place for several months was because Gabriel had got involved in the politics of Spain, and because he had yet to overcome a certain air of moral disapproval with which she contemplated his attachment to her sister.

The outbreak of the Spanish Civil War sharpened Gabriel's fanatical Catholicism. It gave her a motive and a spur to action to defend her faith, drawing her into the network of English and Spanish Catholics that supported the Nationalists. She put her energies into helping channel funds to the nationalist side, and organising the transport of medical supplies from the UK, across France and over the Pyrenees, in a fleet of volunteer ambulances.

Overt Catholic fundraising was initiated within days of the military uprising with advertisements in two Catholic newspapers, the *Universe* and the *Catholic Times*. The fundraising then became coordinated by a committee presided over by the Archbishop of Westminster, Cardinal Hinsley, and composed of a selection of the great and good in the Catholic laity. The chairman was Lord Howard of Penrith, a former ambassador to Washington and Madrid, and a relation of the Dukes of Norfolk, with a formidable array of social and political contacts on both sides of the Atlantic.

In the UK, Howard was active in Catholic intellectual circles. He was a close friend of Fr D'Arcy, and his son Francis – educated by the Benedictines at Downside – had joined the journalistic and publishing circles that revolved round Burns, with whom he had shared a flat in Chelsea after leaving Oxford. Other members of the committee included two other publishing associates of Burns, Christopher Dawson and Frank Sheed, as well as Waugh.

The officially declared mission of the Bishops' Committee for the Relief of Spanish Distress was listed as 'the relief of the sick, wounded, refugees, and destitute children of Spain'. In fact the Committee was overtly anti-communist and determined to counter the attempts by the Spanish left to monopolise public opinion in Britain. The Committee maintained close ties with the Friends of Nationalist Spain.

More than a year earlier, in late September 1936, Evelyn Waugh noted a lunch he had with his sister-in-law-to-be, Gabriel, who was 'off to Spain to relieve insurgents'. That evening both of them went to another fundraising event, this time organised by the Catholic Archbishop of Westminster's 'Spanish Association'. Gabriel opened the event by reporting on a meeting she had had with one of the Duke of Alba's aristocratic friends, the Duchess of Laguna, and urged the Association's committee to meet her demands for medical and other supplies as soon as they could be arranged. Waugh made a recommendation to the committee that Gabriel should be sent to Spain without more ado to see, on the ground, what was needed, and to coordinate the delivery of supplies. It turned into the first of several trips Gabriel made to

Nationalist-occupied Spanish territory with an ambulance unit, mainly staffed by Spaniards. Gabriel's growing enthusiasm for the nationalist cause as she worked as a volunteer nurse and intermediary between the medical team in Spain and the fund-raisers in London was conveyed in a series of private letters she wrote to friends and family members. During an interlude in London in 1937 – the precise date remains unclear – between trips to Spain, Gabriel wrote a report to her mother, Mary Herbert, with instructions that it be distributed among members of the English Catholic Bishops' fund-raising 'Spanish Association'.

Gabriel glowingly depicted the far right *requetés* from Navarre as the main standard-bearers of a heroic Catholic crusade which she claimed had been misunderstood by large swathes of the British media.

She wrote: 'To those men, who watched the creeping disorder spreading over Spain, threatening the Church ... and bringing disaster into the balanced order of their farming lives, who witnessed the powerlessness of the government to restrain the growing unrest to prevent churches being burnt and priests murdered, it was not unnatural to go and fight in defence of their religion and their right to live in their own homes.'

Gabriel had developed strong personal bonds with the *requetés* because during her first year in Spain they were the great majority of soldiers she nursed in hospital on the northern front. But far from a romantic adventure, the experience intensified her ideological commitment to the Franco cause, and her blind acceptance of its propaganda for which she acted as an energetic conduit. 'To a people tired of injustice and misrule, Franco appeared as their only hope – a hope which has been justified,' she wrote in notes prepared for a book she planned to write but never did.

It was a project for which she earned the approval of her spiritual mentor Fr D'Arcy whenever she returned to London. It also gave a fresh frisson to her on-off courtship with Burns, who retained fond memories of his first dances with Gabriel when she was a debutante. Many years later Burns described the third and final prologue to his main Spanish performance, his reunion with Gabriel, thus: 'A chance encounter with a friend in a London street led her to ask what I was doing for a summer holiday. I told her that I had no plans. She asked me if I could drive an ambulance, which had been donated by English

Catholics, to Burgos, the Spanish Nationalist headquarters. I accepted at once and was delighted to know that my companions would be a family friend, General Pereira (retired but, I suspect, not restrained from observing the situation for military intelligence) and Gabriel Herbert, a friend of debutante dancing days who was a volunteer nurse with the Nationalists, later decorated for valour.'

Their destination in Spain was the old Castilian town of Burgos, a city disproportionately populated by soldiers and priests. The birthplace of El Cid, the legendary eleventh-century-conqueror of the Moors, Burgos had backed the military uprising with scarcely a shot being fired in opposition. 'The very stones are nationalist here,' the pro-Franco Condesa de Vallellano told Marcel Junot, a Red Cross doctor. In fact, what opposition there was found itself brutally repressed before it had had time to organise itself. Republican sympathisers who were identified in local police files were taken from their families and shot.

Within days Burgos was transformed into the effective capital of Franco's Spain, a safe haven as well as a gathering place for some of the aristocrats and other anti-Republican civilians who had fled Madrid. By the time the ambulance, driven by Burns, and with Gabriel Herbert as his passenger, reached it, the town was also home to foreign journalists covering the Nationalist advance on the north of the country. Burns and Herbert, identifying themselves as two volunteer Catholic 'aid workers', were initially welcomed by a delegate of the Red Cross, the Duchess of Lecera. Of his meeting with the Anglophile Spanish aristocrat, Burns would later recall: 'A diminutive but dynamic lady with cropped hair, in a peaked cap and khaki uniform. She spoke perfect English . . . Her somewhat bovine husband was rumoured to be at least the would-be lover of Queen Ena. I was to learn later that, unless they moved in a circumambient atmosphere of scandal, Spanish aristocrats would feel themselves unclothed.'

While Gabriel and her team of Spaniards oversaw the distribution of medical supplies, and drew up lists of further orders, Burns went out drinking with the press corps, a convivial group of semi-alcoholics. He discovered that one of their number, Kim Philby, was then out of town.

Philby had first arrived in Spain in February 1937, having secured accreditation as a freelance from the London *Evening Standard* and a

German magazine called *Geopolitics*. As he later recalled, his immediate assignment was to get first-hand information of the Franco war effort and transmit this to his Soviet contacts, who in turn would pass it on to the Republican army. However, his main mission was to assist in an abortive Soviet attempt to assassinate Franco. For the purpose, Philby attached himself initially to the nationalist's southern logistical command in Seville. The assassination plot was aborted after Philby nearly had his cover blown during a visit to Cordoba. He was in the Andalusian town with the aim of watching a bullfight but inadvertently strayed into a restricted military area. He was arrested by Civil Guards and questioned while his luggage and clothes were searched. When asked to turn his pockets out, Philby threw his wallet across the table – a move that distracted his interrogators and, so he later claimed, gave him time to put into his mouth a small ball of paper on which his secret codes were written, before swallowing it.

Philby was released without charge and went back to London where he was debriefed by his Soviet controllers and relieved of further involvement in the assassination plot. He was told to focus on securing further intelligence on Franco and his forces. Having obtained a further letter of accreditation from the London General Press, a news and syndication agency, Philby was subsequently hired by *The Times* and returned to Spain as its correspondent in June 1937.

He reported from Salamanca where Franco had established his first military headquarters in the local bishop's palace. He also spent some time in Burgos where, by the autumn of 1937, foreign journalists accredited to Franco's army were spending more of their time, using it as a base to report on the nationalist advance across the Basque country. Whereas his colleagues were genuine war correspondents, Philby continued to use his journalism as a cover for espionage. He had been recruited as an agent of the Soviet intelligence service in 1934, a year after leaving Cambridge a convinced communist.

In the run-up to the Spanish Civil War, Philby had been encouraged by his Soviet controller to join the Anglo-German Fellowship to cover up his communist background, including his post-Cambridge involvement with the socialist movement in Vienna where he had married a communist student, Litzi Friedman. It was not until January 1963 that Philby's cover was officially blown after the Soviet Union announced it had granted him political asylum in Moscow. The full story of who among Philby's acquaintances suspected his true identity in the preceding thirty years is unlikely ever to be fully revealed. Philby carried many of his secrets to the grave, knowing many people who had as much, if not more, to lose from the revelation of the truth as he did.

Nevertheless there is little doubt that during the 1930s Philby swam in similar waters to Catholic laymen during his stint at the Anglo-German Fellowship, and later when filing pro-Franco copy from behind Nationalist lines, and did so without revealing the true nature of his political sympathies or secret assignments. The fact that in Salamanca, and later in Burgos, Philby had an attractive, socially well-heeled and amusing mistress he could bed whenever he felt like relieving the stress of war was a source of envy for the bulk of his mainly womanless fellow hacks.

But for the visiting 'aid volunteer' Burns, the discovery that the mistress in question was in town while Philby was temporarily absent was a cause of some personal celebration. For Philby's lover, the Canadian-born Lady Lindsay Hogg, was not unknown to Burns. In fact, she was an old friend from pre-war days in Chelsea and Bloomsbury.

Burns had met Lady Lindsay Hogg during the early 1930s when the then Frances 'Bunny' Noble was a young, effervescent star of the London stage. After her marriage to Sir Anthony Lindsay Hogg, Burns temporarily lost track of Bunny, only to rediscover her once she had extended her social network to Spanish aristocrats and other Francoist sympathisers, friendships she had sought to repay by sharing passionately in their cause. The Spanish Civil War lover of the man destined to be exposed as one of the most famous spies of the twentieth century was a thirty-five-year-old divorcee when Burns shared a flirtatiously nostalgic meal with her in Philby's temporary absence, the food selected in the full mutual knowledge of its aphrodisiacal properties. ' "Bunny" was good company,' Burns recalled years later. 'I can see her now laughing at my shock at the effect of lemon juice on fresh clams, wriggling and raising their periscopes in apparent surprise.'

It was in Burgos that Franco's chief liaison officer with the foreign press, Merry del Val, offered Burns a tour of Gernika as part of the extended propaganda battle fought in print and on the wireless following the Basque town's bombing. The two had been contemporaries at Stonyhurst, when Del Val's father was Spanish ambassador in London. Del Val appears to have harboured few doubts that Burns, by now a director of the rabidly pro-Franco *Tablet*, would be receptive to whatever propaganda was laid before him.

'Pablo (Merry del Val) took us to Gernika and patiently explained that the extensive destruction of the main streets had been the work of the retreating Reds. Dynamite, not bombs of the German Condor Legion, was responsible. It was not convincing propaganda and has since been abandoned,' Burns admitted many years later. At the time, though, he chose to keep whatever doubts he had to himself, believing that breaking Catholic ranks on Gernika would threaten Britain's and Franco's best interests – that of maintaining the British policy of non-intervention, however breached it was in practice by its other European signatories, namely Germany and Italy. After Gernika, Burns spent a few more days wining and dining Bunny Noble while Kim Philby continued to be professionally occupied getting as near as he could to the battle front behind Nationalist lines, not without raising some suspicions among his own colleagues.

Some of Philby's English-speaking colleagues, among them Sam Pope Brewer of the *New York Times* and Karl Robson of the *Daily Telegraph*, noticed Philby's tendency to ask more probing questions than other journalists at press briefings, wanting details such as names, numbers and troops strengths. Whenever he returned to base, Philby was as hard-drinking as the rest of his colleagues, but when not with Bunny usually drank alone, maintaining a certain personal aloofness.

The Spanish minders had no problem with Philby. Convinced as they were of his pro-Nationalist credentials, they were happy to offer him any detail they thought might underline Franco's tactical nous and his military superiority. Pope Brewer and Robson later claimed that they suspected Philby was not who he claimed to be, even if neither of them guessed that he was a Soviet spy. Robson, who shared a room with Philby at one point, used to listen to him painting a doomsday scenario of China and Russia dominating the world. Robson thought Philby's anti-communism exaggerated but claimed to have been too preoccupied with the war to give it much thought. Robson was in a car in front of Philby's when, on New Year's Eve 1937, he and a group of journalists left Zaragoza by convoy to cover Franco's bold counter-attack to relieve a besieged garrison near the town of Teruel. Philby travelled in the back seat of a two-door saloon, accompanied by an Englishman, Dick Sheepshanks of Reuters, and two Americans, Ed Neil of Associated Press and Bradish Johnson, a freelance photographer who was on assignment for *Newsweek*.

On the way to Teruel the journalists stopped off at a small village called Caude. It was mid-morning with sub-zero temperatures. Soldiers huddled round improvised fires. Robson walked a few yards and sought shelter with a group huddled by the side of the barn to protect themselves from the wind. Suddenly there was a violent explosion, knocking two nearby Spanish press officers to the ground. Through a thick pale of smoke, Robson could see that the car Philby had been travelling in was on fire. He then saw Philby staggering across the road towards him, blood dripping down his face and on to his clothes, screaming as he pointed to the car, 'They're in there!'

Robson described what he saw next: 'Sickeningly I saw three figures, with grotesquely blackened faces, lolling motionless in their seats . . . When the door was opened, Johnson tumbled out dead. Sheepshanks, who had been sitting next to Johnson, was breathing in quick, deep snores, his temple torn open, and consciousness gone for ever . . . Neil was sprawled in the back . . .'

Robson put Philby's survival down to incredible luck. However, neither Robson nor the soldiers he was sheltering with, still less the two press officers who were blown off their feet, were in a position to see exactly what happened. Of the four journalists hit by the blast, one, Johnson, had died instantly, Sheepshanks died later that evening without regaining consciousness and Neil died of gangrene two days later. Only Philby survived to tell the tale. He had emerged largely untouched except for cuts on his forehead and wrist, telling Robson and others who were first on the scene that his car had been hit by shrapnel as they were entering the village. By his own account, Philby, who was sitting in the back seat, managed to 'jump out'.

After being treated in a local field hospital, Philby went back to Tarragona where he was joined by Bunny Noble. He met her in a restaurant, his head heavily bandaged but neatly, cleanly rolled and stacked like a Sikh turban. Otherwise, Philby was dressed in a fur-lined military coat lent to him by a Spanish officer, as if he had emerged heroically from the trenches, his apparent serenity masking a deeper inner tension. He asked for a drink as soon as he sat down at table. 'His hands were shaking,' Bunny later recalled, 'but his mind was absolutely clear.'

So clear that on that day, the day Neil died, Philby filed a story to *The Times*, reporting dispassionately on the death of his travelling companions and his own extraordinary escape. It was published alongside a photograph of Philby, with his head bandaged, looking more like a man in fancy-dress than an injured hero. In subsequent years conflicting accounts developed as to what really happened that cold day in December 1937. One version had it that the car had been hit by a Russian-made shell, and that the reason Philby omitted this detail from his report was that he could not bring himself to tell the world that a country he had secretly sworn allegiance to had not only killed three journalists, but also nearly killed him.

What is known about Philby is that in his years as a spy he displayed utter ruthlessness in betraying British agents in the field, and was also a master at covering his tracks. Philby's own version of what happened that winter in Spain leaves more questions than answers that, with detailed forensic investigation, might have got at the truth that was lost in the fog of war.

Philby emerged from the incident with his reputation as a loyal journalist enhanced in the eyes of Franco, who promptly honoured him with the Cross of Military Merit for bravery in the line of duty. Similar medals were awarded posthumously to the journalists who had been killed after their corpses had been returned for immediate burial to their own countries – Sheepshanks's to the UK, Neil's and Johnson's to the United States. Philby recovered, spending more time with his mistress in Zaragoza, and later in France. Then, feeling confident enough to resume his cover as a *Times* journalist, he returned to Burgos. There he continued to report on Franco's military planning and political manoeuvrings, including the institutionalisation of the *Generalísimo's* rule on 30 January 1938 with the formation of Franco's first cabinet.

The Spanish Civil War was now entering its third year. By then, some left-wing intellectuals who, like Philby, had studied at Cambridge, had been killed fighting against Franco. They included the poets John Cornford and Julian Bell and the writer David Haden-Guest. Philby showed no regret or sense of grieving. Instead he enthusiastically went on to report for *The Times* on the 'liberation' of Barcelona by Franco's troops. The city that George Orwell had witnessed in a state of euphoric revolution in the first months of the civil war in 1936 now greeted Franco with a mixture of hysterical abandon and disbelief. As one of his biographers later put it, it was in this moment of disaster for the international left that Philby celebrated the fact that his Spanish cover story had acquired perfection.

By then the civil war had secretly defined Philby politically, as it had done, in quite different ways, those English Catholics he so resented, not least Tom Burns, whose influential role as a publisher was by now well known to journalists on *The Times*. While in Burgos, Philby and Burns had separately made the acquaintance of a German officer named Ulrich von der Osten, or Don Julio, as Franco's soldiers called him.

According to Philby, the German spent much time in Burgos entertaining him, with the hope of recruiting Bunny Noble to the Nazi cause, preferably in bed. Philby later boasted that he thought he had deceived the German into believing he had done him a good turn by suggesting he could have Noble for one night, an offer she indignantly turned down.

Philby made much of von der Osten, inflating his importance as a member of the Abwehr, the German military intelligence service. The two men would make a habit of meeting in the Convento de Las Esclavas, a convent which had been converted into a logistics depot and media centre. Philby, who was by this time passing his secrets to the KGB, would later claim it was in Burgos that he had first managed to infiltrate German intelligence, a boast he used to get himself recruited by the British secret services for similar anti-Nazi work after the beginning of the Second World War.

3

MINISTRY OF INFORMATION

'Mass and Communion. After breakfast the Prime Minister broadcast the war had begun.' Thus Evelyn Waugh wrote in his diary at the beginning of September 1939 when news came through that German troops had crossed the Polish border. Much as the cause of Franco had stirred British Catholics into taking sides during the Spanish Civil War, the menace of Hitler had largely been neglected. 'Despite his impressive evidence and formidable eloquence, Churchill was not taken seriously – Parliament ignored him,' recalled Burns. 'I remember thinking that he was aggravating dangers in the very act of denouncing them. The prospect of peace receded with each new barrage of insults and accusations hurled against Hitler. Mine was a view widely shared among many of my friends.'

Even after the Munich crisis, many of them still hoped that a peace pact with Hitler was possible. The painter and poet David Jones – an integral figure in the coterie of friends that Burns had formed around him – wrote to Harman Grisewood at the BBC, following Chamberlain's first encounter with Hitler. 'Yes, I heard Chamberlain's grand little speech on his first return. I did like that more than I can say. He is simply the real goods, there is no doubt about that – the only bright spot. But, Lord, what a weight the poor man has to carry, and hardly any bugger to give him proper support.' Hitler stirred more complex emotions. In April 1939, Jones was staying at the Fort Hotel, Sidmouth when he wrote again to Grisewood thus, after reading a full edition of *Mein Kampf*. 'I am deeply impressed by it, it is amazingly interesting in all kinds of ways – but pretty terrifying too. God, he's *nearly* right – but this *hate* thing mars the whole thing, I feel. I mean it just misses getting over the frontier into the saint thing – he won't stand any nonsense or illusions or talk – but, having got so far, the conception of the world in terms of race-struggle (that's what it boils down to) will hardly do. But I do like a lot of what he says – only I must admit he sees the world as just going on for ever in this steel grip. Compared with his opponents he is grand, but compared with the saints he is bloody.'

Burns sought inspiration and hope from developments at the Vatican. On 10 February 1939, the ultramontane Pope Pius XI died. Within minutes Burns received a telephone call from Grisewood, with an urgent request that he accompany him immediately to Rome to help facilitate the BBC's coverage of the funeral. 'You'll be able to pull strings for me – I know nobody there. The BBC will pay all expenses,' Grisewood told Burns, who was more than happy to assist.

Burns had a key contact in the Vatican, a raffish prince, William Rospilgliosi, of Italo-American parentage, who ran the Italian state radio network. Thanks to the contact, the BBC was given unparalleled access to the funeral ceremony inside St Peter's, and provided with the equipment it needed.

Grisewood went on to organise the BBC's coverage of the election of the new Pope by the College of Cardinals in just three ballots and the subsequent crowning of Pius XII on 12 March, the eve of Hitler's march into Prague. The new Pope was Cardinal Eugenio Pacelli, a brilliant young Vatican lawyer who had played a major part in the drafting of the Code of Canon Law, a legal instrument which helped transform papal primacy and infallibility into an unprecedented principle of papal power.

In the early 1930s, Pacelli, by then promoted to Cardinal Secretary of State, the most important post under the Pope, negotiated a concordat with Hitler under which the Vatican secured certain privileges and protection for German Catholics in return for their withdrawal from politics. Pacelli proclaimed the Reich Concordat an unparalleled triumph for the Holy See, a total recognition of the Church's law by the German state. But Hitler interpreted it differently, seeing in it the Vatican's blessing of his policies, not least his increasingly virulent anti-Semitism.

Nevertheless when Pacelli was elected as Pope, many British Catholics saw him as a man capable of providing moral authority in the midst of the turmoil of European politics, strong enough to see off the threat of communism and to contain the ambitions of Hitler and Mussolini. Pacelli's coronation marked much more than the advent of a skilful mediator: it symbolised the Vatican's potential as a universal power.

Three days earlier, Burns had written to Grisewood in a state of spiritual and emotional euphoria. 'This is the first chance of writing to you or anyone. I've thought a lot about Rome these days and imagined you are at various times and places. Ann read me your letter and I saw and felt with you in St Peter before the conclave. I wonder if this is the time – what I think we both feel (and hope) – that this Pope really can be and do a great thing – something in a different order from others – as if he were a Gregory. Never before have I had such a personal devotion to a Pope, a personal trust as in leader and not just this supremely important ecclesiastic but really Christ's vicar . . . People are just longing for a spiritual leadership and he has all of them waiting for him and him only. It is positively momentous – This Papacy . . .'

Ann was Ann Bowes-Lyon, a member of the Royal family, with whom Burns had embarked on a passionate if doomed affair. The precise circumstances and timing of their first meeting remain obscure, with both parties taking a deliberate decision to keep their relationship protected from public scrutiny in later years.

But letters and other material discovered by the author in the later stages of researching this book have helped bring to light one of the more intriguing social encounters of the 1930s, when a generation was forced to set aside the frivolity of its party days and face up to the slow drift to world war with a sense of urgency as well as vertigo. Ann was the daughter of Patrick Bowes Lyon, a retired army officer, and the fifth son of the 13th Earl of Strathmore. She was the youngest of four children. The oldest in the family, Gavin, was killed in action in the Great War, aged twenty-one. A second brother, Angus, fought and survived the same war and committed suicide in 1923, aged twenty-three. Ann's sister, Jean, was three years older than her, and never married. The extended Bowes-Lyon family of cousins and second cousins had a history of early death, neurosis, and alcoholism. Ann was descended from an ancient aristocratic Scottish family, although rumour had it that the blue blood had been mixed by the time Ann was born due to the ancestral dalliance with working-class maids. The family seat, Glamis, was a legendary castle, the fictitious setting for the murder of King Duncan in Shakespeare's *Macbeth* and the real-life childhood home Ann had shared with her cousin, Elizabeth Bowes-Lyon, the future Duchess, Queen Consort, and eventual Queen Mother.

Of those childhood days, prior to the outbreak of the Great War, royal biographer Hugo Vickers has remarked on the structured aristocratic society that manifested itself at Glamis, as it had done for centuries. 'Following the three month London season, the aristocrats retired to their estates, where they remained from August to November . . . they invited other aristocrats to join them in their sport, be it shooting or hunting.' During the First World War, Glamis was converted into a Red Cross home for wounded servicemen. While Elizabeth stayed in the castle helping her mother and older sister look after the soldiers, Ann remained closeted in her parental home in London's Queen's Gate, taught by governesses.

Yet Ann was eleven years old by the time the war ended and not unaffected by the anguish and trauma which the Bowes-Lyons, like so many other families, suffered at the battlefield deaths of family members. The men of the Strathmore family, according to Vickers, were 'damaged for life', with a heavy strain of alcoholism affecting sons and fathers, and breakdown and suicides affecting the next generation.

Ann survived her teenage years, living comfortably between Mayfair and a large country house in Kent and watching her older female cousins emerge in society, the normal events of the season – balls, races, hunts, and shoots – re-established despite crippling taxation.

She came of age at eighteen in 1925, at a time when the old social boundaries of the Edwardian age were, in the words of D.J. Taylor, 'annually dissolving'. Alongside the formal entertainments of Ascot and debutante balls there emerged the 'smart bohemia' of the 'Bright Young Persons', with hedonistic parties open as much to aspiring avant-garde intellectuals as to young Ladies and Honourables.

How frequently Ann stepped out of her protective seasonal programme and into the racier nights where social convention was self-consciously flouted is not clear. There is an undated letter to her from Harman Grisewood offering an introduction to Olivia Plunket Greene, among the more notorious female members of one of the chief Bright Young Persons groups. She also corresponded as a young woman with academics and the occasional artist. But Ann did not earn a reputation as a fast aristocratic young lady with a particularly adventurous private life. It would take her some years before she found someone capable of breaking through her emotional self-control and gained sufficient trust in men with which to build a relationship.

Burns's own memoirs suggest that he spent most of the 1920s without ever falling seriously in love. It was a period during which he avoided deep commitments, including proposals of marriage, or complex affairs, preferring instead to live, as so many of his 'set' did, in a state of fluctuating and frivolous affections.

Before moving to Glebe Place, on the King's Road, Burns lived in a flat in St Leonard's Terrace from where he straddled social milieus with an eclectic group of friends, several of them active members of the Bright Young Persons set, ranging from homosexual painters like Cedric Morris and his anonymous 'saturnine lover' to writers like John Betjeman and the poet's friend from Oxford days, the extrovert Etonian Lord 'Cracky' Billy Clonmore.

During 'the season' Burns emerged from his modest quarters in Chelsea 'like a butterfly from a chrysalis', in white tie and tails for events often given by hostesses he barely knew.

He later recalled, 'I discovered that I was on some sort of hostess register, my entry read: "Smart young man, dances well, safe in taxis."' When there were no balls, Burns visited the venues appropriated by the wilder party-goers and sexually liberated intellectuals of the Bloomsbury set. The Gargoyle, the Café Anglais, and Hell were habitual haunts.

Life however had moved on by the time Burns met Ann Bowes-Lyon. By the 1930s, in common with many of the Bright Young Persons, Burns had put behind him the unbridled extravagance of his youth and replaced it with a deeper yearning to make sense of the gathering storms moving across the world stage. He was a committed publisher, dedicated to weighing up the possibilities for co-operation and resolution of conflict between the modern world and Catholicism at every point where contacts could be established – in arts, politics, economics, and, last but no means least, human relationships. Their first meeting is thought to have taken place on 19 June 1935 during the first performance in the Chapter House of Canterbury Cathedral of T. S. Eliot's *Murder in the Cathedral*. The play had Robert Speaight, a mutual friend of Burns and Grisewood, in the main role of Becket and all three were there that night, as was Ann, invited by – drawn by – veneration for Eliot. Ann at the time had become increasingly drawn to the Catholic faith through her friendship with a Cambridge academic couple, Dorothy Hoare and her husband Jose Maria, otherwise known as 'JM' De Navarro – both Catholics – much to the disapproval of her Protestant parents.

While Burns had befriended Eliot in 1932 during the poet's year-long professorship at Harvard University in the US, Ann's acquaintance was more recent, and was linked to her developing interest in poetry as a writer of it herself, and her growing interest in religion. Like several aspiring poets, Ann had sent Eliot some of her own tentative verses to him at the publishing house Faber & Faber, where he was director, with the hope of obtaining his blessing.

Within two years, by 1937, Eliot liked Ann sufficiently to publish her first and only collection of verses with the coveted Faber imprint. The edition was entitled simply *Poems by Ann Lyon*, had a very small print run, and limited publicity. It was subsequently circulated among friends rather than family, suggesting a tension between Ann's public persona and private life.

Of the fifty-four poems, mostly written in the haunting elegiac style of the early-twentieth-century 'Georgian' poets, three – 'To Have Loved Enough', 'Hypnos from a Bronze', and 'The Lover' – stand out because of the intimacy linking the poet to an unidentified person. They are love poems, intensely expressed, with feelings of longing underpinned by a prevailing sense of vulnerability and foreboding. The lover was Burns.

> *So bound in you, I scarce can draw breath*
> *But your quiet breathing stirs against my breast,*
> *Under my heart I feel your heart's unrest*
> *The close quiescence of your tenderness . . .*

I have no movement shared not-even death
That stills the tumult of a blood to sleep
Shall merge immortally hand and lip
And seal the consummation of our kiss.

It was over a discussion about Eliot, his growing interest in Christian activism, and the way in which the play they had seen in Canterbury seemed to combine faith and poetry in the figure of a solitary and ambivalent martyr, that Burns fell in love with Ann Bowes-Lyon, at twenty-eight years old one year younger than himself.

Burns found Ann – born a Protestant but moving towards the Church of Rome much as Eliot was – intellectually mature and physically attractive in a way that set her apart from and above other women he had known. She was no sexual flirt like Olivia Plunket Greene, nor a religious fundamentalist like Gabriel Herbert. Her royal lineage and self-control challenged him socially and romantically – the commoner pursuing his 'princess'. The suggestion that Ann's blue blood may have been mixed as a result of an ancestor's affair with a Welsh maid appears to have been kept from him, another secret the Bowes-Lyon family thought it prudent not to share with the outside world.

Ann, for her part, found herself initially uneasy at being courted with such passion by a man who evidently was well outside the tightly-knit aristocratic circle in which she had been brought up. A cradle Catholic, born in a foreign land, and educated by the Jesuits, the darkly handsome Burns carried the charismatic air of a bachelor who seemed more content with life than the male members of her family, and with a self-confidence that contrasted with the stiff upright young men she had met when growing up. And yet from their first meeting, he had also shown himself disarmingly thoughtful.

He was not only insightful about literature, and matters of faith, but deeply sensitive and receptive to her views. He began to pay court, writing to her and seeing her whenever he could – whenever she returned to London between extended stints at Glamis and her country home in Kent near Churchill's house in Chartwell. Burns would often follow Ann to Orchard Farm, a large cottage her academic friends the De Navarros owned in Worcestershire, near to where her sister Jean lived.

The De Navarros were happy to provide an intimate environment where the lovers could meet without the intrusion of Ann's parents or some of her less liberated childhood friends. Such was the intensity of the affair that Burns would leave sealed notes around the cottage for Ann to remind her of a particular passionate moment they had recently shared.

In one letter, dated 29 May 1939, Burns while at Orchard Farm wrote: 'Darling, here I am alone in this room, crouched next to the fire – I can hear little padding about above and still the sound of your voice. This is just a "ticket" for your morning – to tell you how very dear you have been all day. From the moment you popped your fuzzy head out of the window – to the moment you laid it back on the pillow after I had kissed you goodnight you were beautiful, really and truly lovely . . . I know that my heart is branded with your beauty, Ann, and no one else can make their mark now. Dearest . . . I'm grateful for you being so much better than when I last saw you . . .'

Photographs the De Navarros snapped of the couple at the time show Burns and Ann standing rather awkwardly before the camera, as if slightly uneasy about their relationship being recorded for posterity. Perhaps Ann's sister Jean was present that day. However intense, their love affair appeared to be based on fragile ground.

Gradually she found herself opening her inner feelings to him in a way that she had never done with anybody else, as if he had laid siege to her Edwardian battlement and breached its defences.

As she wrote in another of her poems:

> If to have loved enough could be its own assurance
> There was no chink left in my armour,
> Never a hidden entry for betrayal
> Only the safety of your tenderness
> Like a firelit room secure from the winter night.

The passionate poetess is barely hinted at in a collection of photographs taken by Howard Coster for the National Portrait Gallery in 1937, about the time her relationship with Burns was becoming more intense. It shows her very posed and controlled – a well-groomed woman with a swan-like neck, face of fine complexion and eyes suggesting an inner intelligence. As a mature young woman, Ann shared some common traits with her cousin Elizabeth, including deep-blue eyes and that 'thrush-like beauty' as Cecil Beaton would later refer to the future Queen Mother. Beneath the veneer of prudence and decorum was a multi-layered personality that Burns discovered only gradually, and which made his relationship with the future Queen's cousin something tense, unpredictable, and for his part certainly, almost obsessive.

That Burns's relationship with Ann came to prove more complicated than his previous somewhat frivolous affairs of the heart had to do with the royal milieu into which she had been propelled as a result of the events of 1936. For in that year her cousin Elizabeth Bowes-Lyon had become the Duchess of York, briefly sister-in-law to King Edward VIII, before finally Queen Consort to King George VI. Suddenly Ann found herself sharing her family duties with an extended royal household that, after the debacle of Mrs Simpson's relationship with King Edward VIII and the ensuing abdication crisis, was less than open to outsiders.

Ann nonetheless stirred in Burns romantic notions of his own Scottish roots, which, he believed, stretched back, as they did with the Bowes-Lyon family, to Robert the Bruce, the great King of Scotland. The turmoil sweeping through European politics, and the growing realisation that world war might not be far off, made the relationship both intense and complicated as it developed during the late 1930s.

When not seeing each other at Burns's flat off the King's Road, or at the homes of mutual friends, the pair maintained a regular correspondence, only Burns's side of which has survived. The letters are punctuated with references to a feline world in which Burns includes sketches of himself and Ann as loving cats in constant pursuit of each other – he a dark tabby, she a sophisticated white Persian. The feline imagery and language show the influence of T. S. Eliot, whose recently published whimsical verses on cat psychology and sociology, *Old Possum's Book of Practical Cats* – fully illustrated – contrasted with the intensity of his early works and the mounting sense of collective unease in the run up to the Second World War.

During the first months of 1939, Ann suffered periodic illness – fatigue accompanied by nausea and fever, symptoms of the depression that affected generations of Bowes-Lyons. Several letters written to her by Burns during this period refer to her either as bed-ridden or recovering from illness. Learning from his experience of living with his friend David Jones, who was also a depressive, Burns tried his best to divert her attention from what he saw as the demons that threatened her from without – in particular the pressures to conform emanating from Glamis Castle and her parents' home in Kent. But there was a part of him that increasingly came to see the darkness affecting those dearest to him as part of a broader pattern of political and social dislocation. As the war drew nearer, it focused his protective thoughts on her, expressing them as a form of prayer, as if by so doing he hoped not only to win her heart but ensure, through God's intercession, that war would be avoided.

In March he wrote, 'My darling Ann, I wish I was with you tonight. Being together in love would put these given things in their place. Poor poor little miaoooo – being sick in the wood – I do indeed understand how you could be but you see, darling, things are much better than they appear to be: and we live in the frontiers of heaven and hell – of which peace or rumblings of war are very sketchy shadows. Live in the reality and the world will do what one expects of it, of good and bad. I mean live in a kind of prayer and you'll be all right . . .'

In August, Ann was with other members of the Bowes-Lyon family in Glamis Castle, attending the usual round of summer house parties as generations had done before them, when Ribbentrop, the former German ambassador to London who had become Hitler's foreign minister, flew to Moscow and with Stalin's foreign secretary Molotov signed the Nazi–Soviet Pact that divided Poland between them. A letter reached her from Burns: 'I keep thinking of you isolated up there with all this wild and grim news flying around: poor darling: I do hope you are all right. The Russian–German hook-up may turn out to be a good thing; if the Germans and Poles both act with generosity and common sense: seeing destruction of Poland as certain if things waver and deciding to play for peace with Danzig and the diminished life of Poland after its gone. Before this pact, you see, the Poles were more likely to fight and the left wing in this country were getting more and more impatient with Chamberlain and keener and keener on the Russians; now at any rate, even Mr Gollancz will have to see the light –

which is simply that the Russian simply cannot be trusted at all. I hope it is not too late – but our left wing has led us a long way up the garden path and it's difficult to come back . . .'

The hope that another world war might be avoided was shattered by Hitler's invasion of Poland. When he heard the news, Burns could think of nothing better to do but go to Fortnum & Mason and invest in a pair of strong brogues and an all-purpose canvas bag, in case he might be called up. Later he went back to his house, and there, in the white room, with Tim on his lap, wrote Ann the first lines that came into his head. In the intimate code language they used with each other, spontaneous notes quickly dispatched by messenger or left on coffee tables came to be known as 'tickets'. This was the first ticket of the war.

'Darling little heart – this is just a scribble in the midst of things to say hello. I think these last days aren't at all without their muse. They make us take stock and see what we stand for and mean to do and be. My Darling – I will write a little ticket very soon – tonight it's impossible . . . What a wind and rain tonight – cats ought to be curled up in boxes on such a night as this – I'll send my love to keep you warm. Blessing you my dreamt one . . .'

Hours after war had been declared, Burns sat at home drinking whisky with a young friend, Michael Richey, discussing the tumultuous events that were unfolding. At twenty-three, Richey was ten years younger than Burns. A fellow Catholic, he had been educated as a schoolboy by the Benedictines, and had for a while considered becoming a monk himself before joining Eric Gill's commune of artists as an apprentice carver.

By 1939 Richey was looking for a job in the wider world, quite where and what he had no idea after the unique if occasionally unsettling experience of working with Gill.

Burns convinced Richey that the best way to reconcile his pacifism with his sense of patriotic duty was to join the navy, serving on a minesweeper as an ordinary seaman. As he told Richey, 'This seemed to me an admirable way of confronting things, as when you sweep mines you are destroying instruments of destruction though you are liable to be blown up yourself.'

Burns for his part made an effortless entry into government service, the outbreak of the war marking his transition from a public figure to an agent of the state playing multiple parts. The BBC's Grisewood and Lord Howard of Penrith were among those who brought to the attention of the higher echelons of Whitehall Burns's background as a leading Catholic publisher and his experience as a consummate communicator and social networker.

Shortly before war broke out he received instructions to report to the Ministry of Information (MoI), and was told he was to be in charge of 'Roman Catholic affairs'.

The Ministry of Information, while officially functional from 4 September 1939, the day after the UK declared war on Germany, had been secretly planned since 1935 by an internal Whitehall committee. Secrecy had been maintained because the government did not want to admit to the inevitability of war.

Senior UK officials claimed to have learnt the lessons of the First World War, when propaganda was the responsibility of various government agencies except for a brief period when there had been a Department of Information (1917) and an earlier version of the MoI (1918) which was subsequently disbanded.

Plans for the new MoI, with overarching responsibility for publicity and propaganda in the Second World War, had been accelerated in response to the well-oiled Nazi propaganda machinery under Dr Goebbels. The MoI's initial functions were threefold: news and press censorship; 'home publicity'; and overseas publicity in Allied and neutral countries. In early 1939, UK government officials predicted a 'war of nerves' involving the civilian population and warned ministers they would have to go further than ever before in 'coordinating and utilising' every propaganda tool at their disposal in order to counter the Nazi threat. Burns was given a broad brief, from encouraging contacts with dissident Germans to liaising with the Vatican, and developing links with Franco's Spain and Salazar's Portugal, as well as with influential Catholics in the United States.

Burns moved into the Ministry of Information's offices in the University of London's headquarters at Senate House in early 1940, about the time his friend the future poet laureate, John Betjeman, was recruited into the Films Division by Kenneth Clark.

Employees of the Ministry were instructed to keep their duties secret from the outside world and worked to a rolling eight-hour shift pattern to ensure 24-hour coverage. And yet for all the semblance of a functioning and efficient government department, the early months proved particularly shambolic as the MoI struggled to define a clear role for itself and to make efficient use of a mixed bag of recruits drawn somewhat haphazardly from a wide variety of professions. One of the MoI's senior recruits, Kenneth Grubb, recalled the initial confusion its creation brought to the machinery of government: 'The permanent civil servants who inevitably handle the higher arrangements of a new ministry were themselves frequently at a loss to perceive the next step, although war presupposes quick decisions. Many different types of personalities and experiences were needed. Someone had to find the scholarly approach on some remote but key territory, the journalist with the right touch, the broadcaster, the advertiser, and many others from the publicity profession. Most of us indulged in an unscrupulous and crazy scramble to secure the best available people before they were snapped up, since everyone knew that war was bound to create a shortage of capable management types.'

In the early stages of the war, the MoI's operations were hampered by the lack of cooperation from other agencies of government, namely the War Office, the Air Ministry and the Admiralty, and the intelligence services that resented what they saw as a weakening of their ability to control and manipulate the flow of information to the public on military plans and movements. Similarly, the MoI's involvement in propaganda in enemy-occupied and neutral countries led to tensions with the BBC and other Whitehall departments such as the Foreign Office and the Ministry of Economic Warfare.

In its attempts to impose itself on government policy, the MoI was further disadvantaged by frequent changes of senior personnel. Between 4 September 1939 and 20 July 1941, the department changed ministers three times – Lord Hugh Macmillan, Sir John Reith, and Alfred 'Duff' Cooper paving the way for a more continuous and successful leadership under Brendan Bracken. There were also mixed blessings in the fact that civil servants outnumbered public relations and advertising experts, with many tasks being left in the hands of writers, publishers and artists with no experience of government, still less of taking on an enemy expert in the art of spin and deception.

In Evelyn Waugh's 1942 novel *Put Out More Flags*, it is the MoI in the early months of the war that bears the brunt of Waugh's acerbic satire as the author tries to capture the mood of a nation changing from frivolity to a deep sense of foreboding, and as the ageing generation of bright young things contemplates division, death and destruction.

The main character, Basil Seal, finds himself at the outbreak of war a man without a job, despite his firm belief in himself as the kind of person who 'if English life had run as it did in the books of adventure' should at this turn in world affairs have been sent for by the secret intelligence services. But hard as he tries to exploit his social 'old boy networks', Basil cannot penetrate the world of propaganda and secrets. The nearest he gets to initial employment is an interview at the MoI, a Ministry also visited by his friend, the camp aesthete Ambrose Silk, who ends up peating bogs in a friar's garb. Ambrose's invitation to visit the MoI is facilitated by his publisher, Geoffrey Bentley, who is working there at the head of some newly formed department. In his introduction to the Penguin edition of *Put Out More Flags*, Nigel Spivey notes, rightly, that Basil Seal falls short of being quite the mirror image of his creator, Waugh – 'too tall, too handsome, too well-born' – but the book is a brilliant satire on the administrative chaos and improvisation that characterised Whitehall, and the MoI in particular, in the first months of the phoney war. It is hard not to see Basil's alter ego Bentley as a thinly veiled if partial portrait of Waugh's friend Burns, who in real life continued to commission books from his literary contacts, while branching out into a world of intrigue and secrets for which he had no formal training.

In the autumn of 1938, Burns approached Waugh himself to write another book, a history of the Jesuits. He also commissioned the eccentric and controversial Hilaire Belloc, whose blend of humour and bellicosity came to be much admired by Catholics of Waugh's generation, not least Evelyn himself.

Burns asked Belloc to write a preface to a book by his old friend J. B. Morton – 'Beachcomber'. Belloc's agreement was conveyed in a letter addressed to Burns care of the Reform, one of several London clubs the publisher used for nurturing his friends and clients.

'Dear Burns . . . I shall be delighted to do such a preface as you propose. I don't mind the terms so five guineas will do as well as anything else, but I shall begin it with the words, "My dear Morton" because I think beginning with the name under which I usually write to him, "My dear Johnnie", would be too familiar for public print.' After Chamberlain's declaration of war, Burns enlisted the help of his friend and political ally Douglas Jerrold to get Belloc to write 10,000 words of pro-government propaganda, entitled 'The Case for the Present War, from the Catholic Angle'.

During the 1930s the fear of Communism had produced ground in which sympathy for fascism had grown among some Catholic intellectuals as well as the members of the British upper classes – hence the support for the Italians in Ethiopia and the Nationalists in Spain, even if this has been described by church historian Adrian Hastings as 'individualistic and idiosyncratic' and 'carrying little weight outside the upper-class Roman Catholic community'. But if Belloc, one of Burns's enduring influences, had made enemies on the left by his support for right-wing French Catholics and his alleged anti-Semitism, his mind about Nazism had been made up once war had been declared, and he was against it.

Belloc grew to despair of the newly elected Pope's apparent inability to speak out unequivocally against the Nazis, 'browbeaten, by people who talk of a large and powerful Catholic body in Boche-land'. As Belloc put it, 'There is no such thing. The Catholic Germans were swamped and dowsed long ago in a flood of horribly vulgar Paganism with Atheistic architecture.'

In fact the need to encourage the stirrings of opposition to Hitler within German Catholic circles was one of the tasks Burns had set himself from his early days at the MoI. In this endeavour he was helped by Harman Grisewood and Bernard Wall, who, after a stint working undercover in Rome, went on to join the Foreign Office research department based at Balliol College, Oxford, under the direction of Dr Arnold Toynbee and Sir Alfred Zimmerman.

'Before the war . . . violent polemics were carried out by literary men, but they hardly ever bothered to check and counter check their facts. Now facts took their revenge,' recalled Wall. 'We had to find out what was true in a world deluged by lies. The lies weren't only Hitler's and Stalin's. Though in Dr Toynbee's department we told no lies, we were surrounded by lies. The British and Americans, once they had set their minds to war and propaganda, pursued both ruthlessly.'

Once again the network of Catholic public school boys had a common point of contact not just in Burns, but also in his old Jesuit mentor Fr D'Arcy. The enthusiasm D'Arcy had put into backing the Franco cause during the Spanish Civil War was channelled into the new war aims of the British government. Appointed to the BBC's religious committee, D'Arcy began to broadcast frequently on the need for Christians on both sides of the Atlantic to unite against the Nazi persecution of the Catholic Church. Later, in September 1941, D'Arcy left for the United States on a mission organised by the Catholic Department of the Ministry of Information. His aim was to influence the Catholic community in the US, namely the Irish and Italians, to drop its opposition to US intervention in favour of the Allies.

D'Arcy's success in becoming part of the Allied war effort contrasted with Evelyn Waugh's failure to join a network of friends at the MoI. In *Put Out More Flags* Basil's own attempt to gain useful employment during the phoney war is drawn from Waugh's own frustrating experiences during that period.

Waugh wrote to Basil Dufferin, the Under Secretary of State for the Colonies, an old acquaintance, in the hope that he might use his influence. This and subsequent approaches failed to elicit a positive response. Waugh himself suspected the dark hand of MI5, the security service, which, after Munich, and especially after the German occupation of Czechoslovakia, was digging up old files and creating new ones on potential fifth columnists it saw as capable of furthering the interests of an international conspiracy of Nazis and communists. Waugh had supported Mussolini in the Abyssinian War, and had been pro-Franco during the Spanish Civil War, declaring his sympathies for both causes respectively in *Waugh in Abyssinia* and *Robbery Under Law*. His social contacts during the 1930s had extended to families like the Mitfords and the Mosleys, who moved on the fringes of British politics and openly sympathised with Hitler's Germany. It was this background, combined with Waugh's reputation as a satirist, that might have contributed to putting obstacles in his way inside Whitehall. Burns, thanks to his friends in the Foreign Office, seems to have been initially more fortunate in ensuring that his pro-Franco leanings were not held against him, although he failed, despite Waugh's recommendation, to enlist for covert military duties with the Special Operations Executive, having been judged to lack a killer instinct.

Burns later recalled: 'Evelyn turned up at the Ministry of Information early in the war. He had fixed an interview for me with some Special Services unit and advised me to go, "Get a haircut . . ." I eventually reached the War Office via Trumper's suitably trimmed. Here a bull-necked officer rushed at me with unexpected questions: "Can you gouge a man's eyes out with your thumbs – *from behind*?" "Can you find the kidneys with a sharp knife?' I must have failed in these and other questions because I never heard from him again. Anyway, I was soon off on other business in Spain.'

Burns's 'business' in Spain was a few weeks away yet. It was still a phoney war for almost everyone except those in the Royal Navy who were already embarked on a dangerous mission at sea. Instead of engaging in full-scale military operations, the British shadow-boxed with the enemy, drawing up secret plans, intercepting secret messages, distributing agents, befriending friendly foreigners and tracking suspect aliens. Priests, public school boys, convent girls came and went at the MoI, a building whose architecture and some of its activities partly inspired the model for the Ministry of Truth wherein Winston Smith laboured at the falsification of history in George Orwell's novel *1984*. 'The Ministry of Truth – Mintrie, in Newspeak – was startlingly different from any other object in sight. It was an enormous pyramidal structure of glittering white concrete, soaring up terrace after terrace 300 metres in the air.'

In fact Senate House is built of Portland stone and not quite 300 metres high. The Ministry of Truth was an amalgam of Orwell's literary imagination, which was also influenced by his experience working as a propagandist at the BBC, and that of his wife Eileen's time working for the Ministry of Food.

At the MoI, Burns was joined by Graham Greene, an appointment he helped facilitate with the help of Denis Cowan, the head of his

Catholic propaganda section. Greene was recruited initially into the Film Division, sharing an office with his Oxford contemporary John Betjeman, and put to work on some scripts. After returning from Mexico, and writing up his account of his time there for his publisher Burns in *The Lawless Roads*, Greene had set about turning this into fiction in *The Power and the Glory*. This was followed by *The Confidential Agent*, a novel set in the Spanish Civil War. Its two main Spanish characters were drawn from opposite sides of the conflict.

Greene had never been to Spain. As we have seen, the nearest he'd got to the Spanish border was his attempt to reach besieged Bilbao in 1937, but the book shows that Greene's literary imagination had not remained idle during a period when some of his closest professional contacts and friends were fully absorbed by events south of the Pyrenees.

The two main characters combine to mirror Greene's own torn loyalties when faced with the stark clash of ideals the war in Spain provoked. The confidential agent 'D' of the title is a Republican but was a scholar of medieval literature before the war. The other agent 'L', who is on the side of Franco, in conversation with 'D' confesses to also being a student of such literature but laments the fact that 'D's comrades had burnt his pictures and books, including a manuscript of St Augustine's *City of God*.

In September 1939, in order to complete the novels he was working on, Greene persuaded a draft board of the Officers' Emergency Reserve to postpone his call-up by a few months. After joining Burns at the MoI, Greene managed to survive the administrative upheavals higher up the management chain by helping to enlist the support of a variety of authors and other contacts for the propaganda effort.

Among those who visited the MoI during this period was the writer Barbara Lucas, Bernard Wall's wife, whom Burns had first introduced to Greene while working as a young publisher for Sheed & Ward. Wall was accompanied by Mike Richey, who had by now followed Burns's advice and enlisted in the Royal Navy.

Lucas recorded in her diary, 'Mike on leave came to see us ... went to the Ministry of Information to see Graham Greene and Tom. We hadn't got passes but Mike said we were parachutists (SOE) so were let in. Had a nice chat with Graham Greene and a horrid one with

Tom who is always a bit stiff when he is in his office. I recall that Tom thought it rather a bore that these two rather scruffy people were dropping in on him just when he was starting in his rather nice new office.'

If the stress of wartime government work occasionally got the better of Burns, he, like Greene, knew how to compartmentalise his existence, compensating for the self-imposed discipline of office life with romantic entanglements. The prospect of war, the pervading sense that life as lived till then was about to change irrevocably, with unforeseeable consequences, fuelled a basic human instinct to live for the moment, and focus on what was achievable, a need Burns and Greene were reminded of no sooner had they stepped out of the cold interior of Senate House and into the surrounding neighbourhood of Bloomsbury.

And yet the woman Burns pursued at the time, Ann Bowes-Lyon, continued to resist marriage, and any enduring emotional attachment. The declaration of war brought back memories of the death in action of her youngest brother in the last Great War and of so many of their generation, making her anxious and threatening another bout of depression not unlike that which had ended in her older brother's suicide in 1923. This time nothing her lover could say to her seemed to motivate her. Instead it was her extended Royal family who saved her, for they fuelled in her a sense of patriotic duty, and determined what action she should take.

A major influence was her enthroned cousin, Elizabeth. For within days of Chamberlain declaring war on Germany, Queen Elizabeth threw herself into a hectic round of morale-boosting visits and initiatives aimed at encouraging the involvement of women in the war effort. A new generation of women – voters and workers – was being called for special duties, many of them separated from their children. This was a war destined to draw women into a whole range of fields, from nursing to special operations. With no medical training, Ann joined VAD (Voluntary Aid Detachment) and was posted to the Royal Herbert Hospital in Woolwich. Just over twenty-five years earlier, in December 1914, the first wounded soldier from the First World War had arrived from Dundee Royal Infirmary at Ann's childhood home at

Glamis. It had taken a quarter of a century for Ann to rediscover a sense of public duty which she believed she carried in her blood.

In May 1939, news had reached Burns from Madrid of two public displays of ceremony that convinced him that he might be well qualified, because of his knowledge of Spanish politics, range of contacts, and Catholicism, to monitor Franco's New Spain. The first was Franco's triumphant state entry into Madrid, and a sixteen-mile parade along the capital's main avenue by 200,000 troops that followed it. Near the front of the parade was a battalion of Italian black-shirted *Arditi*, their daggers raised in a Roman salute. The rear was brought up by General Wolfram von Richthofen and his Condor Legion. In between marched Moorish mercenaries, the Spanish Foreign Legion, members of the neo-fascist Falange party, Navarese carrying huge crucifixes, and regular Spanish troops, goose-stepping. Above, in the clear blue mountain sky, aircraft circled and drew Franco's name in smoke. The second took place next day when there was a solemn Te Deum ceremony of thanksgiving at the main military basilica of Santa Bárbara, where Franco led prayers in thanks for his victory and presented the Primate of all Spain, Cardinal Goma, with a silver and gold sword specially crafted in Toledo for the occasion.

Through the prism of the secular left, the two ceremonies confirmed Franco as Europe's new dictator, a relic of Spain's repressive and unenlightened imperial past transformed into an ally of the new fascism, threatening what peace there was left in the world. But as he sat reading the reverential Catholic media reports in his publishing office near St Paul's, Burns was not alone in seeing the ceremonies instead as symbolic of an opportunity unfolding.

Burns was aware of the debt Franco owed Germany and Italy for the help given during the Spanish Civil War, but he saw Franco as an authoritarian ruler imbued with an almost mystical sense of national identity whose Catholic faith and pride in Spain's past imperialist history would resist full submission to the pagan ideologues of the Third Reich, just as it had effectively blocked the plans of the Russian Comintern to extend its influence south of the Pyrenees. Burns believed that the more Catholicism influenced British diplomacy, propaganda and secret intelligence the greater the likelihood that Franco would stay neutral.

In Spain few English institutions lent themselves more willingly to the concept that there was no inherent contradiction in supporting the New Spain and being a patriotic supporter of the Allied cause than the Catholic seminary of St Alban's in Valladolid. The establishment was a curious remnant of a time when English Catholics were regarded as potential traitors to the English Crown and forced either underground or into exile. It was founded in 1589 by the Jesuit Robert Persons, under the patronage of Philip II, as a seminary for exiled Catholic clergy. The majority of priests executed in England during the reigns of Elizabeth I and James I – the Catholic 'martyrs' – had studied at St Alban's.

And yet, soon after war was declared in 1939, the rector, the Rt Rev Mgr Canon Edwin Henson, received a letter from the MoI asking him to become involved in the propaganda war against Germany. It was signed by Lord Perth, the Catholic peer who had overseen the recruitment of several members of his faith to the MoI. The peer, otherwise known as Sir Eric Drummond, was considered one of the great and the good in British diplomatic and political circles. During the First World War he had served as private secretary to one prime minister (Asquith) and two foreign secretaries (Grey and Balfour), before being appointed Secretary General to the League of Nations, and subsequently British ambassador to Rome.

His letter as diplomatic adviser to the MoI, drafted with Burns's help, defined the role expected to be played by trusted friends at home and abroad. 'It is clear that if friendship and understanding are to be established between England and Spain it must be largely through the Catholic Church . . . In this question of the approach to the Spanish episcopate Cardinal Hinsley feels there is no one else who possesses your special opportunities,' Lord Perth wrote.

Hinsley, the Catholic Archbishop of Westminster, was himself to play an increasingly influential role politically, becoming the first leading Catholic bishop since the Reformation to be trusted by the government in wartime as a true patriot capable of ensuring that the minority faith remained united behind the Allied cause. As for Henson, he became a trusted agent in tune with the main thrust of British government policy towards Spain. Thus, while he was happy to help out in Britain's efforts to counter Nazi influence in Spain, he remained doggedly anti-socialist and anti-communist, and constantly denounced any attempts by the left to influence British policy against Franco.

Henson initially responded to the MoI by suggesting that Burns's department ensure that Pope Pius XI's letter against Nazism, *Mit Brennender Sorge* (With Deep Anxiety), be distributed in a good Spanish translation. Given its broader attack on fascism generally, the encyclical had been deliberately suppressed by the pro-Franco forces during the civil war when it was first published in 1937. However, the MoI had resurrected it, believing that it was more relevant to its Second World War propaganda aims than Pius XII's first 'encyclical', published in 1939, *Summi Pontificatus* (The Function of the State in the Modern World), which, much to the disappointment of Burns and other Catholics, lacked a firm public condemnation of the Nazi onslaught.

In addition to circulating *Mit Brennender Sorge*, Henson also suggested the posting of an English Catholic chaplain to Madrid to counter the influence of two German Catholic priests who were suspected of working for the Abwehr. The appointment of such a priest had become an important point of principle for Henson since the last chaplain, his former vice-rector at St Alban's, Fr A. V. Philips, had left the priesthood during the Spanish Civil War to support the Republican cause as a journalist with the *News Chronicle*, before being arrested by Franco's forces. Thanks to Henson's recommendation, the Madrid chaplaincy was handed to Fr Joseph Mulrean, a Gibraltar-based priest who had served as field chaplain of the *requetés*, the right-wing Carlist militias, during the civil war. His first job was to intercede on Philips's behalf and save him from being shot by a firing squad as an alleged communist.

Henson's links with British intelligence and propaganda grew increasingly close after Chamberlain's declaration of war. The relationship was prompted initially by the posting to the British embassy in Madrid of a kindred spirit. This was Bernard Malley, a politically conservative Anglo-Irishman who had lived in Spain for some twenty years as a teacher and university lecturer specialising in ecclesiastical affairs. When the civil war began, Malley was based near the monastery of El Escorial, built as a retreat by Philip II in the mountains outside Madrid. He took refuge in the British embassy when the capital resisted Franco's forces, before making his way into the Nationalist zone and joining the staff of the British agent Sir Robert Hodgson in Burgos. As soon as the British embassy was established Malley volunteered his services as an informant, adviser and general fixer, making himself an indispensable member of the team thanks to the contacts he had built up over the years.

Correspondence between Henson and Malley began in December 1939, within weeks of Burns's appointment to the MoI. In one letter, Henson complained about the bulletins the press department at the British embassy was publishing, and which he thought chimed with the socialist idea of an international anti-fascist alliance. 'Until England breaks definitely with the USSR, and until England definitely states what her reasons are, I am afraid the "*boletines*" will not do much good.'

The issue of what kind of propaganda should be encouraged in Spain and how it should be delivered became an increasingly hot topic of debate in a series of exchanges between the embassy in Madrid and Whitehall early in 1940 as Britain and the rest of Europe moved inexorably towards world war. Burns was called to a crisis meeting by his immediate superior, Denis Cowan, to be told to make ready for a joint trip to Madrid to try and sort things out.

Cowan was a former member of the Foreign Office's consular section, who had last visited Madrid in the thick of the civil war when the capital was still in Republican hands. He had formed part of a commission led by Field Marshal Sir Philip Chetwode, a hero of the First World War, which Spanish officials on both sides of the divide had agreed to in order to facilitate a general exchange of prisoners. Cowan was later implicated in a plot by Colonel Segismundo Casado, a Republican officer, to wrench control of Madrid from the communists and negotiate with Franco. Just over a year later, in February 1940, Cowan's role in helping secure safe haven in Britain for Casado and others who had fought for the Republic embroiled him in controversy as he set off by car on his journey to Madrid with Burns.

News of Cowan's trip and of the declared nature of his mission – the reorganisation of British propaganda emanating from the Iberian

Peninsula – had reached the Spanish embassy in London and prompted a string of protest letters to the Foreign Office. The Spanish ambassador, the Duke of Alba, accused Cowan of having 'pro-Republican sympathies'. Mention was made of his involvement with Casado and with other Republican elements exiled in London, including members of the exiled Basque government.

Alba's press attaché was Pablo Merry del Val, a contemporary of Burns's at Stonyhurst when his father had served as ambassador in London. With a reputation as an aristocratic playboy and a member of the *Falange,* he had subsequently worked as one of the chief liaison officers for the foreign press during the Spanish Civil War. Del Val wrote to the Foreign Office accusing Cowan of encouraging the former priest Philips to write a series of anti-Franco articles in the *News Chronicle* and a pamphlet following his release from a Franco prison. Cowan was aware of the protests, but went ahead with the trip hoping that the furore would die down by the time he reached Madrid.

Burns accompanied Cowan reluctantly – the thought of separation from Ann Bowes-Lyon pained him – but he also felt politically uncomfortable with the diplomatic divide that threatened to open up between the Spanish embassy and the MoI. Burns left it to another more senior Catholic in the ministry, Alec Randall, an experienced civil servant on secondment from the Foreign Office, to try and resolve the issue. In exchanges with the Foreign Office, Randall initially defended Cowan's reputation: 'The Spanish ambassador is apt to consider anybody "Red" who was not out and out pro-Franco, but otherwise I believe Cowan's relations with the Spanish embassy, particularly with the press attaché, quite friendly.'

By contrast the British ambassador in Madrid at the time, the prickly Sir Maurice Peterson, was furious that the first he heard about Cowan's trip was when he was sent a copy of Alba's protest. Peterson had been in post for less than a year, and knew how delicately poised Spanish neutrality was. He believed Cowan was a diplomatic liability and would 'upset the apple cart' and told the Foreign Office that he had formed this opinion independent of Alba's protest. 'The trouble is that the Spaniards, and particularly those young Spaniards who now control the press, are profoundly suspicious of him,' the ambassador wrote.

Burns and Cowan were oblivious to the brewing diplomatic row as they crossed the Channel and motored south, through France, to Spain. As they drew further away from England, both men appeared to set aside whatever hidden suspicions they might have had of each other, and shared in a spirit of adventure, the open spaces, timelessness and the unpredictability of what lay ahead, a welcome relief from the bureaucratic drudgery and cramped conditions of work at the Ministry. 'He was excellent company as we bowled along in a big grey Humber through unoccupied France. I had told my friends that I would be back in no time. But things happened differently,' Burns later recalled.

By the time they reached the border, an internal Whitehall enquiry had concluded that Cowan's visit to Spain made no diplomatic sense. 'It is fantastic to say the least,' said an internal Foreign Office report, 'that the man in charge of propaganda in Spain should be *persona non grata* to the Spanish propaganda authorities, the Spanish embassy in London, and our own ambassador in Madrid . . .'

Before entering Spain, Cowan and Burns called on the British consulate in Hendaye, in south-west France, to report to London on their progress. The consul handed Cowan a sealed On His Majesty's Service envelope marked 'urgent'. It contained orders from the Foreign Office for Cowan to return to London and for Burns to drive on to Madrid on his own. 'It seemed that Cowan was *persona non grata* with the Spanish government on account of his having served as one of the neutral observers controlling non-intervention during the Civil War,' Burns wrote in his memoirs. 'The non-intervention policy had been suspect with the Spanish Nationalists who were convinced that it was a one-sided affair, favouring the Republicans. I am sure that Cowan himself was innocent of duplicity but that was irrelevant. We parted with sorrow. It was sad to hear much later that he had been killed in an air raid.'

Burns picked up the Humber and drove south. The curling road through the great passes of the mountain border brought back memories of himself as a young schoolboy trekking in Belloc's footsteps. This remained God's landscape, beautiful and majestic to behold, the highest peaks still covered in snow, the lower valleys sprouting fresh green. Yes, Burns mused, Belloc was surely right about Spain, that on entering it through this border pass one finds a strong emotion rising in one, and most strongly does one feel 'the contrast and the change – the interest of exploration, the appetite for the discovery of new things, and the weight of the past'. And most strongly does one feel all these things when one passes into that 'proud, separate and reserved world' that is Spain, 'not by any entry commonly used, but alone, through some chance high notch of the ridge, where, not without difficulty but without peril, the mountains may be crossed and an approach made to Aragon . . .'

The landscape, of hills and valleys, on the way to Burgos also brought back memories, for it was along here that Burns, lovesick for Ann Bowes-Lyon, had felt the stirrings too of an unsuspected political passion and religious fervour when sharing the ambulance with Gabriel Herbert, the bright young thing turned Joan of Arc, and the general who was a Franco spy. And yet the town itself was transformed. 'Whereas uniforms had been everywhere and much bustle and movement of men and machines, and a sense of urgency, Burgos was now, bereft – like a woman with nothing to do but confront the chores and the tedium of a solitary life . . .'

Beyond lay what for Burns was the new frontier, the undiscovered plains of Castile, trod by countless travellers before him but for ever reinvented with quixotic imagination. As he travelled south from the hills of the Basque country and Asturias, Burns may have well have thought of how the philosopher José Ortega y Gasset had described the stark landscape that lay ahead . . . 'the yellow land, the red land, the land of silver, pure clod, naked soil . . . the plain undulating as if in torment . . . sometimes turning in on itself forming ravines and gullies, small hills and unsuspected towns . . . always inhospitable, always in ruins, always the church in the centre, with its fine alert tower, which looks tired, but which rests like a good warrior, on its feet, saddle sunk into the earth, elbow resting on the cross . . .'

The civil war had since grafted a new devastation on to the stark landscape where Quixote had mistaken windmills for giants. The long road from Burgos to Madrid that Burns took was pockmarked with bomb craters, its fields disfigured with trenches, the villages torn and broken as if an earthquake had shaken the heart of Spain. As he drove down through the mountain passes he glimpsed the clear outline of

Madrid on the horizon ahead of him. In 1940, it was not so much
a European capital as a provincial town, more contained and much
smaller than London, and yet dwarfing every village between it and
the border. Its outskirts – where the International Brigades had put
up their last failed rearguard action in defence of the Republican-held
city – were in disarray and partly crumbling; all the major university
faculties, a major hospital, the home of the painter Velásquez, a statue
of King Philip IV, churches, bridges and barracks had been wrecked by
gunfire and explosives during a three-year battle of attrition.

In the third weekend of February 1940, Burns drove into Madrid,
through the Paseo de la Castellana (it was then called Avenida del
Generalísimo). The city centre was undergoing reconstruction and
reform, but the signs of enduring poverty and hunger were still visible
– the gaunt faces of the women in black, the skeletal street urchins, the
scarce traffic, the empty or boarded-up shops, the mutilated trees and
unkempt gardens.

It was evening by the time Burns reached the British embassy, a
Parisian-style *fin-de-siècle* remnant of Spain's imperial past. It stood in
a narrow street off the Castellana, protected by an iron gate and a high
fence. The building was dimly lit and lifeless. A porter advised him that
it was closed and passed him a message that he had a room reserved at
the nearby Palace Hotel and was to report for duty on the following
Monday.

'A group of journalists were predictably to be found at the bar but I
had no inclination to mix with them, as I had no identity at this time,
no reason for being there that I cared to reveal,' recalled Burns. A new
sort of loneliness had been thrust upon him, that of a government
agent in a foreign land, probing the untested and the unknown, even if
he already had an inner sense of belonging to the scene.

4

RECONNAISSANCE

When Burns arrived on his first visit to Madrid in the spring of 1940, one half of Spain was paying the price for being on the wrong side in the civil war, while the other was enjoying the fruits of victory.

The new regime had moved quickly to stamp out all remnants of the Spanish Republic. Political party and trade union activity, except that linked to the pro-Franco Falange, was banned, newspapers were censored, street names changed to honour the victors. Catholicism was established as the official religion of the new regime, with the Church recovering the privileges it had lost when the Republic had separated it from the State in the early 1930s. Masses and pilgrimages were once again an integral part of Spanish culture, and priests and nuns walked the streets in their habits for the first time in years, a symbol as much of rediscovered confidence as of religious orthodoxy. Army officers who had fought for Franco and the Falange formed part of the new social elite, rivalling the returning aristocracy, while the paramilitary civil guard and secret police purged society of lingering 'subversives'.

From the thousands of Spaniards serving indeterminate prison sentences, some one hundred political dissidents were being shot on average every month in Madrid in the early months of 1940. Small daily notices in the newspapers gave the names of some of those tried by military tribunals for 'crimes' committed during the civil war. Other, larger notices paid tribute to those who had died fighting for Franco – martyrs of a heroic crusade against the evils of the red anti-Christ.

The luckier losers had escaped into exile. Those who stayed behind hid or adopted new identities. If you'd fought on the wrong side, living in Madrid in 1940 was to feel humiliated, to fear for one's own safety, to have no faith in the future other than in the fantasy of watching the combined forces of Russia, Britain and France occupy Spain for the anti-fascist cause. Quixotic dreams.

By contrast, those who had emerged victorious felt seduced by the idea of a New Spain emerging, life being resurrected from the culture of death. Conscripts who had fought for Franco were offered jobs in the emerging bureaucracy with which the new regime surrounded itself. Women were encouraged to start new families and be dutiful housewives. Orphaned children were put up for adoption. The children of the poor, from whatever side, just went on begging.

Burns slept his first night in Madrid in the Palace Hotel, in silk sheets and under warm blankets. Such luxury had only recently been recovered. During the civil war, the Palace had been requisitioned by the militias and communist workers committee, its ample rooms and corridors turned into wards for the wounded and dying. It became one of the largest military hospitals in Madrid. The American journalist Martha Gellhorn visited it as a war correspondent. She later wrote, 'The clientele was very young then, though pain ages the face, and wore shabby pyjamas, scraps of uniform. In the corridors . . . piles of used bandages collected on the bare floors. Sleazy cotton blackout curtains hung at the windows . . . food was scarce, and medicines, especially morphine. I don't remember sheets and pillow cases, only grey army blankets . . .'

After Franco's victory, the hotel was among the first buildings in the capital to be restored to its former splendour. Built as one of Europe's largest hotels in 1912 during the reign of King Alfonso XIII, its privileged clientele now once again paraded amidst the marble and the gilt fittings. While much of the city and large areas of the country were surviving on the strict diet imposed by ration coupons – pulses, dried cod, bread – the kitchens of the Palace were once again sufficiently well stocked to offer extended tea and cakes in the afternoons and dinner à la carte, as had been the custom before the war.

A copy of *ABC*, the principal Spanish newspaper, was delivered to Burns's table. It was filled with reports and photographs of Nazi troop manoeuvres provided by a German-controlled local news agency. The overall impression conveyed was that of the Third Reich on a triumphant march across northern Europe – and of Franco's Spain getting on with the peace.

Over the next few days Burns would discover that for those victors of the civil war a sort of normality had returned. Dance-halls and bars had begun filling up again. *Madrileños* took longer over their lunches, found time for their siestas and went to bed later. A municipal decree imposing street silence from midnight to seven in the morning was openly flouted. Thousands turned up to watch bullfights in the Las Ventas ring, the bravery of the emerging young talent from the south, Manolete, enthralling crowds just as Belmonte and Joselito, the two great stars of the 1920s and 1930s, had done in the pre-war years. Large crowds also packed out the Chamartín stadium to watch a re-formed Real Madrid. Of the twenty players who had played for the club during the military uprising in 1936, only four rejoined it in 1940. The others were all new signings. The football pages of the newspaper bubbled with enthusiasm for Jacinto Quincoces, the great Spanish international defender who had spent part of the civil war driving a Red Cross ambulance in the Nationalist zone.

Between the covers of the *ABC* were the funeral notes of nuns 'gloriously martyred for God and Spain', and the latest executed Republican 'criminal'. Advertisements encouraged men to buy a cream that stiffened the fringe upwards and back in a style called 'Arriba España', in honour of Franco's rallying cry. For women, there were anti-spot creams and pills to help develop 'a perfect bust'. The newspaper's entertainment list included the latest concert by Celia Gamez. She had become the capital's most popular star with a song that defiantly mocked the communist leader of the civil war, La Pasionaria's, legendary cry of revolutionary resistance. Instead of *No pasarán* (They shall not pass) Gamez sang *Ya hemos pasao* (We have passed) to the rhythm of the popular tango-style *chotis* music that so enthralled *Madrileños* of every class.

Cinemas were showing a variety of Hollywood films dubbed into Spanish as well as Spanish films, most of which pre-dated the war. These, like the plays put on in the theatres, were selected for being non-political. There was no shortage of comedy – the Marx Brothers topped the bill – and romantic adventure. Spanish women swooned at the sight of Clark Gable and Errol Flynn, while Spanish men enjoyed the refined beauty of Olivia de Havilland, the sexuality of Ginger Rogers and the coquetry of Shirley Temple.

On the Monday, Burns's first working day in Madrid, a crisp wind was blowing down from the mountains and the cloudless sky was luminous as he walked the few blocks to the embassy. He was struck by the contrast between the superficial orderliness of street life in the centre of the capital and the devastation he had encountered in his drive across Spain and the outskirts of the city. The buildings of the diplomatic neighbourhood and much of the aristocratic Barrio de Salamanca which straddled the Castellana had survived the civil war largely untouched by the artillery and aerial bombing that had wreaked such devastation on the outskirts. The British embassy building, evacuated at the time, had been hit by a shell during the conflict, but had since been repaired.

Within minutes of arriving at the embassy, Burns took stock of how under-staffed, under-resourced and disorganised it was. And yet he considered himself fortunate, as a fellow Catholic, to have an immediate and personal introduction to the 'assistant press attaché', Bernard Malley, the former teacher from El Escorial. Malley looked older than his forty years, with pallid skin and prematurely greying hair. He spoke in the lowered tones of a sacristan and shared similar ecclesiastical mannerisms in his gestures, a tendency to bless the air and raise his eyes heavenwards.

A repressed homosexual, Malley excused his lack of interest in women by alleging that he was a celibate. Burns, who was used to celibates of all kinds, found him well informed in the area that most concerned him professionally: Catholic opinion on the war in Spanish lay and clerical circles and their influence on the Franco regime.

If Burns knew anything about Don Bernardo's sexual proclivities, he made light of them in later years. Malley's usefulness as a gatherer of useful intelligence and discreet facilitator proved more important than any personal peccadillo. 'Don Bernardo [as he was known in the embassy and beyond] was a fervent Catholic but would chuckle over ecclesiastical scandals,' Burns wrote in his memoirs. 'He was happier in two-star rather than five-star circles, with captains rather than higher ranks, with parochial clergy rather than bishops. Thus he gleaned information and exercised influence in areas seldom reached by the career diplomats.'

It was thanks to Malley that Burns gained an early insight into the complex politics that lay behind the public façade of pro-Axis unity within the Franco regime, identifying the tensions and self-interest that could be exploited to the greater benefit of the Allied cause. Among Catholics in positions of influence were bishops and lay officials who did not share in the pro-Nazi enthusiasms of Franco's brother-in-law Ramón Serrano Súñer and the more extremist members of the Falange.

As important in marking out the future activities of the embassy in Madrid was the contact Burns made with the naval attaché, Alan Hillgarth. The former British consul in Mallorca had been posted to Madrid the previous summer on Churchill's personal instructions. His specific mission was that of countering German intelligence operations. In the spring of 1940, Hillgarth was in the early stages of building up sources within the Spanish military, helping develop from a very low base Britain's intelligence capability across the Iberian Peninsula.

Burns found Hillgarth a likeable and entertaining tutor in the art of espionage, as well as an excellent guide to Madrid night life. Hillgarth for his part found in Burns – the unexpected emissary from the MoI – someone who seemed to share his understanding of Spanish culture and politics and whose consummate skills as a communicator and networker could prove invaluable for an embassy that was trying to gain confidence and expand its influence.

Burns used his reconnaissance visit to Spain to help Hillgarth press London for more support. A report they drafted together drew attention to the inadequate resources that the embassy's press department and other sections endured compared to the well-oiled local machinery of the Germans. More staff and more money were needed to develop a propaganda and intelligence operation with the capacity to spread out from Madrid and extend across the Iberian Peninsula, north to Barcelona, west to Lisbon, and south to Gibraltar, with additional consulates and agents across the rest of the country, they argued.

On his return to London in April 1940 Burns continued lobbying hard to get approval from the MoI and the Foreign Office for a network of press and information offices in Spain, North Africa and France, under the direction of the embassy in Madrid. He was particularly instrumental in seeing to it that an experienced colleague and friend, Paul Dorchy, was deployed to Barcelona, which was of growing strategic importance because of the Catalan capital's position as a Mediterranean port close to the Pyrenees. Getting Dorchy the resources and back-up he needed under his cover post of assistant press attaché proved somewhat laborious as Burns struggled with the bureaucratic inertia of Whitehall. His efforts were helped by a memorandum Burns encouraged Dorchy to write to the MoI and which was copied to senior officials at the Foreign Office.

In it Dorchy hit out at the stinginess and lack of initiative of His Majesty's Government while drawing attention to the deep economic and social malaise left by the civil war. The memo was circulated in Whitehall on 9 May 1940. The premiership of Neville Chamberlain was drawing to its close, with Chamberlain having to shoulder the blame for the apparent indecisiveness of the Norwegian campaign. Dorchy wrote:

There is an enormous amount to do and people are eager for British propaganda but my hands are tied until someone comes out from Madrid with some sort of credentials . . . in the meantime we cannot get any rations and the wife is having a rotten time. Still as soon as I 'exist' officially, I will be able to draw food (when available). For the moment we are compelled to buy from the 'black' market which means that we pay 5/- a pound for mutton, when available 10/- a pound for butter, 9/- for sugar and eat black bread charitably obtained by our porters. With the peseta down at 44 and going down again soon, owing to the fall of the Pound, my Ptas 1,540 a month get me nowhere – to 'exist' costs about Ptas 3,000. I presume that it is thought that all assistant press attachés have fabulous incomes of their own, which is unhappily not the case. I hope the Treasury will realise it some day.

Two days at a third rate hotel (the Victoria) when we arrived cost me £6 so we presumably looked for and luckily found a very small furnished flat at £4 a week – and lucky to get it . . . I am not downhearted, as all the Services people are out here in the same boat, living more or less like paupers – but it does not enhance our prestige. The Germans and Poles seen to dispose of unlimited quantities of Pesetas (no wonder – they print them) but if we are going to put up a Propaganda show at all, the first thing would be to see that our wives do not have to queue up for food with the enemy's maids – and that is what mine and many others are doing . . . They are good sports and don't seem to mind – but I hate it and it certainly seems to back up the Hun propaganda . . .

Dorchy's exact status and who should ultimately be responsible for him continued to be the subject of argument between the MoI and the Foreign Office for weeks afterwards until it was agreed that Dorchy be given the additional funds, and staff back-up, to do his job.

On 10 May, hours after Hitler's forces struck Holland, Belgium and France, Churchill replaced Chamberlain as prime minister. As the historian A. J. P Taylor put it, for months the government had appeared to be moving into war backwards with their eyes tightly closed, with Churchill the one exception, a 'cuckoo in the nest, restless against inaction . . . fertile with proposals'. Churchill's time had finally come. Within days, Dorchy reported that he was installed in his new office, was distributing British propaganda material on a large scale, had made some important local contacts and was therefore in a position to start supplying some 'valuable information regarding local conditions'.

Burns, meanwhile, busied himself with coordinating cooperation between Kenneth Clark's MoI's film division – where John Betjeman and Graham Greene worked – and the BBC to send regular consignments of British newsreel material to Madrid. The MoI reels had their script translated by the Spanish language service at Bush House for, at the time, only a very small minority of Spaniards understood English.

The material chosen was a mixture of trivia, misinformation and a small element of reportage deliberately picked to show the British at their most ordinary and untroubled. A typical consignment prepared for dispatch to Spain and dated 18 April 1940 included items picked for their propaganda value, among them King George inspecting a garrison at Dover Castle – the 'first monarch visiting this ancient stronghold since Queen Victoria' – and the legendary English outside right Stanley Matthews, 'the best hope of England defeating Wales at Wembley'.

From the front line came news and images of French troops 'getting plenty of practice dealing with mines', and the Allies 'rushing to the aid of the Norwegians'. The newsreel concluded that Hitler was 'accelerating his overthrow by laying his flank open to the joint onslaught of Great Britain's navies of the sky and sea'. With the exception of the clip of Matthews's magic on the wing, most of what the MoI was projecting was 'lies, damned lies', for the German troops were days away from crossing the Maginot Line, the Norwegian campaign was in difficulties and Hitler was looking more of a threat to the democratic world than he had ever done. But, then, in every war the first casualty is truth.

The main concern for the MoI was one of logistics, not so much gathering the material and shipping it as ensuring that it was made use of at the other end. According to intelligence provided by one of Burns's Spanish sources, an Anglophile film distributor and concert organiser, Roberto Martín Palleiro, the problem was not with Spaniards themselves but with their government's authoritarianism and pro-Axis sympathies, as demand for Allied newsreels was high and there was anecdotal evidence that people were getting tired of the propaganda put out by the Germans.

In May 1940, the censorship got worse after Burns had dispatched another deliberately misleading film of French troops holding the Maginot Line, and saving the 'civilised world from the Nazi invader'. Further images showed German infantry in apparent retreat, leaving a number of their dead along the way. The Spanish authorities now demanded heavier cuts, imposing a process that led to a three-week delay in the films being shown, effectively making them useless as a propaganda tool. To make matters worse, further imports of the newsreels were caught up in a complex bureaucratic web involving the Spanish Ministry of Industry and Commerce and the Cinematography department of the Ministry of the Interior, each of which tried to outdo each other in the administrative checks it imposed on the importer.

On 9 May, Vidal Batet, a local agent for Paramount Films in Madrid, one of the distributors of the British newsreels, sent a report to London via his head office in Paris, complaining of the bias the Spanish authorities were increasingly showing towards the Germans, by favouring material distributed by pro-Axis companies that had operated throughout the Spanish Civil War in the nationalist zones held by Franco forces. Batet suggested that Burns was wasting the government's time in processing newsreel material that had no chance of ever reaching a Spanish cinema. He wrote: 'They are hardly suitable for a country which has been declared neutral and which is governed by a totalitarian regime. Commentaries against a certain head of a European state i.e. Hitler cannot be allowed, nor should certain words like "aggressor", "invader" etc. It is necessary to suppress all speeches containing words or references against (German) people . . . propaganda has to be very subtle and the commentaries short with non political references, leaving the audience to form its own opinion of the matters shown on the films.'

British propaganda policy was not helped by the fact that the Franco regime was deeply resistant to any British strategy that smacked of intrusion into internal Spanish affairs. The Spanish embassy in London under the Duke of Alba devoted much of its time to identifying and exposing opponents of the Franco regime that were employed by the British state. Its focus was the Spanish department of the MoI where the pro-Francoists had already claimed a significant victory in effectively vetoing its chief Denis Cowan's visit to Madrid.

After his planned trip to Madrid had been cut short, Cowan had returned to London, conscious that his days in post were numbered, and considering whether he should resign, as the pressure on him mounted. On 8 March 1940 Cowan was working in his office at the MoI when his secretary handed him the latest issue of the *Catholic Herald*, a mass circulation weekly, that, together with the *Tablet*, had taken an uncompromising pro-Franco stand during the Spanish Civil War. It ran a lengthy article, based on information provided by the Spanish embassy, accusing the MoI of employing Spaniards who had gone into exile after the Republic had been defeated with the sole aim of mounting an international offensive to have Franco overthrown.

Unknown to Cowan, the article was circulated in Whitehall and added to a dossier the Foreign Office was compiling on the tensions that were impacting negatively on Britain's relations with Spain. The dossier included complaints, emanating from the Spanish embassy in London, that the BBC was using events of the Spanish Civil War for which Franco forces were held culpable, such as the bombing of Gernika, as examples of the cruelty of the modern warfare with which Nazi Germany was now threatening the whole of Europe.

A separate memo from Lord Lloyd at the Foreign Office expressed concern that anti-Franco propaganda filtering through Whitehall risked upsetting his plans to promote the activities of the British Council in Spain. Similar concerns were expressed by the outgoing British ambassador in Madrid, Maurice Peterson. He fired off a furious memo to the MoI, and to Foreign Office, questioning why it appeared that no pro-Franco Spaniards were employed by the department, and suggesting that if Spanish republicans were to be employed at all it should only be as translators.

In the spring of 1940, Cowan was transferred out of the Spanish department, while a short list was secretly drawn up of his possible replacement. At the top of the list featured Burns, who had become increasingly involved in Spanish affairs from his office down the corridor, the hitherto discreetly understated Catholic sector of the MoI's Religious Affairs Department.

Within days Burns was offered a promotion, but not the one he thought he had been earmarked for. Instead of moving into Cowan's chair, he was asked to return to Spain, this time to assume the title First Secretary and Press Attaché, with responsibility for Spain, Portugal and Tangier, a cover post for a whole range of diplomatic and covert duties.

The posting came at a critical juncture in the war. The importance of the embassy in Madrid in strategic and operational terms had increased following the German invasion of Belgium and Holland and the subsequent fall of France. It was crucial, as far as Churchill was concerned, to ensure that Franco did not throw in his lot with Hitler and Mussolini, for such a move risked the loss of Gibraltar and the Atlantic and Mediterranean ports to the Axis, with an ensuing dramatic shift in the military balance. The leadership of the project to ensure Spanish neutrality and effectively buy time for the Allies was entrusted to one of Britain's most experienced and senior politicians, Sir Samuel Hoare, who replaced Sir Maurice Peterson as the new British ambassador in Madrid on 24 May 1940.

Hoare and Churchill's paths had converged and periodically clashed since they had first met in 1919. As a Conservative MP, Hoare had supported Churchill's military intervention in Russia against the Bolshevik revolution. Later in the 1920s Hoare served as Secretary of State for Air and Churchill was Chancellor of the Exchequer, the two men meeting at Chartwell, both as colleagues and friends, before forming part of the political alliance against the General Strike.

Hoare went on to serve as Secretary of State for India, disagreeing with Churchill over his opposition to self-government. There were further tensions when Hoare as foreign secretary during the late 1930s criticised Churchill's warnings about Germany's rearmament as excessively alarmist, alluding in Parliament to the 'scare-mongers who . . . delight in increasing crises, if there be crises, in making the crises worse than they would otherwise be'. Hoare later resigned after signing an unpopular agreement with the French whereby Mussolini was allowed to retain his conquests in Abyssinia in return for halting the war. The infamous Hoare/Laval pact earned Hoare a reputation as an appeaser.

He later returned to Neville Chamberlain's government as Home Secretary, believing along with his prime minister that the pact with Hitler at Munich would guarantee lasting peace. Hoare was among the MPs who most belittled Churchill's judgement by doubting his claims that Britain was losing air parity with Germany. Five years later, as air minister, he argued that an offensive against Germany should be delayed because more time was needed to build up Britain's air force capability.

Churchill made Hoare pay for his military miscalculation by excluding him from his first wartime cabinet. Many in the diplomatic corps hoped that would be the end of Hoare's long involvement in public life. When Hoare was appointed as ambassador to Spain, the news was initially greeted with cruel cynicism by the government's most senior diplomat. The head of the Foreign Office, Sir Alexander Cadogan, told Lady Halifax, the wife of the foreign secretary: 'There is one bright spot – there are lots of Germans and Italians in Madrid and therefore a good chance of S.H. being murdered.' Cadogan also described Sir Samuel and Lady Hoare's apparent anxiety to get to Spain as indicating they were 'rats deserting the ship'.

While the appointment may have implied that Hoare was being 'exiled' politically, it suited Churchill's strategic objectives. Churchill hoped that Hoare's Anglo-Catholic background, his First World War experience as an intelligence officer and his knowledge of Vatican diplomacy would help his 'ambassador on special mission' get to grips with the intricacies of Spanish internal politics. Hoare's reputation as an appeaser and his proven negotiating skills were, Churchill believed, what made him eminently suitable for his new role. For if Hoare, as British ambassador, couldn't keep Franco out of the war no one could.

How to energise the British presence not just in Madrid but throughout the Iberian Peninsula and keep Spain from siding with the Axis powers was the subject of a secret meeting Hoare attended with Brendan Bracken, Churchill's indispensable henchman, at Stornoway House. The Regency building overlooking Green Park was used as a residence and office by Lord Beaverbrook, the newspaper baron whom Churchill put in charge of a new Ministry of Aircraft Production. Beaverbrook hosted the meeting, away from the intrigues of the Foreign Office and other service departments.

The Stornoway mini-summit confirmed that Churchill had no sympathy for those on the left who argued that British policy in the foreseeable future should have as its principal focus the restoration of Spanish democracy. He believed that Franco could be treated differently from Hitler and Mussolini, and was determined to keep Spain, guardian of the Mediterranean, free from military occupation by the Axis powers. Within this framework, those gathered at Stornoway laid out the main priorities for Hoare to follow in his first months in office. There was a consensus that the Madrid embassy would have to be upgraded and additional resources invested in the British diplomatic network across the Iberian Peninsula and North Africa if the British were to match the power and influence of the Nazi presence. Hoare believed this could not be achieved without a major reorganisation of the embassy itself, centralising under his control diplomacy, propaganda, special operations and intelligence.

It was undoubtedly fortunate for Hoare that at the time of his appointment as ambassador there was already in the embassy in Madrid the naval attaché, Captain Hillgarth, whom Churchill had befriended and whose expertise in intelligence matters was hugely valued. It was entirely in character that Churchill should now think of Hillgarth as a key element in his strategy for Spain. For when it came to key decisions at moments of crisis, Churchill cut through the bureaucracry of the civil service and, acting on instinct, drew on the counsel of individuals he trusted.

Soon after the Stornoway meeting, Hillgarth was summoned by Churchill and charged with helping keep Spain out of the war with a campaign of bribery and corruption of Spanish generals and officials. Initial funds of $10 million were drawn from a special reserve contingency budget held by the Treasury for special operations and deposited in an account of the Swiss Bank Corporation in New York, arranged by the Treasury. The operation, which Stewart Menzies, the head of MI6, helped arrange, involved a crucial third party, the billionaire Mallorcan businessman Juan March, acting as agent and intermediary.

Since helping finance, with British help, Franco's uprising in 1936, March had consolidated his power base and influence. He helped finance Franco's campaign throughout the Spanish Civil War, establishing an office in Rome from where he negotiated Italian munitions and planes as well as fuel for the insurgent forces. With the perfect timing that had characterised his emerging years as an entrepreneur, March set up a shipping company called AUCONA in Burgos, the city chosen by Franco as his campaign headquarters, days before the end of the civil war. Monopolising the Spanish import-export business, AUCONA built up his foreign currency reserves in Swiss and British banks while paying Spanish importers and exporters in pesetas. March's riches and the dubious methods used for achieving them bred resentment. However, he remained untouchable. Too many people in the Franco regime owed him favours, not least members of the Spanish armed forces.

When the Spanish Civil War ended and the Second World War began, March moved quickly to resurrect his links with the British through his old friend Hillgarth. A British intelligence report on March said that he was representing the Spanish government in a 'quasi-official role' and described the businessman as a 'scoundrel', well disposed to serving the interests of the Allied cause. On 23 September 1939, Hillgarth arranged a meeting in London between March and his chief, Admiral Godfrey, the head of Naval Intelligence.

March told Godfrey that his shipping interests and political contacts gave him unrivalled intelligence coverage of most Spanish ports and said he was committed to helping ensure that the future of Spain was bound up with that of Great Britain. The Spaniard offered not only to buy up German merchant vessels as a way of controlling German–Spanish trade, but also to act as Hillgarth's 'eyes and ears' reporting on U-boats and other Axis naval movements.

As Godfrey later recalled: 'In return March asked that the British refrain from sabotaging German ships or creating "fires and explosions in our ports" as they had done in World War I . . . He explained that the port authorities were under his control. He said that Franco would never let the German Army into Spain. He wished the relations of Spain and England to be friendly and tranquil and would do all he could do to achieve this end. We kept in touch and he passed me valuable information that was never incorrect.'

Other contacts March had subsequently with Hillgarth raised the possibility of the businessman acting as an arms broker for the Allies. At the meeting with Godfrey, March had mentioned that he was negotiating a sale of Spanish arms to Yugoslavia. Britain at the time had been asked by Turkey to supply it with arms, an offer it found difficult to meet without dangerously breaking into the reserve it was belatedly building up to deal with the Nazi threat.

As an alternative, March was asked by Hillgarth whether he would help arrange a deal whereby Britain and France would finance the diversion of Spanish arms destined for Yugoslavia to Turkey to bolster the defence of her Thracian border. In preparation for the deal, March's London agent met with senior officials of the Bank of England to discuss it taking over a loan for £1.8 million to the

Spanish government which a private English bank was threatening to call in.

The arms negotiations met resistance from the Foreign Office and the War Office and were eventually dropped. However, another deal was struck. The British loans were rescheduled, the agent got his visa and March was enlisted by the British as an agent of influence in the secret war against Germany. In the autumn of 1940, March was asked by Hillgarth, on Churchill's behalf, to set up a secret system of money transfers whereby a small but influential group of senior military officers would receive secret payments in return for resisting any moves Franco might make to enter the war. The money was also intended to help fund the development of intelligence on the regime's dealings with the Germans. 'The fact that March made his money by devious means in no way affects his value to us at present,' Sir Alexander Cadogan remarked.

Other matters arising out of the Stornoway meeting required following up on both sides of the Atlantic. Hoare was conscious that there was little sympathy for Franco in the US State Department or in the liberal press of the United States, which was still heavily influenced by the memory of the anti-Franco reporting of the civil war of such high-profile journalists and writers as Ernest Hemingway and John Dos Passos. Hoare thought it important that Washington be persuaded to accede to a Spanish request for aid, as a way of influencing policy. Not to do so, he feared, would undermine Britain's own efforts to stop Franco drifting into the arms of the Axis.

Hoare believed the British ambassador in Washington, Lord Lothian, would be of help, while Beaverbrook was expected to pursue his good links with Joseph Kennedy, although his term as US Ambassador in London and political ambitions ended abruptly during the Battle of Britain with the publishing of his controversial remarks that 'Democracy is finished here in England. It may be here (in the US).' Separately, in May 1940, Menzies, the head of MI6, with Churchill's support, sent William Stephenson to New York to help boost Anglo-American intelligence cooperation throughout the Spanish- and Portuguese-speaking world, from Buenos Aires to Madrid.

The other item in the pending tray was perhaps the most delicate to handle in administrative terms, for it involved the creation of a key job in the embassy in Madrid that could meet the requirements of the ambassador's 'special mission'. The job would involve responsibility throughout the Iberian Peninsula and North Africa for propaganda, developing secret sources and useful intelligence, and reporting directly to the ambassador. Hoare believed that such a job was essential to counter the dominance within the Franco regime of the pro-German sympathisers. Such was the enormity of the challenge he believed his embassy faced that he had begun to think of creating two new jobs instead of one.

'You cannot imagine what a racket I have had here, alarms and excursion day and night and a depressing feeling of impending catastrophe. There can be no question of making ourselves popular in Spain. The most I can do is play upon the Spanish dislike of another war at a time when they are exhausted after the Civil War . . .' Hoare wrote to Beaverbrook three weeks after his arrival in Madrid.

'Send me a line when you can as to how things are going. Here I am entirely isolated and know little or nothing. Will you also help in two directions? First a talk with Winston about the plans I have for organising the anti-war movement. He and Halifax know about them and I am sending back Commander Furse of the NID [Naval Intelligence Division] to tell them in greater detail about what I am doing. Secondly, will you give me your advice about the press here? At present it is nothing more than a series of German propaganda sheets. The Press Department is in German hands and all the journalists are in German pay. It is impossible for us to get anything into the papers at all and there is a new decree even prohibiting the circulation of typed bulletins. Do you think that it would be possible for someone really big e.g. Roberts [Walter Roberts, a senior Foreign office official] to come out here and advise me as to whether it is practicable to do anything at all or whether I had better give up the job as hopeless? If you do think there is anything in this proposal, I should indeed be grateful if you could fix it with Duff Cooper and send someone out at once. He could do the whole of what I want in a fortnight. As I have no expert to advise me, I am groping in the dark and I terribly want really good advice . . .'

*   *   *

Later that night in London, the person whose fate Hoare's proposal was destined to seal sat and wrote a letter to his loved one. It was nearly midnight, hours after the end of a long day shift at the MoI in Bloomsbury, and minutes away from the night vigil at the Royal Herbert Hospital in Woolwich, where Ann Bowes-Lyon had been working as a volunteer nurse since the outbreak of war. From his blacked-out Chelsea home off the King's Road, Burns used the light of a candle to write, so tired that he could hardly keep awake as he scribbled his lover's talk. 'Darling, don't be miserable about this job of yours – what a chance it is: you can keep watch over so much more than your ward – everything is easier to communicate in the night, both good and bad: people all over the place are slumping into sleep or despair or loneliness or some sordid sort of luxury and yours is the chance to compensate in some way for all of this. And I shall think of you as awake and vigilant and watching over me as much as over the chaps in the old mortuary . . . I wish I could be working with you: just to be caring for stricken and miserable people. Darling, your faith will tell you of timelessness and I think sometimes that you can really be near to our Lord in his agony in the garden; you can be awake and alive to all that agony when the apostles slumbered and sleep and say, "Yes" when he asks, "Could you not watch over him with me?" Do you see, darling, how there is all this reality with you even though every securing misery is crowding in! . . .'

Faith was surely needed. The military hospital where Ann Bowes-Lyon had turned up one bright morning in the summer of 1939, to find long, half-empty wards, and an atmosphere resonant of a Women's League fête, was now filling up with the wounded and the dying, and forcing new duties and longer hours on those who worked there. None of her letters to Burns from this period survive. But one can only speculate, on the basis of his letters to her, that their intimate correspondence not only reflected the stress of her job, but also served as a reminder that their own worlds were drawing apart, each touched by different experiences, the result of a different calling that seemed to come as much from others as from within.

Ann still felt a need to follow the patriotic example set by the King and Queen Consort Elizabeth, her cousin, who continued to live out their lives with a conscious sense of duty towards the defence of the empire they presided over. It was around this time that the Queen had made the latest of her memorable public statements, a perfect complement to Churchill's speeches, to help raise morale. Explaining why she was not escaping from London she answered quite matter-of-factly: 'The children can't go without me, I can't leave the King, and of course the King won't go.'

The King, like every member of the Home Guard, from the plumber to the top civil servant, practised shooting with his revolver and vowed to die fighting, preferably taking at least one German with him. In fact, no one in London could pretend to remain personally unaffected by the war. It was as if a long, dark cloud watched for weeks and months but seemingly settled in the distance was now moving slowly but surely across the Channel. England no longer had reasons to be cheerful. All the country could do, as Churchill urged it to, was prepare for 'hard and heavy tidings'.

The Germans had invaded Holland and Belgium and split the Allied armies in two by means of the 'dash to the sea'. In the last week of May, the British Expeditionary Force had been pushed back towards the Channel ports. From his minesweeper, Burns's friend Mike Richey wrote to his parents: 'Yes, the war has broken out all right and seems to be more astonishing than the first six months of inactivity. That at any rate was a good idea but this ... whatever explanations there may be given I think it is not lack of resistance or inferiority on the allied part that is to blame ... My own reading is that the new commander in chief of the German chaps Mr Adolph Hitler has that peculiar quality of commanding personal allegiance that all great militarists from Alexander to Napoleon seem to have had ...'

On 3 June, the evacuation from Dunkirk had come to an end. Churchill prepared for a German invasion, as did most of Whitehall and the population at large. Over a million men too old to join the army had by that summer joined the Home Guard. Many of them spent their time harassing innocent fellow citizens for their identity cards as part of the MoI's 'know your enemy' campaign.

For those who worked at the coalface of government these were uncomfortable days. Burns's friend and colleague at the MoI, Graham

Greene, left the department and for the next few months worked as literary editor for the *Spectator* and returned to writing reviews for this and other magazines, including the *Tablet*. Whether Greene was sacked or left of his own accord, pre-emptively, remains another unsolved mystery of his life. However, one of his biographers suggests that he may have been advised to do the latter after his cousin Ben, a Quaker and pacifist, was detained on the advice of a controversial MI5 'expert' on counter-subversion named Maxwell Knight. Working from his London flat in Dolphin Square, Knight had placed small advertisements in newspapers to help him recruit a network of impeachable patriots – 'little ships' he called them – who he infiltrated into factories and offices. He was an eccentric and an obsessive, with a passion for wild animals as pets and an interest in the occult and bisexuality. Knight had taken credit for planting an agent as a secretary at Woolwich Arsenal and exposing an alleged Soviet cell there in 1938. His focus later turned on alleged Nazi sympathisers.

Fortunately for Greene, Knight was blind to the Soviet Union's successes in recruiting sympathisers in British universities and seemingly overlooked the fact that Greene himself had, as a student, been a member of the Communist Party. Greene, moreover, had a brother whose fanatical anti-Nazism had led to him being expelled from Germany before the war, and, crucially, a sister who worked for MI6. Within fourteen months of leaving the MoI, Greene himself had been recruited by MI6, and posted to the colonial West African outpost of Sierra Leone, a job that fell under the aegis of MI6's Iberian section, by then headed by Kim Philby.

Fortunately for Burns, he had succeeded where Evelyn Waugh had failed in getting into the MoI, thanks to convincing influential friends that it was possible to be patriotically pro-Allied and pro-Franco at the same time. Burns believed that every Catholic had an ethical duty to fight Hitler as best he could while never showing himself to have any moral qualms about supporting Franco. To put his conscience at rest, he had drawn from the 'just war' Christian medieval theory dating back to the Middle Ages. And yet he could not have imagined the manner in which this Majesty's Government contrived finally to make the best use of his talents.

One day during the summer of 1940, he received instructions from the Foreign Office that he was to return to Madrid via Lisbon. Burns assumed that this was another temporary assignment to the Madrid embassy, with the added bonus of a couple of days in Portugal, where the British diplomatic and intelligence apparatus was also being strengthened. He was scheduled to have meetings with the new ambassador, Samuel Hoare, and renew contact with the priestly Bernard Malley, and Captain Hillgarth. But he presumed that his visit would be no longer that the previous one, a reconnaissance followed by report back. He scribbled a quick 'be back soon' 'ticket' to Ann, packed a small suitcase and left the flat knowing that his housekeeper Ethel would keep it tidy while his friend David Jones continued squatting there.

On 14 July he wrote another letter to Ann as his flying boat made its way towards Lisbon. It was four o'clock in the afternoon and he had been in the air since nine that morning. Arrival was half an hour away. 'It's like flying in a bungalow this plane with four rooms in it and two lavatories and a kitchen. We had our excitement before starting – we had to get out of the plane and take to a little boat and cruise about because there was an air raid warning. We could just hear the dull thud of the engines, nothing more. We got back in the plane after half an hour. Then I saw two British submarines and one convoy on route but nothing else . . . now we are sailing across the bay towards Lisbon. I can see the little white houses on the shore and the dusky green of olive trees. I wish you were here little cat . . .'

Portugal was a haven for refugees, their numbers drawn from all nationalities since the outbreak of war, among them Jews fleeing Nazi persecution and other exiles. Burns spent much of his time on the beach, between briefings at the embassy and meals and drinks with colleagues, making new contacts and catching up with old friends, among them Rosalind Fox, whom he had met during the Spanish Civil War. Fox was a glamorous English divorcee who provided the British with information while maintaining a long and discreet love affair with Franco's foreign minister General Juan Beigbeder. She lived for a while in some style in the Hotel Palacio in Estoril before opening a nightclub and restaurant called El Galgo which became a favourite haunt of journalists, diplomats and spies.

As Ms Fox later recalled: 'The Galgo had an unforgettable ambience, a unique oasis of conviviality and intrigue amidst a world at war. But that atmosphere was not of my doing. Credit for that belongs to all those many human beings who passed through its doors, lending to it something of their own spirit – their hopes, their fears, their sorrows, their joys. The Galgo was a phenomenon born out of war and man's inhumanity to man. It reflected something of that sense of comradeship that simply being human should engender, yet which sadly enough, seems only to be in evidence in times of great trial . . .'

Burns was alone when, one evening, he visited the Casino in the Hotel Palacio, another rendezvous of choice for the Allies and the Axis diplomats and spies who had turned neutral Portugal into a support base for their activities in the Iberian Peninsula. Dressed impeccably in dinner jacket, he walked through a gauntlet of porters and bell boys, across the thick red carpet to the gaming room. Huge chandeliers on golden painted ropes were suspended above the game tables. Cigar smoke lay thick in the air, dispersed now and then by the scent of Chanel. Glasses clinked, roulette wheels turned. '*Prenez vos places. Rien ne va plus.*' Burns had never gambled for money in his life. He gambled now, partly for fun, but also out of a sense of duty. He took in the faces, tried to pick up bits of stray conversation, and reported back to the embassy. Four days later the visit to Portugal was cut short on the orders of Hoare. Burns wrote a letter to Ann, postmarked Estoril. 'Here I am but actually I'm off to Madrid first thing tomorrow and will be knocking about in Spain for about two weeks, I'd meant to be ten days here but Sir Sam simply pines for me so I must go.'

5

EMBASSY ON SPECIAL MISSION

It was the stiffness in Sir Samuel Hoare – dressed in a dull charcoal suit and severity stamped on his face – that reminded Burns of the least likeable aspects of his own late banker father David, the puritan Scotsman who had only converted to the Catholic faith with the approach of death. Burns believed the Whitehall gossip that the real reason Churchill had left Hoare out of his cabinet and encouraged his posting abroad was that he could not bear the thought of having to cope with someone so abstemious and fastidious at close quarters for the rest of the war. Hoare, so Churchill had once joked, was descended from a line of maiden aunts. The new ambassador's distrust of foreign parts and his belief in their endemic political instability had been engendered by his early experience as MI6's station chief in Tsarist Russia's St Petersburg during the First World War before heading the British Military Mission to Italy. On the other hand Hoare's unwavering belief in the integrity and enduring political, economic and cultural superiority of the British Empire had been engendered by a record in the higher echelons of public office spanning three decades. He had served Britain as Foreign Secretary, First Lord of the Admiralty, Lord Privy Seal, Home Secretary, Secretary of State for India and Secretary of State for Air.

Then, after nine years of virtually uninterrupted ministerial office, Hoare had lost his place in government just as his country was embarking on a defining chapter in world history. He was shocked by the sudden severance from the trappings of high office. From one day to the next he lost his official telephones, 'red boxes' of sensitive documents, office, car and staff. Hoare wandered disconsolately from his house in Chelsea to the Carlton Club and from the Carlton Club to the House of Commons, 'not knowing where to lay my head and wondering how I should occupy my time and energies'. For a short period, his old friend Beaverbrook took pity on him and suffered his advice at the new Ministry of Aircraft Production.

But what happened next came close to humiliation for a man who regarded himself as one of the most experienced politicians of his generation. Faced with the reality of his exclusion from the cabinet and the looming prospect of an extended exile to the backbenches, Hoare wanted Churchill to make him Viceroy of India. He wrote to Chamberlain asking him to force the new prime minister to do this. Lord Halifax vetoed it, saying that Hoare was not up to it. Instead Halifax asked Hoare to go to Spain as an emissary and tasked initially only with the implementation of an Anglo-Spanish trade and economic assistance treaty signed the previous March. Halifax told Hoare that his mission to Spain would take only a few weeks. The politically disgraced and physically fading Chamberlain – for whom Hoare retained enormous respect – tried to warm him against going, on the grounds that he could expect little of Franco's Spain other than it falling into German hands.

Another of his trusted allies advised him that it was precisely such a prospect that made his mission both urgent and necessary. The Deputy Chief of the Naval Staff, Admiral Tom Phillips, warned of the crucial importance of ensuring that the Atlantic ports of the Iberian Peninsula and north-west Africa did not fall into enemy hands, if the Royal Navy was to pursue with any chance of success its ongoing battle with German U-boats. It was equally critical to stop the Germans using Spain as a platform for attacking and taking Gibraltar, a key naval base for Allied Mediterranean and eastern communications.

Thus did Phillips soothe Hoare's wounded ego, restoring his faith in his own importance, and dispelling any notion he harboured that he was being put out to grass. The mission, in Hoare's eyes, was no longer a 'pretext for breaking the fall of an ex-minister, or for finding a job for an old friend'. It was instead 'real and urgent war work of great strategic urgency in which the chiefs of staff and the fighting services were vitally concerned'.

Hoare and his wife Lady Maud – a matronly figure from a staunchly Conservative background (she was the youngest daughter of the Tory grandee Frederick Lygon, 6th Earl of Beauchamp) – set off for his new post via Lisbon, arriving in Madrid on 2 June. For all his foreign experience, Hoare seems to have been ill prepared for what awaited him in the Spanish capital. He was shocked to discover that the Foreign Office, unlike the Indian Civil Service, did not provide its higher officials with fully-appointed houses and a large complement of domestic staff for their missions abroad. He sent urgent word to the Secretary of the Office of Works, Sir Patrick Duff, to remedy the situation. Duff saw to it that a cargo of china, cutlery and linen was collected from noble establishments around London and shipped out immediately to Madrid via the port of Valencia.

Far from being warmly greeted by their host country, the Hoares faced angry anti-British demonstrators outside the embassy, shouting in Spanish, 'Gibraltar must be Spanish.' With no official residence to go to, the Hoares booked into the Ritz Hotel. Like the Palace, which it faced on the other side of the wide Paseo del Prado, the hotel had only recently been restored after being used as a military hospital during the civil war. It had a palatial entrance of wrought-iron gates, topped with gold paint, and was surrounded by manicured gardens. Its rooms were filled with antique Spanish and French furniture, including priceless velvet curtains, tapestries, chandeliers and silverware.

The Hoares had chosen the Ritz on the recommendation of the Spanish ambassador in London, the Duke of Alba. The Duke's sister, the Duchess of Santoña, was among a group of Spanish aristocrats who were regular guests at the hotel, taking suites there while waiting for their palatial houses to be restored to their pre-civil war splendour. Doña Sol, as the duchess was popularly known, made a point of sitting at the same table in the hall by the bar that her family had had before the war. The table was sacrosanct. Every day before luncheon at 1.30 she sat at the same table sipping her dry Martini, in the presence of other members of the aristocracy.

Hoare was struck less by the Ritz's aristocratic inhabitants than by its intrigue, not least the presence of so many Germans. From the moment he and Lady Maud booked into the hotel, he suspected he was being watched and followed, and his telephone tapped. The Hoares found it oppressive and immediately started looking for an alternative residence. House-hunting was not easy, for few good houses had survived the civil war intact and the ambassador had to count on the services of his military attaché, Brigadier William Wyndham Torr, to exploit his contacts among the Spanish senior officer class in his search for a suitable abode.

A large house was eventually secured off the Castellana, within walking distance of the embassy building in Fernando el Santo Street. That Hoare chose to live next to the residence of Baron Eberhard von Stohrer, the German ambassador, was a deliberate act of defiance, symbolic of his determination not to be seen to be intimidated by the Nazi presence in Spain.

Hoare's first days in Madrid were marked by a growing realisation of the importance of his mission. When he had set off from England, Spain was seemingly isolated from the rest of war-torn Europe, but the Nazi military offensive had intensified the nearer he got to Madrid. While he was en route, Dunkirk was evacuated. Then, while he was in Lisbon, Norway followed by Belgium had fallen to the Germans. Almost simultaneously with his arrival in Madrid, France had finally capitulated, allowing German troops to reach the Franco-Spanish border at the Pyrenees and radically altering the whole strategic balance of Western Europe.

It was not just the Atlantic ports of the Iberian Peninsula that were potentially in jeopardy from Hitler's advance. Following Mussolini's entry into the war, the whole of the Mediterranean, and, by extension, the maintenance of access to the Suez Canal and beyond, was under threat. The British could no longer rely on the French fleet with its bases at Marseilles, Bizerta and Casablanca. Instead they faced the nightmare scenario of Hitler pushing through Spain, taking Gibraltar and taking over North Africa so as to dominate continents and seas.

To Hoare, it became evident that, in addition to official German organisations and 'front companies', there were German sympathisers in every department of the Spanish government, with some Nazis enjoying a major influence over the media, and how the war was reported. The German embassy had been built up into a powerful hub of diplomatic, military, commercial, and covert activity, its reach extending as far as South America. The Abwehr ran a European and American network of agents from its Madrid base, while the Gestapo had established close ties with the Spanish secret police, delivering training and equipment and moving its informers backwards and forwards across the Portuguese and French borders in pursuit of Allied targets.

Among the most formidable and sinister players at the German embassy was Hans Lazar, who, under his cover of press attaché, controlled an impressive secret propaganda and intelligence organisation. Lazar's background was as mysterious as much of the work he carried out. The suggestion that he had Jewish ancestry was almost certainly a piece of misinformation mischievously circulated by the British embassy; that he had been born in Turkey and had moved with the Armenian diaspora into Eastern Europe before spending his time between Vienna and Berlin after becoming a supporter of Hitler during the Anschluss, was less in doubt.

A stylish dresser with a trim moustache and swept-back hair, Lazar was indistinguishable from the other well-groomed and cocky young men who dominated key areas of public life in the Spanish capital; only a monocle (when he wore it) gave him a sinister air. Lazar moved with ease in Madrid's social circles, and added daily to his array of contacts. At an early stage in the war he was rumoured to have more than four hundred agents reporting to him, making his department bigger than any other in the embassy.

By comparison, what the British had up and running in Madrid fell well short of what Hoare felt necessary to carry out his mission with any hope of success. The embassy had only been re-established, under Franco's new authority in Madrid, the previous October, after moving from its temporary civil war lodgings in San Sebastián. Hoare's predecessor, Maurice Peterson, had found the small complex housing the residence and the chancery in a state of abandonment, with only preliminary restoration work funded by the British Office of Works.

On 12 May 1940, Peterson received a letter from the Foreign Office bluntly informing him that his posting was at an end. The charge laid against him when he returned to London was that he had grown unpopular with Spaniards, and that he was not 'comfortable' in Madrid.

Hoare arrived in Madrid and was shocked to find just how right the sceptics in Whitehall had been in thinking that the ineffectual Peterson's 'slow-motion machine of a peace time embassy' was totally ill-equipped to deal with the developing strategic imperatives of securing Spanish neutrality. So fragile did Hoare believe the situation to be that he arranged for an emergency aircraft to be on standby to evacuate him and the embassy staff in the event of an Axis takeover. 'It may well be that things may go badly in Spain and that we may have to leave at very short notice and in very difficult circumstances,' he wrote in late May 1940. 'We have to face the facts in the world today and we must not exclude the possibility of a coup organised by German gunmen.'

The embassy struck Hoare at first sight as the most 'horrible building' he had ever been required to work in, its facilities cramped, its staff struggling to remain operational despite the additional funding that Burns and Hillgarth had obtained for their operations. At the time the Secret Intelligence Service, or MI6, had established a relatively small but self-contained office in Madrid in the same grounds as the chancery but in a separate outbuilding. By the end of 1940, British propaganda and intelligence operations within the embassy were seeing unprecedented levels of activity. It had not always been thus.

During the Spanish Civil War, the handful of British diplomatic and consular officials out in the field struggled to provide the eyes and ears of the Foreign Office, while trying to protect UK lives and interests amidst the chaos of the conflict. The bulk of their reports had helped forge the British policy of non-intervention in Spain, turning the country – in the eyes of the professional British spies – into an intelligence backwater. While Abwehr and Soviet NKVD agents swarmed all over Spain, MI6's intelligence gathering was reduced to occasional reporting by its accredited representative, Colonel Edward de Renzy Martin, a veteran of the Great War who had been posted to Spain after serving as Inspector of the Albanian Gendarmerie. When the British embassy was re-established in Madrid in early 1940, Renzy Martin was replaced as 'head of station' by Hamilton-Stokes.

MI6's new local chief tried to maintain his own separate channel of communication to London under the so-called CX system. This consisted in a two- to three-digit prefix on SIS telegrams which identified their recipient to the Foreign Office clerks. 'CX' indicated a personal message to the chief of MI6, while CXG indicated the sharing of information within the organisation. While the system was justified in terms of protecting sources and operations, it also conspired against accountability and effective administration. In Madrid, as elsewhere, there was a tendency built up over the years to keep the distribution of MI6 information to a restricted 'need to know' basis although the agency itself drew on sources from other areas.

When Hoare arrived in Spain, MI6 was drafting plans to reinforce its operations in Madrid, Lisbon, Gibraltar and Tangier. In June 1940, MI6 had lost touch with its agents in occupied Europe, forcing the organisation to build up its stations in the neutral countries of Spain and Portugal as well as Switzerland. Until then much of the information coming out of Madrid had been collated as a result of individual initiative rather than in response to any grand strategy. The embassy's two pivotal operatives, Hillgarth and assistant press attaché Malley, had established their own lines of reporting to London and were responsible for the bulk of intelligence on Spain that reached the Foreign Office and Churchill.

Both men were fortunate in having an experienced deputy head of mission, Arthur Yencken, to hold the fort during the change of ambassadors. An Anglicised Australian who had won a Military Cross during the First World War, Yencken had done some useful intelligence work during his previous posting in Berlin. Drawing on contacts he developed in the German metallurgical industry, Yencken had sent some intuitive reports about Hitler's rearmament programme which eventually found their way into Churchill's hands, thanks to a high-level source he had in the Foreign Office.

As Burns remembered him, Yencken was 'tough, laconic, witty and sometimes rather wild', popular on the Madrid diplomatic circuit and as skilled an operator in obtaining intelligence from local sources as he had been in Germany. In Burns, Yencken identified from the outset a friend and useful colleague, a 'semi-Brit' who could similarly integrate effortlessly into the local landscape because he had managed to resist being drawn into the pompous insularity and phobias that pervaded the British Foreign Service. 'One of your many jobs here will be to keep Sam [Hoare] from doing a bunk,' Yencken told Burns soon after they met.

Notwithstanding the professional talent that existed within the British embassy, Hoare spent his first few weeks in Spain feeling almost overwhelmed by the situation he found himself in. He became paranoid about the German presence in the country, which he believed was paving the way for a full-sale Nazi occupation. 'Things are moving so quickly that by the end of three months there may be no more Mission in Madrid,' he wrote to the Treasury in June 1940.

Just how dire the situation seemed to observers beyond the embassy was summed up in a report published around this period in the *New York Times*. According to its correspondent, compared to the small team of less than a dozen staff employed in the British embassy, there were some two hundred Germans operating in Madrid under diplomatic cover. The report went on: 'Barcelona and other Spanish ports are said to be swarming with German and Italian agents, awaiting Mussolini's signal for the war in the Mediterranean to begin.'

The highly charged political atmosphere Hoare encountered fuelled deepening concern about the survival of his mission. A week into his post he confessed in a private letter to Chamberlain that he found himself 'in the midst of every sort of difficulty with little or no daylight' to guide him through it. He compared living in Madrid to living in a besieged city, 'a shortage of almost everything, prices terribly high. And a heavy atmosphere of impending crisis on all sides.'

Hoare saw armed guards wherever he went, and felt unsure whether they were there to guard or to intimidate him. He became so nervous about his personal safety that he insisted on being shadowed on his daily walk to the embassy by a stalwart Scotland Yard detective he had arranged to have smuggled in from London. And yet Hoare felt a need to redeem himself in Madrid and set about overhauling and shaping the embassy to meet the needs of the mission with which he had been entrusted – that of preventing Franco from entering the war on behalf of the Axis powers.

Taking on the Germans in the propaganda war and winning over Spanish public opinion was placed at the top of Hoare's agenda. On 7 June he wrote personally to Duff Cooper, the newly appointment Minister of Information, asking for his support in developing the operational capacity of the press section. Hoare also wrote to Beaverbrook, asking for his help in ensuring that 'someone really big' – he had suggested the head of the Foreign Office's Western European Department, Walter Roberts – be posted to Madrid as soon as possible to help advise him.

That Hoare was sent not Roberts or anyone of his rank or status within the upper echelons of the civil service, but Tom Burns, a Catholic publisher and relatively recent recruit of the Ministry of Information, partly reflected the ambassador's unpopularity and the resentment he still generated in British political circles.

Those within the Foreign Office who joked about Hoare being murdered by Germans or Italians saw him as a cowardly appeaser and were unconvinced of Spain's developing strategic importance. They were damned if they were going to help Hoare out in his time of need, and wanted to thwart his plans if they could. There were also those in the Ministry of Information who had no difficulty in offering Burns up as a sacrificial lamb. Coming as he had done from outside the civil service and largely through the recommendation of his Catholic network, Burns had made enemies among his own colleagues. Religious bigotry, politics and envy all conspired against him, and in particular the fact that he had backed Franco.

Burns's own record of his first meeting with Hoare on a hot July day in 1940 suggests that neither man expected to survive long in Madrid. 'I protested my inadequacy and lack of experience, but all objections were brushed aside. Perhaps he [Hoare] thought that job would be too short-lived anyway,' he later recalled. Fate and circumstances had thrown these opposites together into a coordinated effort that was to survive, for better or for worse, for most of the war. And yet the job Hoare offered Burns suggested there was method in the ambassador's madness. 'What you make of the job is largely up to you,' Hoare told Burns; 'all I insist is that that you report directly to me.'

Thus, having initially asked for a senior Whitehall mandarin to come and hold his hand, and seen the request turned down, Hoare felt he had no option but to make do with what he'd been sent and to try to turn the appointment to his advantage. The ambassador calculated that

Burns's relative inexperience would make him more manageable, easier to fit into the grand design he had for the embassy and for British policy towards Spain generally. The fact that no single department would, under Hoare's design, be able to claim ownership over Burns meant that his appointment could be turned into a pivotal post, straddling civilian and military departments and diplomacy and intelligence – in effect, the ambassador's eyes and ears.

Given their differences in background and character, both men faced a formidable challenge in ensuring an effective professional relationship between them. What separated them was rooted in geography, blood, faith and history. Hoare seemed ill at ease in Spanish society. Burns believed his ambassador's alienation stemmed from an indelible insularity reinforced by puritan convictions. And yet these personal failings, thought Burns, were largely overcome by Hoare's own dynamism. 'He was,' Burns would later comment on his ambassador, 'absorbed in his station and its duties, restlessly determined to advance or initiate whatever might help in his mission.'

Burns's own advancement under Hoare's tutelage was largely thanks to the fact that he found the official policy the ambassador pursued for much of the war entirely in accord with his personal opinions. The urgent necessity of bolstering Britain's presence in Spain was, after all, the proposal Burns had reported back to the Ministry of Information and his friends in the Foreign Office when he had completed his earlier visit to Spain in February 1940. Moreover, he hoped for and worked towards Spanish neutrality with a passion that perhaps Hoare lacked. Ever since his friend Douglas Jerrold had helped plot Franco's uprising, Burns had argued, contrary to the view held by many fellow British men and women, that the Spanish Civil War was not by design a rehearsal for the Second World War, thus linking Franco ineluctably with the Axis, but was a phenomenon specifically of Spanish political history. It was not that Burns ignored the Axis support for Franco. He saw this as an undeniable fact, just as he regarded as an undeniable fact the support given to the Republican government by the Soviets and worldwide communism. But he had no doubt that if these 'giants' had been off the scene, the 'fatal clash in Spain' would still have come about.

Now Burns saw in the mission dedicated to preserving Spain's neutrality the answer to the question posed by his friend Mike Richey during that night of shared whisky and revelations on the eve of the Second World War. What, in all conscience, could those who could not bring themselves to kill but who wanted to do their bit for the war do? Burns had signed up to his ambassador's 'special mission'.

And that was how, scarcely a week after his arrival from Lisbon, Burns found he was staying on in Madrid, keenly aware that he was joining, as he put it, an embassy of 'many talents and many tensions that over time came to be transformed into a closely-knit unit family'. This time he didn't stay at the Palace Hotel, but for some weeks took up residence in the no less luxurious if smaller and more discreet Gaylord's Hotel, which was operating under the name Hotel Buen Retiro. One of Franco's first decrees on coming to power was that hotels and other such establishments should have Spanish names but Gaylord's was what its customers continued to call it, immortalised as it was thanks to the pen of Ernest Hemingway.

During the civil war, communist officers and Soviet spies had stayed at Gaylord's, displacing the bourgeoisie with the same disdain they had shown for the previous occupants of churches, convents and palaces. It was there that Robert Jordan, the young American volunteer in Hemingway's *For Whom the Bell Tolls*, had ended up during his three-day leave from the front, because there you could get 'good food and real beer and could find out what was going on in the war', thanks to Karkov, the Russian KGB colonel. Jordan had at first felt bad about being there – it seemed too luxurious and the food too good at a time when most of the city was starving – but Jordan corrupted very easily, or so he thought. He felt he owed himself some decent food after taking on the dangers that living at war in Spain brought along.

It was in the room once slept in by an NKVD officer that Burns found himself one night when, towards the end of July 1940, he sat and wrote his first long Spanish 'ticket' to Ann Bowes-Lyon. He imagined her on night duty in the military hospital at Woolwich, listening to the groans and cries of the wounded and the dying, trying to distinguish between the pain and the nightmares. 'I am in shirt sleeves after a sweltering day,' he wrote to her. How inadequate, by comparison, seemed his existence, but what else was he supposed to write that was not invention? 'Nothing is emptier than a hotel when you're alone,' he continued. 'Even the furniture is dead and gone and the room seems to soak up one's life like blotting paper so that one has to get out every now and then to survive it all.'

Writing that seemed a corruption of the language: 'survival' in a hotel room without a shot being fired or a bomb dropped? He had to explain as best he could that his peace, Spain's peace, was deceptive. So he wrote on, telling her that Madrid that summer was an all day burning sun and dust – 'not a heavy humid heat, but dry hard bright heat and a gentle warm tender sort of night'. He went on: 'People creep along the shade of walls from house to house in the midday and sit for hours in the evening round their little tables on the pavement . . . It is all peaceful as far as you can see, you would not guess the intrigue and threat behind it all . . .'

And then he told Ann what he had been dreading having to tell her – that he wasn't coming back to London, to her, not for a while at least, because of the 'special mission' he had been recruited for. This meant that for the first time since they had met they faced the prospect of a prolonged period of involuntary separation. He tried to think of a way of reassuring her. It was duty not betrayal but he thought it best to deflect the issue. He turned instead to the cat language, a frivolous code but one they had learnt to share. 'Sam Hoare seems – *miao* – to think he is a much better sort of cat than I am. Any way he has asked me most insistently if I would stay here and cope with things for a month . . .' Hoare had in fact given Burns no time limit but had insisted that the job should be open-ended, and include assignments in Lisbon, Gibraltar and North Africa. Like the rest of the embassy, Burns was secretly warned by his ambassador that he might have to flee Madrid if Franco joined the war on Hitler's side. The 'month' Burns had mentioned to Ann was a white lie conjured up to reduce the blow of a less predictable separation. What followed reflected a sense of calling, on Burns's side, and the need to overcome any vestiges of self-doubt: 'Do see darling a bit and help us by being all right as I shall try to be . . . How I am plunked down with much too big a job for my furry head and having to work like fury . . . if only one can keep this heavenly place from the main flood of war, that will indeed be worth all one's sweat and life.'

He ended, as he always did whenever he wrote to her, wishing God's blessing on her 'dreamt heart', and wishing 'her safe and well, and his enduring love'. He sketched her as a white cat looking at him, similarly transformed into a black cat, sitting in a building marked British embassy. 'Oh dearie, he *is* grand!' the white cat mocked. And, yes, there was a sense that Burns had found something he could be proud of telling her, that he had finally got somewhere special before her, that he had found his own Glamis Castle, one whose bridge was not drawn up on him even if walking into it risked losing her.

Burns placed the letter in the diplomatic bag for urgent dispatch to London, acutely aware of the distance that separated him from England now that he was flying the flag in a foreign land. 'She looked jolly nice . . . in her tight fitting tailored blue coat and black tie and white collar,' David Jones wrote to Burns after a visit by Ann. 'She seemed all right and pretty cheerful, but of course sad that you were going to be longer away than you thought.'

It was the summer of 1940. London, like Madrid, was experiencing a heatwave. Jones, the artist, struggled to remain above the fray, as nearly everyone else got dragged into it. Jones continued to live rent-free in the basement of Burns's Chelsea house, his meals dutifully cooked by Ethel, the housekeeper. Her wages were still paid out of Burns's London account, as was much of Jones's general unkeep, thanks to an informal arrangement the painter had reached with his friend at the outbreak of war. Such generosity sprang from a sense of enduring loyalty and protectiveness Burns felt towards the neurotic artist.

Of the original close group of Catholic friends, Harman Grisewood, by contrast, was working flat out and almost to the point of exhaustion at the BBC, a key link man between the Corporation and Churchill's war effort. In his letters to Madrid, Jones also reported on the occasional visit by Bernard Wall, down from Oxford where he was working as a researcher on a 'secret Foreign Office project'.

Periodically Jones dined with Douglas Woodruff, the former *Times* leader writer who was now writing regular leaders for the *Tablet* as its editor, strongly supportive of Spanish neutrality and Britain's ongoing relations with Franco, while his wife Mia helped coordinate nursing support across London. Jones shared occasional leisurely lunches with his literary patron, Hilaire Belloc, the religious apologist and social prophet who had lived his life with an irredeemable grief and an embittering sense of failure. Belloc lived in Cheyne Row, around the corner from Burns and Grisewood. With the local church named after the recently beatified Catholic martyr Thomas More, this small part of Chelsea had developed into a faith-based community in the heart of London.

Belloc was looking older than his seventy years. Italy's declaration of war had struck at the old Catholic's heart, while the fall of France, where his beloved daughter Elizabeth lived, had filled him with anxiety. It was only several months later that he heard through his one-time disciple Burns that she was safe. Burns sent word that Elizabeth had crossed into Spain, before making her way back to England. Belloc, meanwhile, continued to urge the Pope to speak out against the Nazis but the head of the Catholic Church continued to confine himself to generalities.

Meanwhile, Eric Gill was working on his autobiography despite periodic bouts of sickness. Unaware of the cancer beginning to creep up on him, he was busily making plans to emigrate to America with his family to join Graham Carey in the founding of 'another cell of good living'. He had lost none of his mistrust of industrial society and its ability to create a proper human world. He now saw war as a death wish once again made reality, with mankind drifting towards self-destruction.

Months before the start of the war, Burns and two other Gill disciples, Harman Grisewood and Rene Hague, while on their way to visit the sculptor, had narrowly escaped serious injury if not death when the brakes on the MG sports car Burns was driving failed, leaving the vehicle to crash into a brick wall on the outskirts of London. Hague put the three friends' survival to divine providence. 'Now, *that's* the sort of accident I like – just time to make an act of contrition,' he had remarked after stumbling out of the crippled car, good-humouredly.

And yet the accident was an omen of sorts. For the extended community of family and friends that had stayed at Pigotts and which

Burns had come to know so intimately had long been in a process of dispersal, and in the case of one of its female members, disintegration.

At the time of the accident, Gill's one-time model and apprentice and David Jones's muse, Prudence Pelham, was suffering from depression and was under treatment for a creeping multiple sclerosis that would eventually lead to her death in 1952, at the age of forty-seven.

'What a real sod and bugger this neurosis is for this generation – it is our Black Death, all right,' wrote Jones.

Prudence's husband Guy Branch was flying increasingly dangerous missions with the RAF and had once been reported missing, only subsequently to reappear. The news had been brought to Glebe Place by Paul Richey, brother of Mike, who was on short leave from duties with Bomber Command. Richey had turned up to borrow Burns's sports car for an outing with a girlfriend. As he watched the car disappear down the King's Road, tooting as it went, David Jones recalled the day when Burns had taken him and two other friends for a drive to one of their favourite country pubs, only to misjudge a curve and end up in a ditch, laughing their heads off like schoolboys breaking rules. Those days of carefree merriment seemed gone for ever. Those who got drunk and made love now did so in the knowledge that their days might well be numbered.

Mike Richey had tried as best he could to keep in touch with the network of Catholic friends that Burns had helped build up in the run-up to the war. Earlier in the summer he had written to Graham Greene with some critical comments on *The Power and the Glory*, arguing that he had found the novel too long and the portrait of the priest theologically unconvincing. Greene wrote back defending his work: 'You are objecting to him (the priest) on the same grounds as people who object to a book because it has no nice characters. The answer is: they are not meant to be nice.' It was a courteous exchange nonetheless, born from a growing friendship. Greene extended an invitation to Richey to come and visit him when he was next on leave, before adding, 'You certainly live now in a stranger world than the priest's.' Mike, the younger of the two Richeys, was in some secret part of the ocean, blowing up mines while avoiding German U-boats when he wrote to Greene. Soon afterwards, while on shore leave, he visited

Jones at Glebe Place. 'He looks like a young lion with a blue anchor tattooed on his vest and hairy fore-arm – he's just the same,' Jones wrote to Burns.

Richey collected a gift Burns had organised for him before leaving for Madrid. It was a brandy flask inscribed with the legend: *love to Mike from David* [Jones], *Tom* [Burns], *and Ann* [Bowes-Lyon]. The flask was later lost at sea.

Letters continued to arrive at Glebe Place for Burns, and Jones took care to sift them. One letter arrived with Burns's name neatly typed on a large brown envelope. Jones opened it and saw that it came from Burns's tailors in Jermyn Street, Mayfair. It was an unpaid bill with a warning of imminent legal action to recover the debt. Jones rang and secured an indefinite deferment after telling the manager that his friend was on 'a top secret mission of huge national importance'.

'I bet it is bloody hot in Spain,' Jones wrote to Burns days later. 'I think about you a lot and wonder how you are liking it all. It's weird to think of you there. Rum when chaps are away doing something quite different and all looks the same – the room etc – as if you might walk in any moment and say, "Come on, Dai, let's have a pint – I'm absolutely dying for a quick one." '

It *was* bloody hot in Spain but that was not what most concerned Burns in those early days in Madrid. It was his conscience. In a letter to Jones he confessed to feeling wonderfully suited to the heat and the shade, the long lunches, the two-hour afternoon siesta, then the long, balmy evenings, drinking and dancing and feeling that the Spanish lifestyle was good for the soul. But it was then that he remembered how he had left London just as the capital and the entire country was bracing itself for an onslaught by Nazi Germany. He had settled in Gaylord's – just as the Battle of Britain had entered its preliminary stage. German attacks had also begun on convoys of merchant ships, those which his friend Mike Richey had volunteered to protect with his minesweeper.

Then the Luftwaffe began bombing RAF bases in southern England, before turning on London. Burns thought of Paul Richey, and Prudence's Pelham's husband Guy, flying Spitfires off the English coast. Both were eventually shot down. Paul survived but Guy was lost in action. He thought, too, of Evelyn Waugh and Graham Greene, from whom he had not heard since leaving London but who, he imagined, were now closer to mortal danger than he was.

Waugh's tortuous search for military employment had finally borne fruit the previous November when his application to join the Royal Marines was accepted. Months of indoctrination in military history and training followed until the end of May 1940. Then, while stationed at a tented camp at Bisley, near Aldershot, he received a message to call Burns. It was Saturday 25 May and his old friend and publisher – at the time Burns was still at the MoI – had somehow managed to track him down to the Swan Hotel in Alton, where he was spending a romantic weekend leave with Laura Herbert, his second wife. 'We went to church, read P. G. Wodehouse (who has been lost along with the Channel ports), watched old men in panama hats play bowls, and forgot the war. Burns made strenuous efforts to get in touch.'

Three days later, on his return to Bisley, Waugh received an official summons to report 'soonest' to the MoI. Arriving there on 28 May, he recorded:

'I found the news of Belgian surrender on the streets and women selling flags for "Animal Day". Had hair cut and bought pants. Went to M of I [Ministry of Information] where Graham Greene propounded a scheme for official writers to the forces and himself wanted to become a marine; also Burns. I said I thought the official writer racket might be convenient if we found ourselves permanently in a defensive role in the Far East, or if I were incapacitated.'

Waugh's biographer Christopher Sykes described the Official Writers Scheme typical of the 'empty-headed utopianism of the "Phoney War"' which was already out of date by the time it was proposed. Within weeks Waugh had been appointed an intelligence officer with 8 Commando brigade and was on his way to Freetown in Sierra Leone as part of an Anglo-French attempt to wrest Dakar in Senegal from the Vichy government and install General de Gaulle and the Free French in its place.

The operation turned into a military fiasco late in September 1940. But long before then Burns had fixed in his imagination the image of Evelyn bravely fighting battles to which he was physically and psychologically unsuited, a heroic example which darkened his own early days in Madrid with a sense of guilt. That he should feel like this was somewhat ironic for, unknown to Burns, it was his mission in Spain that Waugh had looked to with some envy at a time when Madrid was filled with Germans and Aldershot had no Germans at all. Waugh had learnt of Burns's sudden appointment from their mutual friends Douglas and Mia Woodruff during an evening in London on leave, drinking champagne. 'They [the Woodruffs] were full of tales of the interesting jobs all my friends are getting – Tom [Burns] in Madrid, Chris [Hollis] in Washington. I felt sad to be going back to the confusion of the marines.'

As things turned out, Waugh would reach West Africa only after Graham Greene had got there first – although neither they nor Burns could have predicted how their respective lives would unfold in the weeks and months after their unsuccessful attempt to engage with the Official Writers Scheme.

The guilt that Burns sometimes felt at leaving London for Madrid was accentuated by the German aerial offensive on the capital which began on 7 September 1940 and continued every night until 2 November that year.

The horror of the Blitz was brought home to those who had shared the vigorous literary life of the 1930s by news of a heavy air raid on a leading publishing house in Paternoster Row, near St Paul's. It was there, while working for Longman, that Burns had shared an office with the employees of Burns & Oates, the firm named after its founder, his great-uncle James. It was there, too, that Burns had signed up Greene to write *The Lawless Roads* and discussed other publishing ventures with Waugh.

News of the bombing reached Burns through Douglas Woodruff, whose offices had also ended up reduced to ashes and rubble of broken brick and stone, and charred furniture. Burns also heard about the bombing of Greene's house in Clapham. Miraculously, Greene had been staying at his studio in Bloomsbury with his mistress while his wife Vivien and the children were in Oxford. As Vivien later remarked, not without a sense of enduring pain and betrayal caused by the love of her life, 'Graham was saved by his infidelity.'

Burns would later come to reflect with sadness that the destruction of Greene's house in Clapham, where Vivien had once cooked him and her husband a generous meal, had come to symbolise the beginning of an end of a marriage he had suspected was doomed to failure because of differences of temperament and expectation.

He would learn belatedly that Greene's job at the MoI had come to an abrupt end in September 1940. Greene was allowed to leave by the Ministry's new Director General, Frank Pick, on the grounds that his position in the writers' section – 'an absurdly hilarious time' according to Greene – was no longer necessary. As his friend and publisher, Burns rightly sensed that Greene's ignoble exit from the MoI was providential. It allowed him to draw on material for further novels, and paved the way for his eventual recruitment by MI6 and a posting in early December 1941 to Freetown, Sierra Leone.

In the letters Burns wrote back to London during those months in 1940, he had Greene among others in mind when he told his friend David Jones how bad he felt to be enjoying his posting to Madrid when all the other 'chaps' and the world generally seemed to be having such an 'awful time'. But he also reflected on how the 'love thing' he felt for Ann Bowes-Lyon was not about being 'above and beyond or below and besides', it was on a different plane. And there was a part, deep within him, that confessed to wanting nothing else but Ann. As he wrote to Jones, 'Hell, bugger them all. I will be as near to Ann Bowes-Lyon as I bloody well can be, even if she does not write another letter back and is completely indifferent. Empires can crash and the lands be waste – let the buggers get on with it – I must be near the extraordinary girl – I can do no other come what will.'

A Catholic with a conscience needs a co-religionist to set him free. So it was that David Jones came to act as Burns's informant, confessor and counsellor. Jones's surviving letters to Burns gave a vivid if sometimes rambling account (one letter was fourteen pages long) of how the London they had experienced together was changing under the impact of war. Right up to the beginning of September, Jones continued to visit their favourite pub on the embankment, the Cross Keys, and hear mass at the Church of the Holy Redeemer in Cheyne Walk, where the statue of her patron Thomas More served as a constant reminder of Catholic witness and martyrdom for the faith. 'We get raid warnings a good bit at any old time in the 24 hours, one has got quite used the sound of the old sirens, occasional bumps and "noises off" etc. It is a bloody curious type of war ... odd in many ways, everything goes on as normal except that if one makes an appointment it may get put off if there is a warning.'

Then the bombs started falling and Jones found it increasingly difficult not to write more graphically about the devastation they caused. He and the rump of friends that remained in London clung desperately to old habits and old haunts. On 14 September 1940, Harman Grisewood, then working as the BBC's assistant director for programme planning, married Margaret Bailey at the Holy Redeemer in a ceremony attended by Jones and three other friends. They celebrated with a champagne lunch at the Hyde Park Hotel and a visit to the zoo during an air-raid warning. There was no one there except for the animals. They ended the day having tea back at Grisewood's home at 61 King's Road, before he went off to the BBC on night duty.

It was, as Jones put it, 'very phantastical now, this curious compound of ordinary private life in the old haunts, mixed in with the violent stuff'.

Despite the Blitz, Burns's dark tabby, Tim, for ever immortalised in his letters to Ann, seemed to flourish, his coat full and glossy as he devoured pieces of liver bought for him by Jones from the local butcher. Ethel continued to cook meals for Jones and tidy up after him, thanks to the cheques Burns sent from Madrid. She was by now also working part-time in an air-raid shelter.

Number 3 Glebe Place survived the Blitz unscathed physically, but bombs hit a house across the street, the crypt of the Holy Redeemer, and the local public library on the King's Road, killing dozens of civilians. Jones made plans to evacuate his paintings. Wherever he walked he saw a church damaged, books burnt. Winston Churchill had no doubt that the ultimate scalp the Luftwaffe was seeking was St Paul's Cathedral because of its iconic status. It all added to Jones's growing sense of seeing Hitler as an anti-Christ, destroyer of faith and art.

In a letter to Jones, Burns said he felt that what he was living through in Madrid was 'uncontemporary' in the sense that it seemed existentially dislocated from the horror sweeping through Western Europe.

Jones tried to put Burns's mind at rest. 'I think you ought to do whatever you bloody well feel inclined to do, and, sweet Tom, don't let it get you down. It is difficult for anyone else to know a person's mind. Anyway it is not a moral question. But it would seem that if you can be of use in any place, stay put. We've all got ourselves to think about – and by doing what we can best do and most want to do, ourselves, we best do what is best for the jolly old "community" in the end. I'm sure of that . . . to an on-looker, however intimate, you seem to possess all of the requirements and qualifications for the kind of job I imagine you are doing.'

In fact, for all his years in publishing, cudgelling authors of the likes of Waugh and Greene, inherent empathy with the Catholic faith, and networking abilities extending from the higher echelons of Whitehall to Buckingham Palace, nothing could have quite prepared Burns for the job he found himself doing in Madrid.

His tasks went well beyond the normal duties of a press attaché. In peacetime this would have been reduced to keeping tabs on what the local media were reporting and acting as an information service, if not informal tourist office, on UK affairs. Such duties were neither relevant nor practical in Spain after the outbreak of the Second World War, given the censorship imposed on the Spanish media and the pervading influence of the Nazis based in Madrid, not least in the areas of propaganda and secret intelligence.

6

OF PRINCES, PRIESTS AND BULLS

When Burns arrived in Madrid in the early summer of 1940, the youngest member of the Spanish government was Pedro Gamero del Castillo, a Minister without Portfolio whose anaemic sounding post belied the influence he had at the highest level of the regime. Gamero was a rising star within the Falange party who had served as governor of the Andalusian capital of Seville after its 'liberation' by the Nationalists during the Civil War. Gamero was also a close ally of Ramón Serrano Súñer, the Secretary General of the Falange, Minister of the Interior and Franco's brother-in-law, the most powerful figure in the regime after Franco himself.

In 1940 Gamero had taken temporary lodgings at Gaylord's Hotel, waiting to move to more permanent accommodation after being transferred to the capital from the south. Burns booked into the same hotel and discreetly made plans to meet Gamero unofficially. He used as a go-between someone he knew from his publishing days, the minister's brother-in-law José Antonio Muñoz Rojas. Another Andalusian Francoist, Muñoz Rojas had spent the civil war teaching in Cambridge, developing close ties with the English Catholic network in academic, publishing and government circles.

Knowing of Burns's own pro-Franco stance during the civil war, Muñoz Rojas had no hesitation in recommending him to Gamero as a secret point of contact at a time when official diplomatic encounters between Ambassador Hoare and senior figures in the Spanish government remained strained and unproductive.

Burns for his part looked on Gamero as a radical idealist deeply committed to his Catholic faith, who, beneath his pro-German exterior, was alienated by what he saw as the godless nature of the Nazi vision and was prepared to offer discreet support to British efforts to keep Spain out of the war. During Burns's posting in Madrid, Gamero not only became a close friend but also a useful source, keeping him informed of the inner machinations of the Franco regime as it struggled with its internal divisions as well as the contacts the Falange had with the Germans.

In developing his mission in Spain under cover of press attaché, Burns drew on his intuition and charm as well as a slush fund provided, with Churchill's approval, by London to win over further 'agents of influence' to the Allied cause. While he never had as much money as his counterpart Hans Lazar with which to bribe Spanish officials, Burns used the funds he was given selectively and generally to good effect.

Burns was helped by the sheer simplicity of the system of censorship that the Falange had imposed. Nothing could be published without the permission of high-ranking officers of the party, among them Gamero and Serrano Súñer. While there is no evidence that Burns bribed Gamero personally, he did channel secret funds to some of his more junior officials in exchange for information on the inner workings of Spanish government policy and support for British propaganda operations.

That Spaniards generally at the time took a somewhat cynical view of their highly censored media, ensuring that Spanish newspapers were often not only unreadable but also unread, was of some comfort to Burns. It certainly put a premium on a bulletin his department, under his management, began to publish, with material drawn from a special wireless service provided by the MoI.

Each afternoon Burns and his team prepared and printed off thousands of copies of the bulletin before having it distributed across Madrid and in several Spanish towns by a clandestine army of locally recruited messenger boys, most of whom were orphans of the civil war or the sons and nephews of Republican soldiers who were in prison or awaiting execution.

Remembering those days long after the end of the Second World War, Burns recalled the tragic juxtaposition he witnessed on a daily basis between the continuous queues of young volunteers shuffling through the porter's lodge to his office, and the lorryloads of political prisoners who daily passed the embassy on their way to some detention camp with 'cheerful shouts, clenched fists and cries of *Viva Inglaterra*'. While the British embassy helped find employment and housing for the children of the Spanish Civil War, it generally adopted a policy of scrupulous non-intervention towards older Spaniards thrown into jail – many of whom were subsequently executed – with the exception of those who had some connections with British government service.

In his old age a certain sense of guilt nagged at Burns's conscience on this issue, so that he wrote in his memoirs: 'I could not help reflecting that this luckless mass of men would quickly stifle their *vivas* if they knew what British policy was: to keep Spain neutral by doing nothing to disturb Franco's hold in the country and when possible to aid it economically. To prevent the Germans marching through to attack Gibraltar was our major objective.'

Over the weeks and months that followed, local staff employed by Burns were periodically verbally abused in the streets by fascists. Embassy secretaries were detained by the police and questioned about the precise nature of their duties. Some of the messenger boys were beaten up by plain-clothes fascist thugs and their bulletins set on fire. Under pressure from Lazar and some of his more pro-Nazi allies within the Spanish government, a note was delivered from the Falange headquarters to the British embassy accusing its press department of spreading 'Red propaganda'. But the bulletin continued to be widely distributed, with Burns's allies within the Franco regime blocking any attempt to suppress it officially despite an ongoing campaign of intimidation. The messenger boys bravely continued to carry Allied propaganda through the neighbourhoods of Madrid and across Spain throughout the war.

Nowhere was the embassy's propaganda strategy better served than in Valladolid, where the Rector of the English Catholic College of St Alban's, Fr Henson, remained as committed to the Franco cause as he had been during the Spanish Civil War while working for the British. On his rare visits to Madrid, Henson insisted on eating his lunch punctually at one o'clock, not later, like the Spaniards, and seemed to glory in the English accent of his spoken Spanish. He also discarded his purple cassock for a clerical coat that might have come out of a Trollope novel. Burns excused Henson his eccentricities, as the camouflage of a good agent, and liked to think of him as the reincarnation of the Jesuit spies who during the Reformation ended up being martyred rather than succumb to the enemy.

From the outset of the war, Henson became increasingly engaged in propaganda and intelligence work, reporting on German sympathisers and recommending Spaniards who could be relied on to help the Allied cause. In one report to the embassy, Henson gave the name of a shopkeeper who was prepared to bribe local officials for the necessary import permits to bring in and distribute wireless receivers from England. The project was organised by Burns through the MoI, with the support of Grisewood at the BBC. It proved less challenging for Burns than having to help deal, soon after his arrival in Madrid, with a Nazi conspiracy to have the Windsors – the former Edward VIII and Mrs Simpson – detained in Spain pending the former monarch's restoration to the British throne.

With the German advance across northern Europe, the Windsors had retreated from their self-imposed exile in Paris, first to the Château de la Croë on Cap d'Antibes before making their way south across the Pyrenees. On 23 June 1940 they arrived in Madrid, and booked into the Ritz Hotel. There they were met by Hoare, against the background of mounting German propaganda in the Spanish press claiming that Churchill wished to arrest the Duke as soon as he returned to England.

Hoare tried his best to reassure the Windsors, and suggested that the sooner they returned to England the better as this would help stem the campaign of Nazi misinformation.

Intelligence had reached the British embassy that the German foreign minister Joachim von Ribbentrop had persuaded his Spanish counterpart Beigbeder to invite the Duke to remain in Spain for as long as he wished as a guest of the Franco government.

The Windsors did not immediately take up the offer of residence in the Palace of the Moorish Kings in the Andalusian town of Ronda, but chose instead to extend their stay in Madrid, where they were entertained separately by the Franco regime and the British embassy while becoming the subject of intense diplomatic wrangling behind the scenes.

Seemingly encouraged by the Foreign Office, Hoare ensured that he saw as much as he could of the Windsors, making them feel appreciated with regular invitations to the embassy. The cocktail party given in their honour was the biggest held since Hoare had taken over as ambassador. It subsequently fell to Burns to ensure that a tight rein be kept on the Windsors' dealings with the local press, so that no statements were forthcoming that could be interpreted as critical of the Allies. He was also asked to keep an eye on the Duke's contacts with the Franco regime during the short time they were expected to remain in Spain.

Much to Burns's relief, the Spanish government raised no objections to the Windsors' decision on 2 July 1940 to leave Madrid and travel to neighbouring Portugal, to await there a more positive response from London to their request that they be allowed to return to the UK. Over the next month, the Windsors played for time, hoping for positive news from London, while letting it be known that they had not ruled out, as an alternative, returning to Spain, seemingly unaware that the Germans were behind the original 'invitation' to take up residence there. While in Portugal they stayed in a large villa near Cascais, along the coast from Lisbon, belonging to Ricardo Espirito Santo, a rich and powerful local banker, in an atmosphere of intensifying diplomatic intrigue.

Early in the morning of 4 July a telegram arrived via the British embassy for the Duke from Churchill advising him that he had been appointed Governor and Commander-in Chief of the Bahamas. It was delivered personally to the Duke by David Eccles, an experienced diplomat who had become a key figure in the Lisbon embassy.

Sent to the Iberian Peninsula in the first year of the war by the newly created Ministry of Economic Warfare, Eccles had spent a period in Madrid using the British control over navicert shipping licences – and thus Spanish imports – to secure a trade deal with the Franco regime with which to counter German commercial interests. His colleague Burns would later recall that the 'over-elegant' Eccles created a formidable working unit in the 'Economic Section' with Hugh Ellis-Rees from the Treasury.

In Lisbon, Eccles's rank of economic counsellor provided adequate cover for a post that straddled trade, politics and secret intelligence. With his responsibilities extending across the Iberian Peninsula, Eccles liaised closely with Marcus Cheke, the somewhat aloof and aristocratic student of Portuguese history who served as press attaché in the Lisbon embassy under Burns. All three were drawn operationally into the saga of the Windsors.

July saw Lisbon becoming increasingly immersed in a feverish atmosphere of spying and propaganda activity, with a renewed attempt by the Germans to have the Duke detained in Spain. Eccles was among those entrusted with keeping socially close to the Duke. He resolved to 'watch him at breakfast, lunch, and dinner; with a critical eye'. For his part, the press attaché Cheke, instructed by Burns, used his contacts with local Anglophile politicians and newspaper proprietors to counter Axis misinformation, ensuring that the Duke's access to the media was, as it had been in Madrid, largely controlled by the Allies and heavily restricted.

As a result, it was not just the Portuguese media that found its coverage of the visit being censored. The English language weekly *Anglo-Portuguese News*, which the MoI funded both as a tool of British propaganda and a source of local intelligence, remained strikingly uninformative in print about the Duke and Duchess as if they didn't exist. The newspaper was edited by Susan Lowndes Marques, an English Catholic and niece of Hilaire Belloc whom Burns had befriended before the war. She was married to an English-educated and similarly staunchly pro-Allied Portuguese banker, whom Burns had helped contribute to a collection of articles published by Burns & Oates entitled *Neutral War Aims*, with an introduction by Christopher Hollis.

Such contacts ensured that the *Anglo-Portuguese News* became a key instrument in the Allied strategy aimed at denying the Windsors any official significance that could be exploited by the Germans. Meanwhile, discreet British contacts with senior officials of the Franco regime helped Churchill anticipate German moves, in Lisbon as much as in Madrid.

On 23 July Nicolás Franco, brother of the dictator and Spain's ambassador in Lisbon, told Eccles that the pressure was building from

Berlin for the Duke of Windsor to return to Spain and remain there, pending a decision by Hitler on how to use him after a successful invasion of Britain. Of Nicolás Franco's usefulness to the Allied cause Eccles would later recall: 'He was the sort of self-made person who always seemed to be saying, "Look at me! I'm an ambassador!", and would illustrate the fact by repeating all kinds of things he had got to know recently. We relied upon him for much of our political information. Not only was he indiscreet, but we always felt he was on our side.' It was partly thanks to the ambassador that the British had advance warning of the arrival in Lisbon three days later of the latest Spanish 'emissary' sent with the specific mission of trying to draw the Duke into German hands. Angel Alcázar de Velasco was a fanatical member of the Spanish Falange, who was thought to have taken part in the fatal shooting of Lieutenant Jose Castillo Seria, a socialist paramilitary policeman on 12 July 1936 in the days leading up to the outbreak of the Spanish Civil War. At the time, the only information the British had on Velasco was that he was a former bullfighter who had retrained as a journalist and had high-level contacts within the Franco regime.

The British embassy also knew the identity of the Nazi figure operationally behind the plot, Walter Schellenberg, the head of the *Sicherheitsdienst* (SD), the German foreign counter-intelligence organisation, who was thought to have arrived separately in Lisbon on the same day as Velasco, accompanied by Paul Winzer, the Gestapo's chief in Madrid. The task Schellenberg had set himself appears to have been twofold: to fuel the sense of insecurity surrounding the Windsors, and to ensure that, once they had taken fright, their flight would not be impeded at the frontier. However, unknown to Schellenberg, one of the key contacts used by the Germans in the Portuguese secret police to pursue their interests was a double agent working for the British. The German plot had begun to unravel before Velasco had even met the Duke.

The meeting took place on 28 July in the villa the Windsors had been staying in since their arrival in Portugal. The location was a wooded promontory called Boca do Inferno, the Jaws of Hell. The Duke was handed a letter signed by Miguel Primo de Rivera, brother of the founder of the Falange, reviving the old canard that the Windsors faced the threat of extra-territorial terrorism by the British while remaining in Portugal, and that they similarly risked assassination by the British secret services in the Bahamas. As an alternative, the Duke's alleged friends in Madrid offered the Windsors safe haven on Spanish soil. In the event of Franco entering the war in support of Hitler, the Duke would be given the option of remaining in the country as a 'prisoner of honour'.

Velasco left for Spain later that night without an immediate answer. By then the British government had reacted to the alarming intelligence it was receiving from Madrid and Lisbon and set in motion an exercise designed to stop the Windsors tilting towards the enemy. On the same day as Velasco's departure from Lisbon to Madrid, 28 July 1940, there flew into Lisbon from London a British government official as senior and influential in his country's wartime affairs as Schellenberg was in Germany's.

The latest high-ranking 'emissary' involved in the Windsor case was Sir Walter Monckton, a brilliant and charming barrister who as Edward VIII's lawyer had been involved in the delicate negotiations over the abdication, and was trusted by the Windors. Since the outbreak of war Monckton had been put in charge of a wide range of sensitive operations as Deputy Director of the MoI, including the interrogation of suspect German agents and overseeing the conduct of British government propaganda.

Once in Lisbon, Monckton delivered a letter to the Duke signed by Churchill. It began by reassuring the Duke that the Bahamas appointment would provide him and the Duchess with a 'suitable sphere of activity and public service during this terrible time when the whole world is lapped in danger and confusion'. The appointment, insisted Churchill, reflected his sincere desire to do all in his power to serve the Duke's interests and consider his wishes.

The letter then went on to warn the Duke to be on his guard against loose gossip and fiendish plots. 'Many sharp and unfriendly ears will be pricked up to catch any suggestion that your Royal Highness takes a view about the war, or about the Germans, or about Hitlerism, which is different from that adopted by the British nation and parliament,' Churchill warned.

According to the prime minister, since the Duke's arrival in Lisbon 'conversations have been reported by telegraph through various channels which might have been used to your Royal Highnesses' disadvantage'. Various historians have speculated on the nature of the sources informing Churchill's comment. While it has been claimed that some German ciphers were being read by the Allies at the time, such intercept capability had not yet extended to the cipher code operated by the Abwehr in top-secret German communications between the Iberian Peninsula and Berlin. The first such Abwehr Enigma was not broken by British intelligence until late 1941, well over a year after the Windsors had left Portugal.

It is almost certain, however, that information had reached Churchill through various human intelligence channels developed by the British embassies in Madrid and Lisbon, in addition to secretly coded transmitted communications involving the Spanish and Portuguese governments and diplomats which were intercepted by the Allies as well as the Axis from the beginning of the Second World War. What also seems likely is that by the time Churchill wrote his letter, those feeding information to London about the Duke's state of mind and political inclinations included Burns, who had discreetly travelled to Lisbon from Madrid by train, anticipating the arrival of Monckton, in the Portuguese capital by several days.

Burns revealed his presence in Lisbon at this time in a letter he wrote to Ann Bowes-Lyon. It was in the last week of July that Ann found herself on a break from her ward duty at the Royal Herbert Hospital, opening the latest in a long line of love letters from her persistent suitor. It had been sent in a diplomatic bag, and brought to her by messenger from a secret postal dispatch box in Whitehall.

That it was from Burns came as no surprise. What puzzled her was that it showed that he was back in Lisbon, so soon after she had last heard from him from Madrid, taking up his post there. The letter gave little away. It ran to just a few lines, acknowledging receipt of her letter to him, and saying that he planned to be there for a week, and would write soon at greater length. Given the delicate nature of his assignment, Burns had exercised professional self-discipline while telling no lies.

Two days later Burns wrote the promised follow-up. He was staying in a top-floor flat used by the embassy in the Alfama district, Lisbon's old fishermen's quarter below the city's famous Castle. Though he did not let Ann know of this detail, the flat was one of several 'safe houses' owned or rented by the British in Lisbon and used for secret missions.

Burns had begun writing his letter in the morning and completed it later that afternoon, after attending mass, in time to catch the next day's diplomatic bag run out of the Lisbon embassy. After the moral rectitude of Franco's Spain, and the post-civil war squalor Burns had glimpsed among poorer Madrileños, Lisbon struck him as not just picturesque but refreshingly liberating – a similar feeling to that experienced by Monckton, who had noted the contrast to the depression of the London blackouts. The Portuguese capital was smaller than Madrid and seemingly less developed. But to Burns it seemed a city at ease with itself, less troubled by war (or the threat of foreign invasion for that matter) and enjoying more openly the trading and cultural benefits of neutrality, in an atmosphere both exuberant and sensual, an 'incongruous outpost of prosperity in stricken Europe'.

The near ecstatic rambling goes on for a page before Burns spares a thought for what life must have been like at that time for Ann, with what we now know as the Battle of Britain underway and the wounded and dying beginning to crowd her ward. A sense of guilt nags at him again and he feels a need to reassure her that this is not a holiday for him, so dropping for the first time in his correspondence with her a veiled hint of the secret nature of his assignment.

'Darling Ann, I can't tell you much of my stuff here but just know that I am very well and very busy and just longing for this exile to end and come back and be near you. Of course I wonder each day how things really are with you and everyone – and your dead watchfulness at night keep me safe. I hope it will be impossible for a black cat to be bad at night, prowling because he will think you at your work. Poor darling I suppose the long month of night duty is about over now. Perhaps by the time this arrives you'll have your rest.'

Here the letter stops as Burns leaves to look for a mass. His Portuguese landlady had told him that there were masses aplenty because the priests and monks were saying mass all day in Lisbon. Burns had not imagined a country more Catholic than Franco's Spain, until discovering Salazar's Portugal. He felt truly at home.

'This is a really a happy town,' he continued writing. 'To walk through the poorest part is to go through a vast nursery where children and grown ups aren't separated but squat about on the sun-warm stones and chatter and sew and play games. They are much milder than the Spaniards, there is no hard fierceness, little swagger, and they are very pious.'

The letter ends without giving any hint as to what Burns is really up to in Lisbon. His 'ticket of love', as if written by a euphoric tourist, had finally resolved itself into an exercise in deception. Burns's official appointment as First Secretary had given him responsibility over the press office in the embassy in Lisbon, a similar cover, as in Madrid, for a broad operational remit that took him into areas he was unable to reveal even to the woman he considered then to be the love of his life. It showed that by this stage Burns was operating as a spy as well as a propagandist. His memoirs provide a tantalising clue as to what he might have been doing. He recalls that while he was in Lisbon he met the Duke of Windsor on a return visit to the Casino in Estoril, a 'haunt of spies and many shady characters at the time'. Burns was playing at one of the roulette tables when a voice behind said, '*Dix mille sur le noir.*' It was the unmistakeable voice of the Duke.

The two men had last met in New York in 1937 when Burns was working as a publisher and the Duke was checking some proofs. At the time Burns shared, along with many of his generation and Catholic upbringing, a huge regret that the King perceived as a 'moderniser' had been forced to abdicate the throne because of love. The Duke had thanked him for the way the *Tablet*, under Burns's chairmanship, had showed sympathy for his human predicament. But the war had forced a change in Burns's perception of the Duke. He had become an issue of concern for the British government and potentially detrimental to Allied interests.

The former publisher was in Portugal among the 'watchers', making sure, just as Churchill wished, that the Duke did not allow himself to be irreversibly tricked and trapped by the Nazis. Far from it being a chance meeting, Burns had gone to the Casino knowing that the Duke would see him and renew an old acquaintance.

'The Duke drew me off to a sofa as if I was an old friend and told me of his last audience with the Pope. "We talked about Communism all the time. He was against it," the Duke recalled. The thundering banality of this comment has obscured my memory from anything else he said, but he seemed to be glad to be holding a different conversation from what might be expected from his glitzy friends across the room.' There are no surviving records of the meeting so one can only speculate as to what hidden motives lay behind it. It is doubtful whether it was purely accidental or that what was said was as inconsequential as Burns makes out in his self-censored memoirs.

Brief as the encounter seems to have been, the Duke appears to have deliberately sought out Burns as someone who might lend him a sympathetic ear and rescue him from the minefield of enemy intrigue he had stepped into.

Another possibility is that Burns had taken the initiative to seek out the Duke, as part of a covert diplomatic operation which was stamped with Churchill's personal authority. For Churchill had separately reminded the Duke of his rank of serving major general in the British Army, and of the dangers of disobeying military orders, a veiled threat of court martial.

The Duke and Duchess did not cross the border that summer of 1940. The Spanish invitation was snubbed as sure as the German plot to 'kidnap' the Windsors collapsed. Monckton stayed on in Lisbon overseeing the Windsors' departure on 1 August aboard the cruise ship *Excalibur*. Two days before they sailed, the Duke, with the Duchess beside him, bade farewell and thanks to the Portuguese in a press conference held in the British embassy.

For three weeks any detailed mention of the Windsors had been carefully exorcised from the pages of the Portuguese press and no foreign journalist had been allowed near them. A rare exception was Josie Shercliff, a *Times* correspondent living in Estoril – one of the Windsors' favourite haunts – who served as a wartime agent and was encouraged by the British embassy to help keep an eye on their movements.

Now the British judged that the time had come to turn the Windsors into a vehicle of propaganda. The Duke's statements, like the journalists who were invited (all were vetted by the embassy beforehand), were carefully controlled to convey a simple message of gentlemanly good manners and patriotic duty. Portugal, the Duke told his audience, was a country 'whose beauty and history' he had admired ever since visiting it for the first time in 1931 as Prince of Wales. He now graciously accepted his appointment as Governor of the Bahamas, 'one of the few parts of the British Empire which I have never visited', alluding to the offer Churchill had urged upon him and which in the end he knew he couldn't refuse.

A week had gone by since the Duke had met Burns in the Estoril Casino. As he watched the press conference taking place, Burns could have been forgiven for believing that this was a job well done. One day earlier the Germans had accepted they had lost the battle to get the Duke, or Willi as they had code-named him. '*Willi wollte nicht*' – Willi won't play, the Gestapo's Schellenberg wrote in his log.

Burns returned to Madrid to find his ambassador no longer worried about the Windsors but trying to deal with a crisis nearer to his patch: a fresh German push to try to force a breach in Anglo-Spanish diplomatic relations and draw Spain into the war. Hoare had intelligence that German *agents provocateurs* were behind the latest anti-British demonstrations and the intimidation of British subjects. Escaped Allied prisoners of war were being arrested and thrown into prison or special detention camps by Spanish police working under the influence of German agents. Meanwhile, Hans Lazar, taking advantage of Burns's absence in Lisbon, had installed some rabidly pro-German editorials in the Spanish media, and news coverage suggesting that a weakened Britain was facing a seemingly invincible Nazi war machine.

On his first evening back in Madrid, Burns attended a reception at the British embassy to which senior members of the Spanish government he counted among his sources were invited. 'Sam [Hoare] seemed very glad to see me. He happened to be having a huge cocktail party that night and asked me to go,' Burns wrote to Ann. 'It was a huge affair and lasted from 8 to 11 and was a bit queer as all the Spanish government chaps who are supposed to be our enemies, having said they would not come, at the last minute came. I left a proud cat as I was told to cope with Serrano Súñer and in the end it was jolly as could be and we were punching each other's stomachs . . .'

On a weekend that August 1940, Burns drove in his Humber to the city of Ávila where he wrote another enthusiastic letter to Ann. 'How you would have loved it! It is one more of those places that I vow you shall see with me one day my darling Ann. It is a walled town – a big sandy grey bastion on a hill. It is St Teresa's town, and John of the Cross was often there. It couldn't have changed much since: nothing could alter that stone house or straighten the twisted narrow street or take away the smells of horse and fruit and soup. All the houses have "*patios*" – with courtyards filled with flowers and make shadows or else when everyone is dark the flowers catch starlight and moonlight from the square opening to the sky – Darling can you guess how much you are wanted when I creep out and see such things on my own?'

A postscript suggests that a letter from Ann that had crossed in the post had been written in a somewhat different tone. 'Not nice to hear that *Rosie* is rampaging,' Burns wrote back. *Rosie* was the word he had coined long ago to describe the bouts of depression which periodically afflicted his friend David 'Dai' Jones.

'We must just hang on and hope . . . Lovely to hear of you having drinks with Mike [Richey] and Dai and all. You poor darling – if only you had a little more of that and so rested yourself. I do agree with what you say about how it isn't possible to contemplate the war but only to get on with one's job: that's what I try and do – but one thing is specially awful for me: the Spanish press is always full of the wildest German claims about wholesale destruction and what not and of course I suddenly feel sick with misery and doubt about my darling's safety . . .'

By the middle of August in Britain the Blitz was still raging, with fleets of bombers protected by fighters hitting civilian, industrial and military targets across the country. The Spanish media reported in triumphalist terms on the first raids being carried out on London. One night in his room at Gaylords Burns woke covered in sweat, poured himself a neat whisky and walked over to his hotel window. Apart from the night watchman on the corner, the streets were empty, the whole city humid and hushed and bathed in the light of a tranquil full moon. He could only think of Ann so he wrote: '. . . I kick myself and have to tell myself that it is here where I must fight, and lie, and plot that I can do my job and that there where you can tend wounds you can do yours and we can stick at it and work at it in such different ways. I do love you Ann right across this unspeakable thing. I come to realise more and more that you are all that I want and need in human womanhood and dearest Ann, sweet heart I trust you to be strong and good and well till I come back – as surely I will just as soon as I can . . .' What Burns didn't mention was that he had just been told by his ambassador that British interests in Spain were facing a critical period during which there was no question of him taking leave. He knew that he would not be returning to London for several months. What he did not know at the time was that he had written the last letter of his that Ann would keep. If there was further correspondence between them it is impossible to tell, as none survives, but it suggests, as later emerged, that their love affair had reached a critical fork in the road.

Riven with guilt that his posting might be viewed, from a London perspective, as a holiday under the sun, Burns felt spurred to explore uncharted and potentially dangerous aspects of his embassy job by the knowledge of the war increasingly threatening the lives of those he felt closest to in Britain. He began to expand the scope of his assignment into areas for which he had no special training and where he risked treading on jealously protected fiefdoms.

Among the secret contacts he began to make few proved as fruitful from the outset as the one he established with his American counterparts. Officially, the British and US embassies in Madrid had maintained a discreet if dysfunctional relationship with each other since the two governments had recognised the Franco government in March 1939.

At a time when American public opinion was far from enthusiastic about the prospect of being drawn into another European war, the US government was also slow in waking up to the potential strategic importance of Spain in such a conflict. That the US embassy in Madrid in the first years of the war was smaller than the British also reflected the fact that Washington doubted if there was any real justification for fearing, as the British government did, that Spain would join the Axis.

Samuel Hoare neither really liked the Americans not seriously tried to understand them. In contrast, Burns had used visits to the United States as a young man between the wars to forge long-term friendships and gain privileged access to important areas of American intellectual and government life. During the 1930s Burns's schoolteacher, the Jesuit Fr D'Arcy, had helped him gain a foothold in the US Catholic network whose field of activity ranged from Harvard, the Jesuit universities of Fordham in New York and Georgetown in Washington DC to the State Department, the FBI and the fledgling OSS, the wartime predecessor of the CIA. In Harvard, Burns had been the guest of T. S Eliot, at the time a professor at the university. 'The poet seemed totally at home there in a way that could not be said of him in London where he was an exotic despite his complete disguise as a traditional British publisher,' Burns recalled. He might have said the same about himself. What he liked about America was its racial mix, its openness and its youthful optimism. Burns called it his 'New-found land'. In America, Burns broadened his friendships to encompass characters as diverse as the poet Thomas Merton, the FBI officer Matt Murray, the intelligence officer Archie Roosevelt, the grand Washington dame Mrs William Corcoran Eustis and Ann Fremantle, the English peer's daughter whose brownstone off New York's 6th Avenue became a haven for writers such as Waugh and Auden.

In attempting to bridge the gap between the British and US embassies in wartime Madrid, Burns was encouraged by his friend and colleague Captain Hillgarth. Hillgarth was aware that Churchill had embarked on a private correspondence with President Roosevelt while at the Admiralty and that this personal approach had become another vital channel for Anglo-American relations with the objective of securing US military support.

Within weeks of his arrival in Spain Burns had established a close relationship with several members of the American embassy staff. They included Earl Crain, a young, energetic and outgoing second secretary who used his diplomatic cover to build up a 'press and propaganda section' with a brief as wide as that developed by the British. The fact that Crain was nicknamed 'Tom' by his American colleagues was a light-hearted reference to his operational twinning with Burns. The two men had been posted to Spain at around the same time. Burns's privileged status on the American embassy's books as a friend and colleague became further enhanced when Carlton Hayes, another Catholic, was appointed ambassador. Hayes was a new arrival on the diplomatic scene, recruited from Colombia University where he was a professor, specialising in sixteenth-century Spanish history. An admirer of Isabella, the Catholic Queen who was behind the reconquest of Spain from the Moors and Columbus's voyage of discovery and colonisation, he saw Franco as personifying the Christian values that had dominated large parts of the globe during Spain's golden age of empire. Hayes saw Franco as a phenomenon specifically of Spanish political history, whose sense of national pride would make him resist any attempt by Hitler to absorb Spain into the Third Reich.

The extent to which similar views, shared by Burns, contrasted with Hoare's paranoia about Franco's pro-Nazi sympathies surfaced for the first time when Serrano Súñer became foreign minister in October 1940.

'Tom, I think my mission in Spain is finished,' Hoare told Burns soon after the appointment. Burns replied that, in his view, the mission had only just begun. The appointment to such a post of such an influential member of the regime meant a 'wonderful opportunity to review and renew Anglo-Spanish relations', he told Hoare. There was no doubting that Serrano Súñer was a passionate National Catholic, an eloquent rabble-rouser and a flamboyant womaniser, not unlike his predecessor and rival General Beigbeder; he was also avowedly pro-German. But Burns had formed a nuanced opinion of Serrano Súñer as a result of his personal dealings with him and the intelligence gleaned from his other sources in the Falange.

Burns believed him to be too much of a patriot to allow himself to be used simply as the tool of another country. 'If any man in the Spanish government at that time was a major influence in keeping Spain out of the war and preventing the passage of German troops through to Gibraltar that man was Serrano Súñer,' Burns wrote.

Burns's initiative in establishing a personal channel of communication with the US embassy soon after his arrival allowed him to gain intelligence information from the Americans at a time when the British were over-reliant on their own resources. On 7 September 1940, a telegram with an attached two-page intelligence report was sent by Hoare to the foreign secretary Viscount Halifax: 'I have the honour to transmit an interesting memorandum prepared by Mr T. F. Burns, acting press attaché at this Embassy, of a conversation he had with an American friend of his, who has just returned from Berlin.'

The report was founded on access to the highest level of the German command structure, as well as on a personal observation of how the war was being experienced by ordinary Germans. According to the report, Hitler believed that the war had entered a critical juncture. With the Soviet Union threatening Germany's eastern borders, and Mussolini reluctant to invade Greece, Berlin believed that the war stood to be won or lost in the Battle of Britain.

The source reported that British air raids on Germany had damaged the docks in Hamburg, but that the Krupp armament factory in Essen and other targets such as railway junctions had escaped practically unscathed, with the German air force making effective use of camouflage and decoy fires to deceive Allied aerial photography. While the civilian population was showing signs of 'tiredness and nervousness', and workers had been forced to carry on at the assembly lines 'at bayonet point', most people remained firmly behind the goal of a German victory.

The intelligence obtained by Burns suggested that the German air raids which had so far taken place on England were simply a prelude to the main offensive on an unprecedented scale. The informant provided Burns with two other areas of intelligence: that the Germans had put on hold any plans to invade Spain and that the persecution of the Jews was increasing.

'My informant said that he could see that we in England did not lay nearly enough stress on the absolute inhuman brutality of the Nazi regime and were in danger of letting the war be seen as an ordinary combat of arms – or else were too vague when we talked of a conflict of ideas. The regime was and should be constantly shown to be diabolic,' reported Burns.

According to a weary note subsequently drafted by Walter Roberts, the head of the Foreign Office's Western European Department, Burns's informant was in a position to 'supply useful information' although he had been 'sensationalist in the past'. 'There have even been suggestions that he is under German influence and used by the Germans to plant information.'

On 6 September the codeword 'Cromwell' was sent to all armed forces in the United Kingdom, alerting them to 'immediate action'. It was a false alarm, as Hitler had not even set a date for the invasion. Instead, the real activity, Burns's source had predicted with greater accuracy, was the launching of Germany's entire bomber strength against Britain.

An early draft of Burns's first intelligence report before it was put into code and transmitted to London shows the comment 'I wonder' scribbled alongside his source's claim that the threat of a German invasion of Spain had receded. The scribbler – Hoare – disagreed with Burns's own analysis that Franco's patriotism was of a nature that would resist any attempt by Hitler to absorb Spain into his empire. There was certainly ample evidence to justify the ambassador's scepticism, even if Burns's judgement has ultimately stood the test of time.

Spanish gestures of solidarity with the Axis powers continued through the summer and early autumn, with German influence seemingly reaching a new, particularly threatening stage on 16 October with the appointment of Serrano Súñer as foreign minister.

Four days later Heinrich Himmler, the self-styled Reichsführer SS, began a three-day visit to Spain and was accorded the honours of a visiting head of state. Burns's Gamero was among the senior Falange officials who accompanied Himmler throughout most of his stay. Sitting in an open-air Mercedes-Benz, and flanked by Moorish lancers – Franco's guard of honour – Himmler was driven along the Castellana which was draped in swastika flags and lined with members of the Falange giving the fascist salute and crowds shouting '*Viva!*'

His arrival was on a Sunday, a day normally devoted to masses, football and bullfighting. That day Real Madrid supporters poured into the Chamartín stadium to watch their team beat Deportivo Español 4–1. Himmler was blessed by the monks as he visited the El Escorial monastery. Later that afternoon, he sat in the presidential box of Las Ventas bullring watching three of Spain's most popular bullfighters. It was a dull, overcast day but the bullring was packed and the audience filled with a sense of collective anticipation. The first fighter, Gallito (the Little Cock), stepped out into the ring to huge applause. As he confronted the bull with some deft swirls of his cape, it began raining. With fighter and bull soon slipping and sliding, the *corrida* took on the aspect of a surreal ballet. The crowd loved it as Gallito maintained his composure and imposed himself with a *faena* of effortless skill, and a summary kill that earned him the prize of an ear. The other fighters, Marcial Lalanda and Pepe Luis Vázquez, fought and killed their bulls with similar success, drawing standing ovations. But when the third bull had been dispatched, the arena had turned into a mudbath.

With the rain now a downpour and people beginning to leave the ring, it was decided to suspend the rest of the fight. The three matadors made their way to the presidential box to shake Himmler's hand. It was at that moment, as the band struck up the first notes of the German national anthem, and the crowd of thousands stood and applauded and saluted, that a member of the Gestapo noticed two men who had stayed in their seats.

The two were Burns and one his embassy colleagues, the ambassador's private secretary Gerry Young. A fanatical enthusiast of the bullfight, but ever watchful of the enemy, Burns had installed himself and his colleague in the cheapest seats, to better blend in with the crowds. He had calculated that the German national anthem would inevitably be played, but at the end of a normal *corrida* of six bulls, and had therefore planned to leave before the last bull. He had not counted on the rain.

When the band struck up 'Deutschland über Alles', a mixture of principle and sheer bravado prompted Burns and Young to stay where they were, action that provoked murmurs of disapproval which soon developed into angry roars of protestation from the Spaniards surrounding them. Within seconds they found themselves being unceremoniously hustled out by two plain-clothed members of the Gestapo. It was only as they stumbled down some steps and out of one of the entrances that Burns spotted a group of Spanish Civil Guards talking to their officer. 'I am under Spanish jurisdiction,' shouted Burns as he broke free from his Nazi captors and joined the Spaniards, identifying himself and Young as British diplomats. He was aware that his friend Gamero was almost certainly in the ring as well, but knew that to mention his name would risk exposing a key source.

Just a few yards away the recently killed bull was being hung and quartered by a butcher and his assistants. The mules that had dragged the creature from the arena stood nearby, their coats drenched, their bells silent. In the ensuing conversation, Burns offered the Spanish officer a cigar, explained that Britain acknowledged Spanish – but not German – sovereignty over the bullring, and apologised for any inconvenience caused. Minutes later, the Gestapo officers withdrew from the scene having been persuaded by the Spanish officer that he and his men would take charge. This they did, once the Germans were out of sight, by issuing Burns and Young with a formal reprimand, before taking their money and telling them they were free to go back to their embassy.

That evening word of the incident spread around Madrid's diplomatic circle and Burns was summoned urgently to the ambassador's residence. Hoare was furious. 'Totally irresponsible, Tom, you have come dangerously close to endangering my mission,' he protested before letting the matter rest.

Years later the South African poet Roy Campbell told Burns he had been at the same bullfight on the other side of the ring and had watched the whole incident without knowing who or what was involved. 'You should have been recommended for the VC,' Campbell growled over his beer.

7

SPY GAMES

Autumn faded and with it the memory of Gallito's magical *faena* in the pouring rain. In the Retiro, Madrid's central park, the last of the leaves from the few trees that had survived the civil war shrivelled and fell. An icy wind from the Sierras had arrived suddenly, sweeping down the Calle Alcalá and along the Castellana. The harshness of that winter of 1940 – the coldest any Spaniard living then could remember – created new hardships for *Madrileños*, the divisions, deprivations and destruction wrought by the civil war made worse by the food and fuel shortages created by war in Europe.

Not everyone was badly affected, however. In Madrid, a new, privileged sector had emerged since Franco's troops had defeated the Republicans, with access to black-market luxury goods, restored or new housing, cars, restaurants and nightclubs. The regime had created a new bureaucracy of former soldiers and members of the Falange. It had also drawn back to the capital the aristocratic families with their maids and chauffeurs and English nannies. And then there was the foreign expatriate community, using their embassies for entertainment when not exploiting to the full whatever Madrid had on offer for those with money to spend.

Social life was concentrated in and around the centre of the capital, on either side of the Castellana, the diplomats' favourite haunts within walking distance of their embassies. British and the Germans shared the bars and dining rooms of the Ritz and Palace hotels, but there were places where territory was more delineated. No Germans ventured into the Anglo-American Club – a favourite watering hole for some of the harder drinking members of the diplomatic staff. Also out of bounds to the Axis, and accepted as such by the Spanish police, was the hugely popular 'Embassy' tea room.

Located just a few blocks from the British embassy, and near the homes of Spaniards of wealth and title, the upmarket Embassy tea room was famous for its cocktails as well as its cakes and sophisticated clientele. Its owner, Margarita Kearney Taylor, was an attractive and impeccably mannered Englishwoman of Irish descent who had had a long-running affair with a Spanish Marques and given birth to a daughter named Consuelo. Closed down during the civil war, the tea room had since been revived, using Spain's neutrality and the snobbishness of the pro-British Spanish aristocracy to create a newly burgeoning business. Wealthy Spaniards felt pampered and secure there, as did Allied diplomats. As the war progressed, Mrs Taylor's flat above the tea room provided an additional secret service. It was run by the British embassy as a safe house for Jewish refugees fleeing from the Nazis and on their way to Lisbon.

The Germans had their own club in the style of a Bavarian beer garden, and their own five-star restaurant, Horcher, in the city's fashionable Alfonso XII Street. It was set up during the Second World War by Otto Horcher, the owner of one of the most successful restaurants in Hitler's Berlin, where it was popular with the high-ranking members of the Nazi party and military personnel. Horcher's key staff had been exempted from the military draft on the orders of the Reichsmarschall himself.

In later years it was claimed that Horcher transferred his main business operation to Madrid when Allied bombing of Berlin became too threatening and in anticipation of Hitler losing the war. In the 1940s the restaurant's pro-Nazi sympathies were never in doubt, even if they were hidden beneath a veneer of civilised luxury. Its waiters wore tails and its rooms were decorated with dark wooden panelling and thick velvet, and lit by silver candelabra. Horcher became the German embassy's unofficial canteen. Lazar and the ambassador von Stohrer were among its most frequent guests, with its private dining room also used for visiting high-ranking Nazis with a special interest in Franco's

Spain, such as the head of the Abwehr, Admiral Wilhelm Canaris, and the foreign minister Ribbentrop.

Among the more popular nightspots for male members of the British embassy was Chicote, in the Gran Vía cinema and theatre district. Its owner, Pedro Chicote, had trained as a barman at the Ritz Hotel before setting up on his own in 1931 to cater for the young and rich. When civil war broke out the genial, slightly bumptious Chicote fled the capital and made his way to the Nationalist-controlled northern part of the country. There he set up another bar, making a small fortune serving officers on leave contraband liquor in San Sebastián after the Basque town had been taken by Franco's forces early in the conflict. Chicote's bar in Madrid, under different management, remained open for most of the conflict, its clientele comprising members of the international brigades, foreign correspondents, and a regular posse of working class prostitutes. By the outbreak of the Second World War, Chicote was back in the Spanish capital, at his bar in Number 12 Gran Vía and very much in charge. The establishment earned a reputation for glamorous single women, seemingly of some social standing. They were despised by anti-Francoists as *señoritas putas de derecha*, sluttish right-wing ladies. The bar was nevertheless enormously successful in attracting a generation of Spaniards that sought escape from the war and the moral strictures of the Catholic Church. With its long American bar lined with high-backed stools, dimly lit, squat tables and sofas, Chicote offered an intimate and sophisticated drinking den famous for its special gin and red vermouth cocktail, margaritas and mojitos and the attractiveness of the women who happened to be there each night. The atmosphere of a more sombre and austere Madrid that had suffered coups and revolutions, and been subjected to governments of every conceivable political hue, from liberal monarchies to neo-fascist military dictatorship, is captured in Camilo José Cela's post-war novel *The Hive*. He describes a city bristling with paradoxes and offering more contrasts and inconsistencies than either London or Paris at the time. The central character, Martín, hears the story of the waking city, its 'rioting heart', as he emerges from a night in a brothel. The carts of the garbage men are coming in from the suburbs, emerging from the 'sad, desolate landscape of the cemetery and passing – after hours on the road, in the cold – at the slow, dejected trot of a gaunt horse or a grey, worried donkey'. There are 'the voices of the women hawkers as they make their way to set their little fruit stalls and the first distant, indistinct horns of the cars'. There was also the rumble of the trams and the sound of their bells – the main source of transport – for in those days most *Madrileños* did not have cars. Those who had recovered cars looted during the civil war could hardly run them for lack of petrol. Government officials had access to a special pool of cars with guaranteed fuel supplies, as did foreign diplomats. Taxis ran mainly on 'gasogene', with the burner in the boot contributing another layer of grime and dust to vehicles which dated from the early 1930s.

Madrid had always prided itself on being the centre of the Spanish literary world, attracting writers as well as painters to its cafés and restaurants for the informal gatherings over coffee or drinks known as the *tertulia*. During the civil war, several writers and painters who had supported the Republic had either been killed or forced into exile, their *tertulias* disbanded. Nevertheless, with the outbreak of the war in Europe other *tertulias* formed, providing an opportunity for sharing information among trusted friends, under the cover of a convivial and informal drink or meal.

Early on in the winter of 1940 Burns learnt that one of the most interesting and eclectic *tertulias* had begun to meet regularly in Casa Ciriaco, a popular *taverna* specialising in Castilian country food and plentiful regional wine. One lunchtime he decided to pay a visit alone. He was ushered to a single table in a corner and sat there rather self-consciously reading a copy of a week-old London *Times*, picking at a plate of cured ham and *chorizo*, and drinking from an earthenware carafe filled with Rioja wine. The only other occupants of the tavern sat at a long table, and, judging by their laughter and fluid conversation, had been there for some time. Looking at them discreetly from behind his newspaper, Burns saw two attractive young women he took to be actresses surrounded by men he recognised as an assortment of painters, bullfighters and writers – the very *tertulia* he had been looking for. Minutes later, one of their number detached himself from the table, came over to Burns and, in a strong American accent, asked who he was and what he was doing in Madrid, before inviting him to join the others.

The 'American' was Edgar Neville, the Spanish film-maker who had lived and worked in the United States before turning out some pro-Franco propaganda films during the civil war. The actresses are thought to have been Conchita Montes and Amparo Rivelles, two of Neville's favourite female stars during the 1940s. All three worked for Cifesa, the state-sponsored department of cinematography set up by Franco after the civil war.

The rest of the table was made up of an assortment of Spaniards who would remain vivid in Burns's memory fifty years on. The most loquacious was Antonio Cañabate, the leading bullfight critic of the day, 'a lank owl-like character, droll, and undomesticated'. Next to him sat the 'portentous presence' of Eugenio d'Ors, the Catalan critic, and alongside him the equally imposing Basque painter, Ignacio Zuloaga. Also there that day were Domingo Ortega and Juan Belmonte, two of the great bullfighters in Spanish history.

Ortega, from Toledo, in the region of Old Castile, was then at the height of his powers. Belmonte, from Seville, the capital of Andalusia, Burns had not seen a fight since his first trip to Spain during the early 1930s. Belmonte had by then retired from the ring. He spoke with a stutter and had a picaresque sense of humour. 'Unless it is *per-per*-proved to the *con-con*-contrary, I assume that you, *Bu-Bur*-Burns, like *aa-aa*-all Englishmen are in the Intelligence Service,' he ventured.

By then the *tertulia*, after a lunch lasting four hours, had moved to the Lyon d'Or, a Parisian-style *fin-de-siècle* café opposite the Post Office in the Calle de Alcalá. Intimacies were shared within the circle but went unrecorded. Only Burns felt it his duty to make a mental note of any information he thought he could make use of. During the Second World War there would be many others who drifted in and out of the *tertulia* Burns came to appreciate as a very special private club, Spanish-style. They included learned Arabists, bull breeders, publishers, antiquarian booksellers, mistresses, and Sebastián Miranda, an eccentric sculptor who, together with Belmonte, was destined to become involved in a decisive chapter in Burns's life.

'Those evenings at the Lyon d'Or became a matter of habit; they were convivial but with the austerity that underlines much of Spanish life,' Burns later recalled.

'Imperceptibly I was discovering that life, its language and its lore. I had struck a rich vein of the essential Spain – the permanent *país* – distinct from the polarised passions of the Civil War – which, however, were still far from extinguished.'

And yet it was not from the *tertulias* that Burns learnt about suffering Spain, but in the poor suburbs and the countryside that he also frequented.

A report he sent to London following a trip he made round Andalusia painted a bleak picture of the dire socio-economic conditions that ordinary Spaniards were enduring beyond the world of privilege and power that was only too apparent in Madrid. It prompted the Foreign Office to conclude that even Nazi Germany might hesitate to take on a country in such a plight. It also informed British policy in encouraging the offer of economic assistance as a carrot for ensuring Franco's neutrality, backed by an intensified campaign of pro-Allied propaganda.

Burns wrote: 'All this region is in a very marked contrast to the highly charged political atmosphere of Madrid. In these southern provinces the political machinations of the Government have hardly registered. The obsessing problem is a domestic one: food . . . The war is only seen in relation to the means of life. I cannot over emphasise the extreme need of the people in this region: it verges on the desperate. Whole villages have been without bread for weeks, large peasant families are living for days on less than one British workman's supper.'

Burns felt reassured by what he described as the 'quite markedly friendly' general attitude towards the Allies that he found among ordinary working-class Spaniards. He felt less sure about the loyalties of the 'more or less comfortable bourgeois' who had yet to be convinced that 'we are not wantonly continuing this war and that a Nazi victory will leave him and his way of life unaffected'.

Given the lack of a developed middle class in Spain, the category applied to the emerging class of state functionaries, mostly drawn from the nationalist so-called *Movimiento*, or Movement, Franco's amalgam of the military, the Falange party and the traditionalist right-wing monarchists, the *requetés*, who had spread out across towns and villages. 'We must face the fact that with a veering of Spanish opinion away from Germany comes the necessity for more, not less, British propaganda,' Burns reported. He recommended that additional money be provided from a special contingency fund within the MoI to ensure that the daily British bulletin that was circulating in Madrid and Barcelona would also be distributed in the south of Spain.

Within days Burns was in Tangier, where British diplomatic and intelligence officials and their agents liaised closely with the other Iberian 'hubs', Madrid and Lisbon, as well as Gibraltar, a growing network which effectively provided strategic coverage for the western end of the Mediterranean, the Atlantic coast of Spain and Portugal, as well as the border with France.

Tangier had been a danger spot for the great powers of Europe for decades, because of its strategic location overlooking the Strait of Gibraltar and as a potential bridgehead between Spain and North Africa. In the lead-up to the Second World War, Tangier was nominally ruled by the Sultan of Morocco, while actually being administered by foreign forces, with the French maintaining a predominant influence. In June 1940, Spanish troops marched into the town after convincing the British and the French that it was a temporary but necessary move to ensure Tangier's security against any attempted takeover by Mussolini.

In Madrid, the Spanish occupation fuelled an outburst of patriotic fervour, drawing parallels with the expansion of the Spanish Empire in Africa under the Holy Roman Emperor Charles V in the sixteenth century.

Tangier was drawn deeper into the war in Europe when the Germans boosted their intelligence and propaganda operations there, forcing the Allies to do likewise. In the winter of 1940, however, there were no British troops available for turning the Spaniards out. Instead, the embassy in Madrid was instructed by the Foreign Office to negotiate an agreement with the Spanish government guaranteeing the protection of British interests with the free entry and departure of British subjects, and the continuing existence of a British newspaper, the *Tangier Gazette*, and a post office.

Negotiations were coordinated by the embassy's deputy head of mission, the resourceful and dynamic Arthur Yencken. His close friendship with and professional trust in Burns led Yencken to depend on his colleague's contacts inside the Spanish regime to facilitate an engagement with the foreign minister Ramón Serrano Súñer on the issue. While negotiations were ongoing, Burns arrived at the British mission in Tangier. 'Two retired colonels ran the Information Office. They had little to do and seemed to be doing it very well. I left them in peace in the turbulent city,' recalled Burns in his memoirs.

The two colonels were Toby Ellis and Malcolm Henderson, whose work covered intelligence and propaganda. Burns reported to the Foreign Office: 'It now appears that the *Tangier Gazette* is to be allowed to continue publication; its circulation, however, has been forbidden in certain parts of the Spanish and in the entire French zone. This is our sole means of propaganda – the Press-attaché's industry has increased its quality and scope. It is the best-selling paper in Tangier and will make big inroads in Spain.'

Burns believed that Tangier, for all its enduring international status, was not sufficiently used by the British for what it was – a vital bridgehead not just into Spain but also for pursuing Allied interests in North Africa. He used his report to press the case for the British mission to be expanded, along with an enlargement of the consulate network on the Spanish mainland. 'I am not satisfied that we are sufficiently equipped in Tangier to maintain contact with the French and to keep check of the constant German effort to drive the Spaniards to further adventures and the occupation of important French possessions . . . Information and intelligence services are so bound up with each other in Tangier that I cannot but remark on this,' wrote Burns.

For much of its history, Tangier had retained a certain exotic allure, a city which played to its own rules, offering refuge and excitement, escape and indulgence. At its most tarnished, it was, in the words of its biographer Iain Finlayson, 'a city of illusory vanities . . . the ante-room of failure, the casualty ward of desire'. When Burns visited it, he found Charlie's Bar, a 'more fruitful source of information' than the 'two colonels'. Part-gambling den, part-nightclub, it was presided over by its eponymous owner, a tall, elegant dark-skinned North African who spoke in a somewhat affected upper-class British accent reputedly picked up while studying at Cambridge. There was no shortage of drinks, cigars or women at Charlie's. Its clientele was almost exclusively expatriate. The British and Americans in particular met there to swap notes, as did the Germans with the collaborationists among the Vichy French.

The smoky, jovial atmosphere around the bar and the piano, along with its darker recesses, provided neutral ground where refugees on their way to Lisbon evaded their pursuers, agents touched base with their handlers and escaped prisoners of war shared their adventures over endless rounds of contraband whisky. It was a place where one could find or lose oneself.

At that time a fictitious version of Charlie's, based in wartime Casablanca, was being created in a Hollywood studio. The film, *Casablanca*, starred Humphrey Bogart as the cynical owner of Rick's Café Américain, who finds himself torn between the love of his life and a rediscovered sense of duty and self-sacrifice. Rick finds resolution in helping Ilsa, his lover (played by Ingrid Bergman), to escape with her husband, a heroic leader of the French Resistance. The film – a beautifully crafted propaganda movie – was rush-released within a year of the Allied landings in North Africa, and went on to become one of the most popular films of all time.

In the winter of 1940–41, it was in Tangier, where the family of Ann Bowes-Lyon happened to own property, that Burns unwittingly found himself playing out a critical scene from his own real-life story of intrigue and romance. With the world he had known in London disintegrating, he had travelled from Europe to Africa as part of the only cause that, apart from his Catholic faith, made any sense to him in the chaotic world – the defeat of Hitler. But in so doing he had crossed an emotional Rubicon.

'Everything happens here,' Charlie told Burns the night he drank himself into the ground in Tangier; 'if you bring your wife I will have to charge you corkage.' The irony of the quip was not lost on the Madrid embassy's press attaché. For not only did Burns not have a wife at the time but the prospect of having one had suddenly vanished just a few hours earlier. Before crossing the Strait to Tangier, Burns had spent the morning in Gibraltar, with the military governor and intelligence, signals and defence personnel discussing plans to turn part of the military base into a wireless station from which to broadcast propaganda across into Spain. Another idea advanced at the meeting was boosting local printing facilities so as to enhance the quality and distribution of a locally produced pro-Allied Spanish-language newspaper. Discussions over, Burns was invited to lunch by a local contact to the Rock Hotel, where the restaurant and rooms had been turned into an officers' mess for the duration of the war. It was there that, during a casual conversation with one of the officers, Burns learnt that Ann Bowes-Lyon was engaged to be married to Francis D'Abreu, a Stonyhurst old boy who was serving as an army doctor.

This was the only news of Ann that had reached Burns in weeks. The last letters he had written to her from Madrid had gone unanswered and those he had received from mutual friends had dropped all mention of her without explanation. While he knew that his departure to Spain had put a strain on their relationship, the correspondence they had maintained after his arrival in Madrid had for a brief period rekindled the relationship with a sense of urgency and longing.

When her letters had suddenly dried up, Burns blamed the Germans and an unpredictable post, while also making himself believe that she had been diverted by the increased workload at the military hospital where she worked as a volunteer nurse. Neither had made any solemn commitment to marriage, but they had parted with mutual trust – or so Burns had imagined. Since arriving in Madrid, he had clung on to the thought of her, despite the fact of their very different circumstances, and he had remained faithful to that thought. Such misplaced loyalty showed how out of touch he had in fact become with Britain and what moved those who remained there.

For at the Royal Herbert Hospital, Ann had been drawn into a world not of spy games, diplomacy, propaganda and expedient neutrality, but one in which men and women fought and were killed in a war they believed was between totalitarianism and democracy, and all she was left with was the wounded, the dying and the dead. It was in such circumstances, not in the romantic candlelit evenings she had spent with Burns at Glebe Place, or the privileged family gatherings at Glamis Castle, that Ann had met and fallen in love with the Jesuit-educated army doctor she had decided to marry.

Burns was emotionally shattered, and he never entirely eradicated the memory of that loss. As he later wrote in his memoirs (in which Ann Bowes-Lyon is never mentioned by name): 'Any budding affair of the heart had been checked by what seemed a beckoning purpose in my life. Suddenly all of this vanished: no presence, no trust, and no discernible purpose. It would take a long time for this to be changed from a vacuum to a new vision, freed from the bondage and illusion of years.'

Purged of love for a while, Burns returned to Madrid to find his embassy still grappling with the uncertainty of Franco's intentions. Would he or would he not join the Axis? And how long did Churchill have before he had to confront the nightmare scenario of German troops marching across the Pyrenees, taking Gibraltar and pushing across to North Africa? If there was no easy answer to these questions it was because Franco was a master at playing one belligerent against the other, to his own advantage.

On 23 October 1940 Franco had met Hitler on the French–Spanish border at Hendaye, for their first and only encounter. Neither leader had got what he wanted. Hitler stalled on making any formal promises on Spain's claims to further territory in North Africa. Franco, for his part, had told Hitler that he would not cede to any foreign power, including Germany's right of conquest over a sovereign territory (Gibraltar), warned Hitler that England was far from defeated and was likely to fight on with the help of the United States, and made no commitment to dropping Spain's neutrality. The summit involved the participation at close quarters – apart from Franco and Hitler – of just five people: the German and Spanish foreign ministers, Ribbentrop and Serrano Súñer, two translators, Gross and Barón de las Torres, and a German foreign ministry official named Paul Schmidt. While the meeting was supposed to be secure and protected from enemy intrusion, it was infiltrated by British intelligence through an individual code-named T.

While the identity of the agent has never been conclusively established, it is likely that he was the translator, Barón de las Torres, otherwise know as Luis Álvarez de Estrada y Luque, a Spanish aristocrat whose Anglophile sympathies led to him providing information to the

British about Spanish policy throughout the war. The information the British obtained from the summit was that Franco had resisted entering a formal military pact with Hitler and Mussolini. This released Churchill from any immediate pressure to refocus his military campaign on the Iberian Peninsula at a time when the British had not enough forces to invade the continent, and had been pressed into a war of attrition with Allied air power now seconding the previous weapon of naval blockade. Nevertheless, it left little room for complacency. Hoare remained hugely mistrustful of Serrano Súñer's pro-Axis sympathies, and believed that the British embassy needed to step up its efforts to counter German influence.

The poverty and hunger which Burns had reported on during his travels reinforced Hoare's belief that the Allies could use trade in foodstuffs to win over hearts and minds. Equally, Burns's reports – urging greater use of propaganda and boosting the loose network of agents from Barcelona to Tangier – had convinced the British ambassador that he could neither relax his vigilance nor, as he put it, 'ignore any straw that showed the direction of the wind'.

On one point Hoare was insistent: any gathering or dissemination of secret intelligence by the British on the Iberian Peninsula should be consistent with his mission of keeping Spain neutral and should be under his control.

From the moment he had taken charge as ambassador in Madrid, Hoare had made every effort to centralise key aspects of the embassy's operations, holding daily meetings to ensure proper liaison between departments and an uncluttered line of reporting on priority issues. He felt he had every reason to be wary of career intelligence officers whose first loyalty was to their line managers in head office rather than to the interests of British foreign policy, as identified by the ambassador.

Hoare's experience as an intelligence officer in St Petersburg in the lead-up to the Russian Revolution and his later dealings with the British embassy in Rome during the crisis in Abyssinia had left him with an enduring memory of failed diplomatic missions, whose weakness he blamed on divisive internal departmentalisation. In both missions, the developing international importance of the politics of the host country had meant the grafting on to a relatively small diplomatic staff of a large number of so-called technical experts 'who owed their primary allegiance to different offices in Whitehall'.

Hoare believed that intelligence officers were potentially isolationist, with a tendency to keep a proprietorial guard over the information they obtained, and with a cavalier attitude to the discipline imposed on civil servants. 'Important branches of the mission would be ignorant of each other's programmes, whilst the Chancery, instead of being the nerve centre of a multifarious organisation, would be left stranded on the outskirts of a field almost entirely occupied by the technicians,' Hoare wrote of his previous missions.

It was in Petrograd in 1918, after he had left Russia, that SIS officers had become embroiled with a group of Latvians in a disastrous plot against the Bolsheviks, involving an attempted assassination of Lenin. The failure of the plot led to hundreds of revenge executions and the dismantling of the British mission, so that the SIS subsequently stood accused of fuelling the Red Terror, and poisoning for years Anglo-Soviet relations.

The memory of the Petrograd debacle confirmed Hoare in his belief that intelligence operations needed to be carefully controlled and that policy was best pursued through diplomacy with military intervention an option of last resort.

His appointment in Spain gave him an opportunity to breathe new life into an embassy that, under the lacklustre Maurice Peterson, had struggled to have any influence on the Catholic, right-wing and militaristic Spain which had emerged victorious from civil war. Hoare wanted to mould an embassy around his leadership which had the capacity to take on and outmanoeuvre its German counterpart, while ensuring that nothing was done that might alienate Franco and tip him into the enemy camp.

His core team was made up of his deputy head of mission, Yencken, the naval attaché Captain Hillgarth, and Burns. Of the three it was Burns's department that, with Hoare's encouragement, and thanks to the personal and professional ties developed with Yencken and Hillgarth, was gradually transformed into a powerful and influential nexus straddling diplomacy, propaganda and intelligence.

Burns had arrived in the summer of 1940, protesting his inadequacy and lack of experience to his ambassador and suspecting his job would be short-lived anyway, given what appeared to be the imminent threat of a German invasion. He had found his first meeting with the professional spies in the embassy an unnerving experience. 'They were at first fish-eyed, aloof and polite to this foreign body thrust into their midst,' he recalled.

The embassy's intelligence operations – until Hillgarth, with Hoare's blessing, took overall charge – was headed up by the MI6 'head of station' (code-numbered 23100), Hamilton-Oakes, with a small staff of assistants. The more experienced spies showed themselves cautiously friendly to Burns no sooner had he arrived, while the young cipher-room girls, high-born, high-spirited and largely unmarried, had no qualms about voting him the most handsome and charming of all embassy bachelors.

Within a year of the fall of France, the Madrid embassy had grown into a formidable centre of Allied diplomatic and covert activity, its network of agents spread across consular posts in the Iberian Peninsula, beyond the Pyrenees in the north, to North Africa in the south. By March 1941, Madrid and Lisbon were two of only four (the others were Stockholm and Berne) MI6 stations remaining in Europe. In Madrid, the secret services' separate annexe of the embassy was referred to as the 'attic' by the attachés. Hamilton-Stokes ran a staff of fourteen under cover of the Passport Control building in the Montesquinza section of the Madrid embassy, running some 168 agents and sub-agents throughout Spain. His staff included the wives of two British diplomats, Joan Bethell, the sixteen-year-old daughter of the Vice-Consul of Cartagena, and a nanny. In the spring of 1941, Kenneth Benton, a member of Section V, MI6's counter-intelligence section, arrived in Madrid after previous postings in Vienna and Riga. Accompanied by his wife of three years, Peggie, he had flown out from England to Lisbon and then driven across the border in a second-hand Buick, alleged to have once belonged to the secretary of Léon Blum, the former French prime minister of the short-lived Popular Front government in France.

Benton's first night in Madrid's Ritz Hotel nearly ended in disaster. He had left Lisbon with a pistol in one pocket and a bulb filled with ammonia in the other, to protect him from bandits along the way. With the items still on him, Benton had stepped into the hotel lift. It was crowded with other guests and when one of them pressed against him the bulb blew its stopper. 'By the time we reached our floor, the people were gasping for breath, but we pretended to be as mystified as they were,' he later recalled.

The next day Benton went to see Hoare. The ambassador listened attentively as Benton told him about a top-secret plan the Bletchley Park cryptographers, MI5 (B Division) and MI6 (Section V), were developing after successfully decoding German radio traffic, known as ISOS. This was particularly significant, as it meant that British intelligence would soon have the capacity to intercept some of the key messages being transmitted between Berlin and German 'stations' on the Iberian Peninsula and in North Africa.

Benton also went on to explain the changing tactics the British secret services were developing in the gathering and planting of intelligence, true and false. In the first year of the war (1940–41), the main aim of MI5 and Section V was to identify and disrupt German attempts to infiltrate spies into the UK. But after the setting-up of the XX Committee in January 1941 to supervise all double-agent work, a further plan got under way to use turned Abwehr agents in a process of strategic deception. 'That is all extremely interesting,' Hoare said, after Benton had concluded his monologue. 'Only mind you don't fall foul of the Spaniards.'

Meeting Hamilton-Stokes later that day, Benton discovered that exactly the same warning had been issued to the MI6 station chief. It was not that Hoare did not want any secret intelligence or other covert activity to take place while he was in charge; what he wanted was to protect his mission from the development of autonomous fiefdoms which might get out of his control and leave him with the job of picking up the pieces diplomatically.

Hoare came to trust Burns rather more than any of the other spies. The ambassador employed his press attaché as a covert diplomatic tool, using his links with the Franco regime to keep abreast of its intentions and to identify areas for negotiation, providing intelligence that was not obtainable by any other means.

The fact that Burns had never formally been recruited by either MI6 or MI5 as an intelligence officer, but nonetheless ran his own sources, was viewed by his ambassador as an advantage. It gave Burns the operational flexibility to collaborate with both agencies when necessary while maintaining ties with other key departments in the embassy, both gathering and channelling information through the ambassador and directly to the highest levels of government which might otherwise have been lost, overlooked or deliberately ignored. However, from the early stages of the war, a marked tension had began to affect Burns's relations with some of his colleagues at the MoI and the secret services who questioned his professional competence and political motives, given his reputation as a right-wing Catholic with pro-Franco leanings.

It was while he was serving at the MoI's headquarters in London in 1939 that Burns decided he would try and make use of some of the contacts he had made during the civil war by engaging their services as agents of the Allied cause. It proved a high-risk strategy at a time when some of the more fanatical Francoists moved in the same social circles as Nazi sympathisers, and were as likely to betray the British as to help them. An early target was the Marqués del Moral, a Spanish aristocrat who, like Burns, had been educated by the Jesuits in England before marrying Gytha Stourton, a member of one of the oldest English Catholic families, whose position in the higher social circles dated from before the Reformation.

During his country's civil war, Moral had based himself in London running the Francoist propaganda and intelligence organisation in Britain. In a family memoir, Gytha Stourton's niece, Julia Stonor, describes Moral, or 'Mos' as he was affectionately called by his family, as having been a 'spy, and an important one'.

Stonor, who as a young girl developed a close relationship with her aunt Gytha, tells how Moral became a close friend of Joachim von Ribbentrop, Hitler's ambassador to London, whom he met in England and Spain, while also maintaining close links with British and Spanish arms traders who brokered deals during the Spanish Civil War.

'Gytha was horrified by the politics of these men, by Mos's open friendship with committed admirers and such enthusiastic followers of Hitler. But she was unable to do anything – as an obedient wife, and very Catholic woman she could hardly oppose her husband, let alone her friends so well disposed to the German and Spanish regimes.' Thus the new Marquesa resigned herself to the role of a 'pretty, occasionally useful ornament' to her older and 'very busily occupied Spanish husband'. When not in London, Moral spent the civil war period travelling frequently between Portugal, Spain and France, issuing safe-conduct passes into Nationalist-held territory to Englishmen considered sympathetic to the Franco cause, including Burns and other members of the fundraising organisation Friends of Nationalist Spain. Once Franco was in power, and the war in Europe had broken out, Moral was approached by Burns, under the official auspices of the Ministry of Information, but with support from the Foreign Office, to work for the Allies.

The idea that Moral should be recruited as an informant on Spanish internal affairs and relations with the Germans was channelled through to a senior contact in the Foreign Office by a right-wing Tory MP, with connections in the Foreign Office and an interest in Anglo-Spanish relations, Sir Nairne Sandeman, in April 1940. Sandeman reminded the contact that Moral had had, as he put in a private letter, 'considerable dealings of a cooperative nature' with the Foreign Office during the civil war, and strongly recommended that he be put on the MoI's payroll.

A file on Moral giving additional details on his life was attached. It focused almost exclusively on Moral's pro-British credentials. Moral had fought for the British in the Matabele War, the Boer War and the First World War, and had a son, of British nationality, who had recently enlisted in the British Army.

Sandeman died a few days later, but Moral's recruitment as an agent was actively pursued by Burns, with the support of the MoI and the Foreign Office. The MoI channelled secret payments to Moral via Burns's department under the broad heading of 'private propaganda in Spain'.

While Burns appears to have made use of Moral to extend his own contacts with the Franco regime, little additional benefit was drawn from the operation. The first report delivered by Moral, after Burns had been installed in Madrid, was judged 'practically useless' by one senior MoI official, Leigh Ashton. In a memo to Roger Makins, one of the top diplomats at the Foreign Office, Ashton wrote: 'The report contained some very dubious information about Germany which was passed on to DMI (military intelligence) and a certain amount about Spain and Portugal which did not contain anything we did not know already.'

Moral had been charging for information, some of which he had already shared with Burns, in effect double-billing the British government at a time when budgets were tight. Discovery of the scam led to the immediate suspension of any further payments to Moral after he had been declared *persona non grata* in British embassy circles. Burns was lucky to escape with a reprimand.

While the Moral blunder was quietly and quickly forgotten, it was not an isolated incident in the history of British wartime intelligence-gathering in Spain. During the early years of the war, further cases would expose not only the amateurism of some Spanish agents, but the ineptitude of the British spies running them. Early in the autumn of 1940, the British embassy in Madrid sponsored a visit to the UK of Miguel Piernavieja del Pozo as a representative observer of an influential political study group based in Madrid. Pozo was a Falangist who had spied for Franco during the civil war. He had since become a journalist. Pozo arrived in the UK on 29 September 1940. The tour arranged for him by the War Office with the blessing of the Foreign Office and MoI included visits to aerodromes in Scotland, various army units in England and the BBC's studios in London.

And yet, before the tour got under way, Pozo was approached by Gwylm Williams (GW), a former Welsh police inspector and Welsh nationalist who had been recruited by MI5 as a double agent after he had offered his services to the Germans. GW later informed his handler in MI5 that Pozo – or Pogo as he was code-named by the security services – had given him £3900 stashed in a talcum-powder tin and told him to report on military factories in the west of England, and on the Welsh Nationalist Movement (GW had posed as a Welsh nationalist eager to throw off the English yoke when first contacting the Abwehr in 1939). Pozo had also, so GR alleged, asked for some initial sabotage plans to be drawn up.

'He is a rather unpleasant type who is obviously on the make.' Thus did Guy Liddell, the director of MI5 counter-espionage B division, describe Pogo for the first time in a diary entry dated 10 October 1940. Liddell claimed he had only just discovered that Pozo had come to the UK under the auspices of the British Council and on the recommendation of Hoare. The plan, so Liddell had been led to believe, was to have Pozo file pro-Allied news reports as a counterweight to the German propaganda that was flooding the Spanish media, from Berlin. Liddell believed this to be an odd tactic. 'It seems a curious thing that our authorities should not be really wise to the fact that any member of the Falange, which is in fact a Spanish Nazi Party, must be right in the German camp,' he wrote.

Whatever the embassy's motivation, MI5's B Division needed little persuasion that Pozo was someone they could make use of for their own purposes. The German spy scare had intensified as the Nazi war machine moved across Western Europe. The fear was of the development of a fifth column which, it was believed, had aided the German invasion of France, Belgium, and Holland and was the explanation as to why these countries had fallen so quickly. Emergency laws were brought in suspending the right of habeas corpus and protection against mistreatment of anyone suspected of being an enemy agent. Within MI5 a belief was growing that Nazi Germany was using any trick it could to infiltrate its agents behind lines. The fact that the internment of some 18,000 German, Italians and other enemy 'aliens', along with members of Mosley's British Union of Fascists and other figures who were deemed to have their primary loyalty to Germany, within the first year of the draconian new powers being decreed had failed to uncover any major plot, only resulted in efforts being redoubled to catch other agents suspected of still being at large or recently infiltrated under cover of a neutral state.

In October 1940 MI5 installed microphone and telephone taps in Pozo's London apartment and put him on their official watch list, with officers of D.6, the surveillance unit, tailing him night and day. Despite the blanket coverage, MI5 struggled to come up with anything that suggested serious espionage activity, other than what they suspected were deliberate counter-surveillance measures typical of a trained spy.

An MI5 report accused Pozo of evading his pursuers by 'boarding moving buses and dodging into doorways'. It also drew on intercepts of his girlfriend's phone calls suggesting she was not who she claimed to be.

'According to the person she is speaking to she employs at various times a marked foreign accent, a slightly American accent, a Cockney accent, and a comparatively educated and fluent English accent,' wrote Liddell. 'When speaking to Pogo she appears to be a rather elderly woman with a poor command of the language, just as on other occasions she speaks fluently, quickly, and with no accent at all.'

Pozo was drawn into further meetings with GW, who continued to report to the Germans as well as the British, although the Spaniard's activities became increasingly erratic due in no small part to a heavy drinking habit. Early in November the *Daily Express* published what it claimed was an interview with Pozo in which he expressed his hope that Germany would win the war. Quite why the Spaniard would willingly want to make such a public confession if he was indeed a fully paid-up German spy was not explained. GW nonetheless reported the matter to the Abwehr in Madrid, saying that it had become too dangerous to work with 'such a man who tends to give cause for the attention of the authorities and will eventually lead to his deportation if not something worse'.

In his diary Liddell suggests that the incident had come dangerously close to undermining a plan of deliberately letting Pozo continue to operate as an unwitting feeder of false information to the Germans. He also reflects a continuing concern that rival agencies were struggling to control him, not least the Ministry of Information. 'Pogo has badly blotted his copy-book by getting tight . . . We have sent over a violent protest to the other side who have replied apologetically. It seems that Pogo has been superimposed on their system by some outside body, probably the Propaganda Ministry.'

Days later the *Sunday Graphic* published its own very different 'interview' with Pozo – a piece of crude Allied propaganda – in which he was quoted as declaring his belief that the war was far from over (contrary to the list of victories claimed in German news reports) and that the morale of the British armed forces and the country at large was very high. Within days, an unidentified agent working for MI6 reported that Pozo had suggested to him the Spanish people were becoming more Anglophile and had written to his unidentified 'chief' in Spain stating his conviction that Great Britain was invincible.

This was suspected by some in MI5 of being an exercise in deception rather than the betrayal of a double agent. But government departments remained divided as to what to do with Pozo. The MoI had growing doubts about his use as a propaganda weapon and thought he should be sent home. MI5 and MI6 wanted to give Pozo more rope with which to hang himself and entrap other agents. The Foreign Office wanted to avoid creating a diplomatic incident, and in effect threatened an administrative paralysis across Whitehall over the case. 'The case of Pogo is getting rather difficult,' wrote Liddell on 2 December 1941.

Pozo continued his meetings with GW, some of which took place at the Spanish embassy where the ambassador, the Duke of Alba, still considered the Spaniard a *bona fide* journalist who had had his papers cleared by Burns, with Hoare's blessing. In his dealings with GW, Pozo's alleged demands for information seemed increasingly fanciful. At one meeting he is said to have asked GW to make enquiries about the water purification plant and reservoir at Swansea with a view to introducing a 'poison' or else something to blow up the main pipeline.

And yet Pozo remained extraordinarily indiscreet for someone supposed to be an important German spy. A report he allegedly wrote in invisible ink giving details of bomb damage reached Spain and fell straight into the hands of the British embassy. He also arranged to have a meeting with the Duke of Hamilton, an aristocrat of questionable loyalties. The Duke was under MI5 surveillance, even if his reputation as an appeaser of the Germans may have served as a front for his work for other sectors of British intelligence. (It was because he believed in Hamilton's credentials as a pro-Nazi, high up in the British state, that Rudolf Hess had flown to Scotland to see him.) According to MI5's 'Tar' Robinson, head of the double-cross section, the 'slow-witted' Hamilton, while belonging to the peace party, came to believe that the only thing Britain should do was fight to the finish. Hamilton may well have informed on Pozo's alleged pro-German views.

Towards the end of January 1941, Pozo returned to Spain. The ease with which he was allowed to leave England infuriated some sectors of MI5 who had wanted him interned. But it appears to have represented a calculated risk taken by those within the British secret services who believed they had bigger fish to catch. Instead of bringing in Pozo, MI5 let him swim a little longer with the aim of identifying whatever wider network he was part of, a strategy that was to complicate still further its relationship with the British embassy in Madrid. The spies were in danger of running away with themselves and tying themselves in knots.

It was at the beginning of January 1941, or perhaps even earlier, that Burns became embroiled with a German agent who purported to be in the inner counsels of Serrano Súñer, Franco's brother-in-law. According to the skeleton account Burns gives of his dealings with Angel Alcázar de Velasco – he gives no precise dates – the Spaniard came to visit him at his suite at Gaylords Hotel with a request for accreditation as the new press attaché at the Spanish embassy in London. Velasco told Burns that Serrano Súñer mistrusted the Anglophile tendencies of Spain's ambassador in London, the Duke of Alba, and wanted his own man on the spot to assess more accurately British morale and Britain's capability of continuing the war.

Velasco explained his project with a 'wealth of colourful personal detail about himself', most, although not all of which Burns already knew about. The one-time bullfighter had joined the Falange before forming part of an extreme right-wing faction that had fallen out with Franco halfway through the civil war. He had been under sentence of death but had been reprieved. Over several glasses of whisky, he told Burns that he had become the champion masturbator in the military prison. To emphasise this, Velasco suddenly produced a pistol with a silencer and fired at the ceiling above Burns's head.

'It seemed to be his way of sealing a bond. Gaylord's had been the Soviet headquarters in the Civil War and perhaps more than one bullet had lodged in the elegant moulding round the ceiling,' Burns recalled many years later. 'Anyway to have a spy easy to tail might lead to others and Velasco's idea was welcomed by MI5.'

So there was method in the madness – but what method and whose madness? Velasco claimed in his memoirs that the Abwehr suspected the press and information department in the British embassy in Madrid was playing a discreet but important part in British intelligence activities and that he was tasked with infiltrating the department. According to his account, he began his mission by arranging a meeting with Burns's assistant Bernard Malley.

Over lunch and a series of subsequent meetings, Velasco claimed, Malley became convinced that he was simply an extreme Falangist who felt so betrayed by Franco that he was willing to provide the British with information about the political vulnerabilities of his regime. There is no record anywhere of such meetings taking place although it is probable that Malley may have been involved and that he may have suggested that Velasco meet his boss.

Burns's version of his own meeting with Velasco suggests that he agreed to it with the approval of his ambassador and aware that the Spaniard was a German spy who would be trailed more easily in London, and perhaps even turned into a double agent. A British intelligence file held on Velasco, which Burns had contributed to, shows that he had pro-Nazi sympathies dating back to the civil war, and may have been recruited as an agent of the Abwehr as early as 1935. By the summer of 1940 Velasco was being groomed for espionage work against the British on the recommendation of Wilhelm Oberbeil, a member of the Hitler Youth the Spaniard had befriended during the 1930s. And Velasco had also been involved in the German plot to 'kidnap' the Duke of Windsor before he took up his post in the Bahamas.

Burns nonetheless left the meeting with Velasco convinced that this 'preposterous character' could be manipulated to serve British interests.

By the time Alcázar de Velasco arrived in the UK in early 1941, the small community of Spanish journalists and diplomats then living in London was in the process of being heavily infiltrated by British intelligence.

Of growing interest to certain officers of MI5's counter-espionage B Division was Luis Calvo, the London correspondent of the newspaper *ABC*. Calvo had started his journalistic career as a trainee with United Press International before joining *ABC* as a theatre critic in 1926 at the age of twenty-eight. Despite the conservative monarchist leanings of his newspaper, Calvo became involved in liberal Republican circles, and, following the abdication of King Alfonso XIII in 1931, was posted to London as press attaché under the Republican ambassador Ramón Pérez de Ayala. During the civil war, he changed political allegiance and wrote pro-Franco articles for the London *Observer* and the Buenos

Aires newspaper *La Nación* from behind Franco lines. When war broke out in Europe, he returned to London as *ABC*'s correspondent, having been vetted and cleared by the British embassy in Madrid.

Calvo was by now a fluent English speaker with a good understanding, thanks to his previous posting, of British politics and institutions. He moved effortlessly in diplomatic and Whitehall circles, and was an assiduous reader of British newspapers. Calvo was a hard-working and observant foreign correspondent whose regular articles for *ABC* during the first months of war had exposed some of the more disarmingly absurd aspects of the 'phoney war', before vividly depicting the destruction of the Blitz and the evident refusal of the British people to be bombed into surrender. If, for a while, Calvo managed to escape any censorship by the MoI, it was because Burns saw him as a helpful counterbalance to the pro-German propaganda that was being widely disseminated from Berlin and occupied Europe. Burns's initial views on Calvo contrasted with those of a close group of friends inside the British intelligence community who, by the middle of 1941, were at the heart of UK-based covert activities against Spaniards whom they accused of pro-Axis sympathies and of association with German spies.

The informal unit was made up of MI5's B Division officers, the art historian Anthony Blunt and an Anglo-Spanish art dealer called Tomás Harris, and a third, Kim Philby, who had been recruited by MI6's Section V counter-intelligence section after reporting for *The Times* during the civil war. As well as meeting socially, between them the three men straddled activities which ranged from intercepting incoming and outgoing mail from the Spanish embassy in London (Blunt), through running double agents and interrogations and liaising with the MoI (Harris) to analysing intercepted German communications (Philby). They worked closely together on identifying targets for their agencies, setting priorities and trying to manipulate British policy against Franco's Spain.

The three collaborated in pursuing the case of Velasco and tainted by association the Spanish journalists and diplomats who came into contact with him, thus drawing Calvo into the double-cross system overseen by Major John Masterman's XX Committee and managed by MI5's Thomas 'Tar' Robertson.

On 24 May 1941, MI5 set a trap in which they hoped to ensnare Calvo. They got the double agent Gwylm Williams (GW) to write to Calvo, identifying himself as a friend and contact of Pozo and asking his whereabouts as there had been no communication between the two men for four months. Out of journalistic curiosity, Calvo agreed to meet Williams. By now MI5 had bugged Calvo's flat and was tapping his phone. The main conversations recorded were those between Calvo and a Russian exile called Natasha Antonovsky, the mistress he shared with a former US consul who was working in London for colonel Donovan's recently formed US intelligence organisation, the OSS.

The US diplomat, identified only by his surname, Fellner, was regarded as a 'bit shifty' by Guy Liddell, the head of MI5's counter-espionage division, but not half as shifty as Calvo. While Fellner was allowed to get on with his affair, undisturbed, the relationship between the Spanish journalist and the ravishing Natasha was assiduously monitored by MI5, with transcripts of their intercepted telephone conversations included in the incriminating personal file the security service was building up on Calvo. One alleged recording had Calvo mentioning Velasco's name in terms that suggested a professional arrangement.

Days later Calvo was returning home from work when he discovered Williams waiting in his car outside his flat off Sloane Street. Williams suggested they go for a walk in Hyde Park. According to a report subsequently filed with MI5 under Williams's name, Calvo agreed to operate a 'dead letter box' for any information that might be provided on military factories in Wales and the impact of German bombing raids.

In July, Velasco returned to England after a short visit to Spain. Within Whitehall, there were some, including Lord Swinton, the chairman of Whitehall's Security Executive, who argued that Velasco should be declared *persona non grata* and refused entry. But the move was overruled by the Foreign Office on the grounds that it risked reprisals against British embassy personnel in Madrid. By all accounts, Velasco was a Walter Mitty character – an adventurer as well as a fantasist – whom British diplomacy struggled to understand and who willingly played to his own advantage the intrigue and double dealing of spies on both sides. While the bulk of the information he provided to both the Allies and the Axis proved inaccurate, sectors of British intelligence were happy enough to make use of his services to entrap other suspect German agents.

Encouraged by MI5, Williams made renewed contact with Calvo who, in turn, introduced him to Velasco. Williams offered further false information about sabotage plans by Welsh nationalists and the movement of Allied ships and aircraft from Welsh ports and airfields for which he demanded payment of 'expenses' of at least £500. Velasco agreed to pay the sum in instalments.

Further meetings between Velasco, Calvo and Williams took place over the summer of 1941. At each, Williams told his Spanish contacts of the latest plans being hatched in the fictitious plot by Welsh nationalists, but kept delaying the supply of the 'top secret documents' on British military movements he had promised at their first encounter. Early in September, Velasco abruptly left for Madrid, and was never to return to London. He left behind him a complex web of agents and double agents that permeated out from the higher echelons of the Duke of Alba's embassy and its associated journalists and across the Spanish expatriate community of exiles.

One of the more active informants run by MI5's counter-intelligence division was the assistant press attaché, José Brugada, codenamed Peppermint, who in the early stages of the war shared a flat with Calvo. Another agent, codenamed Duck – possibly another unnamed senior diplomat – passed on to his British 'minders' copies of telegrams sent by the Duke of Alba, while a third – a female secretary at the Spanish consulate in Newcastle codenamed Tangerine – similarly shared secret documents earmarked for the Spanish ministry of foreign affairs.

It was thanks to Brugada that MI5 was tipped off about the betrayal by an alleged SOE operative of Catalan origin called Fernández Martínez Casabayo. The Catalan offered the Spanish embassy details of British commando raids in Norway and of planned operations on the Iberian peninsula in return for money and diplomatic protection. Casabayo was arrested and was not heard of again for the rest of the war.

The incident contributed little to clarifying the relationship between the British on the one hand, and the Catalans and Basques that formed an influential part of the Republican exiled community in London on the other. While Catalans and Basques together with Galicians helped in the transfer across of the Pyrenees of escaping allied POWs, only a select group of republican exiles were trusted as agents by MI5 and MI6, with the Foreign Office generally wary of letting its diplomacy be dictated to by a clearly defined anti-Francoist agenda. Among the more notorious Catalan agents run by Philby at SIS and subsequently by his friends at MI5 was an industrial chemist called Josep Terradellas, codenamed Lipstick. Terradellas initially provided MI6 with what Philby reported was useful information on German spying activities in Argentina, via Spain. But he was cut loose by British intelligence well before the end of the war, after being judged too indiscreet in his ties with Catalan separatists.

Other public figures involved in wartime Anglo-Spanish relations would have files compiled on them by MI5 as being suspiciously pro-axis during the Second World War. They included the Duke of Alba's deputy José Fernández Villaverde (the later Marquis of Santa Cruz), the military attaché Alfonso Barra, the commercial attaché Mariano Iturde, and the Spanish consuls in Newcastle, Liverpool, and Cardiff.

But of all the names to be chosen as a subject for one of MI5's potentially incriminating personal files few were to prove as politically sensitive as Tom Burns. From at least the spring of 1941, communications between Burns and the head of the Iberian section at the MoI, Billy McCann, were being copied and passed on to MI5's B Division in an attempt to build up an incriminating personal file. Alarm bells had been set ringing in April 1941 when Burns recommended that the MoI approve the accreditation of Méndez Domínguez as the London correspondent of the official Spanish news agency EFE. Burns told the MoI he was concerned that the Spanish media carried a disproportionate amount of German-based reports, dominating coverage of the war. Burns blamed the distorted pro-Axis coverage of the war on the overwhelming number of reports being filed from correspondents in Berlin and the limited number of Spanish journalists based in London.

In a telegram of recommendation to the MoI, Burns described Dominguez, a former journalist with *ABC* and the Catholic *El Debate*, as 'more reliable and more trustworthy' than most of the Spanish journalists he had come across in Madrid, and potentially more manageable than those who had been posted to Berlin. One of the surviving London correspondents was Luis Calvo, who was already being monitored by MI5. The other was Felipe Fernández Armesto, the correspondent for the Catholic Madrid newspaper *Ya* and the Barcelona-based *La Vanguardia* whose owner, the Count of Godó, was regarded as being sympathetic to the Allied cause.

Armesto, like Calvo, had supported Franco during the Spanish Civil War. He was regarded by Burns as more of an Anglophile than Calvo and had earned the trust of the Duke of Alba as well as other British officials, thanks to what was viewed as his well-balanced reporting from the UK.

While some MI5 files suggest that Armesto, who wrote under the pseudonym Augusto Assía, was not above suspicion, others would indicate that he may in fact have been working as an agent for British intelligence. Whatever the true nature of his work, his loyalty to the Allied cause was judged sufficiently special to earn him a King's Medal at the end of the war, and later an MBE.

While Armesto enjoyed good relations with certain members of British intelligence, the latest journalist to be sent to London by Burns came to be seen in very different terms. Burns believed that Domínguez's pro-Falangist credentials would ensure that his reports from the UK would be published in Spain. But he also argued with his senior management in London that acceding to his accreditation would benefit the British embassy in Madrid's relations with the Franco regime. It was a huge miscalculation that played easily into the hands of those who saw most Spanish journalists as simple tools of British appeasement towards Nazi Germany.

Domínguez's reports were indeed published by the Spanish media, with the blessing of the state censor. However, far from proving sympathetic to the Allied cause, they turned out to be so biased in favour of the Axis powers that Burns was ordered by the MoI to personally reprimand Dominguez and issue him with a veiled warning that he faced detention as a foreign agent if he didn't alter the tone and content of his copy.

Burns's latest propaganda blunder provided useful ammunition for those who wanted to discredit him professionally. But his enemies within Whitehall knew that it fell short of being definitive. Far more damaging examples of collaboration with the enemy were needed to undermine the support and loyalties Burns had built up across government departments.

By now a great deal of intelligence coming in and out of Spain, and the decisions about what to do with it, had become the responsibility of Section V, the counter-intelligence branch of MI6, and in particular the head of its Iberian section, Kim Philby. Among the material that landed on Philby's desk, via Bletchley Park, was ISOS, the intercepted and decrypted coded communications between the Abwehr and its branches and outposts, including those in German missions abroad.

By the middle of 1941, Section V had become an increasingly active arm of British intelligence. It had its own offices in an MI6 building outside London, near St Albans, in Hertfordshire, where ISOS summaries were logged and analysed. It had also set up its own network overseas, with its officers and agents developing their own reporting lines often in parallel with other station sections and with their own independent channel of cipher communication code named XB.

In the early years of the war, the professional liaison in London of the 'merry band of Iberian specialists' at the heart of British intelligence was forged by an close-knit social circle which the MI5 officer Tomás Harris hosted at his west London flat in Chesterfield Gardens. It was there that the likes of another MI5 officer Blunt, MI6's Philby, and Guy Burgess who had been recruited by MI6's Section D at the outbreak of the war before joining the BBC – a cover for his work for Soviet intelligence – could meet, relax and share their world view over drinks.

Philby at the time was the dominant figure in the circle, personable, self-confident and highly professional, regarded by some of his colleagues as the rising star in British intelligence. He was eminently clubbable without possessing any of the stuffy characteristics of an older generation of British intelligence officers, most of whom had a military background. One of his contemporaries, Walter Bell, who had been recruited into British intelligence during the 1930s before being posted to the US, recalled how he had gone to his first meeting with Philby dressed in pinstripes and bowler hat, only to be greeted by the head of the Iberian section, tieless and with his feet up on the desk. By the desk and piled high were intelligence files Philby claimed had been sat upon by his predecessor and which he was now ensuring got to the people who needed to know.

Bell was only one of dozens of British intelligence officers who would later claim to have been unaware of the traitor concealed by Philby's affable exterior – or, for that matter, of the duplicity of Blunt and Burgess, who would later be similarly exposed as Soviet agents, with Harris suspected of being one of the paymasters of the so-called Cambridge spies right up to the time of his death in a mysterious car crash in Mallorca in 1964. Others who woke up belatedly to the treacherous deception practised by the Soviet agents included Desmond Bristow, an MI6 officer who worked closely with Philby in the Iberian section in London before he was posted to Spain.

Bristow recalled a conversation he had with Philby while drinking rounds of Irish whiskey at King Harry's, the pub near where they worked in St Albans. At one point during the evening, Philby asked him what he thought about Franco and his neutrality, implying that he was too pro-German. 'Kim, I don't know, but I find it hard to imagine actually coming out and openly supporting either side; Spain is far too unstable to fight. If I was Franco I would stay neutral,' Bristow told Philby. With the evidence of hindsight, Bristow would later believe that Philby was 'obviously testing me as a potential partner in his work for the Russians'.

It remains unclear to what extent the merry band of Iberian specialists linked to Philby focused the attention of British intelligence on Spain, in a way that may have defused pressure on the London *rezidentura* of KGB (NKVD) officers, agents and communist sympathisers which had been the subject of perfunctory purges by MI5 during the 1920s and 1930s. Some evidence had emerged suggesting that Philby at this time was not wholly trusted by his Soviet masters. Within the KGB there were those who simply could not believe that the British Secret Intelligence Services could be run by such fools that no one had noticed that precious information was leaking to Moscow. And yet the fact remained that Philby, Blunt, and Burgess were Soviet agents at the time and felt their duty to the communist ideal paramount.

What is also beyond doubt is that the pursuit of Spaniards suspected of being pro-Nazi agents proceeded more or less unopposed by senior UK officials at the time given the paranoia that many in British intelligence, and MI5 specifically, felt about German penetration of a United Kingdom cut off from continental Europe. It was against this background that Spain and Portugal came to be seen, rightly or wrongly, as the main conduit for Nazi agents.

Philby helped spin the web of conspiracy around the Spanish spy ring in London, and relentlessly pursued it all the way to Madrid. No sooner had Velasco returned to the Spanish capital than a message was sent by Philby directly to Kenneth Benton, the newly arrived Section V officer, ordering him to follow the Spaniard and secure as much intelligence on him as possible.

According to Philby's message, the intelligence reports for which Velasco was held responsible were still being sent from London to Madrid before being forwarded to Berlin. Philby insisted that only Velasco could provide the answer as to who all his agents were in England and how they were transmitting. Benton was ordered to find out what he could. The subsequent investigation drew on information provided by a drunk who claimed to work for Velasco as a clerk. He told Benton that he hated his employer and offered to provide access to the contents of his safe in return for £2000 – the equivalent in those days of at least £50,000.

Benton was horrified at the idea of paying such a sum to an untested source for what he thought might prove worthless information on a suspect spy who was something of a Walter Mitty character. But Philby secretly wired him the money and insisted he go ahead with the operation. Benton arranged to meet the informant, while Velasco was away on a two-week holiday in Mallorca, on a deserted road at night outside Madrid. Afraid that the clerk might be a stooge for the Spanish secret police or the Germans, Benton waited in his Buick and watched him approach alone before making contact. He then drew an automatic pistol from his pocket and, with his other hand, passed over a package of £1000 in notes in exchange for a large suitcase. Benton said he would only get paid the balance if the contents proved worthwhile. What he found were papers and account books of minimum value in intelligence terms. The account books contained no details of any names of agents or sums paid to them. The papers consisted of cuttings from British and American technical magazines pinned to copies of the reports sent to the Germans and the Japanese. The discovery confirmed Benton in his view that, if Velasco was a spy, he was an amateur.

When Benton later asked Philby why on earth he had agreed to pay such a large sum in the first place, he was told that MI6's Finance Department had also raised their hands in horror at the idea, but had agreed after being persuaded that a 'single broadside from a battleship would have cost more'. It was, of course, Benton noted many years later, a false comparison since the Admiralty's budget was infinitely greater than that of MI6 at that time. More crucially, it left unexplained why Philby and his friends remained bent on pursuing a spy (Velasco) of extremely doubtful value to the enemy and encouraging a conspiracy whose only real impact on the war was in provoking tension between the British and Spanish governments. The answer may have lain in the ideological imperative Philby and Harris shared in destabilising the Franco regime, even though there were many other such blind-alley MI5 investigations during the Second World War.

It was a conspiracy that would undoubtedly have been curtailed rather earlier had it not been for the decision of Philby and Harris to order their double agent GW to resume contact with Calvo in October 1941 and feed him false information about the movement of a British convoy on its way to Malta.

A few days later GW provided Calvo with another piece of false information – an alleged copy of the minutes of a meeting of the war cabinet chaired by Churchill on 6 October. GW reported that he saw Calvo translate the minutes into Spanish, and put a copy in an envelope addressed to the deputy head of mission at the Spanish embassy, José Fernández de Villaverde.

Finally, GW provided Calvo with a report on wartime food stocks in the UK, which Velasco had requested in a letter to the journalist which had been intercepted by MI5 a few days earlier. Over the three-week period of contacts with GW, Calvo received $600 in the diplomatic bag which was monitored coming in and out of the Spanish embassy in London by Blunt and his team of 'night watchmen' from B Division.

By now Calvo had become a mere pawn in the double-cross system. Under the strategy MI5 used double agents like GW to deceive the enemy about Britain's capabilities and intentions. There was perhaps no greater supporter of the strategy than MI5's Dick White, who became executive head of the XX Committee. As White's biographer Tom Bower has put it, 'the mechanics of the tradecraft – secret inks, microdots, radio traffic, channelling money to agents in Britain, couriering documents from Britain to Germany and "recruitment" of the double agents excited White', even if the betrayal of some of his own colleagues would return to haunt him in later years.

A personal file compiled by MI5 on Calvo in October 1941 described him first and foremost as a 'Spanish patriot', who at the same time believed the best interests of his country would be served by a German victory. While the file suggested there was sufficient material to justify Calvo's arrest, a decision was taken to let him run a little longer under surveillance to see what, if any, network might be revived.

Intercepts of telephone conversations Calvo had with the other well-established Spanish London correspondent, *La Vanguardia*'s Felipe Fernández Armesto, a month later, in November 1941, showed them at one point mentioning Burns's presence in London, and referring to meetings the press attaché was planning with his counterpart at the Spanish embassy and with Calvo himself.

For those anxious to portray Burns as a traitor, the conversations provided little useful material. On the contrary, the perception Calvo and Armesto appeared to share of the British press attaché was that he was a man of influence within Whitehall whom they could not depend on to be indiscreet because he liked his job too much.

Days later, Burns, fresh from his meetings with the suspect Spaniards, met Dick Broomham-White, MI5 Iberian affairs officer, at the St James's Club in London. Seemingly unaware of the scale of the double-cross system that the organisation was running, Burns – who was quite open about his contacts with Spanish journalists – tried to win Broomham-White's support for the propaganda strategy that he was pursuing from the Madrid embassy, refusing to accept that it was fundamentally flawed. He justified the sending of Spanish journalists to London as the only means for getting reports from Britain into the Spanish press. He also argued that the MoI should make greater efforts to 'bear-lead' the Spanish foreign correspondents as 'Nazis have learnt to do in Berlin' – by feeding them information and exercising greater control on their copy.

Burns had asked for the meeting with Broomham-White in the hope that it might ensure better coordination between the embassy in Madrid and whatever strategy was being pursued by the secret services in London. However, Broomham-White emerged from the meeting convinced that Burns was the problem, not the solution, just as his friend Philby had warned him, even if he stopped well short of damning him as a traitor.

As he reported to Philby: 'On the basis of the conversation I am reasonably certain Burns is a man with right-wing sympathies who interprets his major responsibilities as keeping in the good books of his opposite numbers in Madrid. I think he is irresponsible and his judgements are superficial. He certainly has no idea of the implications of security work. I do not however, feel that he would consciously do anything which would be harmful to our interests. His indiscretions and mistakes are much more likely to be due to thoughtlessness and an overdose of the "appeasement" outlook.'

Two days later Harris claimed in a report that Burns was closely linked to Calvo and Velasco, and that he had deliberately turned a blind eye to their pro-German activities in order to avoid a major diplomatic row undermining the operations of the British embassy in Madrid. 'Burns is anxious to keep his position as the spoilt child of the British embassy in Madrid at all costs,' reported Harris. 'Burns feels that if any of the Spanish journalists here are molested that reprisals might be taken against him.'

According to Harris, Burns's fear of reprisals was quite unfounded, as 'not the slightest importance is attached to Burns by the German embassy or the Spanish government'. In fact, a Spanish police file on Burns, drawn from information provided by the Gestapo, showed that he was suspected of playing a major intelligence role in the Iberian Peninsula, and had been inaccurately identified as head of the MI6 Madrid station. 'It is suspected that Burns who is the head of English propaganda is in reality the Head of the British Intelligence service in Spain and Portugal. He travels frequently to Lisbon,' the Spanish secret police stated in a report which landed on Franco's desk.

Harris's assertions that neither the Spaniards nor the Germans took Burns seriously was a complete fabrication, designed to suggest that the press attaché could easily be dispensed with without provoking major repercussions. The lie fitted into the conspiratorial web that Harris was weaving with the help of Blunt and Philby to discredit Burns and have him removed from his post.

From within MI6, Philby was anxious to do all he could to ensure that MI5 came to view Burns as a security risk and thus continued to feed false information suggesting that he was aiding and abetting Spanish journalists to circumvent passport controls. He was not short of MI5 officers willing to fuel the conspiracy. One of them was Kemball Johnston, a friend of Philby's and Blunt's whom Guy Burgess had recommended to his Russian handler as a possible KGB recruit.

Johnston's main responsibility was helping oversee the screening and questioning by MI5 of refugees and foreign aliens and drawing up an index file of those suspected of working for the enemy.

Johnston was strongly anti-Franco and anti-Catholic and did all he could to counter anti-Bolshevik propaganda in all neutral countries, claiming that the communist threat was a Nazi exaggeration. He knew that it was not the defence of communism but the suggestion that a good Catholic was, by definition, a bad Englishman that most appealed in some quarters of the British state. Thus did Johnston on 28 December 1941 add this view to the file MI5 was developing on Burns: 'Nobody appears to have realised that Burns is the Burns of Burns & Oates, one of the two most important Catholic publishers in the country – and as such immensely powerful. This is surely the key to Burns' character, which so far as my information goes, is that of an extremely right-wing militant Catholic.'

In fact, Burns had never hidden his background in Catholic publishing or his family roots. Nevertheless, the Catholic conspiracy theory was picked up by MI5's Broomham-White and included in a two-page report he drafted three days later, summarising the case against Burns so far.

Broomham-White admitted that there was still no evidence pointing to treason. But he believed there was enough dirt that could be thrown at him to make it to stick. The allegations against him were that Burns's recommendation of Spanish journalists had been 'to say the least, misguided' and been of no service to British intelligence. The note from Johnston on Burns's Catholic connections, moreover, had thrown 'an interesting light' on Burns's character, making it even more so a target of 'justifiable suspicion'.

Broomham-White continued: 'The impression I have formed of him myself and from statements from other sources suggest that he is also a very slippery opportunist. Though I do not think he is actively disloyal, his sympathies are undoubtedly very far to the right, and he has no discretion or sense of security values.'

He concluded that from the point of view of those who had put him under surveillance (i.e. Blunt, Philby, Harris and their allies in the MoI), Burns was a 'most undesirable person to hold the post of Press Attaché in Madrid'. Furthermore, Broomham-White suggested, if Burns were to be recalled it would have the advantage of having him replaced by a man 'qualified and prepared to serve the interests of SIS (MI6)', in other words a candidate more to the liking of Kim Philby, the Soviet mole at the heart of British intelligence who as yet was a long way from being discovered as such by some of his closest colleagues.

And yet, unlike Harris's earlier report, there was no suggestion that Burns was a minor piece in the intelligence game that could easily be crushed. 'I think we must assume,' Broomham-White wrote, 'that Burns has powerful friends and that any move against him will meet with very strong opposition.'

In the following months a concerted effort was made by Philby and the small cabal of intelligence officers that had come under his influence to enlist the support of some of the most senior government officials behind their campaign to get rid of Burns. At the same time the double-cross entrapment of Spanish journalists entered a new phase. Philby notified the embassy in Madrid that he had no objection from a security and intelligence point of view to having Calvo, the Spanish journalist, return to Britain after spending a few days on leave in Madrid. In fact, Philby and his friends in MI5 had put in place a plan to have Calvo arrested on arrival and charged with espionage.

Prior to Calvo's return, on 12 January 1942 Broomham-White drafted his latest case report on Burns in consultation with Philby, and submitted it to Guy Liddell, MI5's director of counter-espionage. The report unequivocally blamed Burns for sending Spanish journalists with Falangist leanings to the UK and accused him of being complicit in a pro-Axis conspiracy on behalf of the Franco government. While acknowledging there was no proof whatsoever that he was knowingly working for the Germans, it held Burns personally responsible for 'recommending two German agents, and one suspect and highly undesirable individual' as suitable representatives of the Spanish press in the UK. It also alleged that Burns's zeal to have 'another German agent' (Calvo) accredited had led him to take action which had been 'most damaging' to the work of the security service.

Broomham-White concluded that Burns's 'irresponsibility and lack of judgement' was a sufficient justification on security grounds for MI5 to press for his recall and his banning from holding office in any government department ever again.

Those who had prepared the report on Burns intended to have it copied and sent to the executive head of the XX Committee, Dick White, the head of MI5, Sir David Petrie, and the senior civil servant at the Foreign Office Sir Alexander Cadogan. However, just as the copies of the draft were about to be circulated, Burns chose that moment to remind the Foreign Office and the MoI just what a central plank he had become in British operations in Spain.

Stepping up the propaganda and intelligence activities with which he had been entrusted by his ambassador in Madrid, he made a point of logging for the first time the meetings he had, and making copies to all the departments that he felt needed to know: the Foreign Office, MI6, the Ministry of Information and MI5. There is no record to suggest when and how Burns became aware that his enemies were gunning for him. However, the move by Burns suggests that he was aware that he was treading on potentially dangerous territory, and felt it necessary – to protect himself against anyone who might doubt his motives – to make it clear that he was acting in an official capacity and not as a freelance of dubious loyalties.

On 20 January 1942, Calvo flew back to Madrid ostensibly on leave. Burns wasted little time in resuming contact with him. A few days later he reported to London in detail on a meeting he had had with Calvo in the presence of his editor at *ABC*, Losada, during which he protested about the pro-Axis nature of coverage on Britain appearing in the Spanish media. According to Burns, Losada promised to maintain a close personal contact with him, told Calvo there and then that he must consider himself entirely free to write objectively about the situation in England and undertook to exercise a censorship of his own over and above the official one, in order to exclude any commentary that smacked of pro-Nazi sentiment.

Burns was not taken in but pretended to both Calvo and Losada that he had been, and left Calvo with the impression that the clouds of suspicion that had been forming around him in London were lifting. In fact, in a subsequent report to his superiors in London, Burns revealed that he had managed to intercept letters to Losada written by Hans Lazar, the German press attaché, suggesting not only the closest friendship between the two men but also that the *ABC* editor was in the pay of the Germans. He also reported that Calvo had had a meeting with Lazar in the *ABC* offices.

Back at MI5, those wanting to have Burns's head dismissed his latest intelligence report as a belated attempt to cover his tracks. Harris stoked the fires of suspicion again by suggesting that a lunch Burns subsequently had in Madrid with Calvo, the press attaché of the Spanish embassy in London, Brugada, and Velasco showed that Burns was continuing to collaborate with pro-German Spaniards.

By now Brugada – code-named Peppermint – was working as a double agent for Harris. Only Harris's account survives in the MI5 file on Burns. It is based on information provided by another of Harris's agents, Antonio Pastor, the passionately anti-Franco head of the Spanish department at King's College London – code-named Peacock. Despite the fact that Pastor was not present at the lunch, Harris claimed that he and the professor had been briefed by Brugada.

Pastor – undoubtedly influenced by his Republican sympathies – painted a picture of a gullible Burns being taken in by the Spaniards and being used to further the interests of the Franco regime. 'Calvo arranged a number of introductions for Tom Burns and a dinner party for him with Alcázar [Velasco] and Brugada. They regarded Burns as a buffoon and Calvo was trying to put over that he was attempting to come to an arrangement with Losada ... an arrangement that his messages [newspaper articles] should not be distorted on their arrival in Madrid ... Calvo was telling Burns that Losada was a good fellow and not biased, when Alcázar [Velasco] broke in and said that that all this was nonsense as Losada receives 12,000 pesetas a month from the Germans.'

Harris claimed that Burns himself had made no mention of this conversation and was therefore deliberately covering up the involvement Losada and Calvo may have had with the Germans. And yet MI5's own file on Burns shows that he had already reported on Losada's payment by the Germans and Calvo's meeting with Lazar, not on the basis of information he had received from Velasco but on letters that had been leaked to him well before the lunch with the Spaniards.

Burns trusted Velasco no more than he had done when he first met him and nearly ended up being shot. It was only the erratic Velasco who thought that everyone, including Burns, was taken in by him.

If Burns continued to cultivate Velasco and Calvo it was in order to track their movements while in Spain and infiltrate meetings which he was able to do using his press attaché cover. What he seemed not to have fully realised was the extent to which his reports were being deliberately misinterpreted by key sectors of British intelligence, not as evidence of cooperation by a loyal servant of the Crown but of collaboration by an 'appeaser' with the enemy.

On 10 February, Burns reported to London that Calvo had been approached by Enrique Meneses, the owner of an international Spanish-language media group, Prensa Mundial, to be their correspondent in London. Burns himself had earlier been approached to help with the accreditation by the head of the group's Madrid office, Gregorio Marañón, the son of the famous Spanish doctor, writer and politician whom, as we shall see later, the British embassy in Madrid had been courting as a source of political intelligence since his return from exile in Paris.

Marañón Jr was well to the right of his 'liberal' father, having enlisted in the Falange movement as a student and then volunteered to fight for Franco during the civil war. Despite his close links with the Franco regime, Burns considered him pro-Allied, like his father. Burns also believed that the proposal presented an opportunity to make use of Calvo back in London, having him write pro-British reports for publication in South America, as a counterweight to German influence there.

In a letter that was copied subsequently and shared with his enemies in MI5, Burns wrote to the Foreign Division of the MoI, saying that Marañón Jr's plans envisaged the agency in London extending into a feature and photograph service manned by British staff. He suggested that the agency could serve British intelligence and propaganda interests, particularly in South America.

Burns attached a copy he had obtained of an intelligence report prepared by the Spanish embassy in Paris on Meneses. It showed that Meneses had served as a civil governor in Segovia during the Republic, disappeared during the civil war, and then re-emerged in Paris at the outset of the Second World War where he had become involved in propaganda. He had been paid 100,000 francs by the French government and, shortly before the German occupation, a further £10,000 by the British for a series of articles in favour of the Allied cause. He had since visited Berlin and was thought at the time to be in the pay of the Germans. What the Spaniards did not know – and Burns did – was that Meneses had never left the service of the British and was now in fact being run by the British embassy in Madrid as a double agent.

Early in March 1942, Meneses' use to Burns was made clear when he came to Madrid and secured a meeting, along with Gregorio Marañón Jr, with Hans Lazar, the aim being to secure information that might be of value to the Allies. Trusting Meneses as an Axis agent, Lazar disclosed the plans the Germans had for using Prensa Mundial as a propaganda tool, infiltrating a Madrid-based South American cultural centre called the Consejo de Hispanidad, and ensuring that Franco's relations with South America served the interests of Berlin. All of Burns's reports on Meneses, including his account of the meeting with Lazar, were copied by Harris at MI5 and sent to Philby.

The reports in themselves should have been sufficient to bury once and for all any notion that Burns was working for the Germans, but Harris and Philby saw them as a personal threat. For the reports showed that Burns, their arch enemy in the British embassy in Madrid, was once again encroaching on the double-cross spy game, a field of activity they wanted to control for their own ideological interests.

Towards the end of the month Meneses arrived in Buenos Aires bearing a letter of introduction from Burns to the press attaché in the British embassy. It served no purpose. Days before his arrival, Philby and Harris sent a message to the embassy, denouncing Meneses as a German agent and emphasising the operational necessity of disregarding anything that Burns had to say about him.

By then the original proposal to have Prensa Mundial establish an office in London had served its purpose. Encouraged by the prospect of additional employment, Luis Calvo had flown back to Britain and straight into the trap that British intelligence had set for him. On 12 February, Calvo was arrested by Special Branch police officers on arrival at Whitchurch airport near Bristol. He was taken to Latchmere House – renamed Camp 020 – a secret interrogation centre which British intelligence had set up near Ham Common, on the outskirts of London, on the site of a First World War military hospital once used for the care of officers recovering from shell shock.

The main building and its annexes of portable huts were set in secluded woodland in one of west London's leafier suburbs. A tall wooden fence around the entire perimeter kept it hidden from prying eyes, while a double barbed-wire fence and a series of security barriers offered further layers of protection and isolation from the outside world. The few residents in the immediate vicinity were vetted regularly while no one could go in or out without a special security pass.

An earlier British precursor of Guantánamo Bay, Camp 020 was a product of its time. It came into being in July 1940, when the Nazi advance across Europe fuelled British government paranoia about Fifth Column activity, and infiltration by enemy agents, and led to the suspension of habeas corpus and the introduction of internment.

Compared with other neutral countries, a relatively high proportion of foreign inmates – over twenty – were Spanish citizens or of Latin

American nationality with close connections with Spain. During the time Calvo was detained there, Camp 020 was characterised by its secrecy, security, and lack of accountability to the outside world – with the media, defence lawyers, and the International Red Cross denied access. MI5 justified such containment on the grounds that external scrutiny would risk undermining the development of the XX system. But it meant that the inmates were denied the status or full rights accorded to prisoners of war under the 1929 Geneva Convention. The justification for Calvo's indefinite detention, as in the case of other inmates, was that there was secret intelligence suggesting he was a threat to national security, not that there was evidence capable of being brought to court. The best his captors could initially claim was that his name had appeared in a diary suggesting a link to Alcazar de Velasco.

With steely eyes, the man MI5 selected to interrogate Calvo, the monocled commander of Camp 020, Lieutenant-Colonel Robin 'Tin Eye' Stephens, seemed physically more like a Gestapo officer than a British soldier.

Stephens had been recruited by MI5 at the outset of the war after serving in the Indian Army and playing a mysterious, clandestine role in Abyssinia. He had travelled extensively and spoke numerous languages, but his experience abroad had simply fuelled an obsessive distrust and disdain of foreigners, with a thinly veiled racist tendency that expressed itself in cultural typecasting. Thus, Frenchmen were untrustworthy – 'a "good" [sic] Frenchman accepts the German's money' – Italians 'undersized and posturing' and Spaniards 'obstinate, immoral and immutable', according to the notes he took on his prisoners.

Official MI5 historians have made much of the camp's first and unbreakable rule, that physical violence was not to be used in any circumstances (in fact, it was broken on at least one occasion) – even if it has been pointed out that this was derived not from any sense of morality, but from a purely practical assessment that physical torture risked producing answers to please, and thus lowering the quality of the information. There is no doubt, however, that inmates were subjected to psychological torture of a brutal kind. Recalling his experience many years later, Calvo told friends back in Spain how humiliated and vulnerable he felt, being made within minutes of his forced transfer to the camp – without any formal charges being laid against him – to stand naked as questions were barked at him and insinuations made that he could be sexually abused.

For days he was held incommunicado and threatened with execution. His cell, like those of others, was permanently bugged so as to deny him any privacy. Stephens did not tolerate familiarity or signs of friendship with any of his prisoners – even the offer of a cigarette was proscribed. 'Figuratively, a spy in war should be at the point of a bayonet,' according to the Stephens code.

In the commandant's own case study of Calvo, he comes as close as is possible to admitting, but with no sense of remorse or guilt, that the Spaniard was not so much a spy as the victim of entrapment, a mere cog in a complex intelligence wheel serving necessary ends. Calvo was not a professional agent but a journalist who had been 'pitchforked deeply into espionage', with the manner of his induction into enemy service suggesting a 'certain injustice'.

The fact that Calvo had followed the profession of a journalist, not of a spy, and was therefore not trained to withstand interrogation techniques, made things relatively easy for his inquisitors. Stephens took pride in 'breaking' Calvo within hours, and having him kept in detention without charge for months, despite acknowledging that the information he provided in the end was 'considerably more than was known already, but rather less than had been expected', with the additional intelligence gleaned from him 'both limited and vague'.

Calvo's detention sparked an angry protest from the Spanish government led by the Duke of Alba. This was kept from Calvo by his jailers, who instead fuelled his mental breakdown by insisting that he had been forgotten by friends, family and officialdom. It was over a week before anyone from the Spanish embassy was allowed to see him, the first outside visitor since his detention. Calvo had been warned by his jailers that his chances of being freed would be much improved if he pretended he had been well treated. He was then taken blindfolded out of the camp to an ordinary-looking office that MI5 was using as cover.

The visiting Spanish official found Calvo tired and nervous but showing no obvious signs of physical torture. An uncharacteristic security lapse had allowed Calvo to smuggle out on his person a note hastily scribbled in Spanish. Shaking the official by the hand, Calvo transferred the note. In it, he asserted his professional status as a foreign correspondent and declared his innocence of any espionage activities.

The meeting prompted a further protest from the Spanish government and a warning from the Spanish foreign ministry to the British embassy in Madrid that if Calvo was executed by the British, as other alleged German agents had been over the previous year, the Spanish government would arrest those it suspected of being British spies in the embassy in Madrid and would not hesitate to shoot them.

The fate of Calvo was sealed when the British embassy replied, somewhat disingenuously, that Calvo was a Spanish citizen who had spied for the Germans on UK soil, and that therefore there was nothing analogous between his activities and those of any British diplomat in Madrid. By then the Franco regime had long reached the conclusion that Calvo was not worth provoking a diplomatic crisis over and was expendable.

Calvo was abandoned to his fate in Camp 020 for several months – a 'little grey ghost', Stephens noted gleefully, during his final period there, when he was accorded the 'privilege' of serving as prison librarian. His interrogators could think of nothing better to do with him, given the absence of sufficient evidence to hang him. Calvo was eventually released and repatriated to Spain, after the British embassy in Madrid interceded on his behalf, a gesture of pragmatic diplomacy if not humanity he owed to his contact Burns, if no one else in the British intelligence community.

The Calvo affair showed an MI5 interrogator and his colleagues in the secret and intelligence services at their most ruthless and cynical. What makes the pursuit of alleged German agents linked to the Spanish embassy in London in Second World War Britain all the more extraordinary is that it occurred in parallel with the friendship that had developed between the Duke of Alba and Churchill.

The 17th Duke of Alba and 10th Duke of Berwick, Jacobo Fitz-James Stuart was descended on the maternal side from Arabella Churchill, sister of the first Duke of Marlborough, and thus considered himself Churchill's cousin, a link the British prime minister appeared to have had no problem recognising.

On the contrary, Churchill found Alba a kindred spirit – *bon vivant*, monarchist first and foremost, and a virulent anti-communist, who had little truck with Nazism. During a lunch held at the Spanish embassy in December 1940, Churchill had told Alba that what he wished for – and what Franco would expect – were the best and friendliest relations between the two nations.

During most of the war, Churchill paid several unpublicised social visits to the richly furnished embassy in Belgrave Square, considering it one of the best kitchens in London. Alba had a fine cellar of vintage French and Spanish wine and employed a French cook who was a magician in the kitchen. Despite rationing there seemed to be no shortage there of pâtés, succulent game, vegetables served with extravagant sauces and desserts made with real cream and eggs, thanks to the black market.

So much did Churchill enjoy his meals with his cousin 'Jimmy' that he would often not wait for a formal invitation, but rather telephone and invite himself, a request that was never denied. One day the embassy cook told Alba he would love to have a signed photograph of Churchill. At the next luncheon, Alba approached Churchill with the photograph already framed. 'Winston, would you mind signing this for my cook? He has such admiration for you,' Alba asked. Churchill smiled then grunted: 'Admiration? Well, nothing compared to the admiration I feel for the cooking.'

In another intimate exchange on a visit to the embassy, Churchill confided to Casilda Villaverde, the attractive and well-born wife of the deputy head of mission who was suspected of being a spy by a sector of MI5, that one of the things he most admired about Spanish life was the custom of taking long siestas in the afternoon. The conversation took place at the height of the Blitz. 'But how do *you* find time to sleep, Prime Minister?' asked Casilda. 'Sometimes it's just three minutes, sometimes eight . . . but I switch off and rest,' replied Churchill.

The Spanish embassy was not short of beautiful women at the time but it was the slim and cultured Casilda who impressed not only Churchill but also one of the most notorious womanisers among his friends. One evening Casilda found herself seated at a West End society dinner next to Duff Cooper, the MoI minister who became Churchill's liaison officer with the Free French.

Flirting outrageously, Cooper complimented Casilda on her perfect command of English and declared: 'This can't be your first time in London.' Back came the assured reply: 'Oh, it is, I can assure you it is.'

Cooper was insistent. 'But where did you learn to speak such perfect English?' By now he was leaning in to his perceived prey, as was his wont with the women he thought he could seduce. 'If you really want to know, it was thanks to my English nanny while living in the Plaza de España in Madrid.' Cooper smiled. 'Really? I thought you'd learnt it in Oxford. You certainly picked a bad time to come to London.'

The evening ended without a conquest although Cooper and Casilda would settle for an enduring friendship that survived the war and into the years that followed.

Such encounters surrounding the House of Alba in London during the war would have been a mere comedy of manners had they not formed part of a broader stage in Anglo-Spanish relations which embroiled many of the players in a complex plot of diplomatic intrigue and espionage.

Alba, while aware that communications between his embassy and Madrid were being monitored by British intelligence, and that it housed individuals far more pro-Axis than himself, tried for most of the war to keep his relationship with Churchill separate from the complex stratagems of the spies, even if the spies themselves saw him as just another pawn with which they could play.

In early October 1942, MI5's counter-espionage division went behind Churchill's back and drew up their latest plan to entice the Spanish embassy into their double-cross game, feeding Alba and his diplomats with false information about an Allied plan for a massive amphibious landing in North Africa.

On 20 October, the head of MI6, Sir Stuart Menzies, contacted Guy Liddell, MI5's head of counter-espionage, and told him that Churchill was 'hopping mad' with his friend the Duke of Alba after being told that the ambassador had sent a report to his government about the Allies' forthcoming military operations in North Africa. Liddell noted in his diary: 'Personally, I think it is difficult to blame Alba. People will not realise that however benevolent and pro-British a neutral ambassador may appear, it is his duty to report to his government what he sees, hears, and thinks. The fault lies with those who confide in him. He has an immense circle of friends in all walks of life and probably a great deal of information goes west over the second glass of port.' The note is revealing for it shows elements of British intelligence concerned less with Alba than with the indiscretions that might have emanated from the English friends he made in London, not least Churchill himself.

8

HYACINTH DAYS

The wartime Nazi press attaché in the German embassy in Madrid, Hans Lazar, features as one of the more sinister characters in *The Spy Wore Red*, the memoirs of Aline Griffith, the American model working for New York designer Hattie Carnegie who turned secret agent for the Allied cause and came to Spain in 1943. With a stylish dress code, good looks and outgoing character, Griffith was recruited by the American OSS, the precursor of the CIA. Her mission was to immerse herself in the more pro-Axis circles of wartime Madrid's high society.

Griffith first met Lazar while she was dining 'under cover' with a Spanish friend at Horcher, the German restaurant in Madrid. The rumour already sweeping diplomatic circles in the early stages of the war was that Lazar had developed the habit of using his monocle to reflect light into the eyes of his victims when he interrogated them, when not using it as a simple magnifying glass to scrutinise secret documents.

Other Allied intelligence suggested that Lazar was not only an important figure in the Nazi world, the *éminence grise* of the German embassy, but also a man with strange tastes. His bedroom was decorated like a chapel, with two rows of twelve figures of saints and an altar on which he slept.

Lazar's standing as an important social figure in Madrid and a loyal Nazi was underlined by his choice of companion, the Countess von Furstenberg, a ravishing beauty and friend of the Third Reich who, on the night Griffith saw them together for the first time, was dressed in a long sable cape, a black satin gown and a necklace of gleaming pearls.

Days later Griffith met Lazar again at a party thrown one evening by a German businessman suspected by Allied intelligence of being a Nazi agent at his home near El Escorial. The German's palatial mansion, tucked away in the Guadarrama Hills, was frequently visited by leading members of the Spanish aristocracy who had returned to Madrid after Franco's victory in the civil war.

Griffith's cover was nearly blown that night when she was interrupted secretly photographing a document Lazar had inadvertently left on his dressing table. Luckily for Griffith, her intruder – a fellow guest – was extremely drunk and assumed that the attractive American woman before him was available for sex. According to Griffith, she managed to avoid his advances by slipping a capsule of sodium amobarbital, a 'truth serum', into his drink, which incapacitated him while eliciting from him the information that he was acting as a messenger for the Gestapo. When not attending private parties, Griffith spent her evenings at the Ritz and the Palace. One of her favourite dance spots was Pasapoga, a nightclub in the Gran Vía where a big American-style band from Paris played every night except Sundays. The club was managed by an amiable, fun-loving French Jew called Bernard Hinder who had a keen ear for gossip when not serving as a more serious source of secret intelligence for the Allies. At various times during the war, Griffith and Burns would find themselves with different partners on the dance floor at the Pasapoga pretending they didn't know each other. Madrid was a spy stage and they were merely players.

'In Madrid, people like me had a busy nightlife,' Griffith recalled years later, 'a lot of espionage went on there . . . in Pasapoga you'd be dancing around, bumping into English agents, German agents. Some of us knew each other but I pretended to be totally unimportant Señorita Griffith, just an American girl having a good time.' During the day Griffith worked in a secret code room which the OSS had set up in the offices of the US oil mission on Miguel Ángel Street, a few blocks from the American and British embassies. She helped run a small network of Spanish maids, secretaries and cooks, all of them as agents. During the war the OSS came to have several officers in Spain, mainly based in Madrid and Barcelona. They rented hotel rooms and owned several apartments which they used as safe houses for escaping prisoners of war and informants and agents, including those operating north of the Pyrenees and in North Africa. While it increasingly boosted its presence in Spain as the war progressed, the OSS remained an organisation in gestation in Spain, regarded as very much the junior partner by the British.

'The British had many more people than we did in Madrid. They knew much more than we did,' Griffith recalled. 'They had been doing intelligence for much longer than we had. The English were terribly polite and correct but we knew they had a terrible opinion of us . . . and of course everything we did was new . . . we thought spying was like being in the movies. The British were more sophisticated.'

Much of what Griffith was tasked with finding out at considerable expense when she was posted to Madrid in late 1943 followed a trail already well trodden by the British. From the moment of his arrival in the late summer of 1940 Burns had realised the formidable challenge posed by his German counterpart. Fate had determined that he and Lazar should track each other's movements while seemingly avoiding meeting face to face, playing a cat and mouse game in a world of smoke and mirrors, where no one could be fully trusted and nothing was quite what it seemed. Both men used their diplomatic cover to compete for the attention of the Spanish, socialising as much as they could, when not engaged in the more covert art of psychological warfare and the cultivation of discreet informants.

The British embassy's press office saw as its main official mission that of countering the German triumphalism that manifested itself in the pages of the Spanish media. In addition to circulating its clandestine news bulletins, it invited local journalists, academics and government contacts to showings of morale-boosting British documentaries and feature films. Funded as part of the MoI's 'Programme for Film Propaganda', the films idealised the common struggle that helped forge British national identity, providing an image of stoicism and cheerful resistance. The message to Spanish audiences was that the British were not only determined to win, but that victory over the Axis powers was a foregone conclusion. Films shown included *In Which We Serve*, an account of the heroic exploits of the captain and crew of a British destroyer in the Mediterranean, and *Pimpernel Smith*, in which the main character helps refugees evade the Gestapo. Among the documentaries was *London Can Take It*, which celebrated the spirit of the Blitz – ordinary Londoners getting on with their lives by day while fighting the German bombs by night, 'the greatest civilians the world has ever known'.

The Madrid sessions of Churchill's cinematographic propaganda warfare were initially run from within the main British embassy building with seating space for up to 150 people. Within weeks of the hearts and minds operation getting underway, Burns found a very ready response to the embassy's expanding invitation list, which he put down partly to the quality of the buffet that was laid on. While there was virtually no bread in Madrid in the first year of the war, the British embassy secured ample supplies from Gibraltar. The white rolls – nicknamed Churchills – were sent to Mrs Taylor, the owner of the 'we-never-close' tea room Embassy, where they were transformed into sandwiches. For Burns and those who came to watch his shows, those sessions became 'little oases of optimism in the darkest times of the war'. The press department's duties included overseeing the safe passage through Spain of British subjects and their loved ones. This was not without some risk, as many right-wing Spaniards had developed strong anti-British feelings as a result of the Spanish civil war, when most British volunteers had fought for the Republic in the International Brigades.

Among those helped by Burns was Henry Buckley, one of the most distinguished of the thousand or so foreign correspondents who had reported on the Spanish Civil War. A journalist with the *Daily Telegraph*, he wrote with an unrivalled and scrupulous adherence to the truth. Buckley was a devout Catholic and politically conservative but with a radical social instinct that had led him to report on the struggles of the industrial workers and landless peasants in the 1930s without sharing in the anti-communist hysteria of many of his fellow Catholics. Later during the civil war, he came to be horrified by the ideological blindness and intolerance of Spaniards on both sides.

In 1940 Buckley reinforced his credentials as one of the most astute observers of Spanish politics when he published in London his seminal *Life and Death of the Spanish Republic*, a personal record of one of the most tumultuous periods in European history, from the end of the monarchy to the rise to power of Franco. After the civil war Buckley was posted to Berlin, where he worked until two days before the outbreak of war when, in common with other British nationals, he was ordered to leave by Hitler.

After a brief period in Amsterdam, Buckley worked for a year and half in Lisbon and it was there that he developed close ties with Burns, as a friend and an informant. Despite their political differences over the civil war, Burns trusted Buckley as a fellow Catholic, and considered his experience of Spain invaluable in helping develop British policy towards the Iberian Peninsula. He came to feel very much in Buckley's debt.

When, halfway through the war, Buckley became a war correspondent attached to British forces in the Mediterranean, Burns personally arranged safe-conduct passes and other documents so that the journalist's young Catalan wife, María Planas, could travel from her home in Sitges to meet him in southern Spain whenever he was on leave in Gibraltar.

'I will write to thank Burns for helping you when you went through Madrid for our lovely little holiday in Algeciras,' wrote Buckley to María on 16 April 1943. 'It was good of him. He is a very nice fellow indeed.'

Burns's covert activities included helping the work in Spain of MI9, a branch of the intelligence services tasked with the specific brief of assisting escaped prisoners of war and refugees, both as a way of replenishing the depleted strength of the armed forces, and gleaning information from behind enemy lines. By the end of 1940, MI9 had developed a highly effective Iberian operation headquartered in the British embassies in Madrid and Lisbon, and with satellite bases throughout the consular network, under the direction of Michael Creswell and Donald Darling respectively. Creswell's codename was Monday while Darling's was Sunday.

Escapees handled through the embassies in Madrid and Lisbon ranged across a wide variety of nationalities – French, Russians, Dutch, Belgians, Yugoslavs, Greeks, Czechs, Poles, Austrians and Germans. These included soldiers and deserters from European countries occupied by the Nazis, and Jews escaping from increasing persecution.

Secret lines involving local contacts and safe houses were established across France all the way to the Pyrenees. There they would be met and taken across and into Spain by pro-Allied locals – French or Spanish – with a good knowledge of the terrain.

A successful operation involved escapees then finding their way secretly to a British consulate or the embassy in Madrid, from where they were smuggled down to Gibraltar or across the Portuguese border to Lisbon. Because of the proximity of the French border, both Catalonia and the Basque country became particularly important staging posts for Allied special operations.

In both Barcelona and Bilbao, Allied intelligence gathering was facilitated by the long-term presence British shipping and trade interests had in the respective ports. Among the local expatriates recruited by British intelligence early on in the war was Frederick Witty, the son of Arthur Witty, one of the founding players of FC Barcelona, who ran a very successful trading company in the Catalan capital.

In Barcelona one of the most efficient escape runs was coordinated by Paul Dorchy, one of Burns's appointees at the British consulate. 'A brash and robust young man who rightly regarded his duties as being adaptable to circumstances rather than what London regarded as proper to a press office' was how Burns described him. Among the agents who came through on Dorchy's watch was Mavis Dowden, a young English music teacher who left Mussolini's Italy for Barcelona at the end of the Spanish Civil War and was recruited by the British after the fall of France. Her task mainly consisted of meeting Polish escapees and helping transfer them to the safe houses that the consulate had rented around the city.

By the spring of 1942 Dowden's escape network was fully operational and increasingly well organised by her 'controller', a British expatriate she code-named Mr Eckys. 'We now had working for us, two Spanish policemen, several bandits, a school master called Muñoz, and a Belgian priest, a delightful fellow of gargantuan proportions, a schoolboy's dream of Friar Tuck,' she later recalled.

The network was eventually infiltrated by the Germans and Dowden was arrested while meeting a contact in a café off the Ramblas. She was imprisoned first in the Jefatura, or police headquarters, and then in the women's prison, Las Corts, run by nuns, near the site of the present-day FC Barcelona stadium. During her captivity, Dowden was subjected to continuous interrogation by pro-Axis Spanish policemen, while being held in cramped cells. Unlike some of her fellow inmates, however, she was never physically tortured, thanks to early diplomatic intervention on her behalf by the embassy in Madrid.

After more than a year behind bars, Dowden was given conditional liberty and ordered to report weekly to the Military Tribunal next to the statue of Christopher Columbus that overlooks Barcelona's port.

Life had changed dramatically for Dowden since her arrival at the same spot in 1939, after crossing the Mediterranean from Genoa, carrying her violin and musical sheets. She was later deported and returned to England, where she carried on her work for the British government in political intelligence at Bush House.

Many others were not so fortunate. While the Spanish escape lines remained open throughout the war, many escapees and agents were intercepted by the Germans. In one black week, reported by the embassy in Madrid, four key British agents were captured by the Gestapo. Such was the courage and ingenuity of many of those involved, however, that no sooner had one individual fallen than another was found as a replacement.

POWs who managed to reach Madrid were housed for a period within the confines of the British embassy before being smuggled out by car once the remaining stages of their escape route to Gibraltar had been arranged and secured. The embassy laid on games, books and food. It also provided the POWs with money with which they could supplement their diet with fruit and wine sold on the black market and brought in by trusted Spanish members of staff. Occasionally, one or two of them slipped into the cinema sessions, where they posed as members of staff so that their presence was not leaked to the outside world by any of the other guests. It must have seemed like a holiday camp compared to the rigours of army life and the clandestine existence under German occupation, although their hosts were only too aware how fragile was the political situation beyond the embassy gates.

According to Kenneth Benton, the MI6's Section V officer in Spain, of more than twenty spies identified directly by the embassy in Madrid during the Second World War, about a third were 'walk-ins', individuals who came and pretended to offer their services to the Allies when in fact they were working for the Abwehr.

While serving in the embassy, Burns was personally targeted by several 'walk-ins', some drawn by the fact that he was a Catholic, others by his close liaison with other key departments, and his influence on many of the political decisions made by the ambassador.

In his account of his time in Madrid, Benton described how Burns helped MI6's counter-espionage Section V secure an important asset in the form of a German Jew who volunteered to work for the Allies out of Spain.

'For most of my time in Madrid I had the services of an excellent agent, a German Jew,' recalled Benton. 'He was an educated man, liberal-minded, and he hated the Nazis, so he made an approach to Tom Burns, the Press Attaché, who informed me.' Benton credits Burns with providing him with the contact that developed into one of the most useful agents the British government had in Spain for the rest of the war and beyond. Benton arranged to meet the prospective agent on a lonely stretch of road outside Madrid, where he could be sure he had not been followed. He was offered a source inside the state security apparatus, the DGS (Dirección General de Seguridad).

The DGS was under Franco's orders not to close down the activities of the British embassy even though it was the subject of intense surveillance by Spanish agents and the Gestapo. Documents discovered by the Allies at the end of the war show that the Germans kept lists of everyone who went in and out of the British embassy, while Spanish police files in Franco's own personal archive reveal that Burns was among the diplomats allowed to carry on operating by the Spaniards despite being suspected of spying. Franco benefited from regular information on most of the intelligence operations that were being conducted by the Axis and the Allies against each other on Iberian soil and was content to let them run as long as they did not directly threaten his hold on power. Such a policy appears to have come under pressure in Spanish towns where the influence of pro-Axis Falangists was more prevalent.

In the southern port town of Huelva, for example, William Cluett, the British manager of a British electricity company, Joseph Pool Bueno, an Anglo-Spanish employee of Rio Tinto, and Montagu Brown, the head of the local railway company were expelled for suspected spying activities. The British embassy successfully intervened to secure the release from detention of two other British businessmen. On the whole there was nothing similar in scale to the pursuit of Spaniards suspected of being German spies by MI5 in the UK. Franco's repression remained focused on what he perceived as the internal enemy of Spaniards who had fought against him.

If Burns enjoyed additional protection in wartime Spain it was because of his Catholic credentials, his anti-Republican stance during the Civil War, and the allies and 'agents of influence' he had forged in the higher echelons of the regime.

It was Burns's faith that appears to have prompted at least one attempt by the German secret service to infiltrate one of their agents into the British embassy, in a case of ecclesiastical espionage redolent of the counter-Reformation.

The agent in question was a German Benedictine monk called Fr Hermann Keller. Born with a hole in the heart, Keller had been barred from military service, prompting him to volunteer instead for espionage work. Keller was recruited as an agent both by the Abwehr and Himmler's secret service, and tasked with informing on alleged plots involving the Vatican and British and German Catholics. At one point Keller was also sent to Rome to find out who, in May 1940, had betrayed to the Pope advance information on Germany's impending attack on the Western Front.

Keller continued to work for the Nazis in Paris and from there extended his operations south, attempting to infiltrate the Benedictine monastery in Montserrat, near Barcelona, a traditional refuge for political dissidents high in the granite mountains. The Gestapo had received a tip-off that Friedrich Muckermann, an anti-Nazi Jesuit it was seeking all over occupied Europe, was staying there. He was indeed, but Keller never found him. Undeterred, he travelled to Madrid in search of Muckermann and other pro-Allied German Catholics. There he approached Burns, claiming that he had been in Montserrat on a retreat, and posing as a messenger for the German 'resistance'.

Burns checked with his Catholic contacts and concluded that Keller was a plant. Since Keller was operating mainly out of Germany and had no plans to go to England, the issue of arrest, internment and trial did not arise. Burns, however, knew how to turn the attempted infiltration into an opportunity and suggested to Keller that he should become a double agent providing information on officers in the German army who might be opposed to Hitler.

Whether Keller adopted a new role as an Allied spy is unclear although, if he did, it proved short-lived. The little that is known of him suggests he suffered a crisis of conscience in Madrid and shortly returned to the simple monastic life.

The Keller incident provides a clear example of Burns being drawn unwittingly into the darker reaches of espionage. Burns had never been trained as a spy. Like others in the war, he had become one by default, initially filling the gaps left by the professionals, and then learnt the trade as he went along as his ambassador loaded an increasing burden of reporting, liaison and analysis on his shoulders. During the early period of his involvement with British interests in Spain, Burns was on a steep learning curve, and mistakes were inevitably made. Among his more eccentric recruits was the poet Roy Campbell with whom he had maintained close links during the civil war. Despite their shared admiration for Franco, it was Burns's influence on Campbell as a fellow Catholic that in the end deterred the poet from embracing fully the cause of British fascism. Weeks after the outbreak of civil war, Campbell went to London and met Oswald Mosley, the leader of the British Union of Fascists. They were introduced to each other by the poet and painter Wyndham Lewis in the belief that 'these two men would be on the same wavelength'. They were not and Campbell refused to join the BUF.

Campbell, however, only belatedly came to view Nazism as alien to his concept of Christianity, lacking its spiritual dimension and humanity. With the end of the civil war, Campbell travelled to Madrid to celebrate Franco's victory parade on 19 May 1939, in which Spanish troops were joined by Germans and Italians. Days earlier he had written a letter to his mother in which he expressed sympathy for Hitler and a cynical disregard for the plight of the Jews. Campbell wrote: 'What Catholics realise is that Hitler is a civilised and human adversary, compared to the only alternative, and they suffer cheerfully as they can . . . What we realise is that the world is going to become either Bolshevik or Fascist, and we know that with one exception the fascist states are eminently Christian, and allow Christians to live whereas bolshevism simply kills and degrades everything – it is against morality – and against every form of religion.'

And yet Campbell's politics underwent a further shift when Hitler signed his non-aggression pact with Stalin, and later when German troops marched into Poland in open defiance of the pact between the Polish and British governments.

On 4 September 1939, the day after Britain declared war on Germany, Campbell took a train from Toledo to Madrid to try to enlist at the British Consulate, as a soldier in the British Army, the decision prompted, according to his daughter Anna, by fear that he might be thought of as being 'on Hitler's side'.

His offer to join up was turned down ostensibly on the grounds of age: Campbell was thirty-eight. The consul chose to ignore Campbell's fascist sympathies, instead describing as 'Quixotic' the fact that a South African living in Spain would want to volunteer for the Allied cause. Initially Campbell was relieved at being able to carry on his life in 'glorious Spain' as an expatriate, but as the phoney war gave way to serious hostilities, his conscience stirred and he became frustrated that there was nothing he could do to help the war effort.

He returned to Madrid, this time confident of being enlisted in some shape or form, for news had reached him that among the more influential individuals in the British embassy staff was his friend Burns – publisher turned diplomat with a special mission, whose devotion to the Catholic faith remained unflinching.

Campbell visited the British embassy and was enlisted by Burns as one of his agents. Burns told Campbell to use Toledo as a base for travelling around Spain, reporting regularly on friends and acquaintances and identifying the extent to which their sympathies lay either with the Allies or the Axis powers. Campbell was also asked to make ready to join a clandestine resistance force as and when the Germans decided to occupy

Spanish territory. It remains unclear whether the recruitment had the official backing of MI6 or SOE, although by now Burns was trusted as a conduit by colleagues working for both agencies, and Campbell was personally satisfied that he was now working on Her Majesty's Secret Service. It seems likely that Burns was acting with the approval of his ambassador, with secret funds he had secured from the MoI.

According to his daughter, Anna, after the war was over Campbell kept his role secret from his family and it was only after his death that they discovered he had worked for British intelligence at all. In her unpublished memoir of her father, *Poetic Justice*, Anna suggests that his role in covert operations had a longer lifespan than Burns recalled: 'Roy rushed off to Madrid to join up at the British Embassy, but since he was over age it was suggested that he should join an intelligence unit in Spain instead. He was terribly disappointed that he could not immediately become a soldier, a life-long ambition that kept getting thwarted. I never knew what he was doing in Intelligence, but he did seem more contented than before. He always refused to talk about his work, except to say he was helping to catch some bandits in the Sierra Nevada.'

Quite what 'banditry' Campbell was referring to is unclear. While it suggests he may have seen his role as helping Franco identify the straggling elements of the communist-backed resistance movement, it may also have been a deliberate attempt to divert attention from his somewhat unheroic and brief experience working as one of Burns's informants.

What is true is that Campbell liked to drink, which he often did to excess. His autobiography contains an elegy to the delights of drinking large quantities of wine from an earthenware *botijo*, to which he attributed miraculous powers of transformation. 'This way of drinking brings out the flavour and perfume, both of wine and water, and once one has mastered the art without choking, drinking wine or water out of a glass seems flat and insipid compared to it. The longer, thinner, and more forcible the jet, the more it aerates the bouquet of the wine or the water.'

While in Toledo, when not drinking out of a *botijo*, Campbell would normally make his way in the evening to a café with a large open terrace in the town's main square, the Plaza de Zocodover. It was there that, on a hot summer's evening in 1935, Campbell's propensity for binge drinking, as well as hospitality, had been experienced by the nascent poet Laurie Lee. At the time Lee had barely turned twenty and was busking his way through Spain with a violin. Identified as an Englishman, he found himself invited to the Campbell table and ended up staying for a week, drinking endless *botijos* of wine. Lee would later volunteer to fight in the civil war, on the opposite side to Campbell, against Franco. But in the flush of youth, he held Campbell in awe both as a poet and a free spirit. 'I was young, full of wine, and in love with poetry, and was hearing it now from the poet's mouth,' Lee recalled.

Some six years later, Campbell was back in his favourite café (exactly when in 1941 remains unclear), celebrating his appointment as a secret agent. That morning Burns had driven to Toledo in his Wolseley and, during a lengthy lunch at a local *taverna* with Campbell had confirmed his recruitment. Wine and *tapas* had flowed as the two friends sealed the engagement. 'I found him more than eager to have an active part in the war, and that he would be an agent in place seemed a fine idea to both of us,' Burns recalled.

The two conspirators then devoted the rest of the meal to memories of women and men friends they had once had in common, as well as bullfighters they had come to admire as geniuses, such as Belmonte and Manolete. Burns, like others on wartime service, had developed an ability to drink a great deal while retaining concentration. Campbell had a less self-disciplined attitude towards life generally. After Burns had set off back towards Madrid, Campbell had continued drinking. In the course of the evening, he drew friends and foes to his table, offering to buy them another round. He became paralytically drunk before declaring that the celebration was to mark the start of a new job as a British spy. The next day, when word got back to the embassy, Burns, seemingly under orders from a not-best-pleased ambassador, contacted his friend Campbell and, with regret, informed him that his services were no longer required.

A few weeks later, in early spring 1941, Burns was given permission by his ambassador to visit London on leave, his first break since his posting to Spain. As we have seen in an earlier chapter, he appears to have had some inkling that his pre-Franco leanings and mishandling of certain operations may have stirred his enemies in the intelligence community. Burns saw the trip as a convenient cooling-off period after the Campbell debacle, which he considered a minor incident in the broader context of the work he was doing in Spain. It also offered him the opportunity, on a personal front, to catch up with the news of those he considered his enduring friends.

In March 1941, days before Burns arrived in the UK, the basement dance floor at the Café de Paris, one of his favourite pre-war nightspots, received a direct hit from the Luftwaffe, leaving eighty-four society party-goers dead, among them the bandleader 'Shake Hips Johnson' and his entire orchestra. The news shocked Burns, reinforcing his guilt that his posting to Madrid had left him safer than most of the men and women he had mixed with in peacetime, although it was with a sense of relief that he discovered that none of his friends were among the victims.

Among several old girlfriends Burns wanted to look up was the eccentric author Lady Eleanor Smith, whose memoirs, *Life's a Circus*, he had edited and published while working at Longman in 1939. They told of how she had been resuscitated by a brandy massage after being born 'dead' in 1902 in a small cottage in Birkenhead.

Eleanor was the daughter of the 1st Earl Birkenhead, a tall, olive-skinned lawyer and prominent Conservative politician with a reputation as a brilliant if pugnacious advocate, a hard drinker and a womaniser. As Lord Chancellor he became, with Churchill, a leading figure of the Lloyd George coalition government in the early 1920s. By then he had left an indelible mark on Eleanor, the oldest of his three children. During her childhood he told her macabre fairy tales, took her to boxing matches, advised her to be 'cheeky before solemn statesmen', and in her youth encouraged her to bounce up and down on the Lord Chancellor's woolsack.

Eleanor grew up with a consuming interest in gypsies, circuses and flamenco, passions she owed to reading George Borrow's classic account of gypsy life in Spain, *The Zincali*, and the gypsy blood she claimed to carry within her from a great-grandmother called Bathsheba.

Voluptuous and carefree in her youth, the dark-eyed Eleanor took the hedonistic lifestyle of the Bright Young Things of the 1920s to unparalleled limits. Her escapades on both sides of the Atlantic included an affair with a Chicago gangster called Kid Spider, and turning a pack of Irish wolfhounds on the crowded ballroom of the British embassy in Dublin. In one of her more bizarre exploits, Eleanor spent a night with Zita Jungman, another notorious Bright Young Thing of the 1920s, in the Chamber of Horrors at Madame Tussaud's in London after first moving the wax effigies of the Princes in the Tower from their bed. Zita, together with her sister Teresa, known as 'Baby', went on to part-time modelling, hoping to get their portraits in magazines like *Tatler* and *Vogue*, and caught the eye of the aspirant photographer Cecil Beaton. Boyfriends caught up in their wild escapades outside the studio recalled them as ideal training for wartime special operations. Zita later described some of her Anglo-Saxon suitors as 'horrid' and 'intensely vulgar'. Eleanor, by contrast, found what she was looking for – half-naked gypsies in the caves of Almería and the red-light district of Barcelona. *Los gitanos* fed her existentialist fever with rhythmic dance and song that seemed to be drawn from deep within the soul. In Eleanor, four years older than he was, Burns found his own love for Spain taken to an edge of surrealism which he found fascinating, if occasionally disturbing. He also respected her as a writer, although her time as a society reporter and cinema critic on a London newspaper proved short-lived. 'She was an eternal high-spirited tomboy delighting in the company of gypsies and circus folk,' Burns recalled. 'We saw a lot of each other, without the intrusive pangs of sex, to our mutual relief.'

The war came and he saw nothing and heard nothing of Eleanor for over a year. Then, on leave from Spain, he heard from a mutual friend that she was in London, looked her up and took her to dine at the Mirabelle. The couple were deep in conversation over wine and oysters when there was a hush then a stir and a collective turning of heads towards a group of heavy-coated men at the entrance. It was Churchill, in the company of Brendan Bracken, the newspaper magnate turned Minister of Information, and other close aides. With a cigar in one hand, Churchill shuffled over to the couple's table, smiling broadly. Eleanor's late father, Lord Birkenhead, a witty, reckless man, 'naughty but never nasty', just as his daughter liked to portray herself, had been Churchill's closest friend until his death, aged fifty-eight, in 1930.

By attending one of Mayfair's better-known restaurants Churchill was acting with characteristic bravado and indulgence, for these were the very darkest days of the war, a time of bombs and rationing, when Britain was still having to face the enemy 'alone', to use a word from one of his more famous broadcasts. The United States had yet to make up its mind even if some of its citizens had defied their government's official neutrality by volunteering as pilots in the Battle of Britain. Acknowledging Burns's presence with a smile, Churchill turned to Eleanor and said: 'Well, at least we have the gypsies on our side.' The pair, left to themselves, spent the rest of the evening pondering whether he had been referring to the naked boys in Andalusia or the men in uniform in Madrid, or possibly both. After that evening Burns kept in touch with Eleanor but never saw her again. She died before the war was over, of a sudden mysterious illness, but the memory of that evening stuck with him all his life. It seemed to him typical of her starlit life that she had managed to rekindle his spirit just when it seemed at its lowest point.

If, as the novelist Mary Wesley remarked of her own experience of that time, 'war was erotic', it was because, with death threatening every street and two million people taking up arms, life needed to be reaffirmed. At the height of the Blitz small private parties, like so many sexual encounters, relieved the tension. While in London, Burns wasted little time in seeking one such party out. It was filled with debutantes, and suitably camouflaged spies. Noël Coward was there, his ostensibly glamorous lifestyle barely covering his morale-boosting work as an agent of His Majesty's Secret Service. As Burns and the other guests huddled round the piano, Coward was persuaded by his hostess to sing 'London Pride', the song of the moment, of which the MoI was making much use to lift morale. It spoke of London's endurance and defiance, graceful in its pervading sense of freedom and engaging familiarity. This was a city, defined in terms that were familiar to a social class that had read George Bernard Shaw.

Coward's song romanticised the flower girl Liza and the vegetable marrows, and the fruit piled high in Covent Garden, while similarly exalting the delights of Mayfair's posher basement nightspots, before the bombs fell.

The song moved Burns more than any other, for it reminded him of times past, of love lost, London personified by the woman he had believed to be the love of his life, the Queen's cousin, Ann Bowes-Lyon. 'Coward's song brought back a violent nostalgia for my beloved and now suffering city,' he recalled later. The shock of hearing of Ann's engagement to another man had barely dissipated during the previous months, although it reflected wounded pride rather than a real prospect of early reconciliation. 'I do feel for you about what you say about not being able to get this Ann thing happy in your mind – these things take years and years to burn out,' David Jones had written to Burns.

'I can't say anything consoling,' wrote Jones, 'only just that this 'ere vale of tears, or, as you say, fears, is a sod anyway – not a very original conclusion I admit!'

During his posting in Madrid, the memory of Ann would be periodically rekindled by other mutual friends who came across her now and again. Although such contacts became fewer and further apart as the war proceeded, the fact that they took place at all suggested that she herself struggled to put the past behind her. As late as October 1943, she wrote to Michael Richey, knowing full well that he would communicate the fact with his friend Burns. The letter was so emotionally strained and confused that he had concluded that her proposed marriage was no longer on or at least delayed indefinitely. Frank D'Abreu, the man to whom she had become engaged, had been posted to the Middle East as an army doctor, and she was at Glamis Castle recovering from her latest bout of depression after poisoning a finger.

Most of Richey's correspondence with Ann has not survived, but on 11 October 1943, soon after receiving a letter from her, he wrote to his parents while sailing towards the Falklands on board HMS *Carnarvon*. His letter expresses admiration for her, in contrast to the disdain he felt for others in her aristocratic social circle.

'Ann seems to be working very hard. I think some of the fair ladies one sees so much in *The Tatler* etc would do well to emulate her a bit. Her address is Military Hospital, Shenley, near St. Albans. At least it will be by the time you get this. She was at Glamis recovering from being very ill when she wrote, but was due to go back to hospital in a day or two. Talking of *The Tatler* few things annoy me more now than to see pictures of young Lord this and that and the other at some nightspot with a bottle of champagne on the table and a Guards uniform on. Some of them are on leave and all that but I always have the impression that a lot of them have been there since September 3rd 1939.'

When Burns arrived in London that spring of 1941, nearly a year had passed since Michael's older brother Paul, a pilot with the RAF's Number 1 Squadron, had been drawn into the increasingly violent air battles preceding the fall of France. Between 10 and 19 May 1940, with the squadron confronted by the full might of Hitler's Blitzkrieg invasion of France and the Low countries, he was shot down twice. He baled out once, and later crash-landed after sustaining a serious bullet wound to the neck. After a long period of rehabilitation during which he served as fighter operations sector commander, in the spring of 1941, Richey was declared fit and posted back to operational flying with 609 squadron at Biggin Hill. He spent the next four months flying a total of fifty-three missions across the Channel.

Knowing of Richey's heroic exploits, Burns felt deeply humbled by the fact that a letter Paul wrote to him about this time barely mentioned his extraordinary deeds, but was instead a note of gratitude. Paul said he wanted to thanks Burns for the continued use of his sports car and to apologise for only belatedly sorting out the insurance cover.

Burns heard separately that Mike Richey was at sea again after surviving the sinking of his minesweeper the previous November. In the intervening months, while his brother Paul wrote a journal about his own experiences, Mike penned a no less graphic account of his own scrape with death.

He wrote: 'I remember the disposition of everything, its exact character, as clearly as though the eight or nine months' work we had done in the ship had been a prelude to its destruction and to the overthrow of the small society that had lived within it. I believe that a clear realization of the look of things just before something happens is quite common. In any case, it has stuck in my mind . . .'

His account reads like a chronicle of a death foretold, the transformation of a 'little ship' from homely fishing vessel to protector of a military convoy, underlying the improvisation and endemic fragility of the Allied war effort. Mike would almost certainly have been killed had he been on watch or sleeping on his bunk below deck at the moment the ship hit a mine. Instead he was sitting on a bench huddled over a small stove, contemplating his shipmates with an almost biblical sense of God's presence among them.

'They were no longer a man on watch or a man in his bunk, but they were Peter, Alec, Horace and Tom, with excited, innocent gleams in their eyes, and you felt the unity of the crew which cut across the boundaries of environment, upbringing, and occupation . . .'

When the mine explodes, Richey describes the ensuing devastation as he struggles to escape through the narrow cabin hatchway. He watches the young cook, 'whimpering, his face covered with blood and burns', his lieutenant floating near him, and then the little bows with the boat's name on them going down. 'The craft looked gallant enough and pathetic, being sunk like this after what it had done. It was something personal, like seeing a man drown.'

Afterwards, when the survivors, himself included, were taken to hospital, Mike describes how he had limped up and down shouting, before sobbing like a child. Weeks later, he called in an old favour and submitted an early draft of his account to Lewis Ricci at the MoI. It was Ricci, a retired paymaster captain of the Royal Navy, who at the outbreak of war had secured Mike's recruitment after Burns had convinced him that minesweeping was compatible with his pacifist principles. Ricci read the draft and found it deeply moving but he was no more successful than Burns in having it cleared for publication by the MoI. Senior officials argued against authorisation on the grounds that publication would risk lowering morale.

Burns remained undeterred, however. He was convinced that Mike's writing would raise awareness not just of the sacrifice of British seamen but also the critical importance of protecting Allied convoys across the Atlantic, a message worth conveying to the American people. He encouraged Mike to hand his draft to their mutual friend the author Barbara Wall, née Lucas, who in turn passed it on to her sister, Sylvia Lucas, a literary agent in New York. The result was that 'Sunk by a Mine: A Survivor's Story' was published on 11 May 1941 in the *New York Times Magazine*, later winning the Llewellyn Rhys Memorial Prize for literature.

The Richeys were not the only ones from Burns's group of Catholic friends whom war was in the process of dispersing. A pattern of displacement and separation had set in which would last until well after Hitler had been defeated. A year had passed since Greene had published *The Power and the Glory*, a venture he owed to his Catholic publishing contacts. Burns had subsequently suggested that Greene write the biography of Father Damien, the Belgian leper colony priest who died from the disease, but this time nothing came of the idea. Instead Burns, on returning to London, discovered that Greene was close to joining MI6 and taking a posting in Sierra Leone after severing his links with the MoI. 'The MoI asked me to return the other day which gave me an opening for a cheery raspberry,' Greene wrote to Mary Pritchett in March 1941. While separated by geography and officially working for different departments, Burns and Greene were destined to move in similar intelligence circles in subsequent years. They were both drawn unwittingly into a world of deception and betrayal.

During the Second World War, Sierra Leone came within the orbit of Kim Philby's Iberian section, just as Madrid, Lisbon and Tangier did, with both Greene and Burns having to become involved in work that troubled their Catholic consciences. In his memoirs, *Ways of Escape*, Greene tells how he found himself abandoning an interrogation of a young Scandinavian seaman from Buenos Aires suspected of being a German spy. 'It was a form of dirty work for which I had not been engaged,' Greene reflected. Similarly, as the war progressed, Burns felt increasingly uncomfortable with the thought that one of the Spanish journalists posted to London, Luis Calvo, had ended up being humiliated at the hands of MI5 interrogators in a London detention camp.

But Burns still counted on as many friends as enemies within the

British Establishment. Over at the BBC, Harman Grisewood had leap-frogged from a relatively obscure post in Broadcasting House to a strategically key role as deputy head of the European Division in Bush House at a time when another Catholic, Ivone Kirkpatrick, a senior Foreign Office official, was promoted to the post of Director-General. 'Two Catholics,' Kirkpatrick warned Grisewood; 'some people will make trouble.'

But the expected protest never materialised. Instead Kirkpatrick and Grisewood forged an effective team while maintaining the loyalty and cooperation of other BBC staff. The partnership secured key allies for the policy being pursued by the British embassy in Madrid, an alliance Burns and his friend from debutante days, Grisewood, consolidated over several meetings at the Garrick Club.

Of the original coterie of friends, only the painter and poet David Jones continued to resist, diverting his creative energies away from what smacked of government service. And, unlike the poets Spender and Auden, he did not escape from the war by moving to America. Jones shared Burns's nostalgia for the life that had existed in London during the 1930s, as did Evelyn Waugh, and the bonds of faith-based friendship that struggled to survive.

Of the impact war had on such bonds, Burns would later write: 'There was realism in our own consciences, making for an independence of spirit, born of a dependence on God. That was the ultimate lesson of those years, ringing freedom from fear. Such a growth was like that of plants, best brought up in the dark. Call them hyacinth days. We were curiously happy when everything exploded.'

Jones knew that Burns's relationship with Ann Bowes-Lyon had ended and dissuaded him from trying to win her back. He wrote Burns another letter as he was planning his trip to London. 'I am sorry, dear Tom, about all this Ann thing. It's a bloody awful world, and these personal things are so intricate and chancy – and far worse to bear than these old stupid bombs . . . She appears to have made up her mind about this chap – and that being so – well, one has to take it so.'

Jones encouraged Burns not to cancel coming to London on leave, stressing how much he longed to meet up again and take up where they had left off, old friends bonding again over matters that endure. Jones wrote: 'As you say, you and I are mates, and I do hope we can scrape through these nasty years and have a nice breather afterwards somehow or other. I don't feel we shall be changed much, I don't think anything changes chaps really – jolly tough types, the human species.'

While Burns later alerted the Foreign Office and other government departments that he was coming to London, a letter to Jones detailing the date and time of his arrival never reached him. So Burns arrived at his house in Glebe Place unannounced. Given the bomb damage suffered by the neighbourhood, Burns was relieved to find number 3 still standing. He found Jones where he had last left him, in the sitting room, with Prudence Pelham, the artist's model and platonic lover.

Pelham's husband, the RAF pilot Guy Branch, had been killed in action and she was showing the early symptoms of the degenerative disease that would kill her after the war. Virtually bankrupt after unsuccessfully suing the Air Ministry for compensation, she was as delighted to see Burns as Jones was. It felt like a homecoming, however short-lived it turned out to be.

After Pelham had retired to bed, the two old friends stayed up drinking a great deal of whisky and reminiscing about old times. Burns's dark tabby cat Tim had followed the cleaner, Ethel, to another house. Jones had drawn Tim for posterity, and this image of him now occupied one side of the room, much as he had always done in reality, and they laughed, imagining him twirling his tail before diving off the sofa. It was the surest sign that Burns had begun to put the memory of Ann behind him. But nothing else could really stay the same. The only certainty was that the war would bring more destruction and death before it ended.

The next day Burns loaded his books and various items of furniture into a van and drove to a storage depot further north of the river he judged safer than Chelsea. Jones, for his part, reluctantly agreed to move himself, Prudence and his paintings to an artist's studio he had been lent in Onslow Square, in South Kensington. He was unconvinced by Burns's assurance that life would become cheaper and safer. Burns had taken heart from the fact that, in the early months of 1941, the air raids on London had virtually ceased. A tense interlude prevailed without any major German air strikes. Parliament now returned to its traditional

Tom Burns with publishing colleagues on a trip in 1929

Fr D'Arcy (*front, second from left*) at the opening of Campion Hall, with (*behind him*) Evelyn Waugh, (*to his left*) the Duke of Alba, (*second from right*) Mary Herbert and others

Hilaire Belloc
G. K. Chesterton
Evelyn Waugh
Graham Greene

Gabriel Herbert climbing mountains during the 1930s

Civil War in Madrid, 1936: Mabel (*left*) as a volunteer nurse

July 1936: Red Cross workers carry a victim of the Civil War fighting in Barcelona by stretcher to a waiting ambulance

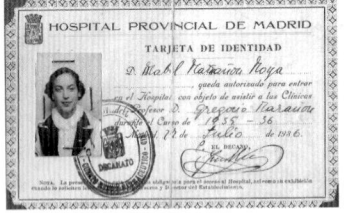

1936: Mabel's Civil War ID card

Gregorio Marañón Junior as a Franco volunteer before he worked in pro-Ally progaganda

Spanish Civil War refugees aboard HMS *Active*, bound for Marseille

Christmas 1936, voyage to exile: Francis Warrington-Strong, the Naval Officer on board HMS *Active*

May 1937: A Nazi parade aboard the German *Cap Arcona* as watched by Mabel and her father, on their return voyage from South America

Nelly Hess, the Jewish girlfriend who disappeared in German occupied Paris

1940: Mabel (*left*) with friends in German occupied Paris

June 14th, 1940: Dr Gregorio Marañón and colleague in Paris as the Germans march in

Irish journalist and Conservative Minister of Information, Brendan Bracken, looks on as Harry Lloyd Hopkins and Winston Churchill shake hands outside 10 Downing Street

Captain Alan Hillgarth, naval attaché and Churchill's eyes and ears

Two nurses watching British sculptor Eric Rowton Gill at work

David Jones, poet and artist

Ann Bowes-Lyon, 1937

Paul Richey in his Spitfire

Michael Richey in Naval
uniform, aboard HMS *Goodwill*

Courting Royalty: Burns and Ann Bowes-Lyon in 1938

January 1941: St Paul's during the Blitz. Nearby publishing houses, including Tom Burns's,
were destroyed.

French refugees c. 1940 fleeing the Nazi invasion to Spain

Niños mendigos

Demonstration of the Falangist Youth. Spain, 1941

Nazi leader German Chancellor Adolf Hitler shakes hands with Francisco Franco at Hendaye train station on the French–Spanish border, 23 October 1940

German press attaché in Madrid, Hans Lazar

Admiral Canaris, German spy chief

Tom Burns, winter in Madrid, 1941

On Her Majesty's Service: Burns with Spanish diplomat and propagandist the Conde de Foxa

Kim Philby

Guy Burgess

Anthony Blunt (*left*) at Cambridge

Enriqueta Harris with her brother Tomás in southern France in the 1930s

Serrano Súñer, General Franco and Mussolini

Alberto Martín Artajo, Spanish Foreign Minister, speaking to the Spanish military

Registration Certificate No. 659475.
Issued at Bow Street W.C.2
on 11th February 1938.
Name (Surname first in Roman Capitals) CALVO Luis
Left Thumb Print (if unable to sign name in English Characters)
Metropolitan Police Aliens Registration Office 14/2/38 Bow Street Station
Signature of Holder L. Calvo
Nationality Spanish
Born on 5/6/1898 Madrid
Previous Nationality (if any)
Profession or Occupation Journalist
Single or Married Married
Address of Residence Spanish Club, 5 Cavendish Square W.1
Arrival in United Kingdom on 1/2/1932
Address of last Residence outside U.K. 49 Palma Madrid, Spain
Government Service Spanish Army 1919 Spanish Embassy London 1/3/1932 until Sept. 1936
Passport or other papers as to Nationality and Identity. Spanish Ppt No 4 issued Guadalajara 28/1/1924

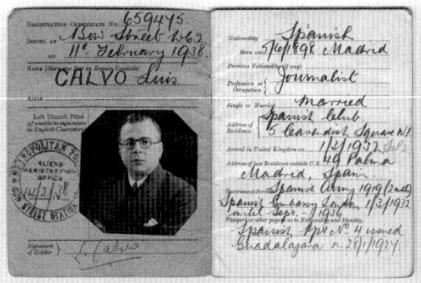

Luis Calvo's identity card at the time of his arrest by the British

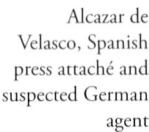

Alcazar de Velasco, Spanish press attaché and suspected German agent

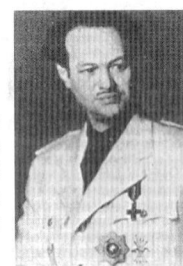

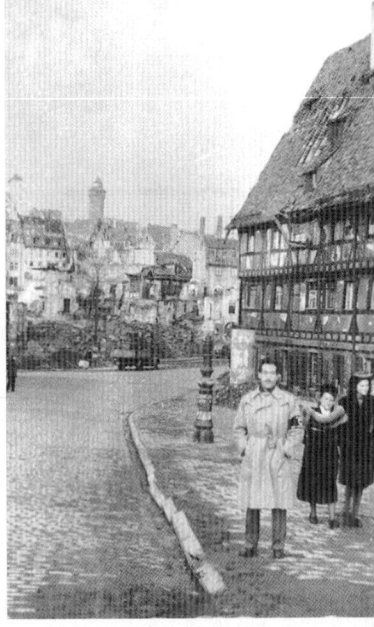

Spanish journalist Carlos Sentís in Germany, reporting on the Nuremburg trials

By permission of Juan Fernández-Armesto

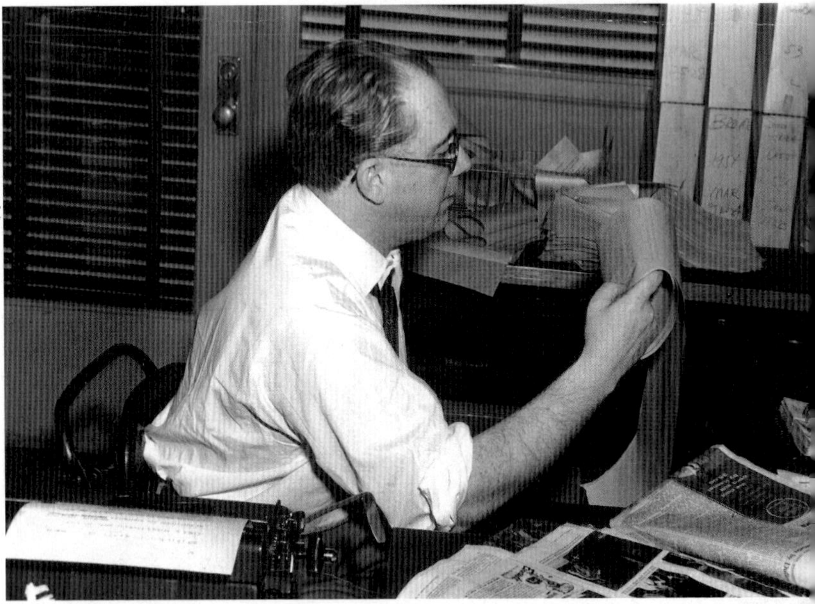

Spanish wartime journalist Felipe Fernández-Armesto

The Carcano sisters, daughters of Argentina's wartime London ambassador

The Duke of Alba, Spanish wartime ambassador

1943: 'Tana' Alba, Duchess of Montoro, by the pool in Albury Park

Tom Burns: Madrid, 1943

Mabel Marañón: Madrid, 1943

The Windsors on their arrival in Madrid, 1940

Tom Burns with embassy staff

Madrid, May 1943: Tom Burns plays host to Leslie Howard and Spanish actress Conchita Montenegro

Mabel at Belmonte's ranch

February 1945: The Burnses with embassy friends in a 'safe' restaurant on outskirts of Madrid.

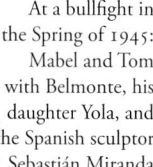

At a bullfight in the Spring of 1945: Mabel and Tom with Belmonte, his daughter Yola, and the Spanish sculptor Sebastián Miranda

The Burns wedding, April 1944: Mabel with Sir Samuel Hoare

Hoare's wife Lady Maud with Mabel's father Dr Gergorio Marañón at the Burns wedding

Juan Belmonte, bullfighter and best man, signs the register

The newly married Burnses leaving the Church of Los Jeronimos

Cutting the wedding cake

The wedding cake made by
Mrs Taylor, showing Spanish
and British flags

The reception: cocktails by Chicote

May 1944: on honeymoon
on the Costa del Sol

May 1944: Burns at Arthur Yencken's funeral in Madrid

8th May, 1945, Madrid: British embassy staff celebrate VE day

The author with his father

home in the House of Commons, and Churchill began using Number 10 Downing Street rather more often than his underground cabinet rooms to conduct government business. But such 'normality' proved short-lived. The Luftwaffe resumed its bombing with a vengeance, first on the ports around Britain and then on London, again. There were two heavy raids on the capital on 16 and 17 April, just after Burns had returned to Madrid. There was a third, much heavier raid on 10 May, the anniversary of Churchill becoming prime minister, during which a bomb hit the depot in which Burns had recently stored his books and other possessions, destroying everything.

9

BLACK ARTS

Hours after bidding his latest farewell to his London friends, Burns found himself bobbing about in a dinghy in Southampton Water, waiting to be ferried to a flying boat that was due to take off as soon as the all-clear sounded.

The flying boat belonged to the old Imperial Airways fleet which had been taken over by BOAC in 1940. Its route was London to Cairo via Lisbon and Gibraltar. It was one of two passenger services operating between the UK and the Iberian Peninsula. The other involved a squadron of DC3s that were operated by KLM out of Heston.

Neither these planes, nor those flown by Lufthansa from Madrid to Berlin or the transatlantic Pan Am Clippers to Spain, were attacked by fighters of either side in the first two years of the war. Nevertheless, by 1941 pilots knew they were running greater risks and their routes were becoming circuitous.

The flight Burns took from Southampton flew several hundred miles out into the Atlantic before landing in Lisbon, some seven and half hours later. From there Burns took the overnight train to Madrid. The Spanish capital, as spring turned to summer in 1941, had been badly affected by an outbreak of typhoid, as had many parts of Spain, a reminder of the poor hygiene and diet that persisted in a country recently ravaged by civil war and denied normal trade by a partial embargo imposed by the Allies and the corruption of local officials and middle men who benefited from it.

Nevertheless, for those lucky enough to be employed by the British embassy in Madrid life seemed peaceful, the weather seductive, with a working day that accommodated a long lunch and siesta and no shortage of decent provisions. The food was brought up in unidentified vans direct from Gibraltar or across the border from Lisbon.

'I am installed at present in a luxurious hotel (which I can neither pronounce nor remember exactly its whereabouts!) ... everything is extremely expensive and I was wise to get stocked up with some "extras" in Lisbon where the exchange is better ... office hours here follow the Spanish custom – 10–2 and then 4.00 till 8.30. I shall get ravenous until I get used to it', wrote Rosemary Say, a recent young embassy recruit from the Ministry of Economic Warfare in a letter to her parents.

By the second year of the war, Burns was himself living in some comfort. He had settled into a large apartment in Calle Serrano, Madrid's smartest street, lined with fashionable shops and cafés, that cut through, as it does today, one of Madrid's wealthiest neighbourhoods. Its balcony caught the fresh breeze coming down from the Sierra in the early morning and the sunlight in the early evening.

In addition to a full-time maid, cook and team of messenger boys, and a car, Burns had acquired a vivacious black spaniel he named Juerga – which in Spain means a 'riotous time'. Most evenings Burns went out for dinner, to a private party or a nightclub where he showed off his tango and rumba. As it did for other spies, the Pasapoga became a favourite haunt, its large, ornate ballroom usually so packed that it was easy to lose oneself in the crowd.

As a single, good-looking diplomat, Burns found himself even more in demand than when he and Evelyn Waugh had mixed with the bright young things in the hedonistic pre-war London days. In the British embassy, young female recruits – employed in activities ranging from administrative secretarial tasks to transmitting top-secret coded messages, the so-called 'cipher girls' – outnumbered the male members of staff.

Far from home, in a relatively relaxed posting, with the added frisson of feeling that one was part of a covert mission against Nazi Germany – all this ensured that embassy life in wartime Spain was characterised by fleeting affairs and marriage break-ups due to the infidelity of one partner or the other.

'Poor Peter, it would never have worked,' one of the embassy secretaries confided to her friend Rosemary. The unidentified lover was one of several the letter writer maintained both before and after getting married while posted in Madrid. 'I felt (I feel) so much for him but it isn't the kind of emotion, or the calm friendly relationship, on which to base a permanent relationship. Domesticity would have killed it in two months . . . But I still derive much comfort from feeling he is in Madrid and not too far away and I can see him sometimes.'

War service in Spain included time off for travel and leisure within a country that, unlike most of the rest of Europe, was no longer a battle ground. Rosemary Say combined her secret work for the embassy with travel across Spain. Her letters home reflected the excitement of an English girl finding Spain and its culture different from anything she had experienced before – and loving it.

Nonetheless the menace of Nazi Germany often seemed to be close at hand, however apparently idyllic the setting. Her boyfriends included a Spanish bullfighter and a Dutch POW escapee.

After visiting Barcelona, Rosemary wrote to her parents about a group of German Nazis she had come across during a romantic weekend she had spent at a villa on the Costa Brava. 'It seemed unreal to be suddenly on a sandy beach, with a very bright blue Mediterranean (lovely and warm) and the mountains coming right down to the water . . . I went on a very riotous flamenco party, and managed to restrain my partner from hitting a particularly blond version of the "chosen race" fair and square – it is extremely difficult to "share" small restaurants and cafés with these people as they are always nauseatingly aggressive.'

Rosemary worked from a separate building to Burns but the two moved in similar social circles. They remained good colleagues for most of the war without becoming emotionally attached. It was not always thus for the press attaché. As he tried to put his infatuation with Ann Bowes-Lyon behind him, Burns engaged in a number of short-lived relationships, his girlfriends ranging from bluestocking personal assistants from the Home Counties to aristocratic *Madrileñas*. If Burns still longed for true love, the spy in him played havoc with his emotions, his job a continuing juggling act between diplomacy, deception and subterfuge and his apparent philandering a subject of obsessive interest to those who wished to undermine him.

Among Burns's young Spanish girlfriends few attracted as much attention as Conchita Olivares. The vivacious aristocratic socialite and fluent English speaker regularly attended parties at the British embassy, where she was often to be seen in intimate conversation with Burns.

At least, that is what one of MI5's agents, José Brugada, the assistant press attaché at the Spanish embassy in London, code-named Peacock, claimed on the basis of a visit to Madrid in July 1943. 'Source says that Burns is madly in love with Conchita Olivares,' the agent's handler, Broomham-White, subsequently reported to Philby and Harris.

The agent had drawn attention to the well-known fact that Olivares was the daughter of the 'anti-British' Spanish consul general in London and the sister-in-law of the Marqués of Murrieta, suspected by elements within MI5 and MI6 of being actively pro-Axis.

Broomham-White went on to report: 'The source says girl, who is constantly in touch with the Germans and Italians, trails Burns round in her wake to all the Madrid parties, and that he is the laughing stock of the town. Source's own view is that Burns, who he likes personally, is bringing a lot of discredit to the British name, and should be recalled at once.'

For all her family connections, there was no collaborative evidence or information to substantiate the idea that Burns was betraying state secrets to Olivares. On the contrary, Burns made no attempt to hide his short-lived affair with Olivares from his ambassador, and was happy to pass on to his most trusting colleagues in the embassy the small bits of intelligence he gleaned from her on pro-Axis Spaniards and the Germans.

The personal file MI5 kept on Burns contains two entries on the alleged 'German agent' Olivares, after which the subject is dropped, presumably because of a lack of any further incriminating facts on what, anyway, proved a relatively short-lived mutual passion.

Burns's enemies in British intelligence nevertheless believed they had detected a human weakness in their target, and around this time tasked one of their female agents working in the British embassy to seduce Burns and build a case against him as a potential traitor.

What was fed back by the small-time Mata Hari, identified only as M 12, but probably his personal assistant Olive Stock, suggested that a traitor he was not.

While M 12 confirmed that Burns had 'right wing political sympathies', he was not, in her view, 'an extreme fascist'. Her report went on: 'Burns interprets his duties as being chiefly to keep as far as possible in the good books of the Spanish authorities . . . the reason, or one of the reasons for this is . . . the fact that Burns is "half-Spanish" and finds himself perhaps more in sympathy with the Spaniards than others of his purely English colleagues.'

M 12 thought it 'quite possible' that Burns was too easily influenced by the over-enthusiasm of some of his Spanish friends and thus might interpret 'what may be a warm interest in his work and information as evidence of genuine friendship'. Nevertheless she had concluded that 'Burns is fairly shrewd and better informed about Spain – or at least Franco's Spain – than many of his other compatriots'.

If MI5 had hoped to find evidence that agent M 12 had successfully drawn Burns into a honey trap, they were surely disappointed. As her handler reported: 'M 12's opinions . . . were arrived at quite coldly and do not seem to be biased by any friendship which may exist between her and Burns . . . M 12 cannot remember any indiscretions – or evidence of a tendency towards indiscretions – made by Burns . . .'

M 12's own views, based on a considered assessment of the target, were largely sympathetic towards Burns, identifying him as a man prepared to think outside the box of government bureaucracy and be guided by his instincts and specialist knowledge.

'M 12 thinks that Burns may quite easily have given the impression of being a difficult man from the FO [Foreign Office] point of view in so far as he may think that our propaganda in Spain is not suited entirely to the needs of Spain at the moment and may give it a twist to suit what he thinks to be the best line of attack,' her report concluded: 'Further that he may think that our Foreign Office is not as well informed as to the Spanish situation as he is himself.'

It was clearly not what those who had commissioned the report wanted to hear. It confirmed Burns as a dynamic entity within the British embassy, and, in effect, at the sharp end of Anglo-Spanish relations.

By 1942, Burns's 'press office' had mushroomed into the British embassy's biggest section with its own separate building and more than 120 British and local permanent and part-time employees. Burns's team of assistant press attachés had been boosted to include John Walters and John Stordy, fellow Catholics trained in intelligence and propaganda with specialist knowledge in Spanish affairs.

Walters came from a prestigious newspaper family that owned a majority shareholding in *The Times*. Before being recruited by Burns, with his ambassador's approval, Walters had been working in the intelligence corps in Gibraltar. Stordy had previously worked in the Spanish department of the MoI in London and was relocated to Madrid with the backing of MI5's Harris, MI6's Philby and his former boss Billy McCann on the assumption that he would act as a further informant on Burns.

'Although Stordy is a strong Roman Catholic and has a leaning towards the Right, he is very moderate in his views on Spanish Affairs. McCann describes him as unbiased loyal and a fine character and adds that he is not a protégé of Burns,' Harris reassured Philby on Stordy's appointment in January 1942.

They had overlooked the fact that Stordy had as an adolescent been at the Jesuit Stonyhurst College with Burns, and that the old schoolboy ties had endured. As the war developed, Stordy, along with Walters, came to consider Burns a good colleague and confidante. Stordy counted on Burns's help to extradite him from a short-lived marriage, with Burns providing a witness statement, as a fellow Catholic, that suggested the union should be declared null and void in the eyes of the Church. Walters, a heavy drinker, came to increasingly rely on Burns to protect him from those within the embassy that thought his alcoholism was a liability.

The location of the embassy's press section was equidistant between the passport/visa building used as cover by a section of the intelligence services, and the main chancery building which housed the ambassador, several attachés and the special annexe for POWs and refugees.

Viewed from the street, the press section's three-storey stone building in Orfila Street had little to distinguish it from the other turn-of-the-century Parisian-style buildings of the neighbourhood. Access to the ground floor was through an unassuming garage door behind which was a store room filled with paper and magazines and next to it a library and reading room. The printing works were in a windowless annexe which gave on to an inner courtyard. A staircase wound up to the first floor where there was a reception area and behind it two large interconnected living rooms leading to a corridor of small offices and a back room filled with radio transmitters, communications equipment and a film projector.

The two main rooms were transformed into a cinema at least once a week, with seating for more than three hundred, a gathering place for the firmly pro-Allied local community, and those sitting on the fence waiting to see which side in the hostilities would prevail – although, as the war progressed, the invitation list drew increasingly on the firmly converted.

An invitation list surviving from early 1944 shows the degree of support on which the British counted for their well-oiled propaganda machinery. In addition to senior US and other Allied diplomats, guests ranged from leading representatives of the Spanish nobility, such as the Marqueses de Quintanar and Miraflores, to sources the British had developed within the Franco regime such as Pedro Gamero and the dictator's interpreter, Barón de las Torres. Others included the film maker Edgar Neville, the painter Zuloaga and the leading newspaper columnist Manuel Aznar, grandfather of a future prime minister of Spain, José María Aznar.

In a separate room Burns's assistant Bernard Malley ran an additional enterprise assisted by qualified medical staff as part of the UK's hearts and minds campaign: an unofficial emergency health service free at the point of delivery. For, stored in a refrigerated back room of His Majesty's Government's press section, was a stock of imported medicines which were financed by another secret British government slush fund and smuggled in through the diplomatic bag.

Other core staff employed under Burns's management included shorthand typists, cipher clerks, radio transmitters and a resident priest who liaised with senior figures of the Catholic Church.

The third floor, officially part of the British mission, acted as cover for the operations of local representatives of the French Resistance, who worked closely with the escape routes the embassy organised. The majority of non-administrative staff in the building was made up of Spaniards working eight-hour shifts on the printing machines that day and night churned out pro-Allied information, much of it thinly veiled propaganda drawn from the BBC, the Ministry of Information and the Special Operations Executive (SOE). Burns's network of messengers, couriers and general dogsbodies included a group of some thirty Spanish boys aged between eleven and fifteen. The boys were summoned by a system of internal bells linked to the main embassy and paid five pesetas a day. Underage and underpaid, they nevertheless felt themselves lucky to have survived the civil war, privileged to be serving the Allied cause not least because it provided them with regular meals.

José Luis García was among those employed as a messenger by Burns at the time. An only child, he was eight years old when, on 31 July 1939, days after Franco's victory, his father and uncle – both Republican sympathisers – were taken out of a detention centre and executed by firing squad for alleged subversion. Three years later, he was told by his widowed mother that she could no longer afford to support him and that he would have to find work and not go on begging in the street. Franco had introduced a new law on anti-social behaviour, whereby child beggars were forcefully taken from the streets and placed in boarding schools run by nuns and female volunteers of the Falange movement.

Widows of Republican prisoners shunned such institutions, believing that their only purpose was to brainwash a new generation of destitute working-class Spaniards into allegiance to the fascist regime. José Luis was encouraged by his mother to seek work she believed was more in keeping with his late father's ideals.

The boy worked principally for the British embassy's press department, helping distribute the bulletin or running personal errands for Burns, including walking his dog, which provided additional cover whenever he thought he was being followed by the police.

'Each in our own way, we were all playing spy games . . . I may not have been conscious of it at the time but I know that the people I worked with would not have been true to their mission if they hadn't also been involved in intelligence. They had the contacts and a lot of information . . .' recalled José Luis many years later.

'What I did feel was that the Germans were all over the place and that there were members of the Spanish police that acted as if they were under the direct orders of the Gestapo . . . They were constantly harassing anyone employed by the embassy . . . I remember they arrested and interrogated for two days Paquita Fernández, the massagist of the ambassador's wife . . . They also beat up one of my mates while he was delivering a package.'

Burns was among the embassy staff that used Republicans who, young and old, had survived the civil war as a source of intelligence in working-class districts of Madrid and other towns. It was a high-risk strategy for the Spaniards involved, for there was little support from the embassy if they fell into police hands. Among the Republicans who returned from exile in France after the Spanish Civil War, and with whom Burns is thought to have had some secret contacts, was the socialist painter and writer Francisco Mateos. According to a report filed by Burns, a Spaniard answering to that name and profession was arrested and tortured by Spanish police after being observed on several occasions meeting the British press attaché. Weeks later, Mateos wrote to Burns, telling him he had been freed after denying that he had supplied the British embassy with information on Republicans who had been shot but signing a statement that he had been commissioned to write some anti-fascist propaganda. He said he was anxious to resume his work as an agent.

In his report, Burns raised the suspicion that Mateos had been released with the purpose of feeding him with false information. The MI5 file in which the report is included contains no further information. Francisco Mateos survived the Second World War and died in 1976. The details of what further covert contacts he may have had with the British remain unclear.

While dozens of Spaniards like Mateos were used as agents by both the British and the Americans during the Second World War, the encouragement of political opposition to the Franco regime was restricted under the terms of an official policy of non-intervention in internal Spanish politics.

Only with one sector of Spanish politics did the British embassy pursue serious covert discussions about a possible alternative regime to Franco's. Throughout the war Burns was among the few members of the embassy staff authorised by the ambassador to maintain contacts with exiled non-communist political figures in Lisbon such as José María Gil Robles and Pedro Sainz Rodríguez who favoured the restoration of a constitutional monarchy.

Burns used his visits to Lisbon to gain intelligence on the political manoeuvrings of Spanish exiles. He discussed possible Allied support for a negotiated transition to constitutional rule in Spain but remained unconvinced that the opposition to Franco was sufficiently united to offer a stable political alternative.

As Burns saw it, part of the problem lay in the political ambiguity of the so-called monarchists who had strongly backed Franco in the civil war only then to profess themselves democratic constitutionalists. British intelligence reports from Rome drew attention to the close friendship the exiled King Alfonso XIII had developed with Mussolini. The democratic credentials of the monarchists had been further undermined as a result of a lunch a close aide to Prince Juan had had in Madrid with Hans Lazar. At the meeting, the German press attaché had been reassured that the monarchist camp supported the Axis.

'A mild form of wishful thinking conspiracy was kindled occasionally by lengthy luncheons but I learnt to expect nothing by way of action,' Burns wrote later. 'The court of Juan Alonso, pretender to the [Spanish] throne in remote Estoril, had an Oriental immobility about it.'

It was a year since Hillgarth had been personally entrusted by Churchill to use a British intelligence slush fund of $10 million to dissuade a group of senior Spanish army officers – referred to by the British as the 'Knights of St George' (because of the image of St George on the face of the British gold sovereign) – from siding with the Axis powers and entering the war on Hitler's side.

US intelligence documents declassified in recent years have suggested that the more influential 'Knights' included General Antonío Aranda, the Captain-General of the Valencia region, General Luis Orgaz, commander-in-chief of Spanish Morocco, and General Alfredo Kindelán, commander of the Balearic Islands, and that monies intended to suborn them and other generals were deposited in a New York bank account. The plot nearly fell apart in 1941 when the US Treasury suspected that Juan March – the Spanish entrepreneur who had helped finance Franco's uprising in the Spanish Civil War and acted with some of his generals as a conduit for the British – was using the money to support Hitler, although this suspicion subsequently dissipated.

In May 1941, General Juan Vigón, Franco's chief of staff during the civil war, warned the Spanish head of state that he would face a mass resignation by his military ministers if he did not curtail the power of his brother-in-law Serrano Súñer. Franco reacted by carrying out a cabinet reshuffle which left Serrano Súñer in post but ostensibly strengthened the hand of the generals against the pro-Axis Falange party. The outcome of the crisis was viewed by one of Churchill's most senior ministers as evidence that Hillgarth's plan had borne fruit. 'In Spain, the Knights of St George have charged: it is thanks to them that certain recent changes have been brought about,' enthused Hugh Dalton, the Minister of Economic Warfare. His enthusiasm, based on supposition rather than firm evidence of a link between the cabinet crisis and covert bribes, proved premature.

In July 1940 Dalton had taken charge of the fledgling SOE, an organisation devoted to sabotage, subversion and black propaganda. In what became knows as the SOE's founding mission statement, or 'high command', Dalton had declared: 'We have got to organise movements in enemy-occupied territory comparable to the Sinn Feín movement in Ireland, to the Chinese guerrillas now operating in Japan, to the Spanish irregulars who played a notable part in Wellington's campaign.'

SOE officers based in Madrid prepared excitedly for the worst-case scenario – a German occupation of the Iberian Peninsula – and proposed to Burns that his department provide extra cover for some additional operatives. The Foreign Office separately sent the embassy secret instructions specifically aimed at protecting the department Burns was in charge of.

Under the heading 'arrangements for Press Section Staff in the event of German Invasion of Portugal and Spain', it recommended that the Barcelona and Lisbon staff be reassigned to the Portuguese colonies, initially leaving Burns behind in charge of a 'compact unit' together with Bernard Malley for the purpose of 'advice, information, and liaison' prior to a full-scale occupation. 'If Spain enters war against us and relations severed suggest Malley invaluable in London. Burns should go to London or South America', the telegram recommended.

Under the contingency plans drawn up by SOE, Burns agreed to help recruit additional agents, and – rather than agree to a redeployment outside Spain as suggested by the Foreign Office – volunteered to go underground in Spain. 'The "merchants bankers" [SOE] suggested that I lie low in a monastery for a spell. I do not think they had any contact with any religious community, or with much else for that matter,' Burns wrote in his memoirs.

The comment reflected the growing scepticism with which Burns came to regard the usefulness of such proposed 'gung-ho' special operations in Spain. That scepticism had its roots in the summer of 1940, when Burns was being transferred from the Ministry of Information in London to the British embassy in Madrid. At the time, the as yet undiscovered Soviet agent Guy Burgess was working in Section D (for Destruction), a branch of the War Office, as a propaganda expert.

In July 1940, Burgess had already recruited to his section his friend Kim Philby. That Burgess, with Philby's blessing, went on to draft a scheme for a training centre called 'Guy Fawkes College' was not without irony. The two communists had named their scheme after a fanatical Catholic whose conspiracy to blow up the Houses of Parliament – against the wishes of many of his Catholic peers – had been foiled by Sir Francis Walsingham, the British state's first spymaster.

Later that summer Section D was disbanded and some of its operations transferred to Dalton's SOE, although the influence of Burgess and Philby within the political and intelligence establishment would continue for a good while yet. One of Dalton's first acts was to appoint Colonel Colin Gubbins as Director of Training and Operations.

Burns met Gubbins while on a visit to London. In a rare reference to his links with the world of espionage and special operations, Burns writes: 'There had been very short visits to London . . . the third was spent in more colourful company: with various Intelligence officers and the SOE where Colonel Gubbins reigned. He took me to dinner with Guy Burgess whom I disliked on sight. "Set Europe ablaze!" had been Churchill's call to SOE. I scented contingency plans to apply this injunction to Spain if necessary and argued against it forcibly, knowing more than they did of the desert that it would create.'

Burns feared that unleashing the SOE on the Spanish would reignite the revolutionary agitation he had opposed during the civil war and which he regarded as a source of division and brutality.

Plans for a twin-tracked policy of propaganda and subversion within SOE continued to be put forward for Spain and Portugal. A strategic directive from the Chiefs of Staffs (COS) in November 1940 included preparing for guerrilla warfare and the destruction of communications on the Iberian Peninsula. A case was also made by SOE's headquarters in Baker Street for an expansion of 'irregular political activities', encouraging the SOE's stations in neutral Europe to cultivate contacts across the political spectrum, from government officials to clandestine members of the opposition who might offer an alternative government system.

Under some pressure from London, Hoare allowed SOE to open a base in Spain in February 1941, but on the condition that its operations were vetted by the naval attaché Hillgarth, who in turn liaised closely on the issue with other trusted members of the embassy staff, with a direct line to the ambassador, notably Burns. While SOE trained bands of Republican volunteers in Scotland, and established some discreet contacts in Spain, it was kept on a tight rein, and had little involvement with Hillgarth's bribery of Franco's generals, which was designed to keep out Germans rather than to provoke an internal anti-Franco coup.

When Burns, Hillgarth and Hoare were recalled to London for consultation in the summer of 1941, all three argued strongly in their meetings across Whitehall and with MPs against any British military intervention in Spain, because they believed Britain's war effort was better served by a 'quiet Peninsula'.

While Burns was in London he also touched touch base with his old department at the MoI on an issue that troubled him as much as it did many people, including Churchill – the continuing refusal of the American government to declare war.

Burns believed that US support both in terms of economic aid to the country and military involvement against the German army elsewhere in Europe and Africa would help bring Spanish public opinion firmly behind the Allied cause, convincing them that a German victory was no longer possible.

In September 1941, at Burns's request and with the backing of the MoI, Father D'Arcy flew to the United States. He was to use a series of lectures, interviews with local media and discreet meetings to generate support for US intervention among the Catholic community in which the majority of Italian and Irish immigrants remained largely against the war. D'Arcy's presence in the US coincided with the growing involvement in anti-Nazi propaganda of Joseph Hurley, an influential American bishop who had previously worked in secret diplomacy at the Vatican. During the war, Hurley worked independently of the Vatican bureaucracy and other American bishops, developing secret ties with the Roosevelt administration, the US office of War Information, and what his biographer described as 'the lower echelons of British intelligence' in a pro-Allied propaganda campaign.

The following spring, weeks after Roosevelt had declared war following the Japanese attack on Pearl Harbor, ill health forced Alexander Weddell, the American ambassador in Madrid, to resign. The move was greeted with relief by Burns, who had to come believe that no good was to be gained by the ambassador's conflicting relationship with the Spanish authorities, and that a more tactful approach to dealing with the idiosyncrasies of local politics was needed to ensure neutrality.

Weddell's succession by Carlton Hayes seemed heaven-sent to Burns, who had managed in a remarkably short time to manoeuvre himself into a key position of influence with some of his American colleagues. A professor of modern European history at Columbia University, New York, Hayes had been pulled out of academic life and thrown into his new job with a clear objective in mind. Both the US State Department and the White House hoped that Hayes's knowledge of Spanish history, Catholicism and sympathy for the Franco cause would help him navigate better the tortuous politics of wartime Spain, and guarantee its neutrality as the Allies prepared a new offensive against Hitler.

On 1 June 1942 Hayes wrote to fellow Catholic General William J. 'Wild Bill' Donovan, Roosevelt's special envoy on Spain and founding head of the OSS, sharing his conviction that, although the Spanish government was still outwardly pro-Axis, the Spanish masses felt first and foremost Spanish and were more anti-German than anti-American. The case Hayes put for a steadily intensifying and expanding barrage of propaganda as a key weapon to be used against Nazi influence in Spain was influenced by the example set by the British embassy and the arguments put forward by one of its members of staff in particular: 'The British have a large organisation which is doing splendid work, but its director, Mr T. F. Burns, frankly admits that Spaniards will pay more attention to Americans than to the British and that the British work does not touch certain basic matters which American propaganda can and should deal with, such as American war preparedness and production, American scientific developments, American films, attitude of American Catholic prelates and intellectuals towards Nazism, the relations of the United States to Latin America (and vice versa) and the grim determination of America to win the war and to help impose a just peace . . .'

In the following weeks, Hayes was granted the financial resources to develop the US presence in Madrid in a way that mirrored the British, increasing its diplomatic staff, building up a new propaganda unit and developing its intelligence-gathering capability.

British intelligence for its part came up with an ingenious plan aimed principally at breeding distrust between Franco and the Germans while disrupting the operations of the Abwehr. Kim Philby, by then head of the Iberian section of MI6's Section V, delivered to the British embassy in Madrid a dossier alleging that the Germans were developing a secret submarine-tracking system across the Strait of Gibraltar.

The information on so-called Operation Bodden, according to Philby, was based on the breaking by the British of German intelligence ciphers covering communications between Berlin and Abwehr stations in the Gibraltar area. It was in no small measure due to Philby's access and use of these decrypts that the Soviet spy managed to win the trust of the head of MI6, Sir Stewart Menzies.

In his memoirs Philby claims that by the middle of 1942 he had considered and then discarded the possibility of engaging SOE agents in sabotage operations against the Germans on Spanish soil. Somewhat disingenuously, he suggests that the decision was his only, when in fact it was taken under pressure from others in Whitehall who did not share his ideological belief in fuelling revolutionary turmoil in Franco's 'fascist state'. He wrote: 'I doubted whether anyone on our side would welcome a James-Bond-like free-for-all in Spain, where the authorities would have been against us. On reflection, it seemed that the diplomatic approach would be the best.'

Information about Bodden was shared within the British embassy in Madrid and a decision taken to bring it to the attention of the Spanish authorities in the form of a formal diplomatic protest. However, the position of those like Burns who argued against anything that might risk a subversive 'free-for-all' by British special forces had been strengthened by two badly bungled SOE operations which provoked embarrassing diplomatic fallout.

The first involved Jack Beevor, SOE's main representative in Portugal, where President Salazar was regarded by the British as a more reliably pro-Allied head of state than Franco. At the outset of war, Beevor was working as a junior partner at the London law firm Slaughter & May when he and several other members of staff were recruited by SOE and other intelligence departments. (Another of the firm's partners, Harry Sporborg, served as assistant to the SOE chief Gubbins, while a third, George Vickers, became Director General of the Foreign Office's Economic Intelligence Division.)

Beevor was posted to Portugal under cover of assistant military attaché with the brief of coordinating clandestine resistance to the Germans, and, if needs be, to the Salazar government, using sabotage and helping the general intelligence-gathering effort in neighbouring Spain. By the end of 1941 Beevor believed he had succeeded, against the odds, in putting together a network of agents, and in countering German influence by working closely with Captain Hillgarth, the intelligence supremo in Madrid, and his Spanish business ally Juan March. Beevor followed Hillgarth's lead in deploying the 'cavalry of St George' – in other words, bribing certain officials in the Salazar regime to support the Allies and neutralise German influence.

One of Beevor's more notable successes was in organising the kidnap of a senior Abwehr officer, using a female MI6 agent to draw him into a honey trap. The agent was told by Beevor to arrange an assignation on a secluded beach outside Lisbon. When he arrived for the meeting, the German was snatched by an SOE team, and flown back to England before his embassy had time to alert the authorities that he had gone missing. In early 1942, however, SOE's operations in Portugal were severely disrupted when the Portuguese secret police infiltrated and exposed Beevor's underground networks which included members of the local Communist Party.

Within days, a British diplomatic bag sent from Gibraltar exploded in the port of Tangier, killing a number of Moroccans and Spaniards as well as a British consular employee. The news provoked instant recriminations between the various British intelligence and military departments that operated in wartime Gibraltar, competing for control under the nominal leadership of the colonial governor.

A subsequent internal British government enquiry revealed that limpet mines which SOE had planned to use in an operation against the Germans had detonated prematurely after being assembled and packed on the Rock and transported by ferry across the Strait. Fearing that Franco would react by expelling British embassy and consular staff, and that other intelligence activities might be compromised, MI6 and MI5, as well as the Foreign Office, moved quickly to distance themselves from any involvement in the incident, and blamed it on SOE's professional incompetence, as well as political naivety. The row forced SOE's chief in Gibraltar, Peter Quennell, to resign and reinforced Ambassador's Hoare's demands to have all SOE military operations in Spain and Portugal effectively closed down.

Philby's subsequent caution about the use of special operations in Spain was part of a general reining in of SOE's operations across neutral countries in the aftermath of the Lisbon and Tangier incidents. Thereafter, Allied intelligence in Spain and Portugal was forced to rely on the decryption of the German Enigma cipher by the Government Code and Cipher School at Bletchley Park, with propaganda, deception and diplomacy – overt as well as secret – as the favoured non-military tools in combating the enemy.

For what remained of the war, and during its aftermath, Philby barely managed to hide his dislike for Hoare, a man whose innate conservatism was at odds ideologically with the spy's communism and who had a tendency to rely on the counsel of Catholics sympathetic to the Franco cause in the Spanish Civil War. 'It is difficult to write nice things about Sir Samuel,' he wrote, but he conceded that, over Operation Bodden, 'he rose to the occasion magnificently' by confronting Franco directly and in effect accusing him of complicity with German covert operations. Hoare, once briefed by MI6, dressed his senior members of staff in full uniform, and took them as a team to see Franco and issue a strongly worded complaint.

At the end of September 1942 Hoare and his US counterpart, Hayes, were secretly notified that the Allies planned an invasion of French North Africa. Burns was among a small group of Allied staff in Madrid with whom the news was subsequently shared on a 'need to know basis'. Those in charge of propaganda work came together in a carefully coordinated plan to ensure that Franco and others in the regime did not react to the Allied operation by allowing the Germans to mount a counter-offensive south of the Pyrenees.

By now Burns had a new American colleague and fellow Catholic with whom he could collaborate on diplomatic and covert activities. Emmet Hughes had been sent as a replacement for Tom Crain, who had suffered a nervous breakdown due to overwork and had returned to the US. Under the cover of press attaché, Hughes worked for the OSS and the Office of War Information, which was broadly modelled on Britain's Ministry of Information.

At the diplomatic level Burns and Hughes made a formidable team, combining to reassure their sources in the highest echelons of the Franco regime – both military and civilian – that Spanish sovereignty was not in jeopardy. They also offered an additional carrot in the form of increasing economic assistance.

As for the 'prescription for propaganda', as Hughes described it, this involved the Allies wielding a big stick. The main priority was to emphasise to the Spanish people and their rulers the swift Allied conversion of war *potential* into war *might*, thanks to increasing US involvement alongside the British, thus countering any notion that a German victory was either possible or preferable.

Two months earlier, continuing tension within the Franco regime between the Falange party and the military had led to the replacement of Serrano Súñer as foreign minister by General Count Francisco Gómez Jordana. Jordana had served as Franco's foreign minister between the end of the civil war and the beginning of the Second World War before being sacked because he was deemed to be insufficiently sympathetic towards the Axis cause.

Jordana's return to government generated positive signals from the British and American embassies. In his memoirs, Burns recalled his own sense of expectation thus: 'The Spain that I had come into was being transformed, power was passing to the new technocrats, and Falangism was on the way out, its fiery foreign minister, Serrano Súñer, had been replaced by the cautious and courteous General Jordana. General Franco remained aloof, enigmatic, in total control.'

Such optimism proved premature. With his well-honed tactic of playing one opposing force against the other so as to ensure his own survival, Franco also sacked the pro-Allied army chief General Iglesias Varela, and replaced him with the pro-German General Carlos Asensio Cabanillas. The latest government reshuffle meant that neither Britain nor the US could be sure that Franco would not mobilise the 15,000-strong garrison in Spanish Morocco to reinforce French Resistance or acquiesce in a German attack on Gibraltar.

Plans for an Allied occupation of the Spanish Canary Islands were revived in London and Washington. From Madrid, Ambassador Hoare, with the support of Hayes, strongly argued against such a move. He warned that an attack on the islands would risk embroiling the Allies in a war with Spain and wipe out any chance of keeping the Spanish as a buffer between the Germans in France and the Allied Anglo-American expeditionary force in North Africa. The Combined Chiefs of Staff were persuaded to put the plan on ice.

Instead, on Saturday 7 November 1942, both embassies received a coded cable confirming that the first great offensive of the united Allied forces, on the success of which depended the fate of the entire war, was going ahead: *Thunderbird november eight two am spanish time.*

Detailed instructions on how ambassadors should proceed, with only a small group of senior trusted officials in the know, were encrypted with a secret British code, deemed safer than any of the American ones. The US ambassador Hayes approached Jordana first with a personal message from President Roosevelt. Hoare, meanwhile, consulted with his deputy head of mission Yencken and Burns and sent a similar message of reassurance from Churchill.

In the preceding hours, Hoare, on the advice of his officials, had spent much of that Saturday adopting 'an attitude of unconcern'. He stayed away from the embassy, maintained communications silence with London and avoided any meetings with Spanish officials. Instead he engaged in the Spanish aristocracy's favourite weekend pastime which Franco had adopted since taking power. Hoare drove out that afternoon and joined a partridge shooting party in Millas, a large estate outside Madrid owned by Luis Quintanilla, the son of the prime minister during the time of the monarchy, Count Romanones.

A few hours later, at two o'clock on Sunday morning, Hayes rang Jordana (Franco himself was on a hunting trip outside Madrid and could not be reached immediately) and reassured him that Spanish sovereignty would not be threatened by the Allied military action that was getting under way. Jordana, whose main concern was to avoid a German occupation of Spain, used his rank to persuade some of the more pro-Axis Spanish generals to remain calm and not mobilise their troops.

The next day the Allies executed Operation Torch without a shot being fired against them by any Spaniard or German on either side of the strait of Gibraltar. The Allied landings coordinated by General Eisenhower followed Montgomery's offensive against Rommel's German–Italian forces across the Western Desert from El Alamein. As US and British forces waded ashore on North African beaches, the Madrid diplomatic circuit was inundated with rumours that German forces were massing in the Pyrenees. In the US embassy several key staff members had been in the words of one of them, 'rushed, smuggled, or bombed out of their previous posts – Warsaw, Amsterdam, and Belgrade'. They now grimly readied themselves 'for the nightmare to descend again, this time in Madrid'. They burnt confidential files, readied code books for destruction and filled gasoline containers to prepare for an evacuation of Spain via Gibraltar. Similar measures were taken in the British embassy.

In the event, Hitler decided to hold off his plans to invade Spain. Historians remain divided as to the reasons why the Germans appeared surprised by the landing and failed to react as some had feared by striking back through Spain. There is some evidence that Hitler and his generals calculated that their forces might be better used elsewhere. It has also been suggested that there was an intelligence lapse provoked by tension between the German High Command and the Abwehr.

The role of the head of the Abwehr, Admiral Canaris, has been the subject of a dispute unresolved to this day. Sympathetic biographers would have us believe that he was sufficiently anti-Hitler by this time and at loggerheads with the Gestapo and the various other German secret services to deliberately withhold intelligence he was given by his own agents in Spain. What is beyond doubt is that Franco did nothing to prevent the thousands of Allied troops that gathered in Gibraltar before crossing within range of Spanish guns on both sides of the Strait. That Spain's neutrality held firm was in no small part due to the efforts of the Allied diplomats in Madrid.

'Well, here we are, safe and sound in the anchorage to the west of Algiers,' Randolph Churchill wrote to his father Winston. 'Nearly everything has gone according to plan.'

It was the morning of 8 November 1942. Thousands of British and American troops had landed and overwhelmed the pro-German French colonial troops of the Vichy government, taking the strategically important ports of Algiers, Oran and Casablanca. Randolph was among them, reporting on what a privilege it was to be taking part 'in these great events' and reassuring the British prime minister that 'all goes well between us and the Americans'. Winston Churchill later told his commander-in-chief in the Middle East, General Sir Harold Alexander, that he wanted to ring church bells all over England for the first time since the outbreak of the war.

After more than two years of European war in which Britain had been brought to the brink of disaster, only to be saved by a mixture of luck and resilience, the success of Operation Torch raised hopes that the tide was now turning in favour of the Allies. Churchill told his chiefs of staff to prepare for a huge offensive against Hitler, attacking mainland Europe from the Mediterranean, using North Africa as a springboard.

On 13 November 1942, as the Allies consolidated their hold on French North Africa, Montgomery's forces entered Tobruk, marking the Allied victory in the Western Desert. This time the bells rang out all over England. But as Churchill conceded in a letter to King Abdullah of Jordan, while the 'end now seemed sure', there was still a 'long road to tread.'

In Madrid, the British and US embassies separately received personal telegrams of congratulations from Churchill and Roosevelt for the critical part they had played in smoothing the way for Torch. Allied ambassadors, attachés and spies had spent the days leading up to the landings engaged in one of the most intense periods of diplomatic brinkmanship since Chamberlain's fateful meeting with Hitler in Munich in 1938.

Undoubtedly it was Allied military success that helped provide persuasive arguments against those within the Spanish armed forces and Falange party who trusted that Hitler would prevail. But it was also true that, for over two years, Hoare and his closest advisers had doggedly persisted, against considerable odds, in winning over friends in the Franco regime and countering German influence within the population at large with a range of tools, from economic assistance and discreet diplomacy, to propaganda, bribes and counter-intelligence. In doing so they had been ably assisted by the Americans, increasingly so after the appointment of Carlton Hayes as ambassador.

The policies and strategy were pursued successfully by both embassies despite the huge organisational abilities and power that the Nazis exercised in Spain, and persistent opposition from the left in the UK from those who dismissed engagement with Franco's neutrality as an act of cynical appeasement with fascism which served the interests of the Axis powers much more than it did the Allies.

As things turned out, Hoare and Hayes emerged from Torch with their reputations enhanced while their German counterpart, Baron Eberhard von Stohrer, was unceremoniously sacked before the year was out. Not only was he blamed for failing to predict the Allied landings, but he was also accused of not being sufficiently pro-Nazi. He was replaced by Hans Adolph von Moltke, who although having none of Stohrer's long experience of Spanish politics and not speaking the language, was unambiguously pro-Nazi. But despite the Allied success of Torch, and von Moltke's sudden death from acute appendicitis, his appointment helped strengthen ever more the Nazi power base in Spain which had been developed in Madrid by Hans Lazar.

Furthermore, despite the success of Torch, the situation in Spain remained tense, with Allied forces to the south and Axis forces to the north, and with increasingly elaborate intelligence activities involving both sides. There was also increasing maritime and air activity around the waters of the Peninsula, with a growing number of escaped Allied POWs crossing the French-Spanish border. 'The American Embassy at Madrid will have to be all eyes and ears – and, on occasions, many-tongued,' US ambassador Hayes wrote to Myron Taylor, the US presidential emissary to the Holy See, at the end of 1942.

10

DECEPTION

Dawn was breaking over the Atlantic Ocean off the south-west coast of Spain and the fishermen were hauling in their nets about a kilometre out to sea on the morning of 30 April 1943. As the sun rose over the white sand dunes, one of the fishermen spotted a yellow object floating in the calm turquoise waters. He rowed closer and discovered a Mae West keeping afloat the body of a dead man. The corpse was dressed in British military uniform and had a briefcase attached to its belt. Only years later would the fisherman, twenty-three-year-old José Antonio Rey, discover that he had become an unintentional witness to one of the most audacious acts of deception to be carried out in wartime Spain, in an episode that would gain notoriety as *The Man Who Never Was*.

Months earlier, as 1942 drew to a close, the highly secretive interservice XX Committee, under the chairmanship of the MI5 officer John Masterman, had begun to put in place its latest plans to deceive the enemy. Its basic mission was to fully occupy German and Italian forces in Western Europe and the Mediterranean and thus discourage their transfer to the Russian front. As part of the deception strategy, two British military intelligence officers, Ewen Montagu from Naval intelligence and Charles Cholmondeley, another MI5 officer (both members of the XX Committee) developed a plan to feed the Germans false information about a major Allied landing in southern Europe following the successful Operation Torch in North Africa. The aim: to divert German troops towards Greece and Sardinia and away from Sicily, the area selected for the commencement of a major Allied offensive.

Code-named Operation Mincemeat, the plan was put together in Room 14 (NI D12), a top-secret office run by Naval Intelligence from a basement in Whitehall. It involved a team of a dozen carefully vetted individuals, including secretaries, tasked with handling coded messages and, most famously, Ian Fleming, the creator of James Bond. As a member of the XX Committee, Montagu had access to the 'most secret sources', the information drawn from Ultra, the British system for intercepting and breaking of high-grade German code and cipher signals. He was thus able to plan his operation according to the analysis of the intercepted communications on military dispositions that the Germans in Madrid and Lisbon had with Berlin. These reached him from the communications centre at Bletchley Park.

Patricia Davies was one of those who worked on Mincemeat. 'A colonel in the marines got me into the Admiralty. Most of the people in Naval Intelligence were recommended by somebody in the armed forces because that meant you came from the right kind of family. Everything was incredibly hush hush. "Don't you dare mention anything to anybody", we were warned. I was put in a section that received the traffic from Bletchley . . . the intercepts used to come by teleprinter every day, into the little office of the building we called the Citadel.'

The plan involved creating the false identity of a Royal Marine officer, Major William Martin, and enlisting him in an equally fictitious mission, as the courier of top-secret letters detailing the Allied plans from Sir Archibald Nye, the Vice Chief of the Imperial General Staff in the War Office, to General Sir Harold Alexander, the British commander in North Africa under Eisenhower. An accident whereby the aircraft carrying Major Martin crashed into the sea, but near enough to a coastline that would guarantee his body and the documents being discovered by the Germans, completed the basic elements of the ingenious plan.

To make the plot credible, weeks were spent creating Major Martin's identity, making it as plausible as possible: family background, career record, love letters from a girlfriend, nights out at the theatre, intimate dinners in the West End, bank statements all documented and with the participation of an array of invented characters. Patricia Davies played her part in the deception. 'Ewen (Montagu) handed me the big brown envelope that was to go on the body and got me to forge the address from Nye to Alexander . . . the love letters and the photograph of the girl friend were provided by girls from MI5 . . . I remember being rather annoyed not be asked to do that as well.'

In its final stages the deception took on a macabre tone as the planners put out discreet enquiries to trusted service medical officers and waited to hear that a suitable body had been found. Over sherry at the Junior Carlton club, one of the country's top pathologists, Sir Bernard Spilsbury, advised Montagu that the corpse of a man who had either drowned or recently died from any but a few 'natural causes' could be used. So the quest intensified.

Montagu wrote later: 'There we were in 1942, surrounded all too often by bodies, but no one that we could take. We felt like the Ancient Mariner – *bodies, bodies, everywhere, nor any one to take!* We felt like Pirandello – *Six officers in search of a corpse.*' Eventually a suitable body was found, of a man who had died of pneumonia and had liquid in his lungs. His identity was kept secret, although Montagu told members of his team that he was a down-and-out, originally from Wales, who had spent the last days of his life sleeping rough on the streets of wartime London.

Sir Bernard inspected the body and judged that if a post-mortem were made by someone who believed that death was due to drowning, there was little likelihood that the difference between the liquid in the lungs of a body that had started to decompose and the seawater would be noticed. 'You have nothing to fear from a Spanish post-mortem,' Sir Bernard told Montagu; 'to detect that this young man had not died after an aircraft had been lost at sea would need a pathologist of my experience – and there aren't any in Spain.'

The body was kept in cold storage in a London mortuary, before being dressed up in a Marine officer's uniform and given Major Martin's identity papers, together with a briefcase filled with the fictitious documents. The major was then packed with dry ice into a metal container and driven north to Holy Loch in a 30-cwt Ford van. At the wheel was a racing driver who was on special duty at the War Office. He and Montagu took turns to drive through the night, accompanied by Charles Cholmondeley. Once in Scottish waters, the container was taken out by boat to the submarine HMS *Seraph,* whose crew had been told that it contained a secret weather reporting device bound for waters near Gibraltar.

Eleven days later, at 4.30 a.m., the submarine surfaced in the Gulf of Cadiz, some 1600 yards from the mouth of the River Odiel and the nearby port of Huelva. The local currents and German presence had been meticulously studied over the preceding weeks by a small intelligence unit headed by Captain Gómez-Beare, the assistant naval attaché at the British embassy in Madrid.

The Gibraltar-born Lieutenant Commander Gómez-Beare had worked in military intelligence for Franco's army during the civil war before being recruited for covert wartime duties by Naval Intelligence. With his dark looks and southern accent, Gómez-Beare was one of a small number of embassy staff who could infiltrate the local population without drawing attention to themselves.

Like his commander Captain Hillgarth, he had developed close ties with key sources in the Spanish navy and was familiar with the coastline, its ports, their personnel and the local weather. Huelva had been identified as a hub of German intelligence, with the Abwehr and Gestapo controlled from the German consulate and a Nazi agent monitoring Allied shipping from a house near the estuary. Gómez-Beare reported on close collaboration between the consulate and the Spanish naval authorities. It was considered that as soon as Martin's body was washed ashore the Abwehr would be alerted and given access to the planted documents.

It was still dark when the Royal Navy submarine went about its secret business that spring day in 1943. The new moon had just set and the ebb tide was on the turn. The submarine was trimmed down until the calm sea just lapped its hull. It was then that the mysterious container was raised aloft and unbolted by members of the crew who had been made privy to the secret of its contents by Captain Bill Jewell for the first time only minutes before.

In silence, the seamen raised the body, wrapped in a blanket, and slipped it into the water, commending its soul as they did so even as their captain prayed secretly for its safe delivery into Nazi hands. In preparing for this final stage, the planners of Mincemeat had taken into account the lessons learnt from an incident that had occurred in Spanish waters some eight months earlier. In September 1942 the secrecy surrounding the build-up to the North African landings had nearly been compromised when an Allied Catalina crashed near Algeciras, killing all those on board. Among the victims was an officer who was carrying a letter about Operation Torch to the governor of Gibraltar, Noel Mason-Macfarlane. The officer's body was washed ashore where it was discovered by a Spanish naval coastguard. Within hours the letter had been handed over to the British, but not before it had first been seen by the Germans and dismissed as a fake.

Two aspects of the Catalina crash inspired the planners of Operation Mincemeat. First, no debris or equipment from the aircraft – similar to the one that had now 'crashed' off the coast of Huelva – had been washed ashore. It had thus been decided that there was no need to float a dinghy along with Major Martin to complete the deception. It was also assumed that the Germans, having cause to regret the ease with which they had been taken by surprise by the North African landings, would not again easily dismiss strategic Allied documents if and when they came into their possession.

Martin's body was discovered off the beach of El Portil, near Huelva. After it had been brought ashore by the fishermen, it was handed over to the local police, and eventually to the British consul, but only after a local German agent had taken copies of the documents and sent them back to Berlin via the German embassy in Madrid. The British vice-consul in Huelva, Francis Haseldan, was the only local British agent to be briefed on the operation. In Madrid, only a small group at the British embassy were party to the final stages of Mincemeat, their contribution as critical to its success as the accuracy of the intelligence they had helped provide. The naval attaché, Captain Hillgarth, became involved in a series of separate, carefully orchestrated exchanges with the Admiralty in London, which he shared with his contacts in the Spanish navy, designed to give the impression that the documents were of the utmost importance and needed to be retrieved as quickly as possible. Hillgarth and his superiors in Naval Intelligence accurately predicted that such exchanges would be leaked to the Germans and fuel their belief that the documents were genuine.

As part of the operation, Hillgarth decided to enlist the support of Burns. The press attaché had made some enemies in British intelligence, but Hillgarth was not one of them. The two cooperated on the basis of mutual trust. Burns was asked by Hillgarth to contribute to the deception by telling anyone who enquired about the fictitious 'Major Martin' that he was someone he vaguely recalled having dealings with as an agent of the British government in Burgos during the civil war. Questioned by his Spanish friends, Burns would claim to have forgotten the details.

Gómez-Beare, Hillgarth and Burns were among the unsung heroes of Mincemeat. A fourth was Eduardo Contioso, a young Spanish doctor who was involved in the post-mortem of 'Major Martin'. He had his suspicions about the real cause of death but refused to divulge to the Germans what he believed had really happened.

Undoubtedly the biggest 'hero' of all was 'Major Martin', not an officer at all but an anonymous civilian who died in mysterious circumstances before being transported to Spain. It is there that 'Major Martin' lies buried, in Huelva's main cemetery; a bunch of flowers was dutifully laid on his tombstone on Remembrance Day for years after the end of the war by a member of the local Anglo-Spanish community.

In 1996, a British town planning officer and amateur historian called Roger Morgan claimed that the body used by British intelligence in Operation Mincemeat was that of a homeless alcoholic Welshman named Glyndwr Michael who had died after ingesting rat poison. The discovery, subsequently supported by documentation filed at the National Archive in Kew, fuelled continuing conspiracy theories on the internet, but the tombstone nonetheless now also bears the name of Glyndwr Michael. The rest, as they say, is history. On 1 July 1943 Allied troops landed in Sicily. The Italians appealed in vain for German help, but they were otherwise occupied in Greece and Sardima.

The fall of Mussolini, just over three weeks later, on 25 July 1943, led to a two-day news blackout in Spain, as Franco tried to defuse the threat it posed to his own future. Franco wept as he recounted the events in Rome to his cabinet, but in public and in a meeting he had soon afterwards with the US ambassador Hayes he appeared self-assured, insisting there was no similarity between the collapse of fascism in Italy and the situation in Spain. While Italy had fought against the Allies, Spain had not. And yet, as Hayes pointed out to Franco, the Spanish regime continued to send out too many mixed messages which raised doubts about the genuineness of its neutrality. The Spanish media remained heavily censored and biased against the Allies, with many officials, including civilian and military governors, and members of Franco's own cabinet, openly pro-Axis. Hayes also complained about the continuing presence in Russia of Spain's pro-German Blue Division regiment of volunteers which he regarded less as an anti-communist crusade than as a military alliance against an ally.

If such protests barely dented Franco's complacency it was because there was no suggestion that it would all lead to a move by the Allies to have him removed from power. On the contrary, the central plank of the policy being pursued by both the British and American embassies in Madrid was to maintain low-level interference as far as a change in regime was concerned. To both London and Washington, the strategic Allied interest still lay in a neutral Spain and the avoidance of any pro-Axis military intervention south of the Pyrenees that might threaten supply lines to North Africa and the Mediterranean.

In May 1943, following a secret meeting with a member of the Spanish royal family, Alfonso de Orleans, the British ambassador Sir Samuel Hoare had alerted London to the ongoing activities of those who favoured a restoration of a monarchy in Spain in favour of Prince Juan, then living in exile in Lausanne, Switzerland. The plotters had set themselves a target of toppling Franco within four months and yet seemed to lack any convincing plan for how to go about it.

On 24 May, Hoare received a letter from the foreign secretary, Anthony Eden. It warned that there remained the danger of 'German counter-moves, involving strong pressure from the Spaniards', although the prospect of the Germans taking any effective action if the British invoked the Anglo-Portuguese Alliance and obtained facilities in the Azores was unlikely given the strain on Germany's resources and military commitments.

Despite accepting that the strategic risks of alienating Franco's Spain were no longer as great as they had been, Eden nevertheless remained adamant that British interests were best served by not rocking the boat. Thus he emphasised the need not to stray from the 'guiding principle' of non-intervention in internal Spanish affairs: 'I am . . . convinced that we should not become in any way connected with arrangements to bring Don Juan to Spain from Switzerland,' Eden wrote. 'This is a matter which we must leave to the Spaniards themselves, and we must not lay ourselves open to any subsequent accusations of having aided or abetted his return.' On 27 July 1943 Hoare wrote to Eden with an early analysis of what he thought might be the likely reaction in Spain to Mussolini's fall. He remained sceptical that the Spanish left's joyful reaction to the news would translate into effective action to topple Franco. As Hoare reported: 'If they attempt any movement against the Franco regime, they will be easily suppressed by the Army and the immense force of police that dominate Spanish life . . . So long as the Spanish Army is against them, the Leftists are committing suicide if, elated by Italian events, they at this moment attempt a coup.'

As for the monarchists, despite the support of some generals, 'very few of them have any political sense and, hitherto, Franco's opposition has been sufficient to block any movement in Don Juan's favour,' commented Hoare. As he prepared for his next meeting with Franco, the ambassador planned to press for unambiguous Spanish neutrality, while holding back from issuing any ultimatum on which he knew the Allies would not deliver.

Hoare went on to tell Eden: 'I feel that it is necessary to disabuse him [Franco] of the idea that Falangism and the Allies can jog along happily and indefinitely together, but that in making this clear, I must avoid the danger of appearing to dictate a particular form of government.'

Two days later his US counterpart Carlton Hayes emerged from his meeting with Franco in the Pardo Palace, a former royal hunting lodge outside Madrid, feeling, as he later put it, that 'I had cast a good bit of bread on the water, and wondering how much, if any, might return.' Within a week Burns and the US embassy press attaché were summoned to the office of a sympathetic source they shared inside the Falange party and told that Franco had ordered that the Spanish press, radio and newsreels were to adopt an impartial stance, one at least that did not discriminate in the coverage of the war against the Allies.

While Hayes's account of his meeting with Franco and its aftermath suggests that he alone was responsible for the conciliatory attitude adopted by the Spanish regime, the apparent 'concession' made by Franco had been carefully planned to ensure that his own interests were well served, with more than a little help from within the Allied camp.

Hayes's 'summit' with Franco had been preceded by a more discreet meeting in London between Tom Burns and Rafael Nadal, an exiled Spanish academic whose broadcasts for the BBC's Spanish service had become an important propaganda vehicle. This visit was the latest in a series of short work-related trips Burns had made to the UK since being posted to Madrid.

Towards the end of July 1942 Burns invited Nadal to lunch at the Garrick, the private gentleman's club near Covent Garden which had been founded in the nineteenth century. Burns had developed his network of literary, political and secret intelligence friends among the club's membership since being elected weeks before the outbreak of war in 1939, with the support of the actor Robert Speaight and the influential publisher Rupert Hart-Davies. Among the Garrick members who had already achieved certain stardom in the film world was the actor Leslie Howard, who was destined to play his most dramatic and final role in wartime Spain.

The club's Shakespearian motto, '*All the World's a Stage*', was well suited to the tragi-comedies and intrigues that had traditionally been played out within its walls. While Garrick rules prohibited work-related business being conducted in any of its rooms, the club's ruling committee was packed with individuals already involved in some way or another in the war effort, while the club's reputation for discretion in a convivial atmosphere meant that its members could and did use it as a perfect location for the discussion of sensitive matters of state.

Burns had enticed the poverty-stricken Nadal with the promise of a relaxed and nourishing lunch, during which they would have the opportunity to catch up on news of mutual friends in Madrid. Nadal was late. He found Burns standing impatiently in the entrance hall at the foot of the winding staircase, by a bronze bust of the Victorian actor Henry Irving. Burns, Nadal later recalled, seemed irritated at having been kept waiting and suggested they go straight into the main dining area – known somewhat misleadingly as the 'coffee room', given the relative luxury of its decor and fare in rationed wartime London. Sacrificed was the traditional pre-lunch cocktail or two and the informal banter members and their guests usually enjoyed in the upstairs long bar. Only when the two took their seats at one of the round dining tables did Burns seem to relax and Nadal begin to feel more comfortable with his host.

Burns ordered wine and talked about the informal literary meetings, or *tertulias*, and the bullfights he had recently been to in Madrid; Nadal recalled the experience of living and working in a London that awaited the assault of the Luftwaffe. First it was the firebombs, now it was the flying bombs. Burns confessed to missing his London friends but not the bombs. The claret they shared seemed better than any wine he had recently had in Spain. Nadal looked around the 'coffee room' and was surprised, amidst the studied elegance of the silverware and antique wooden furniture, by the poor taste of the cheap prints that somewhat incongruously lined the walls.

Only later would he be told that, since the outbreak of war, more than two hundred of the Garrick's most valuable pictures had been removed outside London. Some of the windows had been blown out despite the regulation tape criss-crossing the glass. The bombing had led to a drop in attendance in the evenings, and the occasional loss of electricity and gas, leaving the club cold and dark for extended periods. But the committee was proud of the club's wartime record: not a day had passed without luncheon being served. For Nadal, the Garrick certainly made a change from the place at which he usually ate, the canteen at the BBC's wartime location in Evesham.

Over cheese and port, conversation drifted inevitably towards Spanish politics. Knowing of Burns's right-wing sympathies, Nadal couldn't help recalling that one of his best friends, the poet Federico García Lorca, had been among thousands executed by fascist thugs early in the civil war. Burns in turn remembered the writers executed on both sides, and that the left had shot priests and raped nuns. He then moved the conversation to another delicate subject – the political position of the British embassy in Madrid and of the Allies in Spain in general as they tried to defeat Hitler. Franco, he asserted, deserved the support of the Allies so long as Spain remained neutral. Nadal's response was that the Allies had a moral imperative to help restore democracy to Spain as soon as possible.

It was only over coffee that Burns confronted Nadal about the broadcasts he had been making for the BBC. He admitted that they were incisive and well produced and heard by thousands inside and outside Spain. However, the Spanish embassy in London and senior government officials in Madrid had complained that the broadcasts were biased against the Franco regime, and 'subversive'. Burns suggested that Nadal would better serve the interests of the BBC, the British government and of Spain generally if he adjusted the tone and content of his programmes in a way that would widen their appeal to both sides of the political divide in Spain. Nadal recalled the moment: 'I couldn't believe what I was hearing. Then I said, "On no account, Tom. For this operation you've got to find someone else. Don't you realise that to try and embrace the Falange and others who support Franco would be to betray in one act all those who rest their hopes in Great Britain?"'

Nadal had a depressing sense of *déja vu*. It seemed to him that Burns's line of argument was the one long used by British Conservative MPs and their Catholic allies. It dated back to 1936, in fact, when the British government had refused to intervene against Franco's military uprising in the outset of the civil war. And yet Nadal sensed that the policy of non-intervention was also being influenced by longer-term strategic planning, in London and Washington, about the Spain that would best serve Western interests once Nazism had been defeated and the Soviet Union had begun to claim her share of the spoils of victory.

'I still think that you could and should do what I am suggesting. Perhaps at a later stage you will understand why I am right,' Burns told Nadal. Their lunch was at an end. There was no raising of voices. No sudden walkouts. This was the Garrick, after all, and Nadal had lived in London long enough to know how to play by club rules. 'We parted without any apparent tension, although with a better understanding of where we each stood,' he recalled.

It was nearly eight years since Nadal had first arrived in London. He had been studying at the French University of Poitiers and thought the time had come to learn English. Among his letters of introduction to various British academics of a left-wing disposition was one from the communist Chilean poet Pablo Neruda and another from Lorca himself. He was soon studying English at University College London while working as a part-time Spanish teacher.

Nadal's circle of friends included the Spanish ambassador representing the Republican government, Ramón Pérez de Ayala, and two Anglo-Spaniards, Tomás Harris and his younger sister Enriqueta. At that time Tomás, yet to be recruited by MI5, was an art dealer, specialising in El Greco and Goya and selling paintings to raise funds for anti-Franco forces. He worked at a gallery in Mayfair which his Jewish father, Lionel, had set up after marrying a woman from Seville. Enriqueta was doing a postgraduate course at the Courtauld Institute where Anthony Blunt was a lecturer. It was Enriqueta who introduced Blunt and Tomás to each other.

Early in the summer of 1936, Nadal was appointed assistant lecturer in the Spanish department at King's College London, a post he assumed belatedly after being caught up, while on holiday in Spain, in the early stages of the civil war. Nadal considered himself a loyal supporter of the Spanish Republic, having spent his early youth as a militant member of the Spanish Socialist Party. But weeks into the war he chose exile rather than military conscription and returned to London. In exile, Nadal's politics became passionately anti-Franco, all the more so when news reached him of the summary execution near Granada of his close friend Lorca after the poet had been arrested by nationalist forces. Within weeks Nadal expressed his disdain for Franco by embarking on an English translation of a book of Lorca verses in cooperation with Stephen Spender. The literary left was beginning to speak out in support of the Spanish Republic.

The outbreak of the Second World War provoked the closure of the Spanish department at King's College and left Nadal temporarily reduced to scraping a living from giving private classes. His luck turned when, in the final weeks of the phoney war, he met Billy McCann, the head of the Iberian section of the MoI, at a party at the Harris household. Thanks to McCann, he was offered a job at the BBC. But for occasional contributions on Latin American culture, Nadal had no broadcasting experience. He was also ideologically poles apart from Douglas Woodruff, the unashamedly pro-Franco editor of the Catholic weekly the *Tablet*, whose reflections on the war were being broadcast twice a week on the BBC's Spanish service. Nevertheless Nadal managed to convince McCann that, if given an opportunity, he would be able to serve the interests of both the British government and the Spanish people better by offering a commentary that was bolder in projecting the war as a fight against freedom and fascism. British propaganda aimed at Spain, Nadal argued, had to be fine-tuned so that the majority of Spaniards would be left in no doubt that their lives would be better and happier if the Nazis were defeated.

Nadal was appointed assistant producer of programmes. He was told by McCann that this gave him responsibility for the content of Allied propaganda broadcast to Spain by the BBC, but under the supervision of John Marks, a writer and journalist who had been recruited into government service on the recommendation of Burns and others in the British embassy. Both men were required to report regularly to McCann at the MoI.

What Nadal was not aware of was the extent to which he was being drawn into an unresolved power struggle, involving government departments, over who should be in control of propaganda and what the nature of this propaganda should be. Lack of agreement between and within the Foreign Office and the MoI as to what the government's relationship with the BBC should be only added to the tension already created by the divergent ideologies and political views of some of their employees.

McCann's own appointment had been made against the background of continuing disagreement within the British government over how policy should be conducted towards wartime Spain. As described in an earlier chapter, the previous incumbent at the head of the Spanish department, Denis Cowan, had been shifted sideways after the Spanish embassy had used its contacts in the Catholic media in Britain to criticise him for employing Spaniards known for their strong opposition to Franco. The same shake-up had resulted in Tom Burns being posted to Madrid.

*   *   *

Nadal's appointment by a board comprising senior officials from the MoI, the Foreign Office and the BBC was the result of an uneasy truce in the hostilities that had been raging between government and the BBC over policy towards Spain. It involved a compromise whereby concerns about Nadal's politics and lack of journalistic experience were temporarily set aside on the condition that his broadcasts were made subject to careful monitoring and effective vetting by the government. Nadal himself was reminded by one of his interviewers, Ivone Kirkpatrick, the controller of the BBC's European Services, that British policy towards Spain had as its only end that of maintaining its neutrality. 'It is not that we want Spain to enter the war on our side, it is however our aim to ensure by all possible means that she doesn't join the enemy,' Kirkpatrick told Nadal.

Days later, on 17 November 1940, Nadal, under the *nom de guerre* (agreed to by the BBC) of Antonio Torres, began a series of broadcasts in Spanish called *La Voz de Londres*, the voice from London, from a studio in Evesham. One of his first commentaries was a morale-boosting broadcast as London suffered heavy bombing by the Luftwaffe. While Nazi propaganda across Europe, not least Spain, predicted that Londoners would be brought to their knees, Nadal spoke of the heroism of the Blitz, describing Londoners as a bastion of democratic resistance against the forces of fascism. Other programmes were delivered in a lighter tone, with Nadal mocking the inflated rhetoric of Hitler and Mussolini's speeches.

Writing from Madrid, Burns pressed Nadal to continue broadcasting anything that might counter the depressing sight of Spaniards clutching their radios and listening to the Germans triumphantly proclaiming their latest 'victory'.

In the spring of 1941, Nadal, in a moment of almost Chaplinesque brilliance, responded by getting his studio engineer to record the notes of an out-of-tune flute over the military trumpet blast that preceded the official Nazi propaganda broadcasts, fading the flute in with increasing volume as the broadcast progressed.

Days later word reached Burns from one of his Republican informants that in a Madrid suburb the German ambassador's car had been surrounded by a group of Spanish urchins mocking him by pretending to play tunelessly on flutes. Thanks to Nadal, it seemed that the BBC had briefly struck a chord with Madrid's hungry and dispossessed, a sign, perhaps, of the growing popularity of his broadcasts in some working-class neighbourhoods of the Spanish capital.

The honeymoon period between Nadal and his detractors proved relatively short-lived once *La Voz de Londres* began to focus more directly on emphasising the pro-Axis sympathies of the Franco regime. From the autumn of 1941 the British embassy in Madrid began to warn the Foreign Office that its diplomatic strategy in Spain was being put at risk by Nadal's broadcasts. This was strongly refuted by Nadal who claimed that the popularity of his programmes among Spanish listeners was increasing daily.

By now Nadal had friends in MI5 – Tomás Harris – and another ally in the MoI, the deputy head of the Spanish department, Enriqueta Harris. Under the influence of her former tutor Blunt, Enriqueta had learnt to keep her political cards close to her chest at the heart of government. She joined the MoI after her brother Tomás joined MI5, the year Blunt was recruited by British intelligence, in 1940. The precise ideological allegiance of the Harris siblings when war broke out is unclear beyond the fact that they both hated Franco, his ministers and everything they stood for, and secretly regarded anyone who thought differently as fascists. Blunt was already a committed communist and had been recruited by an agent of the Russian secret service when he joined MI5.

In her days at the MoI, Enriqueta Harris was careful not to appear as anything other than a loyal patriot. Only towards the end of her life, reduced by old age and illness to spending long hours in the darkened sitting room of her house in Earl's Court, did she allow her guard to drop when visited by the author. She seemed angry at having been discovered by the son of a wartime colleague she utterly despised after maintaining a relatively low profile for so long in retirement. She remained extremely defensive when asked about the circumstances of her recruitment into the MoI but what little she was prepared to let slip at least hinted at the intriguing possibility that she too may have been working for the Soviets.

'I try and forget all that . . . but why don't you think of the Spanish Civil War, and think what that meant . . . I was in London. Most of my friends were anti-Franco because they were on the side of the people,' she said.

She declared herself absolutely against the strategy the British government had adopted of not supporting the anti-Franco opposition. Despite being brought up as a young girl in the Jewish faith she admitted to being 'anti-religion' and feeling, as Philby did, that Catholics had been given too great a role in influencing British policy towards Spain. 'There were a lot of Catholics in British government service. I thought there were too many,' she told me. 'It seemed to me as somebody who was supposed to be doing propaganda that I had no scope at all because we weren't allowed to do propaganda against Franco,' she added.

She acknowledged she had had dealings with all three known Cambridge spies – Burgess, Blunt and Philby – but her refusal to discuss them in any detail and what she did say seemed deliberately misleading. She described Blunt simply as a 'very polite and good lecturer', Guy Burgess as a 'bad joke', and Philby as someone she didn't like very much. 'He drank too much and at one point started sucking up to Franco.' This last remark I took as deliberately deceptive as it referred to the time when Philby had been working as a pro-Franco foreign correspondent as a cover for his work for the Soviets. She also denied that, as some writers on intelligence have suggested, her brother Tomás was a Russian spy. Only afterwards did I realise that I hadn't even asked her about her brother when she decided, unprompted, to mention his name alongside those of the Cambridge three.

By then it was plain that Enriqueta didn't wish to say anything more. She ended with these words: 'I don't like remembering and anyway I don't know if what I tell you is lies or not, you see. You will have to check it out.' Months later she was dead, carrying her truths and her lies to the grave.

In January 1942 the tensions over the BBC's Spanish coverage stirred internally when the journalist John Marks was encouraged by an unidentified source in government – almost certainly Burns – to write to the MoI questioning Nadal's political objectivity and professionalism.

Until that point, Marks had won Nadal's affection as a friend and colleague. The Spanish academic looked at the journalist-turned-

BBC-producer as a somewhat archetypal ex-public school boy and Cambridge graduate, with a certain hedonistic lifestyle that seemed to consciously defy the stifling bureaucracy of the careerists in the BBC and the insularity of many British government officials.

A chain smoker, with a permanent smear of nicotine round his nostrils, Marks drank heavily and was a serial womaniser. He was also immensely educated in Spanish culture, having developed a passion for its poetry, its music and its bullfighting while travelling round Andalusia as a freelance writer, a trait which the hugely educated, aesthete Nadal much admired.

But whatever feelings Nadal may have felt for the Englishman-turned-Hispanist quickly changed to a deep sense of betrayal when he heard the knives were out and he suspected Marks of sharpening them. Nadal tendered his resignation. Kirkpatrick refused it, declaring Marks's criticism to be unjustified. It proved to be a hollow victory for the BBC as it struggled to assert its independence in wartime. As for Nadal, he had merely achieved a stay of execution. Marks left for Madrid as the London *Times* correspondent where he developed a close friendship and political alliance inside the British embassy with Burns and his two assistants, Walters and Stordy, for the rest of the war.

Nadal was convinced by now that the pressure he had first come under at the Garrick Club lunch was the product of a diplomatic chess game with the Franco regime in which BBC employees had become expendable pawns.

During the summer of 1943, the new Spanish foreign minister, General Jordana, made clear to both Burns and his American counterpart that he expected Nadal's programmes to be reined in as a diplomatic response to his government's decision to ease the restriction on the importation of pro-Allied films and the placing of other British and US news material in the Spanish media.

A Spanish government decree in January 1943 prohibiting the showing in cinemas of raw unedited newsreel footage produced by the official German news agencies and the American studio Fox, and an announcement of their replacement instead by a new national state-run newsreel called the No Do, was seen by the British embassy in

Madrid as an opportunity to establish a more level playing field in propaganda terms.

By contrast, at the MoI in London the creation of the No Do was viewed with some scepticism, not least by Enriqueta Harris, who saw it simply as a cynical manoeuvre by the Franco regime to create a propaganda vehicle for its own internal political purposes. The first No Do appeared to vindicate such fears. It showed no clips of the war whatsoever. Instead it presented Franco as the omnipresent head of state – *Caudillo* and *Generalíssimo* – handing out diplomas to new staff officers, and visiting emblematic locations of his victory in the civil war such as the ruins of Toledo's Alcázar and the Valley of the Fallen.

Alongside such triumphalism, the No Do portrayed a Spain radiating peace, good cheer and Christian devotion at Christmas time and over the New Year. No reference was made to the daily executions and mass imprisonment of political dissidents, and the continuing economic hardships experienced by the majority of the population. The text accompanying the news items commented: 'One of the most interesting and succulent decorations in shop windows at Christmas time consists of traditional poultry hanging there, waiting for the pot – but the true spirit reflected in people's hearts during the festivities is that of the Child Jesus. We all feel a little childish and fancy free on beholding the small painted clay figures . . .'

Despite the blatant Francoist propaganda, Burns urged patience and understanding in London, pleading with the MoI not to desist from sending him more British newsreel footage. On 8 January 1943, he wrote to his head of section at the MoI, McCann, thus: 'I can quite well see how it might appear all together too Falangist, and worse than that. But I think it is important to realise that for all its defects the No Do represents a big step forward in our direction. By merely existing it pushes off screen the UFA and LUCE [Nazi] newsreels which have virtually dominated the screen up to till now.' As an aside, Burns said that the Spanish decision to include inserts from British movietone news rather than Fox was a welcome development. 'Fox, as you know, has virtually had to confine itself to bathing girls, dress parades and pastoral scenes, and was useless from our propaganda point of view.'

Such optimism generated by Spanish action proved premature. Film footage was sent belatedly from London, and the Spanish authorities were even slower in using any of it. In the following weeks, Burns struggled to secure the 'balance' he had been promised by the senior Spanish government officials in charge of the No Do. While the volume of blatantly pro-Axis war footage was reduced, there was no immediate marked increase in war footage showing the military advances being made by the Allies. Burns's official instructions from the Spanish were that anything sent from London should be confined to non-war scenes, and exclude any footage of German prisoners of war. As a result an early edition of the No Do had only one newsreel item devoted to the UK: a scene of horse schooling at the Police College in Imbert Court.

Beyond the embassy in Madrid, in Whitehall, the patience of Burns's enemies began to wear thin. Burns's candid admission to McCann in February 1943 that the Germans might have discovered a covert operation he had been running to buy up and destroy German newsreel before it reached Spanish hands gave ammunition to those who questioned his political judgement and professionalism. In a curt telegram from the MoI to the ambassador he was ordered to abandon the operation forthwith. 'The press attaché in Spain should know clearly that he should not purchase any film material of enemy origin except on specific instructions from ministry headquarters.' After Burns's clandestine newsreel buying enterprise was stopped, Enriqueta Harris pressed her case at the MoI that it should refuse to accept any Spanish No Do shots of Franco on the basis that it was Falangist propaganda. From Tetuán, the British consul, R. G. Moneypenny, wrote to the department in a similarly combative tone. No Do films, he insisted, 'Under the guise of a national Spanish and neutral enterprise are becoming an effective medium for pro-Axis propaganda.'

Within weeks, however, the British and US embassies were reporting to their head offices a marked improvement in the dissemination in the Spanish media of Allied propaganda following the unopposed success of Operation Torch. As the US ambassador Hayes later recalled, 'There was considerable contemporaneous improvement in the attitude of the Spanish press and the Falange censorship towards us. Two outstanding Spanish publicists, Manuel Aznar and Manuel

Halcón, were seemingly unhampered in conducting a strongly pro-Allied campaign. Leading dailies like *Ya* and *Madrid* in the capital were now giving good publicity ... this was a noticeable change ... an increase in news and photographs from United Nations sources; improvement in headlines; and a decrease in volume and less favourable presentation of Axis news.'

In London and Washington, sceptics viewed such developments as a cynical exercise by the Franco regime to save itself now that the tide of war appeared to be turning against the Axis powers. But they were unable to come up with a convincing and coherent alternative. Information gathered by the British embassy in Madrid from various key Spanish political sources outside the regime in late July 1943 suggested 'a growing discontent', according to the British ambassador Hoare, but one that still seemed unable to translate itself into a unified strategy or detailed plan of action.

On the subject of Franco's opponents, Hoare wrote to Eden: 'I fear ... that they all equally seem to show that there is no precise or effective plan for getting rid of it [the regime]. It is this want of a plan and of a leader that is the real strength of Franco's position. It gives him the chance of once again digging himself in and of exploiting the general fear of war, foreign and civil.'

Hoare's memorandum was largely based on information supplied to him by Burns, evidence that the press attaché's role in influencing British policy towards Spain had been reasserted. Burns in turn was encouraged by the strong support he counted on within the US embassy. Over that summer of 1943, the importance the US government attached to not allowing anything to undermine its conciliatory attitude towards Franco was underlined in exchanges between Ambassador Hayes, President Roosevelt and Robert E. Sherwood, the chief of the overseas Office of War Information.

Hayes reported that, thanks to his representations, Spanish newspapers as a whole were publishing more news from the Allies than from the Axis. 'I am glad,' replied Roosevelt, 'that our position in the press is so much better.' Meanwhile, Sherwood had separately signed a propaganda directive for Spain stressing that the US 'does not propose to interfere in the internal affairs of Spain' and that this was the 'best reply to enemy propaganda to the effect that an Allied victory would bring Bolshevism to Spain and curtail Spain's independence'.

On 20 October 1943, Hoare returned to the subject of Nadal. The ambassador wrote to Churchill accusing the BBC's Spanish programming of undermining British policy towards Spain. Hoare threatened to resign unless it ceased. On 2 November, the new Minister of Information at the MoI, Brendan Bracken, wrote to Churchill confirming that Nadal had been suspended from his post as chief presenter of the BBC's *La Voz de Londres*.

Six months passed before Nadal was reinstated, in April 1944, after agreeing not to make any further direct or indirect criticism of the Spanish government. By then the direction of the war had turned in favour of the Allies and it was longer a question of if but when Hitler would finally be defeated.

Nadal was convinced that the self-censorship he had agreed to would prove short-lived and was reasonably content to bide his time. Along with other Spanish exiles, he hoped that British policy towards Spain might still shift in favour of paving the way for a post-war democratic government. Instead Churchill delivered a speech on 24 May 1944 in the House of Commons in which he thanked Franco for helping the Allied cause by keeping Spain out of the war, and argued that the continuation of this policy during Operation Torch had made full amends for earlier Spanish assistance to Germany.

Churchill went on: 'As I am here today speaking kindly words about Spain, let me add that I hope she will be a strong influence for the peace of the Mediterranean after the war. Internal political problems in Spain are a matter for the Spaniards themselves. It is not for us – that is the Government – to meddle in them.'

Churchill's speech came as a terrible shock to Spanish Republican exiles and monarchists who had looked to the Allies to help liberate their country from the Franco regime after Hitler and Mussolini had been defeated. By contrast, the Madrid media painted it as an endorsement of Franco's foreign policy and of his regime. Among many ordinary Spaniards who had lived through the trauma of the civil war there was a genuine sense of relief that they had been saved from another war, as well as the political turmoil and revolution they feared might follow an Allied victory.

Less than a month later, on 17 June 1944, Rafael Nadal was having lunch with Enriqueta Harris in the basement of the BBC's Bush House in the Strand when a loud explosion shook the building, covering them in plaster and dust as they sought cover beneath a table. A flying bomb had destroyed a post office on the ground floor, just a few metres from where they were. Both Nadal and Harris were unhurt, but the bomb injured dozens of civilians, some of them fatally. It was a stark reminder that the war had yet to run its course.

The next day Nadal sat at his desk and typed out his latest *La Voz de Londres* in which he declared his hope that an Allied victory would in time lead to the restoration of democratic government throughout Europe. Without mentioning any particular countries, he laid out a vision of a future international order involving ordinary citizens of every nationality and race recovering their human rights, not least the right to vote for a government of their choice. The commentary was written but then left unrecorded, being judged to be veiled interference in Spanish political affairs by the BBC's censors at the MoI. Nadal resigned that same evening and never again worked for the BBC in a time of war.

11

TO LOVE IN MADRID

In January 1943 the British actor Leslie Howard, best remembered for his role as Ashley Wilkes in *Gone with the Wind*, received a letter from Sir Malcolm Robertson, MP, chairman of the British Council, exploring the idea of a lecture tour in Portugal and Spain to coincide with the Spanish release of the film.

The threat of a German occupation of Spain had resurfaced as a major strategic challenge to the Allies in the months after the North African campaign had got under way in 1942, with supply lines stretched across North Africa.

Behind the Robertson proposal lay a secret plan prepared by the British and US embassies in Madrid to consolidate their influence on the Franco regime following the military success of Operation Torch. The plan was to use Howard as a propaganda tool, and to have him ingratiate himself with Franco by establishing ties with the Spanish film industry which the dictator was keen on developing as popular entertainment.

Over the preceding months the Americans had been expanding their presence in Spain using front companies as cover for the OSS and leasing a separate building for the Casa Americana. This was a thinly disguised propaganda department directly copied from an idea established by the British embassy's press department and the British Council, with dozens of expatriate and local employees involved in the showing and distribution of pro-Allied films and news bulletins, as well as the financing of helpful agents of influence.

Burns almost certainly consulted with his US friends prior to having the British Council make its approach to Howard, who recent polls were showing to be the most popular actor in the Iberian Peninsula. Cover for Burns's involvement was provided by Walter Starkie, the head of the British Council in Madrid, who volunteered to officially host the proposed Howard visit.

Starkie had been posted to Spain in the summer of 1940, after being plucked by government from relative obscurity because of his influential contacts and knowledge of the country and its people.

At the time Starkie was a Catholic professor at Trinity College, Dublin, who had spent his holidays before the war travelling round Spain, writing two books about living with gypsies and earning his keep with his fiddle. A self-taught expert on Irish jigs and flamenco, Starkie also hugely enjoyed Spanish food, wine and bulls. His camouflage as an eccentric expatriate was completed by marriage to an Argentine amateur opera singer of Italian descent.

Years later in his memoirs Burns credited Lord Lloyd, the then head of the British Council, with Starkie's 'imaginative appointment' to Spain. 'For how could official Spain ever say that Starkie was *persona non grata*? He knew more about the country, its literature and folklore than most Spaniards, politics had never concerned him and he could hardly be suspected of being a British agent,' wrote Burns.

Starkie was a British agent, his eccentric public persona belying a background of discreet service to His Majesty's Government as an Anglo-Irishman who strongly identified with the Allied cause and equally strongly opposed his native Ireland's neutrality in the war on the grounds that he considered it part of the British Empire. 'Walter wanted to do anything to help the Allied cause, in contrast to the neutrality adopted by the Irish government,' recalled his daughter Alma years later.

Alma was thirteen when she arrived in Madrid with her parents. Term time was spent in a Catholic girls' boarding school back in Ireland. Holidays were spent riding in the Retiro in Madrid with her best friend, Mary, the daughter of the American ambassador Carlton Hayes. 'The horses belonged to the Spanish army. They had all the best horses,' remembered Alma.

Her Buenos Aires-born mother, Italia Augusta, dropped her first name soon after Starkie's appointment in Madrid. She thought it a price worth paying to avoid being branded an agent of Mussolini and to be allowed access to the exclusive club of British expatriate women.

As a result, during the war years, when not drinking tea or playing bridge, Augusta helped organise knitting groups at which the wives of diplomats and their elegant friends from the Spanish aristocracy made clothes for the poor children of Madrid out of the sacks with which food was transported to the embassy. The 'knitting circle' was presided over by the impeccably correct Lady Maud and regularly addressed with morale boosting speeches by her husband, the ambassador Sir Samuel. It was a joint act they had finessed while campaigning for the Conservative Party back in pre-war London. In their mutual dependence, the childless Hoares came across as a business partnership as much as a marriage. They certainly lived in more style than many of the people of wartime Madrid.

As Alma Starkie recalled, 'The poor people of Madrid were in a bad state in those days,' said Alma. 'I remember the Council doctor having to attend a young woman who had fainted out in the street. He pronounced her dead from malnutrition.'

While the ladies drank tea and knitted rough jerseys for the cold winter, their husbands plotted and intrigued. Some wives and girlfriends volunteered to visit the refugee internment centre in Miranda del Ebro. A few took on the more dangerous task of providing cover for those who had eluded arrest. The Starkies allowed their own large flat at number 24 Calle del Prado – in the old quarter, dating back to the Spanish empire – to be used by the embassy as a safe house for escaping prisoners of war and Jewish refugees.

In his official and covert activities, Starkie found a friend and trusted colleague in Burns. Both men mixed in similar social circles of bullfighters and artists, and looked to each other's foreignness to rescue them on occasions from the stuffy insularity of some of their diplomatic colleagues, not least the ambassador Sir Samuel Hoare, who barely tolerated the 'Irishman' Starkie, despite his declared anti-(Irish) republicanism.

While both shared a love of adventure, Starkie and Burns were physically striking contrasts. The Anglo-Irishman, short – with a height roughly equalling his girth – and with a huge bald head; the Anglo-Chilean with Scottish and Basque blood, tall and lean, with a healthy crop of dark hair swept back from his forehead, whose semblance, as the war wore on, seemed to transform into a disarming cross between Noël Coward and Leslie Howard, as if he had absorbed the mannerisms of the Allied propaganda stars through a process of osmosis.

Inevitably Starkie and Burns came to be dubbed Sancho Panza and Don Quixote by their Spanish friends. One of their more outrageous adventures together revolved around a trip they made to Gibraltar, at the invitation of Captain 'Hooky' Holland, Commander of the *Ark Royal*. While Burns touched base with local intelligence contacts, Starkie played a concert of Irish jigs in the great hangar below deck of the Royal Navy's flagship aircraft carrier, 'the crew crouched or suspended among the overhanging girders giving thunderous applause'. After a night of music and heavy drinking, 'Hooky' accepted Starkie's invitation to accompany him and Burns, strictly incognito, to a flamenco party he had organised the next day in Madrid. It was held in Starkie's flat which was lit with candles for the occasion. Music and dance was provided by a band of wild gypsies Starkie had befriended on his wanderings through the country. Much wine and whisky flowed. In the early hours, the inebriated Starkie struggled to his feet and proposed a toast, revealing his guest's identity for the first time. 'To my honoured guest Captain Holland of the *Ark Royal*!' Starkie declared merrily, lifting his glass.

It had an instant, sobering effect on Burns. 'It was a horrifying and dangerous breach of security. I devoutly hoped that our naval attaché would not come to hear of it, still less his German counterpart,' Burns recalled. Luckily the incident was not reported by either side. 'Hooky' returned safely to Gibraltar, while Sancho Panza and Quixote got back to the Leslie Howard project.

The initial approach to the actor had met with a firm but polite refusal. While delighted that his films were well known in the Iberian Peninsula, Howard claimed he knew very little about the land or its people, had far less lecturing skills than other actors, and, anyway, had yet to finish *The Lamp Still Burns*, a morale-boosting film he was helping to produce in the UK. Undeterred, Burns enlisted the support of key Whitehall figures, among them Jack Beddington, the head of the

Film Division at the MoI who had been helping the British embassy – with mixed results – to get British films distributed in Spain.

Beddington put Howard's obstinacy partly down to lingering depression. His lover, Violette Cunnington, had died suddenly a few weeks earlier having contracted a mysterious skin infection. Beddington believed that the one thing that was driving Howard on was his enduring love of film. He also knew that his agent, Arthur Chenhalls, was looking to expand the commercial success of his client by exploiting the fledgling Spanish-language cinema audience. Beddington visited them both at Denham Studios. He was initially greeted with caution. When he asked Howard how soon he expected to finish his latest film, the actor turned to his director Maurice Elvey and said, not entirely tongue in cheek: 'Ought we to tell him – isn't he a spy from the MoI?'

Beddington kept a cool head and marked time before broaching the subject of the Iberian trip in terms he hoped Howard and his agent would find hard to refuse. He explained that the actor's role would be that of an ambassador for the film industry, and that behind the trip was the potential to tap exciting new opportunities across Spain, Portugal and Latin America. Howard remained publicly non-committal, while privately sharing with Chenhalls his fear that he might present too easy a target for extreme fascists if he went to Franco's Spain.

Such apprehension was not unjustified given that Howard was Jewish and there was a high-profile presence of Nazis in Spain who had the support of the regime. In fact there was evidence of the sort of political passions that Howard might stir a few days later in Madrid when, on 12 February, the US embassy sponsored a gala showing of *Gone with the Wind* at one of the principal theatres in Madrid. The event was preceded by a warning from the pro-German sectors of the Spanish media that the film showed life at its most decadent and was 'immoral'. During a subsequent demonstration, Falangist youths threw nails and shouted pro-German slogans at those attending.

Nevertheless the US ambassador Hayes was encouraged by the huge support the film generated among other Spaniards. They included the Bishop of Madrid who occupied a front seat and stayed, seemingly enthralled, for the full four hours the showing lasted, along with the Spanish foreign minister Jordana, his family and hundreds of others in the audience.

Even more significant and surprising was the reaction to the film when it was later shown to Franco in the private cinema he had built himself in the Pardo Palace. The *Generalísimo* was enormously impressed with the film's depiction of the suffering and survival of war and encouraged its subsequent distribution across Spain in defiance of Nazi advice that it was US propaganda and therefore should be banned along with the book on which the film was based, as had occurred in Germany.

'It proved, indeed, to be a gala affair, and one of our best bits of propaganda,' Carlton Hayes later recalled.

Days after the film's successful showing in Madrid, Howard was subjected to further pressure from senior British government figures. Brendan Bracken, the MoI chief, and Anthony Eden, the foreign secretary, were among the ministers who personally contacted the actor. In response, Howard told Eden that, while he was happy to go to Lisbon, he was not prepared to cross the border. He had no desire to meet leading Falangists at official functions, which he thought unavoidable, and was worried that such meetings might upset the Russians.

Such sensitivity towards Moscow was curious. It suggests that Howard or his agent, or both, may have had some contact with one or other of the Soviet agents who had manoeuvred themselves into departments dealing with Spain, including Philby.

However, there were other elements in Whitehall, among them some of the Foreign Office's top officials, that were unconvinced by Howard's excuses. 'Mr Leslie Howard is going to Spain to lecture on Shakespeare acting and film making. I feel that Mr Howard is exaggerating the damage which his visit may cause to his relations with the Russians . . .' stated a Foreign Office memorandum of 16 April 1943. 'I agree that Mr Howard is making heavy weather of this . . . the Russians understand our Spanish policy perfectly well, and are not going to hold it up against Mr Leslie Howard that he helped to forward anti-German propaganda in Spain,' wrote Walter Roberts, the head of the Foreign Office's European section, a day later.

The Foreign Office had by then received a secret telegram from the Madrid embassy confirming that arrangements for Howard's visit were advanced and arguing strongly that to suspend them would prove hugely damaging in diplomatic and propaganda terms. Anthony Eden wrote to Howard: 'It is very important just now to fly the British flag in Spain and to give encouragement to our many friends there . . . on the whole I think it would be best to avoid Spanish internal politics as a subject of conversation, and to concentrate on explaining the British war effort . . . I do not think either that you need fear that your journey will be misinterpreted by the Russians, who take a realistic view of Spanish affairs and of the importance of Spanish neutrality.'

A week later Howard and Arthur Chenhalls were on their way to Lisbon in an Ibis DC3. The two men stayed there ten days. Between receptions and lectures on Shakespeare and the British and American film industries, Howard spent much of his time in his shorts dictating notes to an young expatriate English secretary at his beachside hotel.

The warm sun and the casino at Estoril reminded him of California. Photographs taken at the time invariably show Howard in the company of young, attractive women. His grief for Violette had given way to the old philandering ways which had troubled his marriage during his Hollywood years. Howard found that the young secretaries at the British embassy and the pretty young daughters of the local Anglophile Portuguese were easily seduced by his charm and good looks and he felt invigorated in their presence.

'He was very polite and *simpatico*, among the most interesting individuals I met in the whole war. Everyone fell in love with him,' recalled Olive Stock, a member of the embassy staff who was appointed to help organise Howard's accommodation and schedule before being transferred to the Madrid embassy as Burns's assistant.

On 8 May, Howard and Chenhalls travelled to Madrid on the overnight *Lusitania Express*, to be greeted at Atocha station by Starkie in the midst of an early summer heat wave. Howard was furious when Starkie began almost immediately going through a packed list of planned engagements. They ranged from meetings with Spanish actors and attendance at embassy cocktail parties to numerous speaking engagements and intimate meetings with a select group of local artists and bullfighters. One of those he was scheduled to meet was the Hollywood Spanish actress Conchita Montenegro, with whom Howard had co-starred in the film *Never the Twain Shall Meet* in 1931, when she had just turned nineteen and he was thirty-seven years old. It was rumoured at that time that they had had a passionate affair. Both had aged well in the intervening twelve years, and they made a striking couple in wartime Madrid – she a beautiful, mature thirty-something-year-old, he a well-preserved and attractive forty-six. Montenegro was by now engaged to – and would marry within the year – Ricardo Giménez-Arnau, one of Burns's contacts in the Falange where he was head of the right-wing party's international affairs department. Her reunion with Howard appears to have prompted a light-hearted flirtation and nothing more serious. Prior to her death in April 2007, Montenegro gave an interview in which she alleged that she had helped secure a private meeting between Howard and Franco during which the actor passed on a secret message from Churchill that was critical in ensuring that Spain kept out of the war, although the evidence for this is largely circumstantial, and Burns, who would have known about it, left no record of it, either verbal or oral.

What is known with more certainty is that, once in Madrid, Howard insisted that his official schedule be cut back drastically so as to spare him the requirement of meeting too many representatives of a Spanish government. By contrast, he was keen to briefly rekindle an old flame in Montenegro, and got his opportunity when Burns sat him next to her at an intimate lunch party he arranged for the actor at a friendly restaurant the British embassy used for discreet encounters on the outskirts of Madrid. While Howard was in the Spanish capital, Burns allowed him three days free of any speaking engagements, a concession which is thought to have paved the way for the actor's fateful amorous encounter with a beautician who worked in the Ritz where he was staying. She was one of several German agents who tracked Howard throughout his stay in the Iberian Peninsula. Among the others was Gloria von Furstenberg, the glamorous Mexican wife of a German count, to whom Howard was introduced by the Spanish actor Luis Escobar. In her memoirs the OSS agent Aline Griffith described von Furstenberg as the best-dressed woman she had ever seen – 'the pure white shoulderless tube of a dress was embroidered with tiny blue stars mixed with geometric patterns that suggested . . . little swastikas'. Griffith believed that, while Howard may have been warned about von Furstenberg, he was so struck by her beauty that he spent much of the evening telling her about his future travel plans, including the fact that he was flying back to London via Lisbon within a week. The information is thought to have been subsequently passed on to the German embassy in Madrid.

Against this background of intrigue, Madrid remained submerged in a relentless war of propaganda between the Allies and the Axis. The British and US embassies were trying to maximise the publicity around the Allied military advance across North Africa and the massive bombings of German factories. For its part the German embassy was spreading rumours of an imminent Allied invasion of Spanish sovereign territory.

To the British embassy, Howard's presence in Madrid represented an exciting new phase in their efforts to win the hearts and minds of Spaniards. In the words of his son Rodney, 'this charming English export epitomised for many Spaniards the best and most admirable of British qualities'. But it was precisely such usefulness to the Allied cause and his record of anti-Nazism that made him a target for the Germans as a suspect enemy agent.

Among the subjects discussed by Howard and Arthur Chenhalls in their talks with representatives of the Spanish film industry was a plan for an Anglo-Spanish production of the life of Christopher Columbus, a project which hugely appealed to Franco. The figure of the explorer and 'discoverer' of the Americas was being resurrected by Franco's government as a symbol of Spanish imperial greatness and of universal Christianity extending on both sides of the Atlantic. Columbus as a Christian hero went down well with the Catholics who were driving American and British policy on Spain.

But while Howard owed his stardom to America, his visit to Madrid was controlled by the British. Social events organised for him included a flamenco evening at the British Council to which Franco's ambassador in London, the Duke of Alba, was invited along with other Anglophile members of the aristocracy and artists and writers who had survived the civil war.

Accompanied by John Marks of *The Times*, Burns also took Howard to a bullfight before introducing him to some of Madrid's nightspots, in exchange for which he was expected to deliver on some of the programme that had been originally devised. The most successful events in propaganda terms were a lunch and press conference with foreign and Spanish journalists, and a lecture Howard gave on *Hamlet*, filled with thinly veiled allusions to the courage and nobility of the Allies in the face of the forces of darkness as represented by Nazism. The lecture was well received by a carefully selected audience of academics, dramatists and art critics, and its printed version – translated into Spanish – was distributed with the daily embassy bulletin across Madrid.

Howard then went to ground, disappearing to his room in the Ritz and not surfacing again for twenty-four hours. His schedule was hastily rearranged, again. Two further official engagements were cancelled, much to Hoare's chagrin. However, Burns suffered Howard's idiosyncrasies more readily that his ambassador, seeing in the maverick actor a kindred spirit with whom he had much in common. Long-term membership of the Garrick Club – where they had met on several occasions informally before the war – a fondness for women and a mixed foreign ancestry all helped fuel a genuine friendship.

Tragically, Burns failed to instil an element of self-discipline and caution into Howard's reckless lifestyle. When Howard re-emerged at the Ritz he did so arm in arm with the hotel beautician. The next day she was with Howard when he took the train back to Lisbon, helping him give the slip to the embassy 'minder', a junior official the ambassador had insisted keep a close watch on him. The lovers shared a compartment while Chenhalls slept alone along the corridor.

Howard and the beautician separated on arriving in Lisbon, leaving the seemingly insatiable Howard to pick up where he had left off last time, sharing a romantic dinner with one of his female friends from the British embassy, in a seaside restaurant near the fishing village of Cascais.

Later that week Howard gave a short speech of introduction to *The First of the Few* before it was run for the first time in Portugal at a private showing organised by the British Council. It turned out to be Howard's final public act of adherence to the Allied cause.

The First of the Few is probably one of the most unashamedly patriotic and propagandist of all the films that Howard acted in, a tribute to the

RAF and a rallying call for continued heroism and perseverance. It was exactly the sort of line the MoI hoped to encourage.

On 1 June 1943, the day after the screening, the Ibis DC3 in which Howard was flying back to England was attacked over the Bay of Biscay by the Luftwaffe. It was the first commercial airliner to be shot down on the Lisbon–UK route in the Second World War. All on board, including Howard, were killed.

In the aftermath of the crash, British intelligence circulated rumours that the Germans had actually intended to kill Winston Churchill, mistakenly thinking he was on the plane. It was a theory that Churchill himself resolutely stuck to, along with others who were with Howard during his visit to Portugal and Spain.

Churchill was at the time in North Africa, at a military aerodrome in the desert outside Algiers briefing an American squadron that was about to bomb the island of Pantelleria, halfway between Tunisia and Sicily. A picturesque volcanic island, its capture was regarded as crucial to the Allied success in invading Sicily in 1943 because it allowed planes to be based in range of the larger island. Pantelleria was heavily bombarded in the days before the landing of the main Allied attack, and the garrison finally surrendered as the landing troops were approaching. Churchill had flown there, after talks with Roosevelt in Washington, by flying boat, first to Newfoundland and then to Gibraltar, a journey of seventeen hours during which the aircraft was struck by lightning. 'There were no consequences, which, after all, is what is important on these journeys,' Churchill commented later.

On 28 May Churchill had flown the three-hour trip from Gibraltar to Algiers in a specially converted Lancaster bomber. On 4 June he flew back to Gibraltar on the same plane. Because the weather was bad, he decided to continue his journey to England later that day in the Lancaster rather than the flying boat as was originally intended. Churchill was back in London by the morning of 5 June. 'We have been rather anxious about you since they got Leslie Howard,' his daughter Diana wrote.

It was only partly due to a British secret service disinformation campaign that the Germans were kept guessing about Churchill's real flight plans, and believed that he might at one stage, during his visit to

North Africa, divert at short notice and take a commercial flight from Lisbon.

As a result German agents were put on alert at Lisbon airport on 1 June. By then the passenger list of the Ibis DC3 flight to England had been changed at least once before Howard and Arthur Chenhalls were observed walking across the tarmac surrounded by other passengers to board the plane. Cigar-smoking, bald, portly and wearing a heavy coat, Chenhalls bore some physical similarity to Churchill but not one that stood up to close scrutiny.

The morning of departure was bright and sunny and both Howard and Chenhalls had lingered to say goodbye to Portuguese friends and embassy staff and to allow the local media to take photographs. It seems improbable that by the time the two men reached the aircraft their identity had not been established beyond doubt. Indeed, the fact that a German news agency first announced the crash, naming Howard and Chenhalls among the victims, suggests that, when the plane was shot down, it was not the prime minister but Howard who was the target of the Luftwaffe, and that British intelligence attempted to cover up the real reason for his death – the suspicion that he was not just a propagandist but also a spy. Perhaps the most disturbing aspect of the whole Leslie Howard affair is the possibility that, by June 1943, the breaking of German codes meant that a small exclusive sector of British intelligence may have known in advance of German plans to attack the aircraft, and that the information may have been deliberately suppressed so as not to compromise the Enigma breakthrough at Bletchley Park.

What is beyond doubt is that the manifest of the fourteen passengers originally booked on that fateful flight included at least two other individuals believed by the Germans to have had some involvement with British intelligence – Tyrrel Shervington, the Shell manager in Lisbon, and Wilfred Barthold Israel of the Jewish Refugee Mission.

It is also true that the young son of a British diplomat based in Washington, Major Frederick Partridge OBE, and his nanny were removed from the passenger list to make way for Howard and Chenhalls, and that a third passenger, a Catholic priest from the local English College, disembarked at the last minute, making the passenger list an unlucky thirteen.

The priest, Fr Holmes, withdrew from the flight after being told by an airport employee that he had received an unidentified telephone message requiring that he urgently call either the British embassy or the Papal Nunciature. When he did so he could find no trace of anyone making such a call. The providence and motive of the telephone call that had drawn the priest away from the flight was to remain a mystery. Although Fr Holmes may have had a premonition and made the call an excuse for missing the flight, he never suggested it. 'It is just possible that the supernatural element has obscured the fact that the unknown caller may, indeed, have had a hot line to someone who really knew what was going to happen,' Geoffrey Stow, the assistant air attaché in Lisbon at the time, wrote later.

Stow died without ever clarifying what he meant, even to his close family. If someone did deliberately warn Fr Holmes off the plane, the motive remains equally unclear since Fr Holmes had no known hidden agenda.

With the passing of the years and evidence emerging of the British government's involvement in Howard's mission, what seems far less in doubt is that the Germans would have had a perfectly valid reason for considering Howard an Allied propaganda tool, if not a paid-up agent of British intelligence. It was this theory that weighed heavily on the conscience of those who had encouraged him to go to Spain in the first place, and who did little to protect him from the prying eyes of German agents.

Only days after the crash did British embassy staff discover that Howard had devoted part of his final days in Lisbon to writing letters while relaxing on his balcony in the seaside Hotel Atlantico in Estoril.

To his long-suffering wife Ruth he wrote a light-hearted if prescient account of the Germans he would occasionally stumble across in the hotel: 'The *Herrenvolk* are not hard to recognise and whenever they see us approaching they drop their voices and stare icily.' It suggested that Howard remained reconciled to hanging on to married life despite his serial infidelity, and that he was aware he was being pursued by the Nazis.

A seemingly perfect gentleman to the end, Howard also wrote several thank-you notes to his hosts in Madrid. As his son Ronald later explained, 'to some he apologised for turning up late and others for not turning up at all'. They were token apologies in the main, perhaps made with one eye on maintaining his popularity and keeping open the prospect of making money in the Spanish film industry in the future. He took particular care with the letter he wrote to Burns. In it, Howard makes clear his belief that he owed him special thanks for his friendship and support during a tempestuous Iberian journey and an apology for his behaviour.

Dear Tom,

After the wild nightmare which in retrospect my Madrid trip seems to have been, I just want to let you know how grateful I am for all you did to get what I hope will have proved successful results. There may have been occasions when I seemed far from grateful, but you will, I know, take that in good part. It was very hot, I was not feeling very well, and the nights were very short. I quite realise that all the visits you arranged to the bull-fight and the film studios were a necessary contribution towards the result for which we are all striving. It may please you to hear that in the view of the Spaniards to whom I spoke to you are one of the aces among the English. Naturally I was most interested in the film situation, which I think merits a good deal of attention, and I do think I might come back one day in this connection. If there ever is such a project, and you are still there, I shall be in touch with you very quickly. If you ever want to reach me in England, Denham Studios, where I have my office, always finds me.

Au revoir, and many thanks and give my love to all the people I really like.

The letter was written on 29 May 1943. It reached Burns in Madrid two days later. By then news was filtering through to the embassy that a commercial airliner believed to be transporting a group of British civilians, including the actor Leslie Howard, had been shot down by enemy aircraft off the coast of Galicia, in northern Spain. There were seventeen people on board, including four crewmen. There were no survivors. Nor were any remains of the aircraft ever found.

*   *   *

Two weeks later, Burns sent a message to the MoI reporting that distribution problems had forced him to suspend the sending of copies of Spanish newsreels with the exception of one piece which he felt was useful in propaganda terms. It was a clip of Howard visiting a Spanish film studio, days before his doomed flight from Lisbon. By then the British and American embassies were reporting that matters in Spain were improving after the embassies had successfully contained the diplomatic fallout from the successful implementation of Operation Torch.

Rumours of a German invasion persisted, however, and the autumn of 1943 witnessed the beginning of the 'last major crisis' the British embassy in Madrid had to deal with as the Allies quarrelled over how best to limit the sale of Spanish wolfram to Germany. Delivery of the metal was vital to the German steel industry, which produced tanks and guns, and made possible the continuation of the war. Nevertheless, the ensuing period leading up to the final Allied victory would also see the betrayals and deceptions of wartime Madrid reach a resolution in diplomatic as well as personal terms for one of its key members of staff. For it saw the unfolding of, arguably, Burns's greatest propaganda coup, his love affair with a Spanish woman of not inconsiderable beauty, charm and influence. On 10 October 1943 Burns received an invitation to visit her father, Gregorio Marañón. A doctor, writer and consummate political networker, Marañón was a man of considerable public standing who had been cultivated by the British. Early that summer, Marañón had been the key guest at a dinner hosted by the British Council's Starkie for a team of British doctors and academics on a Foreign Office-sponsored visit to Spain.

Marañón was subsequently described by one of the English doctors thus: 'I enjoyed meeting Marañón very much, although he speaks very little English, and his conversational Spanish was rather too much for me. He is a *literateure*, interested in art and politics as well as medicine. He had, and still has a great reputation as a physician, the true basis of which I was unable to assess. Indeed I do not recall discussing any medical subject with him at all. I am inclined to think that the diversity of his interests argues a certain superficiality, and that his success has depended more upon his personality than anything else.'

A less grudging assessment of Marañón was sent to the Foreign Office around this time by Ambassador Hoare. In his secret dispatch to London, Hoare described Marañón as 'intellectually, one of the best minds in Spain'. Marañón featured on a named list of four 'representative Spaniards' Hoare regarded as 'important contacts', along with the Cardinal Archbishop of Madrid, Pedro Segura, the writer José Martínez Ruiz Azorín and General Matallana, a senior army officer who had fought against Franco during the civil war.

Marañón made a name for himself in his country's politics in the 1920s, after taking a stand against the authoritarian rule of General Primo de Rivera and earning a prison sentence for his pains. He was later one of a group of leading liberal intellectuals who forced the abdication of King Alfonso XIII and helped bring about the proclamation of the Spanish Republic in 1931. It proved a short-lived engagement with left-wing politics.

Marañón became disillusioned with the political radicalisation of the Republic, and within a year of the outbreak of civil war had led his family into exile in Paris. Although he had been threatened by extreme elements on both sides of the political spectrum, Marañón's sympathies increasingly shifted in favour of a Franco victory, which he saw as necessary to restore a sense of political stability and national unity prior to what he hoped would be the restoration of a constitutional monarchy. Marañón returned to Spain in October 1942.

He was allowed to resume his medical practice in Madrid on the condition that he did not immediately assume his pre-war position as a physician in one of Madrid's major hospitals and kept out of politics. He complied by not publicly criticising the regime, while maintaining discreet political contacts with those, like himself, who mistakenly believed and hoped that Franco would pave the way for a democratic monarchy once the war was over, or even sooner.

The intelligence gathered by the British embassy on Marañón suggested there was still a potential conspirator beneath the skin of the popular doctor: 'Although one of the public men mainly responsible for King Alfonso's downfall, he is now an advocate for Don Juan. He spoke more bitterly than ever of Franco and the Falange and also criticised the Church leaders for not having adopted a more independent attitude.

He declared that a close friend of his who had recently been Minister at the Vatican had told him that the Pope was growing exercised over the want of independence in the Church,' reported Hoare.

The privileged access to Marañón that Burns enjoyed came about thanks to his membership of the literary and artistic clubs that began to re-form after their disintegration during the civil war. Through the *tertulias* Burns won the trust of some of Marañón's closest friends, among them the sculptor Sebastián Miranda. It was Miranda who secured Burns an invitation to the sixteenth-century convent near Toledo that Marañón had converted into his country retreat and which at the time he generally reserved for close family, trusted friends or individuals brought along on their recommendation. 'Marañón is back and you must meet him,' Miranda announced to Burns one day with a characteristic sense of drama.

The invitation was for Sunday *sobremesa*, literally translated as 'on the table' but meaning the extended period over coffee, brandy, anis and cigars, during which Spaniards – and Spanish men in particular – engaged in relaxed conversation on politics, art or bulls.

Burns and Miranda duly set off for Toledo in one of the embassy cars, Burns's dog Juerga sitting on the sculptor's lap in the front seat. The journey took them through working-class suburbs and towns around Madrid that had seen some of the worst fighting during the capital's prolonged siege. The ruins of houses destroyed by artillery, the windows and walls shattered by machine-gun fire and the spreading shanty towns along the way served as a reminder as to why many Spaniards had no desire to go through another war.

As they approached Toledo, Burns found his progress blocked at a level crossing by a long, stationary goods train that seemed in no hurry to move. Miranda jumped out, walked over to the train driver and indicated the Union Jack on the bonnet of Burns's car. It was, Miranda insisted, the emblem of the British ambassador and he was in the car, late for a very important meeting with Toledo's military governor. Within seconds the train was moving again, allowing the two men to proceed, laughing, on their way. The route to Marañón's *cigarral* took Burns and Miranda across the Roman bridge of San Martín and up a hill on the other side of the wide and fast-flowing Tagus. A large wooden gate with a wall made of rough tiles on either side marked the entrance to the narrow, unpaved lane that wound its way down to the house, with its magnificent view of the old imperial city perched over the valley.

Burns drove the final metres to Marañón's house with a growing sense of anticipation, through an avenue of young cypress trees bordering wild rosemary bushes and olive groves, the extraordinary peace and isolation of the doctor's country retreat fuelling a belief that he had been brought to a temple of wisdom across a biblical landscape. Don Gregorio, as Miranda introduced him, was waiting with his wife Lolita, son Gregorio, son-in-law Alejandro, three daughters, Carmen, Belén and Mabel, and two grandchildren – a chieftain among his most intimate tribe.

Apart from Marañón himself, 'powerfully built with head suggestive of a noble Roman', according to Burns's first sight of him, and Gregorio junior – with whom Burns had had brief dealings over the issue of British support for Spanish journalists – only one member of the family came into proper focus that afternoon. That was Mabel. Aged twenty-five, the youngest and prettiest of Marañón's two unmarried daughters, petite, like her mother, with smiling brown eyes, full mouth, fresh olive skin, and short, dark brown hair, she displayed a disarming mix of innocence and alert self-confidence. Burns's memory of this first brief encounter with Mabel – twelve years his junior – is all that remains on record of his first visit to the legendary Cigarral de Menores. From the outset Burns was struck by the fact that Mabel seemed the only member of her family who spoke almost flawless English. She said she had learnt it from her longest serving nanny Miss Burns (a namesake but no relation of their visitor), a Liverpudlian Catholic of Irish descent. Mabel confided that she was going away until Christmas to stay at Gómez Cardeña, a bull ranch in Andalusia, at the invitation of its owner, the bullfighter Belmonte, as it happened one of Burns's Spanish friends. Winter was the season for identifying and rounding up bulls that were suitable for the fight and, having ridden horses from childhood, and developed her father's love of bullfighting, Mabel was looking forward to a working holiday on the ranch.

By chance Burns met Mabel a week later in Madrid, on the eve of her journey south. They had both been invited to a cocktail party given by the Marqueses de Quintanar and Miraflores, well-known members of the Spanish political right before the war who had shifted their allegiance away from the Axis towards the Allies after the success of the joint British and American landings in North Africa.

Parties thrown by the Quintanars were popular and offered the perfect opportunity in wartime Madrid for the exchange of gossip, and above all to be seen in the company of the rich and powerful. And yet Burns was less motivated on this occasion by his professional calling than by a stirring of the heart as he and Mabel spotted each other in the social mêlée: 'It seemed natural that we should gravitate towards each other across the crowded room and that it would seem empty apart from her presence,' he later recalled. Burns felt that his love life was taking a profound turn for the better for the first time in years. From that autumn of 1943, Mabel Marañón became the sole target of Burns's wartime affections as he gradually discovered the extent to which her youth belied a depth of experience he, now thirty-seven, had never imagined could be possessed by a Spanish woman of her age and social upbringing.

Mabel's early memories were of a strict childhood largely dominated by a series of English governesses, none of whom lasted as long or exercised such influence as Miss Burns. The young governess arrived in Madrid in 1926, when Mabel was eight, and stayed in the Marañón household for the next seven years.

Miss Burns was a strict Victorian in attitude, who believed in limiting Mabel's access to her parents, and imposed a regime of lessons and formal meals which included five o'clock tea laid out with milk and cakes. She was blue-eyed and red-headed and extremely prim. She was therefore horrified by the wolf whistles of workers as she walked through the streets of Madrid. Her idea of intimacy was the rare occasions she allowed Mabel to give her a manicure while she read Dickens.

Every month copies of the *Illustrated London News* arrived at the house and Mabel's mother would cut out and frame the photographs of the royal princesses Elizabeth and Margaret. Despite Marañón's Republican leanings, he and his wife had maintained cordial relations with the Spanish King Alfonso XIII and his wife, who was a first cousin of Queen Victoria. They shared a common affinity with the British royal family.

Far from stifling the young Mabel, such tutelage and privileged upbringing merely fuelled a fascination for the world that was apparently out of bounds but which she sensed from an early age to be a great deal more exciting and engaging that the repressed environment in which Miss Burns sought comfort.

The year Miss Burns arrived in Madrid was also the year Gregorio Marañón was thrown into prison for a month after being accused, along with a group of liberal military officers and intellectuals, of plotting the overthrow of the dictator Primo de Rivera. Marañón's subsequent release on payment of a 100,000-peseta fine served as a reminder of his popularity and influence. Throughout his imprisonment his cell was garlanded with flowers sent by well-wishers and he received a constant stream of visitors, from ordinary workers to establishment figures campaigning for his liberty.

Five years later, the Spanish Republic Marañón helped proclaim brought the social and political tensions that had been simmering for decades to the boil; there were agrarian revolts, strikes, and churches were attacked. The left pressed for greater freedoms and root and branch constitutional reform. The bastions of privilege and political reaction – the landed aristocracy, right-wing politicians, sectors of the military and the Church – plotted and conspired. In the midst of the ferment, Mabel felt drawn to a new generation of Spanish women who, rather than marry young or join a convent, took advantage of the educational reforms to emancipate themselves. She volunteered as a nurse in her father's hospital and prepared to apply for university.

Then Mabel's life was brutally interrupted by the outbreak of civil war. Her father initially reacted to the military uprising by signing a manifesto with other leading intellectuals in defence of democracy. He also volunteered to go on working as a doctor in Madrid while the capital remained in Republican hands. Mabel decided to continue as a nurse in order to stay close to her father.

The Marañóns stuck together in Madrid, only to find themselves, like so many other Spaniards, swept up by events which seemed rapidly to run out of control. In the following weeks, Marañón became increasingly horrified by the violence and intolerance that engulfed Spain and tried with limited success to intercede on behalf of those persecuted by one side or the other. But before the year was out he himself was under threat, his liberal politics challenged by the increasingly fanatical elements on the left and the right that were determining the course of the war.

One night he received a summons to appear at a barracks held by Republican militias in the Casa de Campo, the large woodland park on the outskirts of Madrid where hundreds of prisoners were held and interrogated, the majority prior to summary execution. Fearful of what might await him, he asked Mabel to accompany him in his chauffeur-driven car as a witness. As they approached the barracks Marañón told the chauffeur to stop and warned his daughter to stay in the car. 'If I am not out of here in one hour, I want you to get to Madrid and raise the alarm,' he told Mabel before embracing her and leaving her with the fear that she might never see him again.

Mabel would remember that wait for the rest of her life. Time passed neither quickly nor slowly. It was suspended while the best and most valued moments of her life so far – those spent in her father's presence – filled her thoughts, and she struggled with a sense of despair and panic. She desperately wanted to believe he was still alive against the look of hate in the eyes of the sentries, the creeping darkness that enveloped the park and the staccato machine-gun fire which periodically shattered the claustrophobic silence.

Almost an hour later Marañón emerged from the barracks, his face pale and drawn with exhaustion, his suit dishevelled and smudged with dirt after he'd been interrogated about his political leanings by an ad hoc workers' committee. All the way back to Madrid, Marañón held his daughter's hand in silence, squeezing it gently every now and then as a way of reassuring her, a habit Mabel would replicate with her own children in later years. But he had decided that, for the sake of his family and his own survival, he had no option but to go into exile. Two countries had offered him asylum – Mexico and France. He chose the latter in order to stay closer to Spain and to friends who were already in exile north of the Pyrenees. He also had with him an invitation from the French consulate in Madrid to give a lecture at the Sorbonne in Paris where he had been made an honorary fellow in 1932. This helped him secure safe-conduct papers from the Republican government.

Less than a month later, Marañón and his family left Madrid in a small convoy of cars. They were accompanied by another well-known Spanish intellectual, Ramón Menéndez Pidal, and his family and by a young captain of the anarchist militias, a nephew of Angel Ganivet whose seminal essays on the character of Spain and its history hugely influenced the so-called generation of '14 to which Marañón and others belonged. The captain suspected from the outset that the Sorbonne invitation was a cover to help Marañón escape from the execution squads in Madrid, but took it upon himself to help save his uncle's friend and disciple.

Under Captain Ganivet's protection, the convoy drove south-east through territory occupied by anti-Franco forces. They reached the Republican-held port of Alicante where HMS *Active*, a Royal Navy frigate that was helping transport refugees out of Spain under the auspices of the International Red Cross, was anchored off the coast.

The small family convoy made its way to the harbour and there found a young English officer with a team of ratings in a small boat waiting to take the latest contingent of refugees out to the ship. The Marañón and Menéndez Pidal families were just stepping aboard when two local militiamen broke into an argument with Captain Ganivet, insisting that the two youngest male members of the party – Mabel's brother Gregorio and Gonzalo, the son of Menéndez Pidal – should stay behind and enlist in the Republican army.

Of the two, young Gregorio was most at risk because he had enlisted in the Falange youth movement which the extreme left regarded as criminally fascist. But both he and Gonzalo were saved thanks to the timely intervention of the English officer, and the added distraction caused by Captain Ganivet as he officiously waved safe-conduct papers.

As Ganivet engaged the militiamen, Gregorio and Gonzalo were bundled on to the waiting boat, and, shielded by their families and the British sailors, were speedily transferred to *Active*. Only later did the militiamen receive confirmation that the safe-conduct papers did not cover young Gregorio and that he was therefore a fugitive from the Spanish Republic and subject to a military tribunal. By then *Active*'s anchor had been raised and the vessel was steaming out of port.

12

MARRIAGE

The ship sailed to Marseilles via Barcelona where it picked up more refugees, the week before Christmas 1936, the first winter of the civil war.

It was sunny but with a blustery north wind. Mabel spent much of the journey on deck, wrapped in a heavy coat and blanket to protect her from the cold, being looked after by Francis Warrington-Strong, the handsome young naval officer who had helped save her brother's life. The sight of the displaced Spanish families filled Warrington-Strong with a huge sense of sympathy for their plight. But it was Mabel who stirred his emotions most, a young untainted Spanish beauty who seemed to have retained a sense of grace, poise and humour, despite the horrors she had lived through in Madrid.

For her part the eighteen-year-old Mabel found Warrington-Strong a refreshing contrast to the men she had left behind on Spanish soil. He struck her as calm and considerate, and with a fresh, engaging face that seemed as yet unmarked by the experience of killing another human being. On the final night of the passage, Mabel and Francis spent some time together romantically gazing out at the moonlit Mediterranean. They shared their fears that the war in Spain seemed a prelude to a wider European conflict, one in which his ship would be militarily engaged and no longer commissioned for a humanitarian role. Each was resigned to the likelihood of never seeing the other again once the passage was over. In memory of those precious moments they shared together, Warrington-Strong gave Mabel two keepsakes she had inspired – one a piece of poetry, the other a photograph.

The poem, mourning a lost innocence, seemed to foretell with a sense of anguish the fate he thought awaited him once the European war had started in earnest.

> *Steadfastly he gazed,*
> *Down at the bottomless abyss.*
> *To think that life should end like this!*
> *His mind felt cold and dazed . . .*
> *Under the wintry moon*
> *A lonely night not far on high,*
> *And murmured to the velvet sky,*
> *'Too soon – Too soon – Too soon'*

The photograph showed him as Mabel had met him, smiling and relaxed, in his white naval jacket with his arms crossed. It was dedicated to her: 'In memory of a trip which was made so much more pleasant for us by the cheery and delightful company of a certain refugee'.

Two months later, Mabel and her father were at sea again, in a setting that could not have been more different. In February 1937, they boarded the *Cap Arcona*, the luxury German ocean liner, at Boulogne on its journey from Hamburg to South America. Marañón had spent much of the intervening period since leaving Alicante installing his family at the Hôtel d'Iéna in Paris while establishing professional contacts with local French academics and authors. Politically Marañón kept in contact with a wide circle of friends among fellow exiles and the Spanish diplomatic community in Paris. In London and Oxford he corresponded regularly with the Duke of Alba and separately with the liberal writer and former minister of the Republic, Salvador de Madariaga, who became an increasingly vocal critic of Franco. While in Paris, Marañón's own Republicanism had given way to a belief that a Franco victory would bring the stability and order he now saw as more important for Spain than any renewed attempt at parliamentary democracy. While he reached out to those he considered reasonable men on both sides of the Spanish political divide, he felt most perturbed by the communist influence on the Republicans and blamed his exile on the intolerable position he had been placed in by Spain's increasingly radicalised Popular Front government.

While his wife and daughters searched for more permanent accommodation, Marañón wasted little time in making contact with Franco's representative in Paris, Quiñones de León, and interceding on behalf of his son's wish to return to Spain and fight as a soldier with the nationalists. Marañón subsequently found himself becoming increasingly depressed by the news from Spain at a time when Franco's victory seemed far from assured – the relentless violence, the apparent breakdown of law and order, the summary executions by both sides of individuals whose only crime was to be judged politically different.

He found it difficult to concentrate on his work as a doctor, and struggled with his writing. Marañón heeded the advice of friends and fellow doctors and agreed to accept an invitation to go on a lecture tour of South America with his fare and that of his daughter Mabel – enlisted as companion and secretary – paid for by the governments of Uruguay, Argentina, Chile and Brazil.

In that early spring of 1937, the *Cap Arcona* steamed down to Lisbon before making its two-week crossing to the South American mainland, via Cape Verde and Madeira. Marañón had plenty of time to prepare his lectures while Mabel read, took the sun and generally enjoyed herself in the company of similar aged South Americans and Germans between the elaborate dinners and other entertainment laid on for passengers. One evening Mabel dressed up as a gypsy and danced flamenco; on another, she took on the role of fairy princess in the fancy dress ball that followed the traditional rituals as the ship crossed the Equator.

Marañón was spared the company of destitute fellow exiles and found his civil war neurosis improving as he shared the dinner table with a group of rich Argentinian *estancieros* and German entrepreneurs, among them an amiable businessman named Oscar Schindler who would later become famous for his part in saving hundreds of Jews from the Nazi death camps.

Marañón's visit to South America proved both cathartic and a huge personal success. He filled lecture halls and theatres as he spoke emotionally about the Spain that was tearing itself apart. He engaged his audience's sympathy as a true patriot of essentially liberal values, who was suffering the pain of exile because of his refusal to sign formally up to any political dogma. 'I have always been at the service of my country, whether the omens were good or bad. I am now once again at the service of my country, above all else and whatever the consequences might be,' he said in one lecture entitled 'I am a Spaniard'.

In another, entitled the 'Dictatorship of Ideas', he lamented the advent of ideologues that justified intolerance and brutality as a means to an end: 'I never tire of saying that the core of all the ills that afflict this world, or at least this world which is seen from America as an uprising of madmen is the simple fact that men fight each other over ideas rather than conducting themselves as civilized beings.'

Marañón's lectures won him plaudits from the local media, nowhere more so than in Buenos Aires, where the Argentinian commentators noted that he had drawn bigger crowds than the Prince of Wales had on a recent visit to the city. For the eighteen-year-old Mabel, South America was one long holiday, riding along the beach of Uruguay's Punta del Este and across the huge estates of Argentina, on an endless string of horses supplied by the sons and daughters of government ministers and landowners.

Father and daughter enjoyed the return passage on the *Cap Arcona*. Marañón had recovered from his depression. Mabel played ping-pong with a new group of Argentinian friends, and attended a masked ball. She felt excited to be on a ship which was universally considered one of the most beautiful of the time, the most impressive commercial liner to be built since the *Titanic*. Only on 1 May, in mid-Atlantic, did the *Cap Arcona* show its true colours with a well-drilled exhibition of Nazi loyalty. The Marañóns emerged from their cabin to find the main decks covered in swastika flags, and officers and crew in military uniform parading with Nazi salutes and *Heil Hitlers* as a tribute to the Third Reich.

As most of the passengers raised their arms in salute, Marañón put his round his daughter's and held it there, a discreet act of defiance for which the captain of the ship apparently bore him no ill will. The captain chose to observe what he took simply to be a gesture of the love between father and daughter. Three days later he hosted a dinner in honour of Mabel's nineteenth birthday, a full-course menu with champagne and cake. Mabel sat on his right in the seat of honour. Later that night, as father and daughter made their way back to their respective cabins, Mabel asked her father if he was concerned that she had not met anyone yet she wanted to marry. She had two suitors at the time – a friend of her brother's who had enlisted in Franco's army, and a young doctor she had met in Buenos Aires. While flattered by their attentions, she felt unmoved by either of them. 'The only thing that matters,' Marañón advised her, 'is marrying someone you are in love with.' To Mabel, her father was still the most romantic man she had ever known.

On 11 May the ship docked at Southampton and the Marañóns made their way back to Paris by train. Marañón spent the next three years pursuing his calling as doctor, essayist and historian – writing a book on the mysticism of El Greco and an essay on Don Juan – in which he developed the thesis, based on clinical studies of some of his own patients, that the legendary Lothario was a repressed homosexual.

In 1938, Mabel was encouraged by her father to make her first visit to Britain in order to perfect her English and experience something of English life.

Over that summer, she stayed with a family in Norwich where she gave Spanish lessons in Blyth secondary school while improving her knowledge of British culture with occasional visits to Cambridge. A surviving photograph album from that period shows Mabel posing with some Spanish friends outside King's College, punting along the *College Backs* – the most famous stretch of the River Cam – and dressed in academic gown and at Number 15 King's Parade, presumably a student flat but long since converted into commercial premises.

For all her academic regalia, Mabel's involvement with the university city was essentially that of a tourist. At the time, though, she dreamed of staying in the UK and becoming a Cambridge undergraduate. She claimed in later years that an unnamed academic who had interviewed her was a communist and biased against her because she had ended up supporting Franco in the Civil War.

There is no mention of her failed application in the diary she kept at the time. Instead her notes show her generally content, growing in confidence with her first paid job in a foreign land. As one entry put it, 'I like England and I like English men. Most of them seem to have manners.'

In 1939, she returned to Paris, and resumed her studies at the Sorbonne. She was now fluent in French as well as English. During a family summer holiday in the South of France she met a young French girl of Jewish descent called Nelly Hess, the daughter of a Parisian textile manufacturer. By the end of the summer, Mabel and Nelly had become the best of friends. They exchanged addresses and delivered on their mutual promise to continue to see each other in Paris, which they did regularly for the next two years. The memory of Nelly's sudden disappearance in the summer of 1941 would haunt Mabel for the rest of her life.

In early June of that year, as the German army advanced on Paris, Mabel and Nelly were travelling back from the cinema on the Métro when they were confronted by a group of French youths. One of them pointed at Nelly before leading the others in a verbal outpouring of anti-Semitic abuse. The train pulled into the Champs-Elysées station, the nearest stop to where the girls lived. The girls waited till the doors were about to close again, and then rushed out, leaving the boys inside the carriage, gesticulating with their fingers as the train moved on.

Shaken by the experience, the pair walked in silence, arm in arm, to Nelly's house where they embraced and promised to see each other in the morning. The next day Mabel telephoned Nelly's house but there was no answer. When she later visited the house, she found it empty and was told by a neighbour that she and her family had left Paris.

Mabel assumed that Nelly's was one of the richer French Jewish families that had chosen to emigrate across the Atlantic, either to the US or South America. They were lucky to escape when they did. In July 1942 the Germans rounded up 13,000 Jews in the Paris region, most of whom subsequently perished in concentration camps. As the years passed after the war, with no word from Nelly, so Mabel came to believe that her friend had perhaps not survived the Holocaust. She had not been able to do anything to help her. The memory weighed heavily on her conscience.

*   *   *

Mabel was not in Paris when the Germans marched in on 14 June 1940. She and her middle sister Belén had been sent south by her parents, by train to the border, and then across to San Sebastián to visit Marañón's eldest daughter Carmen who was living there with her husband, three young children, and a German *Fräulein*.

On the night of 13 July her father heard on the radio that the Germans had reached the outskirts of the capital and were in in the Bois de Boulogne. The next morning Marañón rose early, ordered his wife Lolita to stay in the family apartment, and, with his medical colleague Teofilo Hernando, walked across the streets of Paris in search of the invaders. The city centre had an eerie, abandoned feel about it, many of its shops and cafés closed, its public transport temporarily suspended. More than half of Paris's population of five million had fled south. Marañón and Hernando were caught by a French photographer in the Place d'Etoile, as they stood on an empty pavement, at the very moment that the first of the German motorcycles with sidecars snaked into the boulevards, followed by the tanks and in turn by German troops, goose-stepping down the Champs-Elysées.

Within days of the Nazi occupation, Marañón witnessed the revival of Parisian life as sectors of the local population settled into a pattern of collaboration. He took notes of what he saw. 'People are beginning to make contact with the soldiers; some women speak to them . . . two or three are laughing, and there are also men talking to the Germans, in German,' he wrote in one diary entry.

Marañón also described the experience of lunching in their local restaurant just after it had reopened for business. 'The owner is eating, alone, in shirt sleeves. We join him, and as we eat together he blames everything that has happened on the politicians and the lack of discipline among his fellow countrymen. When he serves us some food, he adds: "I hate Hitler, of course; but there is something in him which reminds me of Napoleon and Alexander the Great."'

While shocked by the suddenness of the French capitulation, Marañón found himself initially impressed by the discipline of the Germans, believing for a while that they had brought the kind of order he felt Europe so desperately needed. Such was the 'normality' that he sent word to Mabel that she and her sister should return without delay and resume their studies while he continued to write essays, letters and books. 'The years I lived in Paris during the war,' Marañón later told his official biographer, 'were fundamental ones; because I was allowed to work without social obligations, because I was forced to live modestly and because I had the time to get to know myself better . . .'

A wish to find out more about Spain's most famous Parisian exile lay behind the summons Marañón received one day to dine with the most senior Nazi counter-intelligence officer in occupied France, Hans Keiffer, at his residence, a large turn-of-the-century town house from which the owners, a Jewish family, had been forcefully evicted.

The unexpected invitation was made in a telephone call one evening while Marañón was working in his study in the family apartment he had rented in the rue George Ville. He would later tell his family that his first thought was that the Germans were planning to arrest him – perhaps because he and his family had befriended Jews prior to the occupation. But if Keiffer wanted Marañón arrested he would simply have sent troops to his home. Suspecting that other motives lay behind the invitation, or simply as an insurance policy, Marañón almost certainly would have thought of contacting his friend, Franco's wartime ambassador in Paris José Félix de Lequerica, and asking his advice.

Lequerica, under instructions from Franco, had cultivated ties with the collaborationist French right, and with the Germans, while defending Spain's neutrality and resisting Nazi demands for the handing over of Jews who had crossed the border south into Spain. Lequerica, nevertheless, would in all likelihood have convinced Marañón that it was his patriotic duty to accept the invitation from Keiffer as a sign of respect for the Axis while using the meeting as an opportunity to remind the Germans that Franco had no wish to be dragged into the war. Marañón shared the view that the alternative to neutrality was seeing Spain plunge into another civil war, this time with the prospect of the Allies fighting alongside the communists south of the Pyrenees.

In the thin and unconvincing account Marañón's official biographer gives of the Spaniard's meeting, the high-ranking Nazi official is not named, and there is no reference to the fact that his host was by then already responsible for the execution of dozens of resistance fighters and the persecution of the Jews. Nor was any political subject raised. Instead, Marañón claimed he had spent the evening discussing art before being personally driven home by Keiffer. No separate testimony survives of what was said by the two men, though the very fact that Marañón was left alone by the Germans during his remaining stay in Paris would suggest that his freedom was not considered a threat to their interests.

As for Mabel, she appears, initially at least, and in common with several of her non-Jewish French and Spanish girlfriends, to have developed a similarly ambiguous attitude towards the German occupation.

It was only long after the war was over that Mabel recalled her visits to the Paris Opéra and the Comédie-Française when German soldiers were present. She remembered feeling distracted by the smell of leather from their boots mixing with the perfume of the women in the audience. The memory returned as clearly as that of Nelly's 'disappearance' and a separate incident in which a French boyfriend of hers was slapped and then arrested after accidentally pushing into a German officer as he came out of the Métro.

The only German she befriended for a brief period was a Luftwaffe pilot, who had survived the Battle of Britain; he spoke perfect English and French and seemed courteous and trustworthy, at least until the night she agreed to a double date with her friend Chiquita, the daughter of the Argentinian consul César Oliveira, who was a fanatical supporter of Franco and the Spanish Falange party. One night Chiquita persuaded Mabel to join her for drinks in her flat while her parents were away. She arrived to find her alone with her German friend and a fellow pilot.

Within minutes the four of them were laughing and joking. Records were sorted and they paired off, dancing the tango. Then, halfway through the evening, Chiquita announced suddenly that she was going for a walk with her partner, leaving Mabel with her pilot.

Within minutes he had placed cushions on the floor, lit some candles and opened the third bottle of champagne of the evening. To Mabel, what had seemed romantic at first now became a little unnerving. While she thought she liked the German, she had no intention of making love with him. So it was that she told the pilot that she was engaged to be married to a high-ranking officer in the Spanish army who might visit Paris within days. The German immediately stood up, apologised and offered to take Mabel back to her parents' apartment. It was the last night they ever saw each other.

Mabel Marañón never was engaged to a high-ranking officer in the Spanish army but to someone who had served as a subaltern in Franco's army along with her brother Gregorio during the civil war. His name was Clemente Peláez, one of the young founders of the Falange party who had become a stockbroker in Spain. The day Mabel met Tom Burns for the first time, the loyal, well-mannered if somewhat dour Peláez was still officially her fiancé. She wore a bracelet he had given her.

But whatever loyalty she felt she owed him evaporated in the presence of the attractive and charming Englishman who, despite his pipe and dog and heavily accented Spanish, had a charisma almost equal to that of the father she venerated.

It was as if Captain Warrington-Strong had sent his elder brother or best friend to rekindle the romance of that moonlight crossing from Alicante to Marseilles. But just as important was the fact that Burns had come to Marañón's beloved Toledo on the recommendation of friends the two men appeared to share. If Mabel was looking for a father substitute, Burns was the closest she had come to finding one.

It was one of these friends, the bullfighter Belmonte, who, in the run-up to Christmas 1943, took it upon himself to invite Burns down to his ranch in Andalusia while Mabel was still holidaying there, a willing go-between for two individuals of whom he was enormously fond. On 4 December Burns, once again accompanied by his dog Juerga and the eccentric sculptor Sebastián Miranda – now temporarily engaged as an unofficial chaperone – set off from Madrid in an old Ford borrowed from the US embassy (Burns's Wolseley was undergoing repairs) and made the journey south in icy conditions.

Spain was settling into another cold winter, and the car had no heating. It was a bumpy journey, much of it along a badly paved road Burns was familiar with from earlier professional assignments. But with Miranda there were always surprises. The unexpected came after

Burns narrowly missed crashing into a flock of turkeys as he motored through an isolated village. The birds were being driven across the road by an peasant woman with a stick. Miranda told Burns to stop the car, haggled with the old woman and bought two of her turkeys. The two companions journeyed on, each feeling a little warmer thanks to the turkey each had between his legs.

Belmonte's ranch was typical of the region, low-built and whitewashed, and decorated inside with tiles, rugs and hides. Nearby stables were filled with thoroughbreds and cross-breed Andalusian and Arab horses, and there was a small bullring where Belmonte and other friends would practise their bullfighting skills with some of the younger calves. Beyond, hundreds of fighting bulls and cows grazed on grassland which stretched for miles across one of the most underpopulated areas of Western Europe.

The bullfighter was hugely fond of Mabel, who had become a close friend of his only daughter, Yola. He thought the young Marañón girl refreshingly different from most of the somewhat snobbish upper-class Madrileñas – cosmopolitan, a fearless horse-rider, and with a genuine soul, or *duende*, when it came to flamenco dancing. That Christmas, Belmonte dedicated to her a signed photograph of himself on his favourite mare, and dressed in the traditional Andalusian country clothes – the *traje corto*.

Belmonte was similarly taken by Burns, whom he considered the most eccentric Englishman he had ever met – and he hadn't met all that many *ingleses*. From the moment Burns had first infiltrated his dining club, or *tertulia*, in Madrid, Belmonte had taken to this maverick spy who seemed to genuinely love Spain and its culture, not least bullfighting.

Belmonte took a mischievous delight in acting the go-between for his two friends. He proved the ideal host for the developing love-match, providing good company, and matching his other guest, the flamboyant Sebastián Miranda, with an apparently inexhaustible flow of picaresque anecdote at the end of a long day out of doors.

Belmonte's stuttering good humour came accompanied by plentiful wine, *tapas*, and barbecues. But he also showed himself capable of being unobtrusive as circumstances demanded.

Burns had brought with him a book of Lorca poems, *Poet in New York*, which he had smuggled in from the UK, and which he gave Mabel in private. The edition had been published in Mexico because the poems were banned in Spain at the time. Burns had himself been given it by Rafael Nadal, the exiled Spanish academic whose BBC programmes he had had censored. The two men had maintained a friendship despite their political disagreements over Franco, largely through a shared respect for Lorca, whose execution by the nationalists Burns had come to view as inexcusable.

His gift of the Lorca poems to Mabel was an acknowledgement of Lorca's friendship with her father during the 1920s and early 1930s when he had been an occasional visitor to the Cigarral de Menores in Toledo.

While at Belmonte's ranch Burns and Mabel spent most days going on long walks or riding together, watching the cowhands in the distance moving in and out of the bulls, and marvelling at the space and peace that surrounded them. It was hard to believe that a war was still being fought and there were long moments when they were able to forget it.

When the time came for Burns to return to Madrid, Mabel chose to follow soon afterwards. Just after Christmas, they met up secretly for the first time, stole out of the city and spent the day in the peace and quiet of the old university quarter of Alcalá de Henares, before dining at the Mesón de Fuencarral, an old tavern on the outskirts of the capital which the British embassy considered off limits to the Germans. Much of what each had lived went unsaid, and yet they both felt a new dimension was beginning to take form, one built on the common ground of shared secrets, faith and love. His memory of the moment he and Mabel decided to marry would remain the clearest and most profoundly heartfelt of encounters with any woman in his life. 'It was there that what we must have been groping towards in the past few weeks came clearly into sight. Now we were looking not so much at each other as in the same direction. We were going to be married . . .' he later recalled.

Three days later, at a private embassy function celebrating New Year's Day 1944, Burns approached his ambassador and asked permission to marry a Spaniard. Burns had learnt enough about the character of Sir

Samuel Hoare, the inner workings of the British government and the sensitivity of relations with Franco's Spain not to expect an immediate reply. Moreover, it was not immediately obvious whose interests would be best served by the Burns/Marañón marriage, planned for April 1944.

Earlier that spring the US government had decided to step up pressure on Franco, warning him, through its embassy in Madrid, that Spain faced an embargo on petroleum imports unless it suspended exporting wolfram to Germany. The ensuing discussion between the Allies and Franco over the various points at issue – not just wolfram, but the continuing presence of German spies in Spain, a hostile German consul general in Tangier, continuing acts of sabotage, and enduring pro-Axis propaganda in the local media – would probably have been negotiated discreetly had it not been for Germany calling in payment of the debt Franco owed Hitler for his assistance during the civil war.

The 100,000 Marks made it possible for the Nazis to come into the market and purchase wolfram in competition with the Allies. It fuelled a speculative market of international intrigue and double-dealing over a commodity that in 1939, in the words of Ambassador Hoare, had been as 'worthless as dust'.

In a secret memorandum to his foreign secretary Eden outlining the extraordinary story of wolfram trading in wartime Spain, Hoare described the frenzied pre-emptive Allied buying and German demand for the mineral thus: 'Throughout the period there was the wildest possible gambling in the commodity. The South Sea Bubble could not compare with what happened over the Peninsula. Fortunes were made in a night, desperate crimes were committed in making them, smuggling became rife, and the huge sums given for this once worthless rock were one of the principal causes in the rise in the cost of living.' The ambassador's sense of humour, not notable at the best of times, wore decisively thin when dealing with Americans, many of whom he regarded as cowboys, unschooled in the delicate art of diplomacy and the game of intelligence.

Nevertheless, Hoare was wise enough to recognise that, with the tide of war showing signs of turning in the Allies' favour, public opinion in Britain as well as the US was likely to turn against a fascist government remaining in southern Europe. 'It is well, therefore, to reconsider our position from time to time, and to adjust our policy to the general course of the war and the actual facts of the Spanish situation,' he wrote to London on 11 December 1943.

Four weeks later Hoare sent Eden an intelligence assessment based on a series of conversations Burns had had with Marañón since meeting him in Toledo. Burns had been provided by his prospective father-in-law with a useful insight into the current state of internal Spanish politics, not least the continuing divisions of the anti-Franco opposition. 'Spain, however much she may need it, is not ready for a change of regime,' Marañón told Burns. The monarchists, among whom Marañón had several close friends, had spent the past weeks and months plotting a restoration, only to see the efforts come to nought, through their inability to forge a 'really unified, representative and responsible centre'.

Other exiles had proved themselves incapable of unifying except in extremist groups that risked being dominated by the communists. As for Franco, he remained in power more by default than genius, so Marañón believed. Despite his support of the Nationalists in the civil war, Marañón was scathing in his criticism of the *Generalísimo* who he thought history might come to judge as one of the 'most guilty rulers of Spain', out of 'sheer stupidity and from idolatry of self and a few false political ideas'.

And yet, critically, Marañón, in his meeting with Burns, argued for cautious and consensual rather than unilateral diplomacy. 'The fatal thing would be to let the country suffer as a consequence of such pressure [i.e. an embargo] and to allow him [Franco] to appear symbolically as the victim of the whole people.'

Less surprisingly, Marañón described Hoare's mission as a 'triumphant success', for taking the long-term view and maintaining contact with 'so many sides of Spanish life'. It was a strategy, he suggested, that should be used as a model, for dealing with the acute internal complexities of other countries. 'The [British] Ambassador has achieved an almost mythical status which of course held its dangers but implied the highest responsibilities for Spain herself,' Marañón told Burns.

By presenting his ambassador with his report, Burns was in effect gambling his own reputation on Marañón's credibility with the

British government. He was playing for high stakes, in his pursuit of professional recognition on the one hand and the heart of Mabel on the other. Hoare's covering letter suggested that he had won his ambassador over and that a process was under way to convince London of the diplomatic benefits that might be gained from a Burns/Marañón marriage – one that openly linked His Majesty's Government with a Spaniard who was popular and likely to play an important role in the future of his country, with or without Franco.

The higher echelons of the British government took less than a month to decide that the Burns/Marañón union, far from harming British interests, would actually help promote them. Fearing a German diplomatic pre-emptive strike to disrupt the wedding, the Foreign Office sent its official message of approval in cipher. Days later Brendan Bracken, Churchill's propaganda chief, sent Burns a personal letter of congratulations in the diplomatic bag.

The wedding took place on 29 April 1944. The church chosen for the religious ceremony was San Jerónimo the Royal, an impressive piece of architecture, built in brilliant white stone, its neo-gothic exterior resembling a fairy castle, so called because of the royal connections with the restored former monastery near the Prado museum. It was here that King Alfonso XIII had married his English bride Victoria Eugenia on 31 May 1906 before both survived an assassination attempt. The Burns/Marañón wedding proved only marginally less ambitious in its conception. No expense, diplomacy or publicity was spared in making the event the best-organised and best-attended nuptials in wartime Spain, as well as the most eclectic. The invitation list ranged from orphans of Republicans killed in the civil war (the messenger boys employed by Burns's section) and former exiles to members of the royal family and five-star generals of the Franco regime, among them General Aranda, one of the officers bribed by the British. Other guests included English nannies, Spanish countesses, and most of the Allied diplomatic corps, along with doctors, politicians, poets, painters and spies, each of whom had contributed in some way or another to bringing excitement and colour to wartime Madrid.

The atmosphere was captured in the notebook of a journalist: 'the whole of Madrid appears to have been waiting for hours for this wedding . . . a mass of well-known faces mixed in with thousands of ordinary people, who are there out of sheer curiosity, waiting for the couple to arrive . . . there are faces from the days of the Monarchy, from the days of the Republic, from the days of the Civil War, from the present and the future . . . those who have survived on one side or the other are here, many out of friendship and affection towards Marañón who so skilfully has managed with the wedding of his daughter to give a show of unity, a word that is much overused these days, but of which there is scarce evidence . . .'

The best man was Belmonte, the bullfighter. Hours earlier he had attended the funeral of the wife of Domingo Ortega, a bullfighter turned bull rancher like himself. Belmonte had spent most of his professional life risking death. The marriage made him feel as he did after a good *faena* and a decent kill, happy to be alive, among friends.

Burns was impeccably dressed in a morning coat made by his tailor in Jermyn Street, Mayfair, and flanked by embassy colleagues on the one side and Mabel's male relations on the other. Most distinctive among them was the British military attaché, Brigadier Torr, looking the archetypical Colonel Blimp, and Mabel's brother Gregorio, his black hair smoothed back with Brylcreem, and sporting a thin black moustache, as was the fashion among young Falangist veterans of the civil war.

Like the military, the Church was similarly equally represented. Two priests had been called in for the occasion – the octogenarian Marañón family chaplain, the pious, unassuming Monsignor Monreal from Toledo Cathedral, and one of the embassy's more eccentric secret agents, the bumptious rector of the English College in Valladolid, Monsignor Henson.

Mabel, whom Belmonte considered one of the most beautiful women in Madrid, emerged from the British embassy's Rolls-Royce looking very much a fairy-tale Spanish princess – radiant in a flowing lace dress especially designed and sewn by the private seamstress her mother shared with Queen Victoria Eugenia. The dress was covered in damask and crimson velvet.

She was led up the long stairway and the aisle not by her beloved father but by the British ambassador, an arrangement she and Marañón had reluctantly agreed to, for the sake of diplomacy. Burns followed with Marañón's wife Lolita, and after them came the father of the bride with the wife of the ambassador, Lady Maud.

As the procession slowly made its way towards the high altar, Hoare at one point turned towards Mabel and whispered half-jokingly that he believed his Protestant Anglo-Saxon parents were turning in their grave at the sight of him holding the hand of a Spanish Catholic bride. Mabel, her face hidden beneath a veil, replied that, actually, it was her Cuban-born grandmother who was turning in her grave at the sight of a Spanish lady with a Protestant British ambassador.

The riposte confirmed Hoare's opinion that the new Mrs Burns was a woman of character who would need careful coaching by his wife, Lady Maud. Mabel found Hoare's comment typical of a man she considered as personifying the worst characteristics of the colonial mentality: snobbish, mean and inherently racist.

Unaware of the barbed exchange, Burns met his young bride at the altar and, raising her veil, marvelled at her beauty and smiled with undisguised satisfaction at an event her parents and the embassy had stage-managed to perfection. In the preceding days he had persuaded a high-ranking official in the Franco government that the wedding served its interests as much as it did his Majesty's Government, as a demonstration of Anglo-Spanish friendship in its broadest political and social sense.

Tom Burns and Mabel Marañón were married according to the old Spanish Catholic custom *bajo vela*, or under the veil. A large lace cloth was draped over Mabel's and Burns's heads, symbolically representing the union of the couple in one flesh.

The reception was held in the church's ample cloisters. Wartime Madrid's most famous bar owner, Pedro Chicote, marshalled an army of white-jacketed waiters for the distribution of cocktails and canapés of a variety that some of the guests had only dreamed of. Mrs Taylor, the British agent who ran the Embassy tea room, looked on with pride as bride and groom cut a towering three-layered cake she had personally created. It was made of fresh Toledo marzipan and Scottish fruit cake and topped with Spanish and British flags in a sugary embrace.

The wedding was one of the leading items in the official No Do newsreels that showed in Spanish cinemas, with the British mission in Madrid given more air time than at any stage in the war. The final preparations for the ceremony coincided with the Allies and Franco pulling back from the brink of diplomatic rupture. Spain cut its wolfram exports to Germany and the Allies lifted their oil embargo. Much to the anger of Berlin, the nuptials became popularly known in the streets of wartime Madrid as the *Boda de Gasolina*, or the Petrol Wedding.

Since June 1940, Burns had struggled to convince Spain to reverse its disproportionate use of German propaganda in favour of British news. He may not have ended the war but, thanks to his wedding, he had won an important battle.

The next morning, with a copy of the 16mm film of their marriage ceremony donated as a gift by Franco's official documentary maker safely stashed in his bedroom, Burns and Mabel embarked on their honeymoon. They drove to Toledo, for a few days 'solitude and peace' in the Cigarral de Los Menores. From there the couple journeyed south, stopping overnight at a small hotel that British intelligence had commandeered as a safe house near Bailén, beyond the mountain chain that separates Castile from Andalusia. They then continued down towards Gibraltar where they stayed at the Rock Hotel and had lunch as the guests of the governor. German agents still loitered on the Spanish side of the border, but the threat of sabotage had evaporated and talk of an imminent German invasion of the Iberian Peninsula and full-scale offensive on the British colony had long ago ceased.

From Gibraltar the newly-weds motored along the Costa del Sol. Estepona, Marbella and Torremolinos, names that in the second half of the twentieth century would become synonymous with mass tourism, were still small fishing villages. Burns and Mabel found empty beaches all to themselves to play and make love in. In Torremolinos, they stopped off for a drink at a small hotel. It had a good view of maritime traffic and at night they could see the lights of Málaga twinkling in the distance. Its manager, the embassy's local eyes and ears, was on a retainer.

They then journeyed inland towards the Sierra Nevada. The valleys were being replanted with olive trees, and the higher ground with pines, and the roads damaged by the civil war repaved.

In Granada, they booked into a small hotel near the Alhambra and marvelled at this enduring tribute to the architecture of Moorish Spain as they strolled around its perfumed gardens and fountains. Later they walked down to the gypsy quarter where they bought lace, drank a lot of wine and watched an impromptu flamenco, unaware that their honeymoon was about to end abruptly.

They returned to their hotel by moonlight to find an urgent telegram from the embassy. It informed Burns that his friend and colleague, the deputy head of mission Arthur Yencken, and the assistant air attaché Squadron Leader Caldwell, had been killed in an air crash in the mountains of Aragón, on their way to Barcelona. Their plane had crashed into wooded terrain in poor conditions. That night Burns and Mabel drove back to Madrid to attend Yencken's funeral.

It was a solemn affair, with Yencken, as acting head of mission during Ambassador Hoare's temporary absence in London, being accorded full honours by the Spanish government and the Foreign Office. Even if sabotage was suspected by some within the British embassy, London seemed happy enough to exploit the propaganda value of the funeral without turning the cause of Yencken's death into a major diplomatic incident.

As the most senior and longest serving member of the Madrid embassy, Burns found himself among those leading the cortège. He was accompanied by key Spanish government figures, several in military uniform, alongside an equally impressive array of foreign diplomats, led by the American ambassador Carlton Hayes and an emissary of the first post-Mussolini Italian government.

The cortège walked slowly along Madrid's main avenue – the same one down which Himmler had paraded in 1941 – the Union Jack draped over the coffin, the black mahogany funeral carriage flanked by detachments of the Spanish army, navy and air force in the slow march usually reserved for Christs, Virgins, Saints and the *Generalísimo*.

Hoare had spent the last months of his mission in Spain, between June and December 1944, regularly protesting about the prevarication shown by the Franco regime in shutting down the Axis spy networks, and the continuing presence of enemy agents in North Africa and

Spain. According to Hoare, the Spanish police adopted 'every kind of subterfuge' for evading the expulsion orders decreed by their government. Agents altered their passports, had their expulsion orders revoked or conveniently disappeared. Those who were forced out of Tangier were allowed to settle on the Spanish mainland. Hoare calculated that within two months of the Allied–Spanish oil deal being signed, 201 out 220 suspected agents were still circulating freely in Spain, although the figure had fallen to 68 by Christmas 1944.

And yet the diplomatic protests emanating from the British embassy belied the fact that German intelligence was by this stage in turmoil. Admiral Wilhelm Canaris, who had been head of the Abwehr since at least 1936, had been 'retired from his post', his professionalism and political loyalty and that of several of his officers questioned by some of Hitler's closest advisers. Canaris was later executed after being implicated in a plot to overthrow the *Führer*.

On 18 February 1944, Hitler decreed the setting-up of a unified German intelligence service which merged the overseas Abwehr with the domestic security organisation, the SD (*Sicherheitsdienst*), under the control of the head of the SS, Heinrich Himmler. The decision pushed the baby out with the bath water. 'SD officers with the haziest notions of military intelligence procedures and techniques took over positions where networks of agents, painstakingly built up over years, were "burnt" in weeks. As the intelligence war reached its climax ahead of the Normandy landings, the Abwehr was literarily *hors de combat*,' wrote Canaris's biographer Richard Bassett.

In fact German intelligence had already been severely weakened by the cracking of the cipher used in communications between Berlin and the various Abwehr outstations. This had allowed British intelligence to develop successful counter-espionage and deception operations through the extended use of double agents, an achievement which Franco seemed only too aware of. Faced with Hoare's protests, the cunning old fox feigned surprise that the ambassador should be worrying at all about agents, most of whom, in his view, were 'shirkers from the war and double crossers' of no political importance.

In Madrid, MI6 officers had spent much of the war encoding and decoding the decrypted Abwehr wireless traffic, the so-called ISOS material (an abbreviation of 'Intelligence Service, Oliver Strachey' – name of the the officer at the Government Code and Cipher School at Bletchley Park responsible for German intelligence material). After the landings in North Africa, more time was devoted to investigating the links between the Abwehr in Madrid and their agents in Britain. The running of double agents helped British intelligence in Spain to identify their case handlers and other figures linked to German espionage, including their Spanish 'cut-outs' or go-betweens. It also, crucially, allowed the Allied chiefs of staff to continue to deceive Hitler about their planned operations in a way that had a decisive impact on the outcome of the war.

By the autumn of 1944, a Spaniard called Juan Pujol, code-named Garbo, had already earned himself a place in the history books as one of the most successful double agents run from Abwehr Madrid. Three years earlier, Pujol had made his first contact with the British through the embassy in Madrid, using his wife as a go-between. At first the British were unconvinced by the latest 'walk-in'. Pujol claimed to be committed to the Allied cause but his personal history was full of contradictions and impossible to verify. He also claimed to have been born into a liberal middle-class family in Barcelona in 1908. At the outbreak of the civil war he had enlisted in the Republican army but had ended up fighting for the Nationalists during Franco's last major offensive, the Battle of the Ebro. Pujol would later tell his handlers that he had become as alienated by the communism of one set of Spaniards as by the fascism of others. He saw the future of humanity as resting in the hands of the Allies – or so he told the British.

The conversion to the cause of democracy of a man lacking any ideological coherence defied belief, raising doubts about where his true loyalties lay, but Pujol's credentials were no more dubious than those of numerous other agents recruited by the British during the war, not least the legendary Agent Zigzag, the convict Eddie Chapman who worked as part of the double-cross system run by MI5.

Like all double agents, Pujol was a mercenary who cleverly made himself indispensable to both sides. It was only after a year, during which Pujol touted his services among a plethora of British, US and German diplomats, attachés and intelligence personnel in Madrid and

Lisbon, that he was recruited by MI5 and based in the UK. By then Pujol had persuaded the sceptics on the Allied side of his potential usefulness because of the quality of the intelligence he obtained from the Germans as a result of providing them with fabricated information they trusted.

Few cases in the history of British intelligence during the Second World War can equal the Garbo case in terms of its duplicity, deception and betrayal. It was through Garbo that British intelligence managed to recruit a network of bogus sub-agents, each of whom played his part in a complex operation of counter-espionage, both feeding false information and identifying names and addresses of suspect German spies and their agents.

By the time the Allies prepared to make the final preparations for the North African landing, Garbo was regarded as a prime asset by sectors of British intelligence, and by the Nazis. So highly rated was Garbo that all his material was given priority status, with every military report transmitted to Madrid from his network immediately retransmitted to Berlin. While Garbo helped in deceiving the Germans about Operation Torch, his main contribution to the Allied victory was in the false information he fed to the Germans in the weeks leading up to the D-Day landings of 6 June 1944.

Garbo's subsequent role proved more controversial. He and his sub-agents were instructed to feed the Germans false intelligence about the physical damage, or lack of it, wrought by the V1 and V2 bombs. The guided rockets aimed at heavily populated parts of Britain's cities were Hitler's last, desperate throw of the dice. With them he sought to dent Allied complacency that the war was won, by serving notice of Germany's enduring military potential. Early reports by the Garbo network suggested, however, that some of the rockets were missing their targets, and persuaded the German launchers to modify their range. While the aim of the deception was to ensure that the bombs gradually landed in harmless places, this was not always the case, because some of the bombs still went astray, hitting civilian areas. The result was arguments between Whitehall and borough councils, and protests by politicians wanting to protect their constituencies from the diverted bombing. Herbert Morrison, the Home Secretary, was among the cabinet ministers particularly concerned about possible unnecessary loss of life.

Throughout this period of the late summer and early autumn 1944, increasingly elaborate ruses were conjured up by Garbo's handler, Tomás Harris, in order to maintain his credibility with the Germans. At one point, Harris had Pujol arrested on suspicion of spying as a way of reinforcing the idea that the information he was providing Berlin was genuine. Such was Garbo's perceived value to both sides that he was recommended for both an MBE and an Iron Cross.

Within Whitehall, Pujol became the subject of a struggle between MI6 and MI5, both of whom wanted to control him, with each agency accusing the other of inadequately sharing information. The extent to which several members of the British embassy in Madrid and Lisbon may have been involved in initial contacts with Pujol is difficult to judge, given that the intelligence services were selective when declassifying official paperwork dealing with Garbo's activities.

What is known is that it was only after Pujol had applied for accreditation as a journalist from the press office in the British embassy in Madrid – as an initial cover for his work for the Germans in London – that British intelligence began to take him seriously as an agent worth having on side. As for ambassador Hoare, at the very least he seems to have played the part of an unwitting pawn in a complex conspiracy of deception, his diplomatic protests about the lingering threat of German espionage a helpful diversion in allowing Garbo to succeed.

There is evidence, too, that the running of the Garbo network involved other key departments without their full knowledge or approval. In order to explain to his German controllers how he had managed to obtain key pieces of intelligence, Pujol claimed at different stages to be working for the BBC, and to have an 'unconscious source' within the Ministry of Information's Spanish section, a pretence that risked fuelling interdepartmental distrust within Whitehall just when the British embassy was trying to pursue a coherent policy on Spain that would outlive the end of the war.

Undoubtedly, however, it was the success of the Garbo operation in tearing apart German intelligence that ensured the ascendancy within Whitehall of those most closely involved. They included Harris,

Garbo's case officer, and his friend Philby, the head of MI6 Section V, who had oversight and overall management of all the communications between Garbo and the Germans.

Against this background it is perhaps not surprising that one English Catholic who straddled the world of diplomacy, propaganda and espionage began to feel the first pangs of vulnerability.

13

LIBERATION

On 3 August 1944, the increasingly pro-Allied Spanish foreign minister Jordana died of a sudden heart attack and was replaced by José Félix Lequerica, Franco's retiring ambassador to German-occupied France.

It was at this point that Burns re-entered the power play of wartime Madrid, thanks to the close friendship the Basque-born Lequerica had developed in Paris with Burns's father-in-law, Gregorio Marañón, during his exile in France. Following his appointment and before any formal meetings had been arranged with either the British or US embassy at any senior ambassadorial level, Lequerica, an affable bachelor who enjoyed good food and fine wines, received a secret message inviting him to dine at the Madrid flat Burns had moved into with his new bride.

The newly married *Señores de Burns* had coalesced effortlessly into a much-in-demand cosmopolitan partnership on the Madrid social circuit – good-looking, energetic, and intelligent. Burns showed himself to be very much in love with his young bride, a skilful and passionate dancer like himself, who could as easily dance a flamenco as a tango or fox-trot, with a physicality that had rarely been shown by the English debutantes of his youth, and the Queen's cousin he had mistakenly believed to be the love of his life. Daily, the self-confidence Mabel had developed while growing up under her eminent father's tutelage and those of his intellectual and powerful friends transformed into a new maturity, capable of handling the duties required of a diplomat's wife while retaining character and independence. She attended Lady

Maud's tea parties, and occasionally participated in the knitting circle, but always made clear that she preferred coffee and wine and that she had other pressing duties to attend to.

With Mabel as his wife, Burns became more organised, and his contact book even more extensive. Together they turned their newly rented apartment in the picturesque Calle del Prado – one of Madrid's better preserved old neighbourhoods – into a venue of choice for embassy colleagues, anglophile Spaniards, and those in the regime whose allegiance to the Axis cause was diminishing with each military encounter won by the Allies. From early spring onwards, the flat's decorative roof terrace became the scene for extended *sobremesas* – the after-meal discussions that formed such a key part of Spanish culture.

The speed with which the new foreign minister, Lequerica, accepted an invitation to the Burns household that last summer of the war reflected in part the growing influence of the British embassy as Nazi fortunes waned. It reaffirmed the special nature of the Marañón name, priceless in helping gain access to high-level sources within the Franco regime. And it reflected a certain pragmatism on Franco's part. Two months after the Normandy landings, Franco realised it was time to engage more positively with those likely to emerge victorious.

That evening Mabel played her part to perfection, first overseeing the cooking and serving of dinner by her newly hired domestic staff, and then drawing away the bulk of the guests so that Lequerica – fresh from a recent meeting with the German High Command – was given the chance, as Burns would later put it, to 'expand and let his indiscretions roll' in private conversation. On 22 August, as Allied forces closed in on Paris, the indiscretions drawn from Lequerica at his dinner *chez* Burns informed a three-page memorandum from Hoare to the foreign secretary Anthony Eden, giving a detailed assessment of the new minister's appointment and its implications for Allied relations with Spain.

'If history were conclusive, we should be forced to conclude that he [Lequerica] is nothing better than a Falange agent who has in the last four years shown himself to be a flatterer of General Franco and a friend of the Germans,' reported Hoare. And yet, the ambassador continued, such a judgement risked being proved over-simplistic, for friends and foes alike regarded the minister as an 'unabashed opportunist' who was willing to back whichever side looked like winning. 'Being a businessman from Bilbao, the Liverpool of Spain, he is not likely to keep his money in any bankrupt concern,' quipped Hoare.

Hoare had been persuaded by the Foreign Office to delay his planned departure from Madrid until the end of the year and oversee certain changes of personnel within his embassy. Among the new recruits to Burns's department sent by the Ministry of Information, with the blessing of the intelligence services, was Peter Laing, an Old Etonian and Grenadier Guards officer who had been invalided out of overseas military service before being assigned to royal protection duties at Windsor Castle. Laing had a reputation within his regiment as an eccentric prone to indiscipline, raising the possibility that his appointment may have been part of a deliberate ploy by Burns's enemies within MI5 to disrupt the press department's activities and undermine its chief's position. In fact, Laing was befriended by Mabel in a mildly flirtatious way and kept on a relatively tight professional reign by his chief, Burns, who thought him too young for an embassy wartime post but nevertheless possessing some experience that made him useful to the specific mission in Spain.

Apart from his military training and a short spell as an interpreter at General de Gaulle's Free French headquarters in London, the twenty-two-year-old Laing's main qualification for the job as assistant press attaché in the Madrid embassy was that he had unique and unpublicised access to useful Spanish sources in the Franco government thanks to his romantic entanglement midway through the war with Cayetana, the young daughter and only child of Franco's ambassador to the UK, the Duke of Alba, while both were living in London.

In early 1943, Laing was introduced to the eighteen-year-old Cayetana by Chiquita Carcaño, one of the beautiful, fashion-conscious twin daughters of the Argentinian ambassador in the UK he had befriended while studying at the Sorbonne. Cayetana Alba, the Duchess of Montoro, was descended from a noble Spanish blood line, that of Álvarez de Toledo, dating back to the feudal wars of the fourteenth century, her ancestry subsequently interwoven with a history of conquest and aristocratic interbreeding. Her artistic and outgoing personality derived inspiration from the 13th Duchess of Alba, the patron and alleged lover of the eighteenth-century painter Francisco Goya. 'She [the Duchess of Alba] was without question one of the most beautiful women in Spain,' wrote Goya to his friend Zapater of his muse, 'tall, slender, and flashing dark eyes and a fine-boned face.'

Of Cayetana at first sight, Laing would later write: 'She was absolutely divine – piggy eyes, a little plump, but sweet, and terribly attractive.'

Days after their first meeting in the Argentinian embassy, Laing was invited to Albury Park, the Victorian mansion in Surrey which the Duchess of Northumberland had rented to her friends the Albas as a weekend retreat during the war years. Set in more than 150 acres originally laid out by John Evelyn, the seventeenth-century diarist and horticulturalist, Albury would have seemed quite ordinary to the Albas whose palaces and estates in Spain included the magnificent neoclassical Palacio de Liria, in Madrid, where Cayetana was born amid Flemish tapestries, pillars of Siena marble and walls covered in Titians, Goyas and Rembrandts. Nevertheless, it was at Albury that the Duke of Alba hosted weekend lunches for some of Churchill's top officials and ministers while his daughter entertained her own friends. Laing's platonic infatuation with Tana, as she was more familiarly known, blossomed one sultry summer afternoon as he watched her languishing by the swimming pool, her true feeling tantatisingly obscured by dark glasses as she chewed on a reed.

At times Tana's demeanour suggested a melancholic side. She once confessed that she had never got over the loss of her mother to tuberculosis – the same disease that killed the 13th Duchess – when she was only eight years old. Two years after her mother's death, Tana was forced to escape from Madrid with her father at the outbreak of the civil war, first to Paris, then to London, when her father was appointed Franco's chief representative before becoming ambassador in March 1939.

Circumstances had forced Tana to mature rather quicker than most girls of her age while leading a relatively sheltered life. Her studies were overseen by an Austrian *Fräulein* and her outings from the embassy, chaperoned by trusted diplomatic wives and ladies-in-waiting, included sitting for a portrait by the licentious Augustus John. While Alba's trust in his daughter's virtue was not misplaced on this occasion, having her pose for John was not without its risks. The artist had a weakness for attractive young women and is thought to have seduced another Spanish woman – a bride-to-be whose portrait Alba commissioned as a wedding present for her diplomat husband.

Only occasionally did Tana's indiscretions earn her a mention in the local gossip columns, behaviour more characteristic of her later years. One memorable occasion was the night she attended a dinner at the Dorchester Hotel as the guest of Lady Emerald Cunard, the celebrated Anglo-American London society hostess. Early on in the evening, Emerald discovered that one of the waiters was a refugee from the Spanish Civil War, and somewhat flippantly urged Tana to 'say something to him in Spanish'. When Tana did so, the waiter replied in Catalan. There was a pause before Tana announced in English to the assembled guests, 'He's a Red Catalan! He's probably gong to poison us all!' At which point the table erupted with laughter.

In matters of love, the young duchess had yet to find a suitable man to marry. While in wartime London Tana was rumoured to have maintained a formal and platonic relationship with a young air force officer who served as an aide to Prince Juan. But there was another side to her that craved the escapades and follies of youth, and which Laing tried to appeal to by accompanying her to some of London's more sophisticated nightspots, such as the 400 Club in Leicester Square.

Although his feelings for her appear not to have been reciprocated beyond a flirtatious friendship, to Tana and her girlfriends Laing cut a fine figure. An impeccably mannered and dashing young English officer, it was not long before he had secured an introduction to the Duke of Alba and, through him, to any number of influential aristocratic and military contacts in Madrid.

When Laing arrived in Madrid the war was reaching its final stages. In that summer of 1944, the British and American embassies felt it secure enough to move the bulk of their operations to the seaside town of San Sebastián, near the Spanish–French border, away from the heat of Madrid and closer to the German retreat from southern France. At the time, there was growing concern in London and Washington about the unstable political situation north of the Pyrenees, with the German retreat prompting violent revenge on collaborators and also leading to divisions in the Resistance, between those who were communist and those who were not. The Americans and the British were anxious to counter Soviet influence. Burns was assigned to work on a propaganda operation in southern France alongside Michael Creswell, a member of MI9, the unit set up earlier in the war by British intelligence to help run the escape lines of POWs and refugees.

Creswell helped Burns across the border, putting him in touch with a French Resistance group which had good contacts in the local media and cinema. On the way to his first meeting, Burns was stopped on the road by an armed band of *maquisards*. One of them spoke to him in an impeccable Oxbridge accent. He turned out to be a British soldier who had been cut off behind enemy lines during the German advance at the beginning of the war and joined up with the Resistance, preferring to fight alongside them than return to regimental duties. He asked Burns to send a message back to his father that he was alive and well and would soon be emerging from the clandestinity in which he had been submerged for most of the war.

Now that the war seemed to be drawing to an end, the soldier felt it was safe to break cover and asked Burns to make telegraphic contact on his behalf with his father in England. Burns had no problem with that, or with his next encounter with the French – in the person of a local doctor and Resistance leader who invited him home for lunch. On arrival, Burns was led by his host to the end of a long garden where he watched him dig out a large glass jar containing a duck preserved in aspic, which he then shared, with a bottle of wine. 'These were days of great joy,' he later recalled.

Burns was followed days later into France by the British and American ambassadors in a small Allied convoy which crossed the border from Spain into French territory through Hendaye and St Jean de Luz and then on towards Biarritz.

'The road was lined with cheering crowds of French people – men, women, and children, peasants and townspeople, priests and nuns, wounded veterans and "resistance" youths,' wrote the American ambassador Hayes. 'Heaps of flowers were tossed into our path and through the car windows, and when we were halted by the press of people, babies were handed in to be kissed.' When the convoy reached Biarritz, the streets were festooned with British and American, and occasionally Russian, flags.

After the ambassadors had withdrawn back across the border, Burns got to work enlisting the support of trusted members of the Resistance. Initial attempts to bribe a local newspaper, *La Résistance Républicaine*, and to influence the production and mass distribution of special liberation issues – with editorial content suggested by the British – ran into difficulties because of an acute paper shortage, and political differences within its seven-member editorial committee, which included one monarchist and a communist.

Burns had more success in distributing propaganda material sent by the MoI. Large quantities of British press photographs, posters, illustrated reviews and other publicity material were circulated in Bayonne, Biarritz, St Jean de Luz and Hendaye. British newsreels were, meanwhile, shown in local cinemas, from Bordeaux to Pau, including a documentary entitled *Tunisian Victory* from the North African campaign. 'It has gone a long way to reassure the French population that His Majesty's Government was interested in keeping them informed and in countering the subtle effects of German propaganda over the four years [of war],' Creswell reported to the embassy.

Other congratulatory notes credited Burns with a skilful propaganda coup in difficult circumstances, raising morale at a time when the last stages of the war threatened to drain the mission in Madrid of any sense of moral purpose.

Within weeks of his return, across the border, to San Sebastián, his wife gave premature birth to their first child. Mabel had suffered a miscarriage during the first weeks of their marriage, so that the successful delivery of a seemingly healthy baby was initially a source of huge joy. While undecided on his Christian name, Burns and Mabel immediately nicknamed the boy *El Inglesito*, the Little Englishman, in tribute to the Allied cause. Then, only days old, the baby developed respiratory problems and died.

Overwhelmed with grief, the couple placed their child in a small white coffin and took him to the local cemetery where he was laid to rest in the marble mausoleum belonging to Mabel's Basque cousins.

The many letters of condolence included one from Burns's embassy colleague John Walters, who was deeply affected on a personal level – it reminded him of the loss of a dear family member, deepening an alcohol addiction that had been developing through the war. 'This is the most appalling news,' wrote Walters. 'I am so horrified and so sorry for you and for Mabel that the only way I can express a small part of my deep sympathy is to let you know, honestly, that in all my experience of the tragedies of life there have only been two occasions when I have felt the shock of sudden sorrow so acutely . . .'

On 25 October 1944 Burns wrote to Harman Grisewood at the BBC to alert him to the news: '. . . I'm writing just to let you know that we had a sad thing: a baby boy came a month before his time and wasn't quite strong enough and died after 48 hours: there was a strong shock of loss and yet he was God-given, God-taken in such a swoop as to leave more significance than sorrow and Mabel is building up again in a most wonderful way . . .'

A few weeks later Burns wrote to David Jones telling him how he had managed to bear the pain of loss around *El Inglesito*'s death thanks to the deepening love he and Mabel found in each other.

After a period on compassionate leave, Burns returned to his embassy duties, only to find the relations he had built up with the Franco regime under threat. Within days of his return to London, the retiring ambassador Hoare delivered a strong critique of the Franco regime in a talk to his Chelsea constituents and then followed this up, on October 16th 1944, with a similarly scathing memorandum to the Foreign Office. Hoare condemned Franco's Spain as fascist and collaborationist, and, while ruling out direct intervention, suggested that the Allies should use whatever methods were available to bring about his downfall. The statement represented a dramatic personal U-turn for Hoare, effectively throwing to the four winds the cautious crisis-averse diplomacy he himself had imposed on his embassy since 1940.

Burns felt betrayed, and came as close as he could to openly criticising his former chief in a letter he wrote to the Foreign Office. In it Burns argued that the speech risked hurting Spanish national pride and thus boosting support for Franco, although his main concern was that it had badly let down those who had assisted the Allied cause from within the regime. He told Hoare: 'The effect [of your speech] has been frankly bad among many of our friends ... these never had an advocate in their own press, nor were they specially protected by the police, but they felt that they had an understanding friend in you who would wave them a cordial goodbye from London and let it be known there that they were not so bad as propaganda painted them.'

Much had changed since that first encounter between Burns and Hoare in the late summer of 1940 when the two men had buried whatever prejudices – formed by faith and background – might have otherwise separated them in pursuit of what seemed then a straightforward common cause. During the four years of the war, Burns had developed his passionate interest in Spanish affairs in a way that, to his enemies in Whitehall, confirmed him as an unreconstructed pro-Francoist Catholic. Those who wished to tarnish his reputation further insinuated that he had become an enemy agent. By 1944 Burns's beliefs remained unshaken, however misplaced they may have seemed to others.

By contrast Hoare, with one eye on his political future, had in the final year of the war desperately tried to shake off the curse of appeaser that had hung around his neck since Abyssinia, adopting towards the end of his posting an uncompromising attitude towards Franco's Spain just at the time when it appeared to be positioning itself to serve the West as a strategically important ally in post-war Europe.

In truth, Hoare had struggled from the outset of his posting to like a country whose politics and culture he instinctively regarded as alien. His accommodation with the Spanish Catholic Church was the fruit of diplomatic opportunism and only in part based on his theological sympathy, as a member of the Anglo-Catholic wing of the Anglican Church, with the sacrificial nature of the priesthood, and the sacramental aspect of the Mass. But contrary to what the German embassy propaganda mischievously rumoured, Hoare had never converted to Rome, nor did he have any intention of doing so. That would have been a betrayal of his Englishness. Hoare's attitude to the Spanish as a whole was essentially colonialist, regarding them simply as pawns of British interests, while increasingly resentful of the rival influence of the United States. In the end Hoare grew tired of Spain and its idiosyncrasies to the point of being hugely relieved at getting rid of them, with his attitude towards the people, their army and their rulers not unlike that once expressed by Wellington in the aftermath of the Peninsular War. Both men looked upon the Spaniards, as they did the Indians, as a lesser race.

With the Foreign Office in no apparent hurry to send a new ambassador, the British embassy in Madrid was left temporarily under the management of Jim Bowker as chargé d'affaires, with Burns the most senior and longest-serving member of staff as his deputy.

The day after Hoare had made his outspoken criticism of the Franco regime in London, Burns met one of his contacts, Gabriel Arias Salgado, Spain's undersecretary of state for education.

Arias Salgado was not only directly related to Franco but also one of his most trusted ministers at this time. At the meeting, Burns was greeted with a well-calculated counter-blast. The minister told him that it was absurd for Hoare to have complained about the activities in Spain of German intelligence when he knew only too well that British intelligence had been as active in the country throughout the war, if not more so, in defiance of Spain's neutral status, while at the same time protected by it.

Not only this, Arias Salgado told Burns, but all the proof had fallen into Franco's hands, including twenty-six transmitters of British origin seized by Spanish police, and a police report denouncing Burns himself as perhaps the biggest spy of them all, and the dictator had chosen to turn a blind eye.

As for the future, Arias Salgado reminded Burns, Spain should be allowed to choose her own post-war development without foreign intervention. If there was a future for Anglo-Spanish relations, Franco's minister suggested it was in a common Christian heritage capable of resisting the spread of Bolshevism in Europe.

With Arias Salgado 'rattling off with nervous intensity', Burns had thought it prudent to listen patiently before offering a measured reply. It was time, he suggested to the minister as delicately as he could, for the Spanish government to recognise that there were 'moral issues' at stake in the war that were important for the future of the whole world.

Moreover, while Britain respected 'technical neutrality' and, indeed, had asked for nothing more from Spain, London was no longer in the mood to accept 'moral neutrality'.

Asked by Arias Salgado what he meant by this, Burns replied: 'I have never seen a word of blame addressed to Germany in the Spanish press in four years, no criticism of the Nazi threat to Europe or of the barbarities committed by the Nazis.'

Franco's government in the last weeks of the Second World War appeared to be a regime in denial, not just in its refusal to accept any guilt over collaboration with the Axis powers from the outset of the civil war to the final days of the Second World War, but, crucially, in its inability to accept and project through the national media the true nature of Nazism as it had manifested itself in the concentration camps.

The situation presented the press section in the British embassy in Madrid with a fresh challenge in propaganda terms. Its response was to suggest that Spanish journalists should be included in a media visit the combined Allied command was organising to the concentration camp at Dachau. The move drew Burns into renewed conflict with his enemies in British intelligence, for one of the journalists he proposed for the visit, Carlos Sentis, had been placed on a list of suspects by Kim Philby's friends in MI5 because of his pro-Franco leanings.

According to British intelligence files, during the civil war, Sentís had worked as a spy for Franco in Paris, using his cover as a journalist to report secretly on pro-Republican Spanish refugees, among them the fugitive former Spanish correspondent in Berlin, Eugenio Xammar, with whom he shared a flat for a while. Sentís later flew to London and covered the aftermath of the abdication crisis, before publishing a sympathetic if light-hearted book about the British and their democratic institutions. He opened his preface with the comment that he considered journalism to be a great sport in peacetime and espionage in wartime, a statement which even his close friends considered to be crassly indiscreet.

When Franco assumed power, Sentís joined the government administration as a member of the staff of the Falangist minister without portfolio, Rafael Sánchez Mazas. He also pursued his career as a freelance journalist, with his main articles published in the Barcelona-based *La Vanguardia*, whose Catalan owner, the Count of Godó, was regarded by the British as pro-Allied.

With the outbreak of War in Europe, Sentis initiated a discreet relationship with the British embassy in Madrid where he was regarded as a useful source and supporter of the Allied cause despite his links with media outlets of more dubious ideological credentials. They included Radio Mundial, a Madrid-based radio station that broadcast relatively balanced reports on the progress of the war to Latin America and yet was suspected by British intelligence of being financed by the Germans.

It was in the autumn of 1942 that Burns first unequivocally championed Sentís as a useful agent of Allied propaganda, recommending in a letter to the head of the Spanish section at the MoI, Billy McCann, that he be allowed to be posted as the new London correspondent of the Spanish news agency EFE. 'He [Sentís] has been pretty coy in his relations with me but is, I am convinced, very well disposed and certainly would not play the double game,' Burns wrote.

At the time he made the request Burns appears to have been unaware of the protracted secret campaign his enemies in MI5 and MI6 were conducting to have him sacked because of his pro-Franco views and his record of recommending Spanish journalists suspected of being German agents. Burns had survived thanks to the trust invested in him by his ambassador, and the support he enjoyed within the Foreign Office and from other members of the intelligence community. But he now faced additional accusations of furthering the cause of the enemy.

McCann contacted Tomás Harris at MI5 to tell him what he knew about Sentís. He had just read Sentis's book, *La Europa que he visto morir* (The Europe that I Have Seen Dying), and concluded that it contained 'no gibes at England of any kind'. McCann went on, 'Personally I know Carlos Sentís very well: he is a Catalan, and in my opinion, well disposed towards us.' He recalled that he got to know Sentís when they were both living in the Palace Hotel during the first year of the war. 'He was friendly and, when I was having trouble with the Gestapo, he offered to help me if I got into any real difficulties.'

McCann had met Sentís again on a more recent visit to Madrid. Sentís was now married and living in a 'very expensive way' in a luxurious apartment the Duke of Alba had built near the Palacio de

Liria. He asked McCann to use his influence to allow Radio Mundial material into Latin America, arguing that it would help Allied interests by keeping German material out of the local press.

McCann had told Sentís to contact Burns despite lingering doubts over the true loyalties of both men. 'My own personal opinion of Carlos Sentís is that he is a pleasant and gifted young man, who finds the Fascist way of life alien to his own idea of life. At the same time, he has a taste for high living and a great love of money, and if the Germans were paying him enough I am convinced that he would work for them even if he knew it was against his real feelings,' McCann wrote on 7 October 1942. With the Sentís case the subject of ongoing correspondence between the MoI and the secret services, Burns faced intense lobbying by the Franco regime. In December that year he was visited by Gregorio Marañón, the young Falangist son of the doctor and his future brother-in-law, a close friend of Sentís who had also been recruited into the state apparatus.

Marañón showed Burns a telegram sent to Franco's Director General of Press by José Brugada, the assistant press attaché in the Spanish embassy in London. It reported that Sentís would be declared *persona non grata* as a correspondent in the UK. 'This communication from Brugada was shown to me in confidence and naturally you will not let him know that I have seen it,' Burns subsequently wrote to McCann. Neither Burns nor the young Marañón, it seemed, realised that Brugada had been recruited by a section of MI5 as a double agent, code-named Peppermint.

Burns told McCann that Marañón had told him he could not imagine a person better suited to report on British affairs than Sentís, 'judging from his earlier record and his well-known [pro-Allied] sympathies'. It was a view with which Burns concurred. However, as Burns told Marañón, it was perhaps 'quite natural' that in general London was not enthusiastic about giving a positive answer after its experiences with Luis Calvo, Alcázar de Velasco and other Spanish journalists suspected of being German agents. The Spanish regime, moreover, had not helped matters, Burns told Marañón, by continuing to censor heavily the reports sent by the one remaining London-based journalist, Felipe Fernández Armesto, who wrote under the pseudonym Augusto Assia.

Days later Sentís's accreditation request was officially blocked by MI5. The case file on Sentis had been updated by MI5's Iberian desk officer Dick Broomham-White with information provided by Tomás Harris and Kim Philby. Their 'sources' had taken the view that Sentís was 'untrustworthy', 'arriviste' and a 'snake'.

Broomham-White urged the intelligence services not to place any reliance on any recommendations from Burns given the precedent set by the Calvo affair. And yet Broomham-White's file makes clear that his section was opposed to Sentís's arrival in the UK not because they had any evidence that he might be a German spy but on the basis that his professional journalism might undermine the double-cross game the secret services were conducting through the Spanish embassy in London.

'At present the main Spanish source of information to the [Spanish] Embassy is under our control and has been used for passing over deception material. It would be most unfortunate from our point of view if a new Spanish press correspondent arrived in this country who had access to the Fleet Street gossip and provided an independent source which might supply information contradicting that which we were trying to put across through our controlled channel,' wrote Broomham-White. He thus assumed that MI5's double-cross system had priority status over anybody else's handling of agents, however important the latter was in diplomatic and propaganda terms. It was a view shared by several of his MI5 colleagues and those who straddled the influential XX Committee, but which was disputed by other members of the intelligence community, and within government departments such as the Foreign Office and the MoI.

It would take another three and half years before Burns got positive vindication of the accreditation of Sentís, with his enemies in MI5 no longer able to sustain a convincing case against him. In May 1945 Burns successfully arranged to have Sentís imbedded with US troops in Germany after first flying him to London and being accredited there as a journalist. He and his colleague Fernández Armesto subsequently covered the liberation of Dachau and the Nuremberg trials for the two leading Spanish newspapers *ABC* and *La Vanguardia*. The scenes witnessed at Dachau proved particularly poignant for a Spanish readership, as details emerged of the brutality with which the Nazis treated the prisoners, one-third of whom were Jews, in addition to an estimated three thousand Catholic nuns, priests and bishops, some of whom were subsequently beatified by the Pope.

By the autumn of 1944, the Allies had been advancing rapidly across Europe, overrunning towns and villages with minimum resistance, watched by a civilian population that had spent most of the war believing in Hitler's invincibility. The reports filed by Sentís and Fernández Armesto conveyed some of the horror while making clear that Hitler's Germany had been resolutely defeated.

And yet even at this late stage in the war the British embassy in Madrid found itself immersed in fresh controversy from an unexpected quarter. It was around this time, in early May 1945, that Burns heard the news that the wayward – some thought him degenerate – thirty-year-old oldest son of Leo Amery, a close friend of Samuel Hoare, had had his brief career as a Nazi propagandist cut short by his capture by Italian partisans at the end of the war.

John Amery was interned in northern Italy before being brought back to the UK, under arrest, by Leonard Burt, a Scotland Yard detective on secondment to MI5. Four months later, in early September, his brother Julian, later a prominent Conservative MP, arrived in Madrid in a desperate attempt to save John from the gallows.

John, or 'Jack' as he was known to family and friends, had told his defence lawyers that while in Spain during the civil war he had been granted Spanish citizenship. The legal advice he received was that such an admission, if supported by evidence, would make it difficult if not impossible for the British government to proceed with a case of treason against him in a British court.

The Amery case was further complicated by the unpublicised involvement of Hoare. In March 1942, while serving as ambassador in Madrid, Hoare had received a letter from Leo Amery expressing his gratitude for the 'parcel of warm things' that Lady Maud had sent Jack. The letter also thanked Hoare for the contacts he had provided Jack in unoccupied France.

The close friendship which bound Samuel and Maud Hoare to Leo and Florence Amery (John's parents) dated back to the early part of

the century when the heads of each family made their way, thanks
to privileged upbringings and a common political allegiance to the
Conservative Party, effortlessly into the higher echelons of power.
Samuel Hoare was ten years younger than Leo Amery, but both
had long mixed in similar social circles, having been educated at the
exclusive boy's school Harrow, as Churchill had also been. Later, both
Hoare and Amery served in Andrew Bonar Law's government, then in
that of Stanley Baldwin (another Old Harrovian), Hoare as Secretary
of State for Air, Amery as First Lord of the Admiralty and subsequently
as Colonial Secretary. When the Conservatives joined the National
Government of Ramsay MacDonald in 1931, Hoare became Secretary
of State for India while Amery pursued an active political career, as
an MP, a director of several companies and a member of the Empire
Industries Association.

When Hoare was later forced to resign over his apparent 'sellout' to
Mussolini over Abyssinia and another clash with Churchill following
their disagreement over the India Act, Amery was again at his side.

After the outbreak of war, it was Hoare (the appeaser) who became
exiled from Churchill's cabinet, while Amery returned as Secretary of
State for India. Amery was disappointed not to form part of Churchill's
war cabinet, but made the most of the position he was offered, while
maintaining his close personal ties with Hoare once his friend had been
posted as ambassador to Madrid.

By then both Jack and his young brother Julian had become embroiled
in the politics of Spain. Of the two, Julian had the more high-profile
involvement in the civil war, on Franco's side. Julian was a first-year
Oxford undergraduate when, in 1937, a year after the outbreak of war
in Spain, he met Franco's representative in London, the Duke of Alba,
and arrangements were made for him to go to Spain as an observer
attached to Nationalist forces.

Once across the Spanish border, Julian travelled extensively, visiting
a military hospital in San Sebastián and the Nationalist headquarters
in Burgos. From there he joined the international press corps on the
Aragón Front, with Franco's troops poised to cut Barcelona off from
Republican-held Valencia, a defining moment of the war. In Huesca,
Julian came across 'apocalyptic horror': a cemetery which had been

desecrated by Republicans, with some of the skeletons rearranged round a card table, a bottle of wine in one hand, a glass in the other. Other skeletons had been entwined, as if dancing in a grotesque embrace of death.

Joining the Nationalist advance near Lérida, and coming under bombardment from Republican artillery, Julian shared cover in a shell hole with Peter Kemp, another of the few Englishmen who had volunteered to fight for Franco. Julian then drove south to Seville, before returning to England via Gibraltar. Once back in Britain, Julian found himself very much in demand from Conservatives and Catholics in universities, publishing and the media as a public speaker, his pro-Franco utterances fuelling the propaganda war against the left.

He returned to Burgos as an accredited correspondent with the *Daily Express*, reaching Madrid just a few hours after the city was 'liberated' by Franco's advance troops, continuing to write articles broadly sympathetic to the Nationalist cause. Jack was also in Spain during the civil war, although the precise nature of his activity became a subject of dispute. According to Julian, his brother joined the Spanish Foreign Legion in mid-March 1937, although entries in his passport showed him departing from Lisbon and arriving in Genoa at that time. He later suggested to his father that he may have been involved in running German guns to Spain, and had spent some time in secret on Spanish soil.

When Hoare was appointed ambassador to Spain in 1940, Jack was living in Portugal, desperately short of money and under pressure from his father to report for service for King and Country, while secretly suspected by MI5 of being involved in diamond smuggling. Within two years, it was Jack's collaboration with Nazi Germany which was becoming of growing covert interest to British intelligence.

The contents of the diplomatic bag from the British embassy in Madrid, secretly intercepted by MI5, showed that both Hoare and his wife had agreed to act as conduits for clothes, money and letters sent by Leo to his oldest son. Jack was by then living in France, actively broadcasting on behalf of Nazi Germany even as his health deteriorated from alcoholism and TB.

'I wonder if I might trouble you to put a stamp on the enclosed letter and have it dropped into a letterbox in France,' Leo had written to Hoare. A father's protective love for the prodigal son meant that Leo had yet to come to terms with the perception in the corridors of power in Whitehall that Jack was an enemy of the state. Similarly, Hoare appears to have been in denial about the security implications of his actions and those of his wife in deliberately choosing not to use the legal channels open to them for communicating with their son, via the International Committee of the Red Cross.

The suggestion Hoare made in a letter to Leo that Jack might be useful as a semi-official agent of the British embassy in unoccupied France defied credibility given Jack's record of collaboration with Vichy. Hoare's misuse of diplomatic privilege in a gesture of solidarity with an old political chum was at best a serious misjudgement, at worst a conspiracy of betrayal of the Allied cause.

One person who openly admitted many years later to have been with Jack in Burgos was Burns. It was in 1938, at the height of the Munich crisis, and Burns, together with Gabriel Herbert, had driven to the Nationalist headquarters with an ambulance donated by English Catholics. Burns described how one evening he found himself in a room reserved for the foreign press, 'glued to the radio, in the company of John [Jack] Amery and a tall blond man with a Nazi buttonhole badge', listening to the latest BBC bulletins about the invasion of Czechoslovakia. Burns recalled the ensuing conversation thus: '"We'll squash those dwarfs flat," said the Nazi at one point. I glared at him and retorted that in that case he would eventually be squashed flat himself and the swastika banished from the earth. John Amery, the only witness to this clash, was silent, withdrawn.'

Burns described Amery as a 'romantic figure who had taken up the Nationalist cause, leading him into later and deeper involvement with the Axis as a propagandist in Italy'. He was, in Burns's view, 'misguided but never malevolent and certainly not guilty of any bloody act'.

It was on such sympathies in the British embassy in Madrid, together with the friends in the Franco regime he had made during the civil war, that Julian Amery counted when he came to Spain to plead on his brother's behalf.

While Hoare had left Spain in January, the Amerys depended on at least two allies among those who had served under him. One was Burns, the other his most recent recruit, Laing, the young ex-Grenadier guardsman turned spy.

How much Burns knew of Hoare's contacts with the Amerys is uncertain. However, given his close working relationship with his ambassador, it is at least possible that Burns did know and felt comfortable about not reporting it to London. Burns not only had enormous respect for Julian's pro-Nationalist stance during the civil war, he also shared common friends in SOE, which Julian had joined after the outbreak of war.

Now that Julian had 'gallantly' come to Madrid to try and save his brother, Burns was willing to give him all the support he could muster. He had no doubt – for that is what he had been told by his own sources in the Franco regime – that Jack had indeed been granted Spanish nationality, as he had informed his lawyers, and that any trial for treason in a British court was a miscarriage of justice.

Nonetheless, the Foreign Office regarded the Amery case as one of great sensitivity and insisted that Julian's trip to Madrid be handled with maximum discretion. So, rather than booking him into the Ritz or the Palace where the embassy had reserved rooms, Burns arranged for him to stay in the flat of his deputy, Laing. Laing and Julian knew each other from Oxford and had mixed in similar social circles in London. But the accommodation served an added operational purpose which was to keep Julian's visit carefully monitored. Laing's flat was a block away from the embassy and even nearer to a separate building used by British intelligence. It was the best 'safe' house the embassy could offer.

Laing and Burns were more than happy to facilitate his access to senior figures in the Spanish regime in the hope that they might help to save Jack's life. Soon after Julian's arrival, they succeeded in getting Ernesto Giménez Caballero, the regime's main ideologue, to arrange a meeting with Franco, with Laing providing his car and chauffeur. Laing forgot to tell the chauffeur to remove the Union Jack before he set off, so that the visit took on an official note, much to the embarrassment of the Foreign Office.

London was furious and Burns was instructed to give Laing an official reprimand. What Julian was unaware of was that the entire visit was being secretly tracked by a sector of British intelligence with a very different agenda from that of Julian's official chaperones – one that was uncompromisingly anti-Francoist and that wished Jack Amery to stand trial and subsequently to be be found guilty.

This sector was heavily influenced by Philby. By the spring of 1944, Philby, highly regarded by his colleagues and moving fast up the promotion ladder, had been moved from the Iberian section to a new department within SIS with responsibility for setting up anti-Russian networks in Eastern Europe. But he kept a watching brief on Spain, using the influence he enjoyed across Whitehall to counter the British embassy's attempt to engage with leading members of the Franco regime and dissident Nazis.

It is almost certain that Philby would have strongly approved of, if not had a more direct role in, the decision to have the resident SOE officer in Madrid, Squadron Leader Park, join the embassy team officially assigned to accompany Julian Amery while in Spain. Unknown to Amery, Park's mission was to pass as much politically incriminating evidence as he could back to SIS and MI5 to be used in court against Jack. Thus the MI5 officer in charge of Jack Amery's case made much of the fact that his brother not only met with fascist ideologues such as Giménez Caballero but also General Muñoz Grandes, the man who had been in charge of the Spanish Blue Division that had fought alongside the Germans on the Russian front.

Julian pushed on regardless, obtaining sworn affidavits from people who had known Jack during the civil war, a document purporting to show that he had indeed enlisted on 17 March in the Spanish Foreign Legion, and a separate witness statement, supported by Burns, from Serrano Súñer, Franco's former foreign minister, confirming Jack's Spanish citizenship. A defence lawyer in the Spanish embassy regarded the statement as 'conclusive evidence according to Spanish law'.

But such efforts were to no avail. MI5 came up with their own document listing Jack as a passenger on board a Dutch merchant ship sailing from Lisbon to Genoa during a ten-day period in March 1937. MI5 claimed that the ship's log showed Jack to be the only passenger on board, and that the vessel was at sea on the day of his 'enlistment' in the Spanish Foreign Legion. Days later, Major Henry Pakenham, an MI6 officer in Madrid, filed a report to MI5 accusing Julian, and by implication those helping him in his investigation in Spain, of being involved in a conspiracy to manufacture evidence and documents.

In the end the fate of Jack Amery was sealed by the machinations of Spanish politics and the intrigue of international diplomacy. The shifting post-war power balance in the Franco regime, and pressure exercised by sectors of the Foreign Office, resulted in the Spanish Ministry of the Interior and the Spanish embassy in London refusing to back the defence's claim. Franco realised that ditching Amery was perhaps a price worth paying in order to maintain some sort of relationship with the generally antagonistic post-war Labour government. Within Whitehall there were those who did not relish the idea of a protracted trial airing in public the dirty linen of Amery's contacts with the Nazis, and the potentially even more embarrassing tensions and contradictions of British policy towards wartime Spain.

On 28 November 1945 Jack Amery pleaded guilty, having convinced himself and his family that he would be spared the death penalty. In fact being found guilty of treason carried an automatic death penalty in those days. His barrister advised him to plead not guilty and the trial judge went to great lengths to ensure he knew the consequences of ignoring the advice. It has been argued that Amery was dying of TB and wanted to spare his parents the embarrassment of a trial. He never appealed the death sentence, nor did he ask for the sentence to be commuted. He was hanged at Wandsworth prison, three weeks later, on 19 December after the Home Secretary resisted a last-ditch campaign for clemency from family, friends and lawyers, based on a claim of insanity. One member of Jack's family, his uncle-in-law, Hamar Greenwood, made a personal appeal to Clement Attlee based on the apparent inhumanity of executing someone for his opinions rather than his actions. That was also rejected. Jack Amery was condemned on his record of broadcasting Nazi propaganda on a regular basis and also of trying to raise battalions among British POW's to fight the Soviets.

In the end those closest to Jack, led by his father Leo, remain convinced that he had been a victim of political necessity. Having seen the wider conservative establishment saved the embarrassment of a trial, a Labour government was in the mood to teach it a severe lesson, that no one is above the law. Samuel Hoare was nevertheless undoubtedly lucky to have escaped from the whole Amery debacle without having to answer in public for his collaboration. So, too, were Burns and Laing.

On 8 May, VE Day, there were no euphoric mass street gatherings in Madrid, as occurred in other European and American cities. Days earlier, the news of Hitler's suicide had prompted an outpouring of sympathy among certain elements of the Falange and Spanish military. Spaniards in blue shirts and military uniform had turned up at the German embassy in Madrid and its consulates around the country to sign the book of condolence.

'It was a bleak day. It wasn't really sunny . . . I felt the atmosphere was funereal, and terribly distressing . . . It was an oppressive feeling to be surrounded by people who seemed not to be pleased with the fact that we had won,' Helen Rolfe, a secretary at the British embassy, recalled.

VE Day caught the Anglo-Spanish Enriqueta Harris, deputy head of the MoI's Iberian section, on a short work-related visit to Madrid. She had long come to the conclusion that the British embassy was dominated by pro-Franco Catholics led by Burns. She chose, however, to delay the confrontation she had planned to have with Burns, electing instead to accept his invitation to the embassy's modest ceremony to mark the defeat of Nazi Germany.

The victory party took the form of a gathering, organised by the chargé d'affaires, Jim Bowker, and Burns in the main embassy building, of all the British and local staff and small numbers from the expatriate community. They included a large group of English nannies who had spent the last four years looking after the children of Spanish aristocrats. Cakes and sandwiches were laid on at Mrs Taylor's Embassy Bar and bottles of sherry by Ann Williams, one of the embassy secretaries from a family in the wine trade who had married a member of the Domecq sherry family.

Harris later recalled: 'Part of me was furious that I was in Madrid on VE Day. I felt it unfortunate to be caught there with so many people not really caring about the fact we had won. But we celebrated in the embassy . . . singing "God Save the King". It was very emotional in its own way . . . Afterwards I rushed out to the local florist who managed to come up with some red, white and blue flowers – just like I imagined the colour of the bunting back in the UK. I took them like a flag to my Spanish aunt. Do you know what she did with them? She put each colour in a different vase. She didn't have a clue what they meant . . .'

In the Marañón household the celebrations for the end of the war were overshadowed by a particular piece of news that filled Mabel and her father with horror. Four days before Hitler's suicide, and four days before the unconditional surrender of Germany, a squadron of RAF Typhoons had attacked and sunk the *Cap Arcona*, the ship on which they had sailed to South America and back during the civil war. The luxury liner, converted to military use during the war, was in the Baltic transporting both hundreds of SS guards and officers and several thousand prisoners released from concentration camps. While German trawlers rescued most of the SS, only 350 of the 4500 or so prisoners survived.

Following the German surrender, however, Burns received a message from the Spanish Ministry of Foreign Affairs that Franco had broken off diplomatic ties with Germany. However belated and absurd the gesture may have seemed, he took it as a signal that the Allies could now step up their demands for the internment or expulsion from Spain of all Germans suspected of having links with the Nazi regime, a process that had got under way earlier in the year, and the seizing of any related assets by the Spanish state on behalf of the victorious Allies.

A dossier prepared by the OSS's counter-intelligence section X-2, with the cooperation of the British, detailed the extent of 'German penetration of Spain, illegal currency transfers, smuggled works of art, and plans by French collaborators, pro-Nazi individuals, and covert organisations to use Spain as a post-war hideout – as well as integration of German technicians into the Spanish military', reported one of its operatives. X-2 identified nearly fifty Spanish firms suspected of being used by Germany for espionage purposes, some three thousand agents in Spain and more than four hundred members of 'enemy clandestine services'.

Before VE Day was over, Burns was taken by a group of officials from the Spanish Ministry of Foreign Affairs to the German embassy to officially 'liberate' it from Nazi occupation. The Nazis had vacated the building in an operation staggered over a number of months, the exodus seemingly completed just hours before Burns arrived. Missing were works of art, and documents which had been removed or destroyed. The only remaining pieces of furniture were some chairs, office desks and filing cabinets, all of which were empty. In one of them Burns found a Mauser pistol and a large number of Iron Crosses, many of them apparently intended for the Spanish volunteers who had fought for the Blue Division on the eastern front. Burns pocketed them all, then climbed on to the roof and hoisted the Union Jack.

14

AFTERMATH

One day during the final autumn of the war the British embassy in Madrid's long serving military attaché, the blimpish Brigadier Torr, burst into Burns's office and declared: 'Congratulations, Tom, you are a "Call-me-God" in the embassy honours list.' Days earlier, on 19 October, the retiring ambassador to Spain, Sir Samuel Hoare, had written to Brendan Bracken, the Minister of Information, recommending that Burns be awarded 'some honour' for wartime services but without specifying whether it should be a Commander of the Order of St Michael and St George (CMG) or the lower grade Order of the British Empire (OBE), as had been periodically awarded to other chiefs of branches within the embassy.

'He [Burns] has done most remarkable work in Spain, from almost nothing to something very big,' Hoare wrote. 'In addition to this, he has made himself one of the most popular personalities of Spain.'

Hoare's valedictory book of memoirs published after the war paid special tribute to Burns's press and information department. 'Under his vigorous direction, an insignificant section of the Embassy had developed into a great and imposing organisation.'

And yet Burns's enemies returned to haunt him during his final months in Madrid, and many years would pass before he was honoured with any medal for services to his country.

One of his more influential detractors surfaced weeks after Torr's premature announcement, when Burns returned to London on what was to prove his final stretch of leave, granted on compassionate grounds following the death of his baby son.

The new offensive against Burns's reputation was launched by Sir Kenneth Grubb, one of the senior officials at the Ministry of Information. Grubb was a former evangelical lay missionary whose fundamentalist Protestantism put him at odds with Burns. The theological divide fuelled a mutual animosity from the moment each was recruited to the MoI at the outbreak of the war, although a formal confrontation was deferred until the war was coming to its conclusion.

During the war years, Burns grew in his view of Grubb as a fastidious puritan and bureaucrat with a patronising Anglo-Saxon attitude on matters related to the Spanish-speaking world. Grubb, for his part, despised Burns as an insubordinate loose cannon – a 'foreigner' who had been allowed by the embassy to get above himself and had 'gone native' in Spain, defying the MoI's attempts to control him.

Burns spent the war years happily making use of whatever propaganda material and funds that were supplied to him by the MoI while considering his line of duty lay with his ambassador, the Foreign Office and Churchill via his effective intelligence chief in Madrid, the naval attaché Captain Hillgarth, and others with whom he had a mutual trust on intelligence matters.

Only with Hoare's withdrawal from Madrid did Grubb sense an opportunity to punish Burns for his perceived insubordination. To distract him from his real intention, Grubb invited Burns to lunch at the Travellers Club in London for what he claimed would be a routine update briefing on policy matters. It was only at coffee that Grubb turned suddenly and remarked, with what Burns took for a smirk, that he had blocked Hoare's attempts to have him decorated for his wartime work. 'By the way, I'm sorry I had to knock you off the embassy honours list; I thought too many RCs [Roman Catholics] were getting gongs,' Grubb said.

While Burns would later recall the incident as evidence of enduring religious bigotry within the British state, the action against him was taken against the background, days earlier, of a final concerted attempt by Burns's enemies in the intelligence community to paint him as a traitor.

Encouraged by Philby and Tomás Harris, and drawing on a report written by Anthony Blunt on his monitoring of suspect Spaniards, MI5's head of counter intelligence, Captain Guy Liddell, wrote a scathing denunciation of Burns in a secret memorandum to Victor Cavendish-Bentinck, chairman of Britain's wartime Joint Intelligence Committe, and Whitehall's spy supremo. Blunt claimed that while Burns had been on leave in London the press attaché had failed to report his suspicions that six Spanish journalists who were being repatriated from Berlin to Spain via London might have been working as German agents. No evidence was provided to substantiate the claim, but the mere allegation made on hearsay by an unidentified source was sufficient for Liddell to vigorously pursue the case against Burns.

Liddell wrote on 17 July 1945: 'This might of course be considered a minor sin of omission but as you know we have long felt some concern about the activities of Burns who, during the course of the last four years, has pressed for the admission of undesirable Spanish journalists to the UK, on the doubtful grounds that they were going to do so much for Anglo-Spanish relations. In fact three or four of these people whose cases he sponsored have subsequently turned out to be German agents. In fact they were almost notoriously so in Spain before they started. Burns has moreover explicitly stated his view that he is not interested in security and was not concerned to know that the Spanish correspondents whom he was recommending as suitable to work in this country were in fact German agents. I do not know whether there is anything to be done about this but to say the least it does seem that Burns has been singularly ill-chosen for the job.'

Cavendish-Bentinck spent a week looking into the allegations and consulting others in government about Burns. The prejudice felt in some quarters against a spy who had never quite fitted into the Establishment because of his faith and background was deeply rooted, as was evident in the profile that was made of him. 'He is an Anglo-Chilean, aged 39, but we do not know whether he is first or second generation born abroad – at any rate his English is at times of a rather foreign nature,' noted Cavendish-Bentinck in his report on Burns. The comment contained a glaring falsehood. Burns, though born in Chile, had been brought up and raised in England, and his accent was pure public school, without a trace of 'foreignness'.

The intelligence chief did admit nevertheless to finding no evidence supporting the suggestion that Burns was sponsoring the activities of the Germans. All Cavendish-Bentinck unearthed was an administrative blunder earlier on in the war for which Burns was not held directly responsible: the apparent loss of some low-grade correspondence between the MoI and the embassy. 'In 1940 there was some minor hanky-panky regarding misuse of the [diplomatic] bag in which however the Ministry of Information themselves were as much responsible as Burns,' he noted. The 'hanky-panky' had occurred while Burns was still working at the MoI headquarters in Senate House, prior to his posting to Madrid. It had involved the smuggling of propaganda material, paid for by a slush fund approved by his superiors. There may also have been a reference to the unfortunate incident, reported in an earlier chapter, in which Burns, with backing from the Foreign Office, arranged for the pro-Francoist agent, the Marques del Moral, to be paid for information while working in Madrid, only to discover that the agent had been double-billing the British government.

Cavendish-Bentinck reported that any such misdemeanours had apparently been compensated for by the high-level intelligence Burns had secured through his unrivalled penetration of the Franco regime. 'Such reports from Burns which have been forwarded by the Ambassador to this Office have generally met with approval,' he wrote.

Critically, however, Cavendish-Bentinck went on to warn that the vendetta a sector of MI5 was pursuing threatened to be counter-productive, as it risked compromising Spaniards and their handlers who were involved in the double-cross game. He concluded, 'If any action were to be taken [against Burns] it would be necessary to reveal the sources of our information and, as Burns does not appear to have committed many gross crimes in the past I doubt whether any action is desirable in the present case.'

The report saved Burns from any disciplinary action against him. With hindsight it was ironic, nonetheless, that the latest attack on him was prompted by information provided by Blunt, a traitor who, as was subsequently discovered, had spent his time with MI5 during the Second World War sharing all the secret intelligence he handled with Moscow.

If Blunt and his friends were allowed to operate for a while unsuspected and unrestrained it was because Russia was still considered a wartime ally and the political climate in Britain on matters Spanish was turning in their favour. By the summer of 1945 the change in the public mood was reflected in a headline carried in the *Daily Herald* on the eve of the first post-war General Election: 'A Vote for Churchill is a Vote for Franco' reflected the certainty that the majority of British voters saw Franco's Spain as the last bastion of fascism in Europe. And the suspicion that Churchill's policy of non-intervention to keep Spain neutral in the war was also responsible for keeping the dictator in power.

By now the whispering campaign against Burns had surfaced with a vengeance in *Tribune*, the socialist newspaper which, at the end of the war included members of the British Communist as well as the Labour Party on its editorial board. 'Spaniards must be really puzzled over the British outlook. This democracy of ours, which is swinging so hard to the Left, is still presented in Madrid by a Press attaché who is an outstanding friend of the Franco regime and married into the inner ranks,' commented the newspaper's diarist.

The new Labour foreign secretary, Ernest Bevin, had no wish to commit Britain to another military intervention in Europe once the war with Germany was over and opted for symbolic political gestures against the Franco regime rather than any substantive change of policy towards Spain. In a gesture of solidarity with the left, he ordered that any further honours that may have been recommended for the embassy in Madrid be quickly withdrawn, particularly from those most directly associated with the policy of appeasement towards Franco.

Burns was not surprised by the news of his honours snub, which he was told by Whitehall friends had as much to do with politics as with his faith and was no reflection on his professional competence. He was nonetheless furious that it had come from his old enemy, the Protestant Grubb, in an unholy alliance with those who had always opposed him, for ideological reasons, over Spain. The anti-Franco camp in the UK had been reinforced by an opportunistic U-turn by Hoare, and the signing by the Duke of Alba of a manifesto calling for the return of the monarchy.

The political shift against the Franco regime left Hoare's successor as ambassador Sir Victor Mallet ostensibly with little room to manoeuvre when he arrived in Madrid in July 1945, just as the Labour Party was being propelled to power in Britain. Compared to his previous posting in neutral Sweden, where he had been given a reasonably free hand to deal with local problems as they arose, Mallet found that Spain was 'politically gunpowder'. As he later recalled, it soon became only too evident from instructions received from London that official relations with the Franco regime had to be restrained and personal cordiality eschewed.

And yet Franco's determination to stay in power had more coherence than the Labour government's plans for removing him, as the newly arrived ambassador was only too quick to notice. In his first statement to the House of Commons, Ernest Bevin said that it was up to the Spanish to decide their future. The British government would adopt a 'favourable view' if steps were taken by the Spanish people to change the regime, but His Majesty's Government would not itself do anything which would risk provoking another civil war – in other words the overarching policy towards Spain remained passive and non-interventionist, just as it had been under the Conservatives.

Mallet felt frustrated and unconvinced. He wrote: 'A series of suggestions kept reaching me from London that various discredited left wing exiles from the War now living in London like Negrín, or like Giral in Mexico should be encouraged to form a provisional government which would be recognised by the great powers. What this recognition could possibly do to help was by no means clear because Franco was still obviously in full command of the country, his power resting on the three pillars of Army, the Church and Big Business, with the support of the Falange which, however, was becoming rather an embarrassment.'

In a clear strategy aimed at defusing the enmity of the victorious democracies, Franco had appointed a conservative Christian Democrat, Alberto Martín Artajo, as his new foreign minister. His task was to cultivate the image of Franco as an authoritarian Catholic leader, increasingly distanced from the Falange – as opposed to that of the fascist dictator, which is how the Marxist left saw him – and to accelerate the process of denazification the Allies had demanded.

Martín Artajo was a lawyer with interests in Catholic publishing whom Burns had known and maintained cordial relations with since before the war. On his appointment to government he agreed to a series of secret meetings with Burns, outside the official diplomatic protocol, knowing that he would get a sympathetic hearing and that his views would be reported back to London.

It was from these meetings that Mallet drew his intelligence on the political direction of the regime, and tried to influence the Foreign Office, much to the chagrin of those like the Soviet ambassador in London, Feodor Gousev, who wished, like his boss Stalin, to have the Allies break off relations with Franco and offer support to 'democratic forces'.

Gousev was convinced that Franco was trying to consolidate his position and 'throwing dust in the eyes of the Allies' by announcing that he intended to hold elections at some point in the future.

Undoubtedly the Burns/Martín Artajo nexus was used by Franco to help him buy time, resisting foreign pressure for immediate democratic change following the collapse of the Axis powers. And yet British policy of continuing non-intervention appears, nevertheless, to have based itself on an accurate reading of Spain's internal political situation at the end of the war.

Franco's own police reports may have talked up the threat of the left being heartened by the defeat of the Axis, anti-Falangist sentiments may have stirred in Catholic and military circles and some former followers of the regime, including the Duke of Alba, may have dreamt that the restoration of the monarchy was imminent, but the fact remained that the opposition to Franco inside Spain's border and within the Spanish exiled community lacked a powerful unifying organisation, still less a common ideology, ranging as it did from anarchists on the left to virulently anti-communist aristocrats on the right.

In early August 1945, the British ambassador Mallet wrote to the Foreign Office from his summer residence in San Sebastián describing the 'war weariness' that he felt gripped the majority of Spaniards and warning the Allies against supporting or provoking a military uprising, not least because the army remained largely supportive of Franco. In the last stages of the war, the US military had refused to bow to increasing pressure both from domestic American opinion and the anti-Franco resistance fighters that straddled the French-Spanish border to push on into Spain when Allied troops liberated south-east France.

Mallet attached to his dispatch an eight-page memorandum he had received from Burns soon after he had taken up his ambassadorial posting in Madrid, based on the secret conversations Burns had had with Martín Artajo, the minister nicknamed the 'pious elephant' because of his Catholicism and heavy build.

Burns had told Martín Artajo how struck he had been on his recent visit to London by what seemed a unanimity and depth of feeling against General Franco among new members of Parliament.

Martín Artajo, however, had little trouble in persuading Burns of his sincerity in arguing that British public opinion was gravely misinformed about Spanish politics. Far from being an unpopular tyrant, Franco counted on the support of the 'great mass of the Spanish people' who had suffered from the 'reds' during the Spanish Civil War and were enormously grateful to *El Caudillo* not only for saving their country from anarchy but also keeping it out of the Second World War.

But Martín Artajo was much too astute a lawyer to think that an experienced observer of the Spanish scene such as Burns would easily ignore the aspirations of many Spaniards for some kind of democratic opening capable of freeing Spain from its international isolation.

Thus he gave Burns to understand that given time, Franco would be prepared to pave the way for a peaceful transfer of power to the 'most responsible' political elements in Spain, which, in their shared view, were found not on the left but towards the centre, including like-minded Christian democrats and supporters of Don Juan, the Bourbon prince in exile. The future of Spain lay in patience, not revolution in other words. It was a message Burns had no qualms about transmitting to his new ambassador.

On August 6 1945 he wrote: 'A violent or provocative act or gesture from the outside just now . . . might well plunge Spaniards once more into one of the reckless metaphysical moods to which they are so prone, making them defiant of measurable standards and ultimately destructive of themselves and of all understanding . . . any idea that there can be a swift and radical change of the present regime into something more representative without bloodshed and violence on a large scale must be rejected . . .'

In the final weeks of 1945 Burns tried to get his father-in-law Gregorio Marañón named ambassador in London. The idea was conjured up with the help of his friend Martín Artajo but was blocked by Franco. Before the year was out, another contact of Burns's, the former foreign minister Serrano Súñer, had written to his brother-in-law Franco suggesting he name Marañón a minister in a government of national unity which would also include other intellectuals like José Ortega y Gasset and the Catalan politician Francesco Cambó. This, too, Franco vetoed.

According to Franco's biographer Paul Preston, Franco distrusted Marañón as 'someone who would be loyal to higher ideals than the survival in power of Franco'. In their continuing exchanges, Burns and Martín Artajo had concurred that Marañón was among the few intellectuals who could lay claim to the respect of the majority of Spaniards. His political background was that of a founder and one-time liberal supporter of the Republic whose anti-communism had led him, in the end, to back Franco in the civil war, in the hope that, once it was over, he would oversee the establishment of a political system to which most Spaniards could feel they belonged.

But while Franco had agreed, under pressure from his advisers, to allow Marañón back from exile in 1942 – as a way of contributing to a sense of normality – he thought the idea of bringing Marañón into government a step too far and too soon in the direction of democracy. In fact, it would take another thirty-two years for the Spanish people to vote for the kind of regime they wanted in free and democratic elections and by then Marañón and many of his generation were long dead.

In Spain the end of the Second World War brought a reckoning of sorts. Burns's final weeks there saw him helping his British and American colleagues draw up a priority list for the urgent repatriation of 257 German officials and agents considered a security and political risk. It proved a protracted and inconclusive affair, with just over a hundred repatriated by the end of 1946, seventy being given the right to remain in Spain and the rest unaccounted for, having changed their names before starting new lives in South America. Such was the case of Reinhardt Spitzy, private secretary to Hitler's foreign minister Ribbentrop, who escaped to Argentina in 1947, along with countless other Nazis.

Those repatriated to Germany included Wilhelm Leissner (alias Gustav Lenz), who had served as the head of German military espionage in Spain for most of the war. His assistant, Kurt Meyer-Döhner, the naval attaché, got a job working for the Spanish Admiralty. Similarly the police attaché and Gestapo representative Walter Eugene Mosig fled from an internment camp before returning to a discreet post with the Spanish General Directorate of Security.

Other Nazis gave up the spying game and became successful businessmen in post-war Spain, setting up residences and hotels along the country's southern coast in anticipation of what became one of Europe's fastest growing tourist economies from the late 1950s onwards. Among them was Johannes Bernhardt, one of the chief organisers of German military and economic aid to Spain and a personal friend of Franco. Also granted residence in Spain after a short period in a detention camp in Caldas del Rey were two brothers, Adolfo and Luis Clauss, who were working for German intelligence in Huelva at the time of Operation Mincemeat. They returned to the south of Spain and developed a successful family business in construction while becoming substantial landowners on the border with Portugal.

But the most elaborate escape from prosecution involved the Nazi with whom Burns had competed personally in his battle for the hearts and minds of wartime Spaniards. On 6 February 1946, coincidentally the same day that Burns's return to the UK was officially noted by the Spanish authorities, the German embassy's press attaché, spy and propaganda chief Hans Lazar eluded an order for his arrest.

A week later, Lazar reappeared in the form of a letter to the Spanish Ministry of Foreign Affairs saying that he had been recovering in a hospital in Madrid after an operation for acute appendicitis. An enclosed photograph showed the once impeccably dressed Lazar, naked from the waist upwards, looking drawn and emaciated, as if he were dying of some terminal disease.

The photograph, cynically mirroring the image of a concentration camp survivor, was almost certainly fabricated – black propaganda of the kind Lazar was a master at creating. With it came a plea from Lazar that he be granted Spanish nationality, or at worst repatriated to his 'native' Austria rather than Germany. 'The only case that can be held against me is that during a particular period of time I served as a member of the German embassy,' Lazar wrote disingenuously.

Lazar was never arrested. Instead, Franco showed a leniency towards him, and to other Nazis, that he denied to thousands of Spaniards who were either executed or condemned to long prison sentences under his regime. Lazar was allowed to disappear quietly and without trace for several years until his case had ceased to be of interest to the Allies. Eight years passed before Lazar remerged as a freelance journalist and commentator in West Germany. In an article published in a Hamburg newspaper just before Christmas 1953, Lazar lashed out at the evils of communism and portrayed Franco as a bastion of Western Christian values.

By then the Cold War was under way, following the East/West crisis of the Berlin blockade, and London and Washington had long ceased to view pursuing ex-Nazis as a priority. Meanwhile, the majority of those who had played important roles in the British embassy in wartime Madrid had long moved on to pastures new anyway. From the comfort of his Chelsea home, the ennobled British ambassador to wartime Spain, Sir Samuel Hoare – Lord Templewood – wrote his memoirs, entitled *Ambassador on Special Mission*, which aimed to justify his policy towards Franco's Spain and why, in the end, he had turned against it. In the words of Sir Victor Mallet, his successor, Hoare's reminiscences were written in a generally 'spiteful and exaggerated tone with the main object of redounding in his own glory'. For a brief spell Hoare was engaged in an unseemly row with his American counterpart Carlton Hayes, who, in his own memoirs, accused Hoare of imperial arrogance and of failing to understand the true nature of Spain as some of his subordinates, including Burns, had.

Hoare served out the twilight of his political years as an opposition peer, his dreams of leading the Conservative Party shattered by Labour's post-war electoral success and feeling increasingly embittered by the decline of the British Empire and America's emergence as the dominant Western power. He tried to remain active in the post-war parliament, helping get the 1948 Criminal Justice Bill through, opposing capital punishment, and becoming chairman of the Magistrates' Association and the anti-slavery movement. He was also appointed president of the Lawn Tennis Association and became a regular fixture at the annual Wimbledon tournament.

Hoare's trusted adviser on intelligence matters, Captain Hillgarth, spent his retirement pursuing investments in Spain with his old friend Juan March while maintaining his contacts with MI6. Hillgarth converted to Catholicism, and chose Burns as his godfather for reception into the Catholic Church. Out of Burns's team, John Walters returned to journalism, while John Stordy joined the BBC and subsequently the UN. Peter Laing stayed on in the Madrid embassy before turning to freelance writing on Spanish affairs and investing in Spanish real estate.

Among the service chiefs of Hoare's embassy, the military attaché Brigadier Torr became a farmer, and his assistant, Alan Lubbock, a Hampshire squire as Lord Lieutenant of the county. Hamilton Stokes, the MI6 station chief in Madrid, was briefly put in charge of Iberian affairs in London, receiving and distributing reports from Spain, Portugal and West Africa. Suffering from bad eyesight, made worse by the neon lighting in MI6's ageing offices in Ryder Street, he retired in 1945 to become secretary of the Dublin Yacht Club. He was replaced as Iberian station chief under cover of Second Secretary, British Embassy, Chancery division, by Desmond Bristow, who had also served in the embassy in wartime Madrid. In 1947, Bristow replaced the new head of MI6's Madrid station, David Thomson, who had been forced to resign after one of his agents had been caught in possession of Spanish War Office papers. With the cover of Second Secretary, Bristow kept track of Nazis, communist agents and the internal machinations of Franco's regime. Within a year of his arrival, the British embassy found itself having to increase its reporting on the state of prisoners held in Spanish jails, an issue of concern to Labour backbench MPs.

The task of attending political trials and visiting prisons was given to the longest surviving member of the Madrid embassy staff, Bernard Malley, who had worked as assistant press attaché to Burns throughout the war and had subsequently been confirmed on a permanent contract as a locally employed counsellor. With his staunch Catholic views and pro-Franco contacts, the former seminarian continued to play a useful role as a well-placed informant on Spanish internal affairs, although the British remained diplomatically ineffectual in moderating Franco's appalling human rights record.

Burns, like Malley, came to benefit from the fact that the Cold War shifted the focus of attention of the British foreign policy and of the security and intelligence services away from fascism towards communism, putting pressure on the Soviet moles who had infiltrated the British state from the late 1930s. Kim Philby and Anthony Blunt, two intelligence officers who had spent much of the war trying to get Burns sacked for alleged disloyalty to the Allied cause, were belatedly exposed as Soviet spies.

Philby completed his defection by escaping to Moscow in 1963, having betrayed a network of British agents in Eastern Europe, and leaving behind a trail of disillusioned colleagues – senior intelligence officers in MI6 and MI5 – who had looked up to him as a man of impeccable professionalism and loyalty to the Crown, beyond suspicion. The Americans, with the evidence of hindsight, blamed the Philby affair on a very English old boy network's instinct to protect its own. It was, however, a network to which not everyone belonged.

Those who had venerated Philby throughout the Second World War and beyond included Richard Broomham-White, MI5's wartime Iberian desk officer who was part of the conspiracy to get Burns sacked from his Madrid posting. As a post-war Conservative Member of Parliament, Broomham-White stood up in the House of Commons prior to his friend Philby's final exposé as a Soviet agent and insisted that he was innocent, a statement that caused him severe embarrassment and subsequent public discredit. Enriqueta Harris left the Ministry of Information and returned to the art world she had once inhabited with Anthony Blunt. In the post-war years she was employed in the photographic collection of the Warburg Institute which had been incorporated into the University of London. She also earned a reputation as a leading authority on Spanish masters like El Greco and Diego Velazquez, and was honoured by the post-Franco Spanish state. She received the Gold Medal for Merit in the Fine Arts from King Juan Carlos in 1989, and was awarded the Grand Cross of the Order of Isabel La Catolica. She died in April 2006.

Tomás Harris, the MI5 officer who had tried, together with his sister, so consistently to have Burns sacked from the Ministry of Information, was killed in a mysterious car crash in Mallorca in 1964, a year after Philby absconded to Moscow, and a few months before Blunt, by then firmly ensconced in his post-war role as Surveyor of the Queen's Pictures and Director of the Courtauld Institute, confessed to being a Soviet spy in return for immunity from prosecution.

The doubts as to whether Tomás Harris was a Soviet agent were never dispelled. Harris's former colleague Bristow subsequently credited him for his work as a case officer of Juan Pujol, Garbo, who in turn was brought back from post-war anonymity and self-exile in South America and honoured by MI5 as one of the most successful double-cross operators of the entire war.

In his own memoirs, published in defiance of attempts by MI6 to suppress them, Bristow wrote that Harris had been in an 'ideal situation' to further Soviet infiltration, not just as a case officer for allegedly the most successful wartime deception agent in the world, but having also acted as a nexus for a group of friends that included Philby, Blunt, Burgess and Maclean – the four Cambridge KGB 'spies' – and some of the top figures of MI5 and MI6.

Bristow alleged that after the war Harris and Blunt, together with Pujol ran a fake paintings scam out of Latin America until it was cut short by a Venezuelan art expert. It was also alleged that Harris had been the Cambridge four's paymaster, and that some of the fakes Blunt authenticated after the war helped raise money for the Spanish Communist Party. The greatest mystery of all continued to surround the circumstances of Harris's death, with the claim that he was drunk and hit a tree questioned in the aftermath of the crash by his wife who was with him at the time. Subsequently investigators familiar with the road, and who did not consider the site of the accident a blackspot, resurrected the idea that the car might have been tampered with and that Harris had been the victim of an assassination, although no evidence has even been produced substantiating such a claim.

At the same time the absence of any conclusive proof that there was an accident has fuelled the theory that Harris was killed in anticipation that he would eventually have been hauled in for questioning in London over the Philby case and revealed an even greater degree of penetration of Western intelligence by the Soviets than has hitherto been discovered to be the case. The mystery remains unresolved.

After leaving the Madrid embassy, Burns ostensibly went back to his prewar profession as a publisher. A letter from his old friend Douglas Jerrold suggested he take charge of Burns & Oates, the firm founded by his great-uncle, and consolidate it as a leading Catholic books and media enterprise. 'Oblique suggestions from SIS (MI6) that I might wish for some permanent employment with them would now be discouraged with safety for the future,' Burns wrote mischievously in his memoirs.

In fact some of the friends Burns made before and during the war served as spies in the Cold War and he himself maintained a secret informal relationship with the British and US intelligence services after returning to public life as a publisher, a cover for overseas travel and the securing of a variety of sources of information.

His contacts with dissident Christian groups resisting the repression of religious liberty under Eastern European communism and his extensive international network of influential Catholic friends in government and opposition provided him with intelligence from Warsaw to Belfast and across Asia, Africa and the Americas with particularly privileged information on the inside machinations of the Vatican under a succession of Popes, which he would pass on to trusted contacts in MI6, the Foreign Office and the CIA.

Meanwhile, the personal file his enemies in MI5 had built up against him during the war was quietly shelved with the advent of the Cold War, as Franco came to be seen as a strategic partner of American interests – just as the informal network of anti-Catholic conspirators involved in the double-cross system within the organisation was quietly disbanded.

Only one entry in March 1948, two years after Burns returned to Britain from his Spanish posting, served as a reminder that some of the anti-Franco agents Tomás Harris had put in place remained active in the early post-war years. A source code-named Poodle, run by Harris and Blunt's old section B1 inside the Spanish embassy, reported that Burns was by then 'collaborating fully' with the Spanish chargé d'affaires in London, the Marques de Santa Cruz, in 'defending the Franco regime from attacks on it in this country'.

Soon after the new Spanish diplomat had returned to London after a visit to Spain, Burns submitted to him the draft of a letter he suggested might be sent to *The Times* in reply to criticism by a spokesman for the Labour Party. 'Santa Cruz reported to Madrid that Burns's open championship of the regime would have an important effect on public opinion here in view of his high standing,' reported the MI5 agent code-named Poodle.

In the years following the end of the war, Franco survived in power, despite attempts to isolate him internationally, ranging from Spain's initial exclusion from the post-war UN to the temporary withdrawal of British and American ambassadors from Madrid, a measure Washington reversed in 1950 when it authorised military and financial aid to Spain so as to bring it within the anti-Soviet bloc. The resumption of full diplomatic ties with Britain coincided with the return to power of a Conservative government, so that Franco had little difficulty in persuading the Foreign Office to accept the nomination as the new Spanish ambassador to London of Miguel Primo de Rivera, a brother of the founder of the Falange, José Antonio, and a stalwart of the regime.

The subsequent appointment of Santa Cruz – who as José Villaverde had served as deputy head of mission in London under the Duke of Alba – as ambassador in 1958 came as the memory of Franco's services to the Allies was fading and opposition to his authoritarian rule was growing. However, Santa Cruz and his vivacious wife Casilda became the consummate diplomatic couple, making it their mission to assure a wide circle of friends that democracy would eventually return to Spain with the monarchy. Among regular guests at the embassy were Salvador de Madariaga, the Oxford-based academic who had shunned his homeland since the civil war, the ageing exiled former Republican prime minister Negrín and a variety of influential Labour and Conservative MPs including the Tory minister R.A. 'Rab' Butler and future prime minister Sir Alec Douglas-Home.

While the post-war Labour Party had been in power, Burns's sphere of influence had focused on Conservative MPs and their associated networks that extended across the civil service, the Garrick Club and, within it, a convivial dining table known as the Old Burgundians,

which counted *The Times* editor Bill Casey, the cartoonist Osbert
Lancaster, the writer Arthur Ransome and the poet T. S. Eliot among
its regular attendees. His enduring post-war friendships in the world
of intelligence included Walter Bell, who after serving in Washington
in the UK–US liaison committee under William Stephenson went
on to work as a spy in various Cold War postings, including Cairo
and Nairobi. Burns also maintained close links with a number of MI6
officers, including Peter Lunn, son of the Catholic polemicist Arnold
Lunn, whose expertise in tapping Soviet communications was made
much use of in post-war Vienna and subsequently East Berlin.

The return of a Conservative government in 1951 saw Burns playing
an increasingly influential role in bolstering Anglo-Spanish relations
with the help of his wife Mabel, their London home an informal
gathering place for an assortment of Spaniards living in London, well-
connected members of the British political establishment and foreign
service and priests and theologians.

Eight months after Anthony Eden, the new Conservative foreign
secretary, declared he was looking forward to improved relations with
Franco's Spain, on 2 May 1952 Burns gave a keynote lecture at the
Ateneo, the prestigious literary club in Madrid. The invitation had the
official blessing of the authorities as well as the patronage of Burns's
father-in-law Gregorio Marañón. No Englishman had been afforded
such an honour by the Spaniards for years. Burns spoke on English
Catholicism, a subject tailor-made for his audience and to appease the
authorities, as well as one genuinely close to his heart.

He began by noting that, in contrast to Spaniards, the English
were generally by nature reserved when it came to religious matters,
as if slightly embarrassed by them. He went on to identify a growing
and increasing confident Catholic population, comprising traditional
English families, Irish immigrants and converts who had managed
to free the 'true faith' from its social and political segregation before
concluding thus: 'Every thinking Englishman today faces a world
debate between Christianity and Atheism, and increasingly, as he looks
for authentic religion amidst all the confusions, all the darkness, he
finds it in the Catholic community . . . which threatens no one, lest he
be the devil.'

Burns's contacts extended, crucially, to Rome and across the Atlantic, for it was the Vatican and the US administration that led post-war international re-engagement with the Franco's Spain, culminating in its admission to the UN in December 1955.

Key players involved in discreet negotiations during this period included Spaniards Burns had befriended during his time in the embassy in Madrid. Prominent among them was the Christian Democrat lawyer Joaquin Ruiz-Giménez, who was dispatched as Spain's ambassador to the Holy See to secure the Pope's recognition of the Franco regime as a Catholic nation state.

In the US, another of Burns's friends from Madrid days, the former Spanish foreign minister José Félix Lequerica, coordinated a pro-Spanish lobby. For his part Burns used his regular trips to America under his guise of a publisher to help encourage the restoration of full US diplomatic relations with Spain through a network of staunchly anti-communist and powerful American Catholics, who ranged from the Archbishop of New York, Cardinal Spellman, to the CIA's Archie Roosevelt.

The grandson of President Theodore Roosevelt and a cousin of President Franklin D. Roosevelt, Archibald had risen through the ranks of the American intelligence services during the war. In 1953, the year Franco signed a historic pact with the US, Roosevelt was posted to Madrid as the CIA station chief. During his three years there he was a regular visitor to the Cigarral de Los Menores, the country retreat outside Toledo where Burns had first met the daughter of its owner, his future bride Mabel Marañón, in 1943.

'Dr Marañón was a true sage – a great medical doctor, historian, philosopher, and a wonderful human being,' Roosevelt later wrote. He went on to recount how knowledgeable Marañón had shown himself to be about Spain's Mozarabic culture, a theme the CIA man warmed to, regarding himself as somewhat of a specialist in dealings with Muslims.

While Burns travelled frequently across the Atlantic, mentally Mabel never left Spain. It was not just that she returned to the country frequently, taking her children on holidays, and keeping in touch with her parents and their influential social network. She became, in effect, an honorary Spanish ambassadress, founding cultural associations such as the Anglo-Spanish Society with one of the post-war British ambassadors to Spain, Jock Balfour, and charities such as the Spanish Welfare Fund, which helped channel money from Franco's Spain into the growing post-war immigrant community, work for which she was honoured by the Spanish state with the Grand Cross of Isabel la Católica.

It was during these post-war years that Mabel met Franco and brought to his attention the plight of elderly Spaniards who wanted to return home from exile, young single mothers, and children who needed Spanish-language classes. There were still hundreds of political prisoners and periodic executions still took place in Spain, but Mabel refrained from commenting on the country's internal affairs.

Instead she focused on getting a sympathetic response from the dictator to her request for money for her charities when she pointed out that the majority of Spanish immigrants in the UK at the time were from his native Galicia. So moved was Franco by Mabel's special pleading that, at one point in their conversation, he burst into tears. '*Mis pobres Gallegas*' (my poor Galician women) he wailed, for Franco was himself of Galician stock. Behind his tears, Franco had also spotted a political opportunity to counter-balance the opposition to his regime by the old republican exiled community that had established itself in London during the Spanish Civil War. In the post-war years the house – and later the flat – that Mabel shared with her husband in the English capital would leave its doors open as an informal meeting place for a politically wide cross-section of Spaniards. Discussions about Spanish culture or alternatives to Franco's dictatorial regime would take place over a coffee or a glass of wine or an extended dinner of Spanish food.

But Mabel's charities, which she helped run when not working for the BBC's Spanish language service, became the beneficiaries of Spanish public and private funding with Franco's blessing, part of it channelled through the Foundation set up in 1955 in memory of Juan March, the banker who had helped bankroll the Spanish Civil War in the first place and later worked as a British agent.

While using the Marañón name to maintain his own contacts in Spain, on his return to Britain Burns wasted little time in getting back in touch with the world with which he had been familiar as a bachelor. Burns stayed close to the Richey brothers, Harman Grisewood, and his best friend David Jones, who in 1955 was awarded a CBE. When the Queen asked Jones what he did, he answered simply, 'I paint pictures and your mother has quite a collection of them.' He might have added, 'and Anthony Blunt looks after them', which he did at the time, as Surveyor of the Queen's pictures.

While gaining some recognition for his undoubted talent as a poet and artist, work which Burns helped promote, Jones never rid himself of a life-long depression which took hold of him in the trenches in the Great War. Jones spent his last years as a semi-recluse in a nursing home in the outskirts of London. Burns would visit him regularly at weekends, and paid a moving tribute to him in his memoirs. 'I doubt if any other mortal soul has been such a counsellor, such a kind comrade,' wrote Burns eighteen years after Jones's death in 1974.

Among Burns's female friends and one-time lovers, Ann Bowes-Lyon settled into her marriage with Dr Frank D'Abreu, became a devoted Catholic, and helped run charities. The fund-raising events and the Stonyhurst old-boy network meant that the Burnses and the D'Abreus met socially from time to time. The affair between Tom Burns and Ann Bowes-Lyon was never resumed, although Ann secretly kept his pre-war letters until she died in 1999.

For her part, Mabel Marañón found her new post-war life in London as Mrs Tom Burns difficult only when having to suffer some of the old friendships her husband had forged in a different era.

'Back early (11 o'clock) to hotel where just as I was in bed I was telephoned by Burns who came up with his bride, swarthy, squat, Japanese appearance. He says he can arrange a holiday in Spain for me,' Evelyn Waugh noted in his London diary on 21 February 1946.

Mabel, whom most other men considered a beauty, did not keep a diary at this time, but her dislike for Waugh was mutual. She found him physically repugnant, snobbish and rude to the point of cruelty. It was soon after that first encounter that she and her husband invited Waugh for dinner at their first post-war London home in Victoria Square. The author spent part of the evening mocking Mabel for bringing a Spanish maid over from Franco's Spain to serve at table wearing white gloves and also complained about the smell of garlic given off by the *chorizo* stored next to the guest room. Mabel felt it a terrible abuse of her hospitality.

But worse was to come in the conflict between the most brilliant English novelist of his generation and the self-assured youngest daughter of one of twentieth-century Spain's most eminent men of science and letters. Despite the earlier fiasco, Mabel was reluctantly persuaded weeks later by her husband to lend Waugh their home for a party he wanted to give in honour of Clare Booth Luce. The glamorous wife of the proprietor of *Time-Life* was an ardent Catholic convert and Waugh thought the Burns's residence an ideal place to gather together a good sampling of London's Catholic intelligentsia. 'There was a fine mixture of writers and hacks with a sprinkling of selected clergy; the house was awash with champagne; Dr Hyde, so to call the better side of Evelyn, was at his kindliest and most amusing,' Burns later recalled.

And yet Burns was as upset as Mabel by the appearance at their door the following evening of Robert Speaight, the Catholic actor and author. He had turned up a day late because of a misleading invitation Waugh had deliberately sent him.

Some years later Burns had transferred his young family of one daughter and two sons from their elegant Georgian house in Victoria Square to a flat in a Victorian mansion block opposite Westminster Cathedral. No sooner had he moved in than he received a postcard from Waugh. 'I am sorry that you have come down in the world,' Waugh snarled. Burns thought it best not to show the postcard to Mabel.

While Mabel never reconciled herself with Waugh's acerbic wit and brash manner – both of which she found offensive – Burns continued to value him as a literary and social asset, suffering as best he could his idiosyncrasies, over occasional meals together and correspondence, and seeking some advantage in return.

In the summer of 1946, Burns helped arrange for Waugh's first post-war visit to Spain. At the time Waugh was basking in the fame of his bestseller *Brideshead Revisited*. He was 'alternately absorbed in writing and high living, with hard drinking, to the neglect of his wife and family', Burns later recalled. As he would later reflect in his memoirs, Waugh had acquired a persona with a constant scowling glare alternating with an expression of ineffable boredom. 'These masks cracked occasionally with a smile which seemed to me a grotesque grimace,' Burns wrote. And yet Burns considered Waugh's acceptance of an invitation to attend an international congress in Madrid in honour of the fifteenth-century Spanish Dominican Francisco de Victoria something of a diplomatic coup, at a time when the wartime allied powers appeared determined to exclude Franco's Spain from the United Nations.

The congress was ultimately postponed but Waugh and his companion, his old friend from Oxford days, the *Tablet* editor Douglas Woodruff, spent two weeks touring emblemic cities of Franco's Spain – Valladolid, Burgos and Salamanca – and laying a wreath at the Peninsular War memorial in Vitoria. Despite periodic organisational setbacks, the two companions were treated to endless banquets and *vins d'honneur* by the lay and ecclesiastical Spanish authorities and, in the British ambassador Victor Mallet's absence, by his wife Peggy, whom Waugh knew from an earlier trip abroad.

Two years later, in the summer of 1948, Waugh repaid Burns the favour of his free holiday in Spain by editing a book by the American Trappist monk Thomas Merton. 'Tom Burns gave me enthralling task of cutting the redundancies and solecisms of Tom Merton's *Seven Storey Mountain*. This took a week and resulted in what should be a fine thin volume. I gave dinner to Mia, the Pakenhams and Burns. Bill £26. But lavish,' Waugh wrote in his dairy.

Merton's book, with Waugh's amendments, was published in Britain as *Elected Silence*, a title chosen by Burns in consultation with Waugh. This time Waugh did not question his publisher's judgement as he had done with the earlier *Waugh in Abyssinia*.

Burns later wrote to Waugh on the subject of their mutual friend Graham Greene's new novel, *The Heart of the Matter*. The central character is called Scobie, a Catholic expatriate policeman living in West Africa. Scobie's marriage is in crisis, and he falls in love with another woman. When his wife discovers the affair, Scobie pretends he still loves her and, to maintain the pretence, takes Holy Communion with her. Believing that his adultery has placed him in a state of mortal sin, he commits suicide, offering his damnation as a sacrifice for the two women in his life. Whatever its literary merits, as a fellow Catholic

Burns believed that Greene had produced a 'sham spiritual dilemma' with 'a caricature conventional Catholic couple'. He told Waugh: 'He [Greene] almost turns things upside down and hates the sinners whilst he loves the sin. G. G. is becoming a sort of smart Alec of Jansenism.'

Waugh's subsequent review published in the *Tablet* was no less visceral. 'To me the idea of willing my own damnation for the love of God is either a very loose poetical expression or a mad blasphemy . . .' he wrote in a review that provoked a lengthy debate in the letters column of the magazine but which ultimately left his friendship with Burns and Greene unaffected.

Greene had officially left MI6 in 1944 in mysterious circumstances. Just as Burns had facilitated Greene's original recruitment into government service with the MoI in the immediate aftermath of war, so he played a part in helping the author reintegrate into civilian life. Burns arranged for Greene to be offered a job at the publishers Eyre & Spottiswoode. These were days before the advent of the big conglomerates, when publishing was still a cottage industry run by a close social circle of well-known public figures.

Greene was a member of one such coterie, their meetings at the Lamb and Flag pub in Covent Garden recalled by Burns: 'Graham seemed to have a spotlight on him, although his companions were by no means shadowy figures and I recall them with affection . . . there was Douglas Jerrold, the chairman of the company and a tall, saturnine figure . . . all of a right-wing piece . . . in contrast was his close colleague Sir Charles Petrie; an owlish, round and bearded baronet, a learned historian but as much as home in the Lamb and Flag as in the Carlton Club.' Frank Morley made up the trio, a Harvard graduate and Rhodes Scholar who had 'adopted England as his own and had settled near its heart, in Buckinghamshire'.

While Burns's relations with Waugh cooled in later years, his friendship with Greene intensified as publisher and author found common ground in their engagement with the more liberal Catholic theology emerging from the Second Vatican Council and their more discreet and enduring contacts with the murky world of espionage. Burns's friendship with Greene was made easier by the fact that he was much admired by Mabel, who found him thoughtful, kind and attractive, in striking contrast to her feelings for Waugh.

When Burns took over as the editor of the *Tablet* in 1967 from the more conservative Douglas Woodruff, he stepped up his correspondence and informal meetings with Greene, at which conversation would range freely over matters of politics, theology and love. In 1976 Burns persuaded Greene to become a Trustee of the Tablet Trust, along with several of the great and good of the post-war British Catholic establishment led by the Duke of Norfolk and the one-time head of the civil service, Sir John Hunt. Burns came to rely on Greene's voluntary contributions to raise the *Tablet*'s profile at minimal cost, most notably the submission by the author of episodes of what became the novel *Monsignor Quixote*.

A regular visitor to his flat in Antibes, Burns was in correspondence with Greene right up to the final week of the author's life, in June 1991, when he himself had already been diagnosed with cancer – two Catholics struggling to come to terms with their mortality, raging against the night, with their faith in God facing its ultimate test and with the frustration and pain of old age and incurable illness.

Two years younger than Greene, my father died four and a half years later, on 8 December 1995, the iconic Catholic Feast of the Immaculate Conception, having suffered from the same fatal blood condition as his good friend.

More than four decades had passed since the author of this book was conceived. Mabel Marañón, my mother, and my father, Tom, were then staying in their new Madrid flat on the sixth floor of a building on the Avenida Castellana also occupied by her parents and her two sisters. On 27 January 1953, Mabel gave birth in the Spanish capital to Jimmy, her fourth surviving child, the first to be born in Spain since the premature death towards the end of the Second World War of *El Inglesito*. My parents saw my coming into this world as a symbol of a new beginning in Anglo-Spanish relations. Thirty years later, on his retirement from publishing in 1983, Tom Burns was awarded the OBE in recognition of services to Queen and Country.

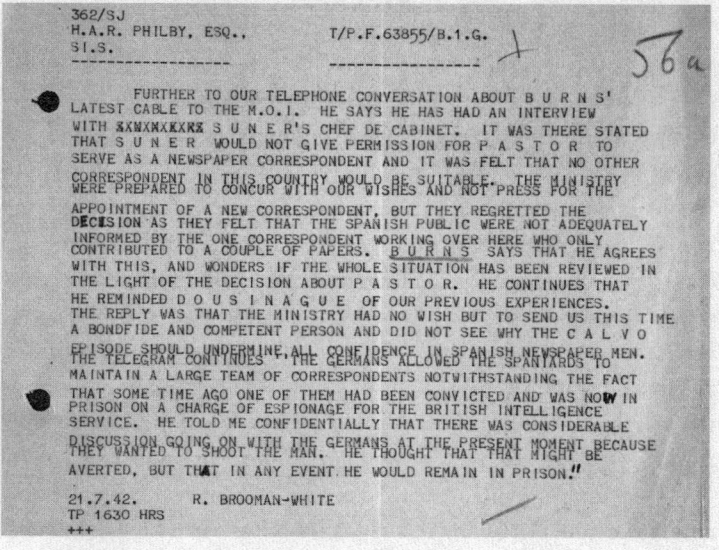

Se sospecha con mucho fundamento que *Burn*, que figura como Jefe de la Propaganda inglesa, es en realidad el Jefe del Intelligent-Service en España y Portugal. Va mucho a Lisboa.

Hablar de colaboracion.

T y U·hablar   Fofroda y Utrillas =

Impresion recogida de personal embajada. II. coincidente con sentir recogido por Otaño señalando que entrevista con Petain fue consecuencia no haber accedido Caudillo peticiones Hitler. Consecuencias

Spanish Secret Police report alleging that Burns is the Head of British propaganda and chief spy in Spain. (Franco Archive)

```
362/SJ
H.A.R. PHILBY, ESQ.,          T/P.F.63855/B.1.G.
SIS.

        FURTHER TO OUR TELEPHONE CONVERSATION ABOUT B U R N S'
LATEST CABLE TO THE M.O.I.  HE SAYS HE HAS HAD AN INTERVIEW
WITH XXWXXXXXXX S U N E R'S CHEF DE CABINET.  IT WAS THERE STATED
THAT S U N E R  WOULD NOT GIVE PERMISSION FOR P A S T O R  TO
SERVE AS A NEWSPAPER CORRESPONDENT AND IT WAS FELT THAT NO OTHER
CORRESPONDENT IN THIS COUNTRY WOULD BE SUITABLE.  THE MINISTRY
WERE PREPARED TO CONCUR WITH OUR WISHES AND NOT PRESS FOR THE
APPOINTMENT OF A NEW CORRESPONDENT, BUT THEY REGRETTED THE
DECISION AS THEY FELT THAT THE SPANISH PUBLIC WERE NOT ADEQUATELY
INFORMED BY THE ONE CORRESPONDENT WORKING OVER HERE WHO ONLY
CONTRIBUTED TO A COUPLE OF PAPERS.  B U R N S  SAYS THAT HE AGREES
WITH THIS, AND WONDERS IF THE WHOLE SITUATION HAS BEEN REVIEWED IN
THE LIGHT OF THE DECISION ABOUT P A S T O R.  HE CONTINUES THAT
HE REMINDED D O U S I N A G U E  OF OUR PREVIOUS EXPERIENCES.
THE REPLY WAS THAT THE MINISTRY HAD NO WISH BUT TO SEND US THIS TIME
A BONDFIDE AND COMPETENT PERSON AND DID NOT SEE WHY THE C A L V O
EPISODE SHOULD UNDERMINE ALL CONFIDENCE IN SPANISH NEWSPAPER MEN.
THE TELEGRAM CONTINUES ", 'THE GERMANS ALLOWED THE SPANIARDS TO
MAINTAIN A LARGE TEAM OF CORRESPONDENTS NOTWITHSTANDING THE FACT
THAT SOME TIME AGO ONE OF THEM HAD BEEN CONVICTED AND WAS NOW IN
PRISON ON A CHARGE OF ESPIONAGE FOR THE BRITISH INTELLIGENCE
SERVICE.  HE TOLD ME CONFIDENTIALLY THAT THERE WAS CONSIDERABLE
DISCUSSION GOING ON WITH THE GERMANS AT THE PRESENT MOMENT BECAUSE
THEY WANTED TO SHOOT THE MAN.  HE THOUGHT THAT THAT MIGHT BE
AVERTED, BUT THAT IN ANY EVENT HE WOULD REMAIN IN PRISON."

21.7.42.    R. BROOMAN-WHITE
TP 1630 HRS
+++
```

Memo from MI5 Iberian officer Brooman-White to Kim Philby reporting on Tom Burns's activities. (The National Archives)

Secret.

In reply, state NUMBER and DATE.

CX '960, dated 18.2.42.
V.D.

Dear Brooman-White,

Our representative in MADRID reports that
CALVO met LAZAR, the German Press Attache in MADRID,
during his recent visit to SPAIN.

CALVO alleged (presumably to BURNS) that this
was a chance meeting. But this news item is nevertheless
worth passing to MILMO for use in HAM.

Yours sincerely,

H. R. Philby

R. Brooman-White, Esq.,
M.I.5.

MI6 memo signed by Kim Philby about a meeting between Spanish journalist Luis Calvo and German Press attaché in Madrid, Hans Lazar. (The National Archives)

Notes

1. Catholic Roots

The main source for this chapter is Tom Burns, *The Use of Memory* (London: Sheed & Ward, 1993)

p. 1 *very English, very respectable, and very traditional*: Sir Samuel Hoare, *Ambassador on Special Mission* (London: Collins, 1946), p. 9.

p. 2 *There is no country*: Ibid., p.102.

p. 2 *a new generation of young intellectuals*: Author's conversations with various English Catholics, including Barbara Lucas and Michael Walsh. Also Bernard Wall, *Headlong into Change* (London: Harvill, 1969), p. 61, and Adrian Hastings, *A History of English Christianity* (London, SCM Press, 2005), pp. 280–81, ibid., p. 279.

p. 4 *Thank you very much*: David Burns's letters from the front are from Burns Family Archive (BFA).

p. 5 *Stonyhurst considered itself unique*: For the most comprehensive history of the school, from its early beginnings to the late twentieth century, see T. E. Muir, *Stonyhurst College* (London: James & James, 1992).

p. 5 *loyalty to the British state*: Francis Irwin, *Stonyhurst War Record* (Stonyhurst, 1927), p. xxxiv. Also contains account of David Burns's death in action, pp. 18–20.

p. 5 *John was infused with an adventurous and polemical spirit*: I have drawn from correspondence between John and Fr D'Arcy from BFA. Also H. J. A. Sire, *Father Martin D'Arcy* (Leominster, 1997), p. 48.

p. 6 *Burns and the much older Gwen*: Ceridwen Lloyd-Morgan (ed.), *Gwen John: Letters and Notebooks* (London: Tate Publishing in association with The National Library of Wales, 2004), pp. 162, 164; Susan Chitty, *Gwen John* (London: Hodder & Stoughton, 1981), p. 189.

p. 8 *On the rare occasion that G. K. was neither on a ritual drinking binge with Belloc*: On the relationship between the two, see A. N. Wilson, *Hilaire Belloc* (London: Hamish Hamilton, 1984), pp. 99–100.

p. 9 *the most innovative if controversial of Burns's early stable of authors*: Fiona McCarthy, *Eric Gill* (London: Faber & Faber, 1989), p. 150.

p. 9 *near his friend Harman Grisewood*: Grisewood papers, Georgetown University (GEO). For other private jokes and references in *Vile Bodies*, see Selina Hastings, *Evelyn Waugh* (London, Minerva, 1995), p. 209.

p. 9 *a BBC news editor he held responsible*: D. J. Taylor, *Bright Young People*, (London: Vintage, 2008), p. 134.

p. 10 *one time fanatics of the party-going scene*: Taylor, *Bright Young People*, p. 166.

p. 10 *the girl that claimed to have visions of the Virgin Mary urging her to a life of chastity*: Sire, *D'Arcy*, p. 79.

p. 10 '*suffered the attention of sea gulls*': Burns, *Use of Memory*, p. 22.

p. 11 *had filled me with foreboding*: Burns, *Use of Memory*, p. 22.

p. 12 *conflict between Burns and Oldmeadow*: Michael Walsh, *Tablet* (London: The Tablet Publishing Company, 1990), pp. 37–8.

p. 12 *royalties going to the Oxford Jesuit college*: Sire, *D'Arcy*, p. 82.

p. 13 '*savagery' comitted by communist regimes*: Christopher Sykes, *Evelyn Waugh* (London: Penguin, 1982), p. 206.

p. 13 '*rather curved*': For Greene's politics at this time see W. J. West, *The Quest for Graham Greene* (London: Phoenix, 1988), pp. 58, 59, also Michael Shelden, *Graham Greene: The Man Within* (London, Minerva, 1995), pp. 89, 140, and Norman Sherry, *The Life of Graham Greene*, vol. 1 (London, Penguin, 1990), p. 161.

p. 14 *It was from Barbara and it was a cry for help*: Author's interview with Barbara Lucas. For Belmonte character and bullfighting, see Ernest Hemingway, *Death in the Afternoon* (London: Classic Vintage, 2007), *Fiesta, the Sun Also Rises* (London: Arrow, 1982) and A. L. Kennedy, *On Bullfighting* (London: Yellow Jersey Press, 1999), pp. 68–79, also bullfighter's memoirs in Manuel Chaves Nogales, *Juan Belmonte, matador de toros* (Madrid: Alianza, 1969).

p. 15 *George Steer, the South African-born correspondent*: Nicholas Rankin, *Telegram from Guernica* (London: Faber & Faber, 2003).

p. 16 *Burns signed up Waugh*: Sykes, *Waugh*, pp. 227, 231 and 234 (for influence of Belloc).

p. 17 *the main army conspirators*: Luis Bolín, *Spain: The Vital Years* (Philadelphia: Lippincott, 1967); Mariano Sánchez Soler, *Los Banqueros de Franco* (Madrid: Oberon, 2005); by same author, *Ricos por la guerra de España* (Madrid: Raices, 2007); J. I. Luca de Tena, *Mis Amigos Muertos* (Barcelona: Planeta, 1971); for Pollard's intelligence links, see documents HS 9/1200–5, NA; Diana Pollard's memoirs were recorded by the Imperial War Museum, London.

p. 19 *On a scale almost Chinese*: Martin Gilbert, *Churchill* (London: Pimlico, 2000), pp. 58–60.

p. 20 '*Blood, blood, blood*': Tom Buchanan, *Britain and the Spanish Civil War* (Cambridge: Cambridge University Press, 1997), p. 87.

p. 20 *Hillgarth, the Naval Intelligence officer*: David Stafford, *Churchill and Secret Service* (London: Abacus, 1997), pp. 236–7; Hillgarth's novel based in Bolivia is called *The Black Mountain*.

p. 20 *Very sure of himself, writes shockers*: Waugh, *Diaries*, 1 July 1927; for account of Son Torella, I have drawn from Mary Hillgarth, 'A Private Life' (privately printed memoirs) (BFA).

2. Authors Take Sides

p. 24 *There's something obscene*: Quoted in Walter Hooper, *C. S. Lewis: A Companion and Guide* (London: Fount/HarperCollins, 1996), p. 25.

p. 25 *When the left-wing Popular Front won*: For Campbell's experience of the 'terror' in Toledo, and other details of his life, I am indebted to his biographers Joseph Pearce, *Bloomsbury and Beyond* (London: HarperCollins, 2002), and Peter Alexander, *Roy Campbell* (Oxford University Press, 1982), as well as Campbell's own memoirs, *Light on a Dark Horse* (London: Penguin, 1971), and Anna Campbell Lyle's memoir of her father, *Poetic Justice* (BFA).

p. 26 *more for my sympathies*: Burns, *Use of Memory*, p. 74.

p. 26 *The Catholic weekly the* Tablet: Buchanan, *Civil War*, p. 179.

p. 26 *Campbell followed Burns's instructions*: Alexander, *Roy Campbell*, p. 172.

p. 27 *the young Cambridge graduate*: For Peter Kemp's own account of his involvement in the Spanish Civil War, see his memoir, *Mine Were of Trouble* (London: Cassell, 1957). Further insights are provided by Priscilla Scott-Ellis, who met Kemp while working as a nurse on the Nationalist side. See her diary, *The Changes of Death* (Norwich: Michael Russell, 1995), and a more critical account of her activities in Paul Preston, *Doves of War* (Boston: Northeastern University Press, 2002).

p. 27 *propaganda efforts*: A detailed examination of media coverage of the Spanish Civil War is provided by Paul Preston, *We Saw Spain Die* (London: Constable & Robinson, 2008).

p. 28 *survey of British writers*: Buchanan, *Civil War*, p. 159.

p. 28 *Burns's takeover of the* Tablet: Detailed in Walsh, *Tablet*. Graham Greene's collected journalism for the magazine is examined in Ian Thomson's edited *Articles of Faith* (Oxford: Signal Books, 2006).

p. 28 *Greene contrasted the political rantings of the 1930s*: the *Spectator* article is quoted in Shelden, *Greene*, p. 225.

p. 29 For this account of the propaganda war waged over Gernika, I have drawn from Rankin, *Telegram from Guernica*. See also Preston, *We Saw Spain Die*.

p. 29 *More recently Basque investigators*: author's interview with Basque journalist and author Iñigo Gurruchaga.

p. 31 *A broader attack on the claims made*: A copy of the Jesuit George Burns's (brother of Tom) letter defending Nationalist propaganda is in the Basque National Archive (BNA), Fundación Sabino Arana.

p. 33 *joined Longman, Green & Co.*: Hastings, *Waugh*, p. 315.

p. 35 *Beverley Nichols entertained leaders of the Hitler Youth to lunch at the Garrick Club*: Taylor, *Bright Young People*, p. 245.

p. 38 *'To those men who watched the creeping disorder'*: Gabriel Herbert papers.

p. 38 *'To a people tired of injustice'*: Gabriel Herbert papers

p. 40 *Philby continued to use his journalism as a cover for espionage*: Preston, *We Saw Spain Die*, p. 165; Kim Philby, *My Silent War* (New York: Random House, 2002), pp. 1–6

3. Ministry of Information

p. 46 *Mass and Communion*: Waugh, *Diaries*, p. 439.

p. 46 *Churchill was not taken seriously*: Burns, *Use of Memory*, p. 83.

p. 46 *Yes, I heard Chamberlain's grand little speech*: David Jones (ed.), *Dai Greatcoat: A Self-Portrait of David Jones in His Letters* (London: Faber & Faber, 1980), p. 88.

p. 46 *I am deeply impressed by it*: Ibid., p. 92.

p. 47 *pull strings for me*: Burns, *Use of Memory*, p. 171.

p. 47 *The new Pope was Cardinal Eugenio Pacelli*: Two essential books of reference on the controversial Pius XII are John Cornwell's *Hitler's Pope* (London: Penguin: 2000) and Gerard Noel's *Pius XII: The Hound of Hitler* (London: Continuum, 2008).

p. 48 *This is the first chance of writing*: Grisewood papers, GEO.

p. 53 *'Darling, here I am alone'*: Burns/BL letters.

p. 54 *thrush-like beauty*: Hugo Vickers, *Elizabeth, The Queen Mother* (London: Arrow Books, 2005), p. 52.

p. 55 *My darling Ann*: All letters from Tom Burns to Ann Bowes-Lyon are from BFA.

p. 55 *I keep thinking of you*: Ibid.

p. 56 *Darling little heart*: Ibid.

p. 56 *Richey was looking for a job*: Information based on author's interview with Richey (24/8/2005) and Richey papers at GEO.

p. 57 *Burns moved into the Ministry of Information*: No government records appear to have survived detailing the precise sequence of events that led to Burns's recruitment although it is possible to deduce from Burns's memoir, *The Use of Memory*, the kind of networking that may have influenced matters. Grisewood was by then a rising star in the BBC and increasingly involved in wartime propaganda. Lord Howard of Penrith was another of Burns's male friends from the 1920s, the first of to achieve a peerage. Francis Howard had just inherited the title following the death of his father Esme, a senior figure in the diplomatic service and former ambassador to Washington.

p. 57 *the future poet laureate*: See Bevis Hillier's condensed biography of the poet (London: John Murray, 2006) and Channel 4's *The Real John Betjeman* (text in Channel 4's portrait gallery). Recalling their first encounter in the 1920s, Burns in *Use of Memory* described Betjeman as the 'first Protestant I've ever met'. They were introduced to each other by a mutual friend, Billy Clonmore, a former Anglican priest who had converted to Catholicism. Betjeman spent only slightly more time at the MoI HQ than Burns before being posted to Dublin as press attaché – his job involved him advocating Ireland's alliance with Britain against Germany and reporting on the activities of the IRA. 'The boy who had been teased as a "German spy" had grown up to be a British spy' (Channel 4, *Real Lives*).

p. 58 *Most of us indulged in an unscrupulous and crazy scramble*: Sir Kenneth Grubb, *The Crypts of Power* (London: Hodder & Stoughton, 1971), p. 107.

p. 59 *if English life had run as it did in the books of adventure*: Evelyn Waugh, *Put Out More Flags* (London: Penguin, 2000), p. 50.

p. 59 *too tall, too handsome, too well-born*: Ibid., p. vii.

p. 59 *history of the Jesuits*: According to Waugh's biographer, Selina Hastings, the author decided not to write the book after his return from his trip to Mexico in October 1938. The decision was welcomed by Waugh's agent A. D. Peters who felt that Burns's proposal 'could not from any angle be regarded as commercial'. See Hastings, *Waugh*, p. 380.

p. 60 *I shall be delighted to do such a preface*: Belloc papers, Burns Library, Boston College (BC).

p. 60 *Burns enlisted the help of his friend and political ally Douglas Jerrold*: 'I am sure this would be invaluable both from the Catholic and national point of view,' Jerrold wrote of the 'pamphlet' he commissioned Belloc to write. Ibid.

p. 60 *browbeaten, by people who talk of a large and powerful Catholic body*: Quoted by Wilson, *Belloc*, p. 365. Belloc's anti-German pronouncements contrast with his more controversial statements on the Jewish race. A more recent biography by Joseph Pearce, *Old Thunderer: A Life of Hilaire Belloc* (London: HarperCollins, 2002), was criticised for 'skating' over the question of Belloc's anti-Semitism, which the reviewer, Hywel Williams, describes as the 'central disfiguring fact of his *oeuvre*' (*Guardian*, 17/8/2002). Critics accuse Belloc of fuelling anti-Semitism among some fellow Catholics through his writings, blaming Jewish elements for the influence they had in promoting the forces of materialism. But in *The Catholic and the War*, published in 1940, Belloc condemned Nazi anti-Semitism.

p. 60 *Before the war . . . violent polemics were carried out by literary men*: Wall, *Headlong into Change*, p. 169.

p. 61 *D'Arcy began to broadcast frequently*: For the Jesuit's involvement in the Spanish Civil War and the Second World War see Sire, *D'Arcy*, pp. 88–9 and p. 121.

p. 61 *Waugh wrote to Basil Dufferin*: see Sykes, *Waugh*, p. 26. On the suspicions agencies like MI5 might have of Waugh's political reliability, Sykes comments: 'He [Waugh] was to show that he was not reliable in the sense of being politically subservient in all things. In the sense of not being prone to treason, he was politically wholly reliable', ibid., pp. 269–70.

p. 61 *His social contacts during the 1930s extended to families like the Mitfords*: The emotional attraction Waugh felt for Diana Mitford (he dedicated his 1929 novel *Vile Bodies* to her) has been well documented by his biographers. See Hastings, *Waugh*, pp. 217–18. For Oswald Moseley's close relationship with the Nazis, and his attempts – aided by Diana and her sister Unity – to support Hitler's regime see Stephen Dorill, *Black Shirt* (London: Viking: 2006). Dorill suggests that a member of Mosley's early circle of friends was a rebellious and polemic Oxford contemporary of Evelyn Waugh's, Peter Rodd, who the author used as a model for Basil Seal in *Put Out More Flags*.

The diaries of Guy Liddell, the deputy MI5 chief during the Second World War, and other recently declassified MI5 files show that British intelligence had been tracking the personal involvement of Diana and Unity with the Nazi regime through the 1930s. Unity shot herself in Munich at the outbreak of the war and lived out the rest of her short life as an invalid. Diana became Mosley's mistress before marrying him in 1936 in Joseph Goebbels's Berlin drawing room. Apart from the witnesses, Goebbels and Hitler were the only guests. Both Diana and her husband were interned by the British until November 1943, when they were placed under house arrest for the remainder of the war.

p. 62 *Burns, thanks to his friends in the Foreign Office*: The most influential of these was Eric Drummond, the 16th Earl of Perth. A descendant of one of the oldest Scottish clans and a staunch Catholic, Drummond developed a close personal and professional relationship with Burns during the 1930s when he served as British ambassador to Rome. With the outbreak of the Second World War Drummond was appointed by the Foreign Office as Director General designate of the MoI and subsequently the department's chief adviser on foreign publicity. Drummond's son, the (Benedictine) Downside-educated John, a contemporary of Burns, served in the intelligence corps in France and was sent, when Burns was at the MoI, to the US to lobby for its involvement in the war.

p. 62 *Evelyn turned up at the Ministry of Information*: Burns, *Use of Memory*, p. 64.

p. 62 George Orwell, *1984* (London: Penguin, 1959). For the topography of *1984*, see D. J. Taylor, *Orwell, A Life* (London: Vintage, 2003), p. 388.

p. 63 Graham Greene, *The Confidential Agent* (London: Vintage, 2001).

p. 63 *Mike on leave*: Barbara Lucas, personal diary and interview with the author.

p. 65 *Franco's triumphant state entry*: A detailed description is given in Paul Preston, *Franco* (London: HarperCollins, 1993), pp. 329–30.

p. 66 *It is clear that if friendship and understanding*: Quoted by Michael E. Williams in *St Alban's College, Valladolid* (London: C. Hurst & Company, 1986), p. 217.

p. 67 *Pope Pius XI's letter against Nazism*: Ibid., p. 217. For an example of how the forthright anti-fascist encyclical was contrasted by Catholics with Pacelli's later failure to publicly condemn Nazism, see Charles R. Gallagher, *Vatican Secret Diplomacy* (London: Yale University Press, 2008), p. 91.

p. 67 *The appointment of such a priest*: Williams, *St Alban's*, p. 217.

p. 68 *Until England breaks definitely*: Ibid., p. 218.

p. 68 *Cowan was a former member*: For account of Chetwode commission, see Hugh Thomas, *The Spanish Civil War* (London: 1977), p. 854. For documentation on Cowan controversy, see Foreign Office files FO 371–245526 at NA.

p. 70 *He was excellent company*: Burns, *Use of Memory*, p. 85.

p. 71 *the contrast and the change*: From Hilaire Belloc's *Many Cities* (London: Constable, 1920), quoted in Jimmy Burns, *A Literary Companion to Spain* (London: John Murray, 1994), p. 3.

p. 71 *Whereas uniforms had been everywhere*: Burns, *Use of Memory*, p. 86.

p. 71 *the yellow land, the red land*: From José Ortega y Gasset, *Viajes y Países* (Madrid: Revista de Occidente, 1957), quoted in Burns, *Literary Companion to Spain*, p. 5.

p. 71 *The long road from Burgos to Madrid*: For a photographic and anecdotal record of the suffering and destruction suffered by the Spanish capital and its inhabitants during the long siege of the Spanish Civil War, see Carmen and Laura Gutierrez Rueda, *El Hambre en el Madrid de la Guerra Civil* (Madrid: Ediciones La Liberia, 2003).

p. 72 *A group of journalists*: Burns, *Use of Memory*, p. 86.

4. Reconnaissance

p. 74 *The clientele was very young then*: Martha Gellhorn, *The View from the Ground* (London: Granta Books, 1989), p. 337.

p. 74 *A copy of* ABC: For source material on this period, editions of the newspaper during the Second World War were researched at the Local Newspaper Library of the Madrid City Council, *Hemeroteca Municipal del Ayuntamiento de Madrid*.

p. 76 *Don Bernardo . . . was a fervent Catholic*: Burns, *The Use of Memory*, p. 87.

p. 77 *Burns found Hillgarth a likeable and entertaining tutor*: For the background to Hillgarth's appointment as naval attaché in Madrid, see British Admiralty files at NA. In August 1939, the Director of Naval Intelligence, Geoffrey Cooke, wrote a memo supporting Hillgarth's posting on the following grounds: politically, Hillgarth would help exploit the Anglophile tendency in the Spanish navy against the influence of German and Italian naval attachés. Hillgarth had an advantage in that nearly all the principal units of the Spanish navy were equipped with British materiel and had been built in the partly British-owned naval shipyard of El Ferrol. Hillgarth had built up his contacts with senior pro-Franco naval officers while serving as Consul in Mallorca during the Spanish Civil War.

According to a Foreign Office report circulated to the British secret services on 22 July 1939, 'Hillgarth is already on excellent terms with the Spanish naval authorities who both like and trust him.' ADM 116/4167 NA.

Churchill considered Hillgarth not only his personal 'eyes and ears' on intelligence on Spain, but as a key player on pursuing a measure of leniency towards Franco's Spain, relaxing the British navy's stringent blockade to allow for some trade with the Iberian Peninsula as a *quid pro quo* for Spanish and Portuguese neutrality. Churchill's decision to delegate authority over policy to the British embassy in Madrid was taken on 29 September 1940. CHAR 20/13 Churchill Archives (CA). See also Richard Wigg, *Churchill and Spain* (Eastbourne: Sussex Academic Press: 2008), pp. 4–6, 11–12 and 14–15.

p. 78 *Burns continued lobbying*: FO 371-24526 NA.

p. 78 *There is an enormous amount*: Ibid.

p. 79 *A cuckoo in the nest, restless against inaction*: A. J. P. Taylor, *English History: 1914–1945* (London: Penguin 1981), p. 568.

p. 79 *Dorchy reported that he was installed*: FO 371-24526 NA.

p. 79 *A typical consignment prepared for dispatch*: Ministry of Information files NA.

p. 80 *According to intelligence provided by one of Burns's Spanish sources*: Ibid.

p. 81 *A local agent for Paramount films*: Ibid.

p. 81 *Cowan was working in his office at the MoI*: FO-24526 NA. The Duke of Alba's influence on his cousin and friend Churchill while serving as Spanish ambassador in Madrid is detailed in Wigg, *Churchill and Spain*. At a lunch in December 1940 – the first of many between the two – Churchill reassured Alba that what he wished for was 'the best and most friendly relations with Spain'.

p. 82 *A separate memo from Lord Lloyd*: FO-24526 NA.

p. 82 *Hoare and Churchill's paths had converged and periodically clashed*: See Gilbert, *Churchill*, p. 544.

p. 83 *he argued that an offensive against Germany should be delayed*: Ibid., p. 626.

p. 84 *There is one bright spot*: Quoted by Preston, *Franco*, p. 356. I am indebted to Dr Peter Martland of Cambridge University for pointing out that Cadogan also separately described Sir Samuel and Lady Maud's anxiety to get to Spain as indicating they were 'rats deserting the ship'.

p. 84 *The Stornoway mini-summit*: Hoare, *Ambassador on Special Mission*, p. 13, also Templewood papers XII-17, Cambridge University Library (CUL).

p. 83 *bribery and corruption of Spanish generals*: See Denis Smyth's essay 'Les Chevaliers de Saint-George' from the series *Guerres Mondiales et Conflits Contemporains*, 162 (Presses Universitaires de France, 1991), pp. 29–54. Also Stafford, *Churchill and Secret Service*, p. 237 – 'at least $2m went to General Antonio Aranda Mata' who was seen as a potential coup leader capable of toppling Franco if the Allies thought it necessary. Stafford questions whether the funds accomplished anything more than the corruption of the generals involved, 'enriching those who would have argued the neutrality case anyway' and who never seriously threatened Franco.

Hoare was also involved in the bribery operation, using 'special funds' of £500,000 to ensure that a 'safe means of approach' could be secured to the then foreign minister Colonel Beigbeder. Templewood papers XII-17, CUL, and FO 371-24508 NA.

p. 85 *March set up a shipping company called AUCONA*: For a broad account of March's involvement in the financing of the Spanish Civil War and the Second World War, see

Sánchez Soler, *Ricos por la guerra de España*. For Hillgarth's relationship with March and the importance of the relationship to British intelligence see Patrick Beesley, *Very Special Admiral: The Life of J. H. Godfrey* (London: Hamish Hamilton 1980). Godfrey, the head of Naval Intelligence, wrote that his running of an 'A1 source' (March) was one of the reasons Hillgarth was a 'super-Attaché'. Another was that he was the uniquely coordinating authority for the Secret Intelligence Service (MI6), Special Operations Executive (SOE) and NID (Naval Intelligence Division).

   March's link to the arms trade is detailed in previously secret British government documents now available to researchers. ADM 1/9809 NA.

p. 88 *You cannot imagine what a racket I have had here*: Templewood papers XII–17, CUL.

p. 89 *you can keep watch over so much more*: Burns/BL.

p. 90 *The children can't go without me*: Vickers, *Elizabeth*, p. 199.

p. 90 *Yes, the war has broken out*: Richey papers, GEO.

p. 91 *Ben, a Quaker and pacifist*: see West, *Quest for Graham Greene*, pp. 100–101. For Maxwell Knight's idiosyncrasies see Tom Bower, *The Perfect English Spy* (London: Heinemann, 1995), p. 26. Some previously secret MI5 files on Knight were released for research in 2004 (NA) although no further light is shed on the Greene affair.

p. 91 *Greene himself had been recruited by MI6*: See Richard Greene's introduction to *Graham Greene: A Life in Letters* (London: Little Brown, 2007) in which Greene's relationship with Philby is described as 'warm'. The author officially left MI6 in 1944 although he continued to have an informal relationship with the agency for many years afterwards. Despite Philby's treachery, Greene agreed to write a foreword to the Cambridge spy's memoirs, describing them as a 'dignified statement of beliefs'.

p. 92 *It's like flying in a bungalow*: Burns/BL.

p. 93 *The Galgo had an unforgettable ambience*: Rosalind Powell Fox, *The Grass and the Asphalt* (Cadiz: J. S. Hartland, 1997), p. 240.

p. 93 *Here I am but actually I am off to Madrid*: Burns/BL.

5. Embassy on Special Mission

p. 94 *The new ambassador's distrust of foreign parts*: 'Final Turn', paper on Sir Samuel Hoare's time in Spain delivered at Cambridge University by Vivek Viswanathan; Keith Neilson, '*Joy Rides?' British Intelligence and Propaganda in Russia, 1914–17* (The Historical Journal, Cambridge University Press, 1981), pp. 885–906. For further information I am indebted to Cambridge University's Dr Peter Martland and his extensive research of the Templewood papers.

p. 95 *not knowing where to lay my head*: Hoare, *Ambassador on Special Mission*, p. 13.

p. 95 *real and urgent war work*: Ibid., p. 16.

p. 96 *Spanish aristocrats who were regular guests*: Author's interview with Peter Laming and unpublished personal memoir by the British diplomat. BFA.

p. 97 *The German embassy had been built up*: The scale of Nazi involvement in wartime Spain was confirmed in documents obtained by the Allies and only declassified in recent years. These documents, held at the NA, have provided an interesting source of information, particularly for a new generation of Spanish investigators. See Carlos Collado Seidel, *España: Refugio Nazi*: (Madrid: Temas de Hoy, 2005) and Ivan Ramilla, *España y los Enigmas Nazi* (Madrid: Espejo de Tinta, 2006).

p. 98 *The suggestion he had Jewish ancestry*: In his memoirs Hoare describes Lazar as a 'very sinister eastern Jew'. It was also rumoured that Lazar had become a morphine addict as a result of an injury suffered in the First World War, although his reputation among Spaniards and the Allies was as a key and energetic figure in the German embassy.

   One Spanish official recalled Lazar as 'quite unlike anyone else in the Franco era . . . well dressed, and self-consciously well-mannered like those operatic Viennese figures created by Straus or Lehar . . . those of us who dealt with him, came to the conclusion that we were dealing with someone very important . . . his ambition had no limit.' During the Spanish

Civil War, Lazar developed his propaganda skills working as a correspondent for the pro-Nazi German broadcaster Transocean, before formally entering the German Foreign Service at the outbreak of the Second World War. From the German embassy in Madrid, Lazar masterminded his 'Grand Plan' to have Franco's Spain move closer to Hitler's Germany, and disrupt Allied propaganda and covert activities. The plan included funding distribution of pro-Nazi parish newsletters, publishing pro-Nazi military action magazines and bribing Spanish journalists and their Spanish government controllers from a slush fund rather greater than that managed by his British counterpart. See 'Los espias Nazis que salvo Franco', *El País*, 26/01/2003.

p. 98 *Hoare's predecessor, Maurice Peterson*: For his period as ambassador in Spain, see his memoirs, *Both Sides of the Curtain* (London: Drummond, 1950). David Eccles, who served under Peterson and Hoare recalled: 'Why was Peterson doomed to failure in Madrid? He couldn't like the Spaniards, not one of them. That was an obstacle no brains, no subtlety could overcome.' See Eccles, *By Safe Hands* (London: Bodley Head, 1983), p. 266.

p. 99 *It may well be that things may go badly in Spain*: Templewood papers XIII (1940–45). See also another letter to Halifax in *Ambassador on Special Mission* (p. 29) in which Hoare foresees the necessity of spending 'large sums [of money] upon propaganda and the development of trade with Spain'.

p. 99 *Britain's official policy of non-intervention had turned Spain into an intelligence backwater*: The lack of reliable information, apart from the secret intelligence provided by Hillgarth in Mallorca, and the often ideologically subjective reports of British journalists (see Preston, *Doves of War*), was belatedly raised as a subject of concern at the Foreign Office when war was declared in 1939. 'I quite agree as to the vital necessity that our intelligence [on Spain] should in these anxious times be of first-class quality' FO-371/231171. See also Nigel West, *MI6, and Service Operations 1909–45* (London: Weidenfeld & Nicolson, 1983).

p. 100 *Yencken was tough laconic, witty, and sometimes rather wild*: Burns, *Use of Memory*, p. 89.

p. 101 *Things are moving so quickly*: Templewood papers XIII.

p. 101 *Barcelona and other Spanish ports*: *New York Times*, May 1940.

p. 101 *living in a besieged city*: Hoare, *Ambassador on Special Mission*, p. 30.

p. 102 *someone really big*: Templewood papers XIII. Letter to Duff Cooper reproduced in Hoare, *Ambassador on Special Mission*.

p. 102 *I protested my inadequacy*: Burns, *Use of Memory*, p. 87.

p. 104 *many talents and many tensions*: Ibid., p. 88.

p. 104 *good food and real beer*: Ernest Hemingway, *For Whom the Bell Tolls* (London: Vintage, 2005), p. 236.

p. 104 *I am in shirt sleeves after a sweltering day*: TB to BL letters (BFA).

p. 106 *She looked jolly nice*: Jones to TB, *Dai Greatcoat*, p. 98.

p. 106 *secret Foreign Office project*: Wall was appointed to work on Italian affairs under the Foreign Office, in the research department based at Balliol College, Oxford, and directed by Dr Arnold Toynbee and Sir Alfred Zimmerman. Author's interview with Wall's widow, Barbara Lucas. See also Wall, *Headlong into Change*, p. 107.

p. 106 *dined with Douglas Woodruff*: For an account of Woodruff's pro-Franco sympathies see Mary Craig's introduction to *Woodruff at Random* (London: The Universe, 1978), pp. 19–20. Also Woodruff's correspondence with Franco's ambassador to London, the Duke of Alba, in Woodruff papers, GEO.

p. 107 *another cell of good living*: Quoted in McCarthy, *Eric Gill*, p. 290.

p. 108 *You are objecting to him*: Graham Greene to Richey, quoted in Richard Greene (ed.), *A Life in Letters*, p. 104.

p. 109 *looks like a young lion*: Jones to TB, *Dai Greatcoat*, p. 98. Also author's interview with Michael Richey.

p. 109 *I bet it is bloody hot*: Jones to TB, ibid., p. 99.

p. 109 *what most concerned Burns in those early days*: BFA.

p. 110 *Burns made strenuous efforts to get in touch*: Waugh, *Diaries*, p. 470. Earlier Waugh had referred in his diary to TB living in a 'land of wild make-believe, where the only problem is to decide what sort of government shall be set up in Germany, immediately, bloodlessly', ibid., p. 461.

p. 110 *Went to M of I*: Ibid., p. 471.

p. 110 *empty-headed utopianism of the 'Phoney War'*: Sykes, *Waugh*, p. 281.

p. 111 *They were full of tales of the interesting jobs all my friends are getting*: Waugh, *Diaries*, p. 473.

p. 111 *News of the bombing*: 'The *Tablet* offices in Paternoster Row were burned out but, like the more famous Windmill Theatre, they could boast we "we never close" ' Craig, *Woodruff*, p. 19.

p. 111 *Graham was saved by his infidelity*: Quoted in *Tablet*, 17 June 2005.

p. 112 *an absurdly hilarious time*: Greene, *A Life in Letters*, p. 106.

p. 112 *Hell, bugger them all*: TB/Jones correspondence, BFA.

p. 113 *We get raid warnings a good bit*: Jones to TB, *Dai Greatcoat*, and p. 105.

p. 113 *curious compound of ordinary private life in the old haunts*: BFA.

p. 114 *I think you ought to do whatever you bloody well feel*: Ibid.

6. Of Princes, Priests and Bulls

p. 115 *Muñoz Rojas had no hesitation*: Author's interview with José Antonio Muñoz Rojas. For additional information on Pedro Gamero, author's conversations with his daughter Concha Gamero and her husband Robert Graham. There are no surviving papers about Gamero's secret dealings with TB. It is thought likely that Gamero destroyed them before his death.

p. 116 *Each afternoon Burns and his team prepared and printed*: Author's interview with José Luis García who was employed by TB as a messenger.

p. 117 *I could not help reflecting that this luckless*: Burns, *Use of Memory*, p. 93.

p. 118 According to Williams, in *St Albans College*, p. 219, Henson was generally happy to engage in clandestine work on behalf of the embassy. Only once did he resist a request from TB on security grounds. Early on in the Second World War TB approached Henson on behalf of Lord Phillimore's pressure group, the Friends of Spain, for help in providing names of contacts. Henson turned the request down on the grounds that putting his contacts into the hands of the group would risk leakage and make them 'marked men'. 'The Friends of Spain might well devote their efforts to changing the attitude towards the New Spain of certain sections of our English Press.'

TB's relations with the previously named right-wing Friends of Nationalist Spain endured throughout the Spanish Civil War and into the first months of the Second World War. However, once recruited by the British government, TB appears to have heeded Henson's advice – shared by the Catholic hierarchy in England – and kept the Friends at arm's length from his projects in Spain, while making use of them for propaganda purposes in the UK.

p. 118 *Edward VIII and Mrs Simpson*: For some of the details of the Nazi kidnap plot I am indebted to the substantial research done on the Windsor affair by Michael Bloch, author of *Operation Willi* (New York: Weidenfeld & Nicolson, 1984). I owe thanks, too, to Patrick Buckley for sharing his researches into certain lesser known aspects of this extraordinary story.

In his study of Hoare's relationship with Churchill in the handling of British policy towards Spain, Richard Wigg argues that the Windsor episode forged an uncharacteristic close collaboration between the ambassador and his prime minister. See Wigg, *Churchill and Spain*, p. 14.

The full story has yet to be written, however, given that the British state still controls and restricts the public release of many documents related to members of the royal family

p. 119 *travel to neighbouring Portugal*: The Duke was reported to have told the Spanish foreign minister that he would only return to England if his wife was recognised as a member of the royal family and if he were appointed to a military or civilian position of influence. The Duke had also reportedly expressed himself in strong terms against Churchill and against the war. The Spanish foreign minister suspected that the Duke was going to Portugal in order to replenish his supply of money.

The subject of the Duchess's status had become an obsession for the Duke. See J. Bryan III and Charles J. V. Murphy, *The Windsor Story* (London: Granada, 1979), p. 528.

p. 119 *The 'over-elegant' Eccles*: Burns, *Use of Memory*, pp. 118, 134. Eccles went on to become a Conservative MP from 1943 to 1960 and in Conservative governments served as Minister of Education. He and TB kept in touch in the post-war years, with Eccles supporting TB's publishing ventures.

p. 120 *Marcus Cheke, the somewhat aloof and aristocratic student*: Ibid., p. 98.

p. 120 *watch him at breakfast, lunch, and dinner*: Eccles, *By Safe Hands*, p. 128.

p. 120 *niece of Hilaire Belloc*: For the sections covering Portugal, I have drawn on information provided by contacts and friends I made while working as the *Financial Times*'s Lisbon correspondent during the late 1970s, including conversations with the late Susan Lowndes, her son Paulo Lowndes Marques, and her daughter Ana Vicente, the author of a family history, *Arcadia* (Lisbon: Gotica, 2006). I am also indebted to the late Josie Shercliff, who aged gracefully as *The Times*'s wartime and post-war Portuguese expert.

p. 121 *He was the sort of self-made person*: Quoted in Bloch, *Operation Willi*, p. 134. In an interview with the *Guardian* published on 15 January 1983 Eccles described his wartime role as that of an 'apostle of bribery', with one of his tasks that of 'buying' unnamed 'eminent neutrals'.

p. 122 *Sir Walter Monckton*: Churchill was by now fully informed by the embassies in Madrid and Lisbon about the plot to 'kidnap' the Windsors. The Nazi SD counterespionage chief Schellenberg mistakenly thought Monckton (which German intelligence reports had misspelt as 'Monckstone') was a cover name for a 'member of the personal police of the reigning King by the name of Camerone'. See Anthony Cave Brown's biography of Churchill's SIS (MI6) chief Sir Stewart Menzies, *The Secret Servant* (London: Michael Joseph, 1988), p. 680.

Monckton was highly regarded by his peers in the MoI. At the end of 1941 he took charge of British propaganda activities in the Middle East in Cairo. See Grubb, *Crypts of Power*.

p. 122 *Many sharp and unfriendly ears*: Letter quoted in full by Bloch in *Operation Willi*, p. 174.

p. 123 *German ciphers were being read*: According to Stafford, *Churchill and Secret Service*, code-breakers at Bletchley Park broke the main Luftwaffe operational key on 22 May 1940. Within a year, the code-breakers made their first significant breakthrough into German's naval Enigma so that by August 1941 every signal to or from U-boats was being read by the Allies.

p. 124 *Darling Ann, I can't tell you*: TB letters to BL (BFA).

p. 125 *haunt of spies*: Burns, *Use of Memory*, p. 70. A transcription error in TB's memoirs sets the encounter in 1943, although TB's own recollection subsequently made clear that the meeting coincided with a time when the Duke of Windsor was 'on his way, through a minefield of enemy intrigue in Spain and Portugal'.

p. 126 *The Duke drew me off to a sofa*: Ibid., p. 70.

p. 127 *a country 'whose beauty and history'*: Bloch, *Operation Willi*, p. 180.

p. 127 *Willi wollte nicht*: Ibid., p. 181.

p. 127 *Sam (Hoare) seemed very glad to see me*: TB letters to BL (BFA).

p. 129 *I kick myself and have to tell*: Ibid.

p. 129 *American public opinion far from enthusiastic*: The reluctance of the US to enter the war has been well documented. See, for example, Taylor, *English History*, pp.60–63.

p. 129 *That the US embassy in first years of the war was smaller than the British*: In his memoirs, Carlton Hayes, the US ambassador, recalled that on his arrival in Madrid in December 1941, the 'British embassy was considerably larger than ours, and names the half British and half-Chilean' TB as among the 'capable (British) officers with whom we were in especially close contact'. See Carlton Hayes, *Wartime Mission in Spain* (New York: Macmillan, 1945). See also Hayes, *The United States & Spain* (New York: Sheed & Ward, 1951), for a critical view of the generally pro-Republic sentiment in the US during the Spanish Civil War, and a sympathetic view of Franco's role in the Second World War. The bad blood that affected the relations between Hayes and his British counterpart, Hoare, in Spain is reflected in each ambassador's memoirs. See Hoare, *Ambassador on Special Mission*, and Foreign Office documents in which Hayes is described by Hoare as a 'very heavy footed professor from Colombia University who, so far as I know, has had no previous experience of public life', FO 954/27 NA.

Hayes also proved unpopular with elements of the US's nascent intelligence agency, the Office of Strategic Services (OSS). According to senior CIA historian Donald P. Steury, 'the OSS mission in Madrid had as a principal function of "economic intelligence" when it was set up in April 1942, despite being very considerably hampered until shortly after VE Day by an ambassador and diplomatic staff hostile to OSS activities'. See Steury, *The OSS and Project Safehaven* (Washington, DC: Studies in Intelligence, 2000).

p. 130 *D'Arcy, had helped him gain a foothold*: For D'Arcy's 'extravagant success in the higher reaches of US Catholic society' see Sire, *D'Arcy*, p. 117.

p. 130 *The poet seemed totally at home*: Burns, *Use of Memory*, p. 73.

p. 131 *Tom, I think my mission in Spain is finished*: Ibid., p. 91.

p. 131 *and preventing the passage of German troops through to Gibraltar*: Ibid., p. 91.

p. 132 *I have the honour to transmit an interesting memorandum*: FO 371/28384 NA.

p. 132 *My informant said*: Ibid.

p. 133 *sensationalist in the past*: Ibid.

p. 133 *the self-styled Reichsführer SS*: Preston, *Franco*, p. 392. Also the newspaper *ABC* issues covering the three-days' visit (HEM).

p. 135 *You should have been recommended for the VC*: Burns, *Use of Memory*, p. 102.

7. Spy Games

p. 137 *Horcher became the German embassy's unofficial canteen*: On arriving in Madrid, the US wartime ambassador Carlton Hayes noted the extensive nature of Nazi social and cultural penetration in the city, within walking distance of the Allied embassies. 'Just beyond the Franciscan Church of San Fermin de los Navarros was a big (German) social club; across the street, the headquarters of the local Gestapo; and directly opposite our embassy (at that time occupying an entire block along the Catellana), a Nazi *Kulturinstitut* with swastikas rampant.' Hayes would soon discover that Madrid was dotted with dozens of other 'annexes' to the German embassy, in addition to the Italian fascist institutes or 'annexes'. Hayes, *Wartime Mission*, p. 25.

p. 138 *Chicote, had trained as a barman at the Ritz Hotel*: At 12 Gran Via, the bar/nightclub had its heyday in the 1940s although it continued to attract the glamorous and famous in the post-war years. Hemingway said of the place: 'The most attractive girls in the city went to Chicote and it was the place from which you could begin a good night out; well, everyone has begun some good night outs from there. It was like a club. It was without doubt the best bar in Spain, and I think one of the best in the world.' Quoted by Elizabeth Nash in *Madrid* (Oxford: Signal Books, 2001), who goes on to remark: 'The clientele during the war was comprised of the international brigades, the foreign correspondents, and a regular church of young women who engaged in prostitution', p. 178.

p. 138 *sad, desolate landscape of the cemetery*: Quoted in Burns, *A Literary Companion to Spain*, p. 33.

p. 140 *Those evenings at the Lyon d'Or*: Burns, *Use of Memory*, p. 95.

p. 141 *All this region is in a very marked contrast*: FO 371/26890 NA.

p. 143 *Two retired colonels*: A thinly veiled reference to the SIS (MI6) station in Tangier where Toby Ellis, a former Indian Army oculist, operated under press attaché cover in the British Consulate-General, alongside Malcolm Henderson, Neil Whitelaw and Paddy Turnbull, three other intelligence officers unnamed by TB. See Nigel West, *MI6* (London: Weidenfeld & Nicolson, 1983).

p. 143 *It now appears that the* Tangier Gazette: FO 371/26890, p. 95.

p. 143 *I am not satisfied*: FO 371/26890 NA.

p. 143 *a city of illusory vanities*: Iain Finlayson, *City of the Dream* (Canada: HarperCollins, 1992).

p. 146 *infiltrated by British intelligence*: The extensive nature of agent T's work on behalf of the British is contained in a three-page British intelligence report which has been previously overlooked by researchers. It is among the records of the Special Operations Executive transferred to the National Archives in Kew in recent years. HS 6/927 NA. An attached note suggests that he was 'run' by Hillgarth and SOE, and paid a regular fee for services that were focused on disrupting the political machinations of the pro-German members of the Franco regime.

Notes on the Hendaye summit taken by Barón de las Torres were published in the Spanish press in 1989 (*ABC*, 'La Guerra Mundial'). In his critical biography of Franco, Paul Preston argues that the notes – detailing how the Spanish dictator resisted Hitler – were 'redolent of the post-1945 propaganda exercise' aimed at downplaying Francoist Spain's pro-Axis leanings in the Second World War. And yet the British appear to have taken some comfort from penetrating 'the inevitable veil of official secrecy' surrounding the summit and concluding that the talks had not gone well. As the British ambassador subsequently put it, 'Franco, not wishing to fight, and never wishing to burn his boats, returned to Madrid without any African trophies, but also without any definite commitment to enter the war'. See Hoare, *Ambassador on Special Mission*, pp. 94–5. On the eclectic nature of agents run by SOE, the historian M. R. D. Foot has noted that they included several nationalities, including 'several score Spaniards' with a social range that reached from head of state (the regent of Siam) to exiled Russian grandees and dukes through 'the whole range of the upper and lower European and east Asiatic bourgeoisie to railwaymen, telephonists, clerks, labourers, peasants, prostitutes and coolies'. See Foot, SOE: *1940–1946* (London: Pimlico, 1999), p. 78.

p. 147 *Hoare had made every effort to centralise key aspects of the embassy's operations*: For Hoare's own account of the lessons he had learnt and how he organised the Madrid embassy, see *Ambassador on Special Mission*, pp.130–31. Also D. Heath, *SIS & British Foreign Policy during the Great War* (University of Cambridge paper, July 2002). The tension that existed between Hoare and senior SIS (MI6) officers is commented on by West, *MI6*, p. 109.

p. 149 *They were at first fish-eyed, aloof and polite*: Burns, *Use of Memory*, p. 131.

p. 149 *The embassy's intelligence operations*: West, *MI6*, p. 134.

p. 150 *By the time we reached our floor*: Kenneth Benton, *The ISOS Years* (*Journal of Contemporary History*, July 1995). Benton's memoir of his time in Madrid appeared discreetly in an academic journal after an original text had been censored by SIS (MI6) with the names of officers, secretaries, informants and agents excised at the request of the Security Section of the Service. Curiously, the version that was published contained TB's name although it was never shown to him, nor permission asked. TB died four months after its publication. The article was drawn to the attention of the author by an MI6 officer during the research for this book.

p. 151 *a spy, and an important one*: Julia Camoys Stonor, *Sherman's Wife* (London: Desert Hearts, 2006), p. 71.

p. 151 *Gytha was horrified by the politics of these men*: Ibid., p. 70.

p. 152 *considerable dealings of a cooperative nature*: The Moral affair is detailed in Foreign Office and Ministry of Information documents; see FO 371/23171 NA.

During the Spanish Civil Sir Nairne Sandeman, a Member of Parliament, was a leading figure in the Scottish branch of the pro-Franco Friends of Nationalist Spain. In the spring of 1938, Sandeman held a fundraising meeting in Edinburgh's Usher Hall which was disrupted by anti-fascist protestors and resulted in mayhem. *Scotsman*, 20/11/2008. Sandeman died in 1940, weeks after Sandeman's letter recommending Moral's recruitment as an agent.

p. 153 *Miguel Piernavieja del Pozo*: For the origins of Pozo's recruitment and details of his subsequent activities and those of other alleged Spanish spies in the UK I am indebted to research undertaken by Javier Juarez. See his *Madrid, Londres, Berlin* (Madrid: Temas de Hoy, 2005), and Eduardo Martín de Pozuelo and Iñaki Ellakuria, *La Guerra Ignorada* (Barcelona: Debate, 2008). I have also examined MI5 files on the subject. KV2/468 NA.

p. 153 *He is a rather unpleasant type*: Nigel West (ed.), *The Guy Liddell Diaries*, vol. 1, *1939–1942* (London: Routledge, 2005), p. 103.

p. 155 *When speaking to Pogo*: Ibid., p. 108.

p. 155 *Pogo has badly blotted his copy-book*: Ibid., p. 110.

p. 156 *The case of Pogo is getting rather difficult*: Ibid., p. 114.

p. 156 *the 'slow-witted' Hamilton*: Dorril, *Black Shirt*, p. 523.

p. 157 *wealth of colourful personal detail*: Burns, *Use of Memory*, p. 97.

p. 157 *It seemed to be his way of sealing a bond*: Ibid.

p. 157 *Velasco claimed in his memoirs*: see Juarez, *Madrid, Londres, Berlin*, p. 47. Also Angel Alcázar de Velasco, *Memorias de un agente secreto* (Barcelona: Plaza y Janes, 1979).

p. 158 *the Spaniard was a German spy*: The British agent code-named T warned his handlers on 18 January 1941 that Velasco was a German agent. The information somehow found its way to the Russians. See SOE document HS 6/927.

p. 158 *Velasco arrived in the UK*: He arrived to take up his post as press secretary at the Spanish embassy armed with a letter of introduction to senior British newspapermen provided by the British embassy in Madrid. It described Velasco thus: 'He is a well known and distinguished Spaniard, having made himself a reputation both as scholar in university life and a fighter in the civil war . . . He is held in esteem and confidence by the Minister of Foreign Affairs and the other members of the Spanish government. A keen Falangist but one of the many Spaniards who believe that Spanish falangism should never imitate German nazism or Italian fascism.' Templewood papers XIII.

p. 159 *Calvo had started his journalistic career*: Biographical details on Calvo are based on information compiled in an MI5 file (KV2/713 NA) and additional personal information obtained by the author.

p. 159 *A hard-working and observant foreign correspondent*: Calvo's reporting for *ABC* from London during 1940 ranges from detailed if dispassionate accounts of ordinary citizens enduring the Blitz to more light-hearted swipes at what A. J. P. Taylor called 'the authorities' misplaced lack of confidence in the British people' (see Taylor, *English History*, p. 599). In a front-page piece published in *ABC* on 31 July 1940, for example, Calvo focused on the Minister of Information Duff Cooper's use of investigators to probe public opinion (dismissed by those investigated, including Calvo, as 'Cooper's snoopers'). Only occasionally does Calvo display a crude political bias, as when he hits out at sectors of the British media for criticising Franco four days earlier (*ABC*, 27/7/1940). On most days, the space devoted to *ABC*'s Calvo reports from London was notably less generous than that enjoyed by the more blatantly pro-Nazi Berlin correspondent.

p. 159 *The informal unit was made up of MI5's B Division officers*: A variety of sources suggest that Blunt was recruited by MI5 in June 1940 by the newly promoted head of the counter-espionage B Division, Guy Liddell, after serving the War Office in military intelligence. The spy writer Chapman Pincher, whose main source was the disaffected MI5 officer Peter Wright, claimed that Blunt was recommended by his friend Tomás Harris, who actually joined the security service subsequently. See Chapman Pincher, *Too Secret Too Long* (London: Sidgwick & Jackson, 1984), p. 389.

B Division was involved in the double-cross system, 'turning' enemy agents, and running agents of its own, as well as surveillance teams. It was where Ultra – the information gathered by the Bletchley code-breakers – was delivered and analysed. Blunt worked for B6, MI5's surveillance section, before he found a 'niche monitoring foreign diplomatic missions', in particular the Spanish embassy. See Miranda Carter, *Anthony Blunt: His Lives* (London: Macmillan, 2001), pp. 249–51 and p. 273.

Harris was a member of a group of Cambridge graduates that included Blunt, Philby and Guy Burgess. It was on Burgess's recommendation that Harris was introduced into the shadowy world of British intelligence, at the SOE training school at Brickendonbury Hall. He was later brought into MI5's Iberian section by Liddell. 'Harris's sociability, wealth, generosity and gourmet tastes made his London home an unofficial club-cum-mess for intelligence officers' including Burgess, Blunt and Philby. See Mark Seaman's introduction to *Garbo: The Spy Who Saved D-Day* (London: Public Record Office, 2000), p. 19.

In his memoirs, Philby credited Harris for helping his recruitment by SIS (MI6)'s Iberian section. See Philby, *My Silent War*, p. 35 His passage into the heart of British espionage was also smoothed by Burgess who recommended Philby's recruitment in 1939 to Marjorie Maxse, the chief-of-staff of SIS's Section D training school for propaganda, sabotage and subversion. See Bower, *The Perfect English Spy*, p. 52.

p. 160 *The US diplomat, identified only by his surname*: West (ed.), *Liddell Diaries*, pp. 186–7.

p. 160 *Velasco returned to England*: In *The Use of Memory*, Burns describes Velasco as a potential Walter Mitty character, a somewhat deranged fantasist who purported to be 'in the counsels' of the Spanish foreign minister at the time, Serrano Súñer, and to have been recruited with the task of assessing British morale and the British capability for continuing the war. Burns anticipated that influential sectors of British intelligence would take Velasco seriously enough as a spy and seems to have gone along with their designs. 'To have a spy easy to tail might lead to others and de Velasco's idea was welcomed by MI5,' wrote Burns (p. 97). It is clear from Guy Liddell's *Diaries* that Velasco was being watched by MI5 from the moment he first landed in the UK and that subsequently MI5 presented a strong case for him to be declared *persona non grata*, banning him from re-entering the UK. However, once Velasco had returned to the UK, he was allowed to effectively 'run' in order to entrap other agents. See West (ed.), *Liddell Diaries*, p. 162.

p. 161 *Williams made renewed contact*: KV2/713 NA.

p. 161 *Further meetings between Velasco, Calvo and Williams*: The story of Velasco's alleged activities in wartime Britain is a good example of the morass into which intelligence history can fall. An official history of MI5 completed in 1946, but only made publicly available in 1999, paints a mixed if somewhat contradictory picture of Velasco. On the one hand it portrays Velasco as somewhat ineffectual spy – the source of intelligence reports sent by the Japanese minister in Madrid to Tokyo – 'much of it invented while some of it based on the reports of another member of the Spanish embassy [in London] who was in fact a double agent controlled by us [MI5]'. On the other hand the official historian subsequently states categorically that MI5's counter-espionage B.1.G. section (Iberia and South America) under Lt Col. Broomham-White had discovered that the Germans had recruited 'at least five journalists and a press attaché for espionage purposes through Alcázar'. John Curry, *The Security Service 1908–1945* (London: Public Record Office, 1999), p. 275.

p. 162 *Other public figures*: KV2/713 NA. As one wartime MI5 officer has written: 'MI5 had no executive function and if they wanted a prosecution they got the police to do it; but prosecution (in those days) came very low down in their priorities; they wanted to watch, wait, and draw in as many others as possible into their view. It was only when their targets became a useless burden that they considered going for an arrest.' Walter Bell's private correspondence (BFA).

p. 162 *But of all the name to be chosen*: Details of the surveillance carried out on Burns, and the secret information circulated about him, are contained in MI5 files KV 2/2823 and KV 2/2824 NA.

p. 164 *a close-knit social circle*: Bower, *The Perfect English Spy*, p. 47.

p. 164 *One of his contemporaries, Walter Bell*: Recruited by British intelligence in the late 1930s, Bell served initially as an MI5 officer and later joined SIS (MI6). During the Second World War he was in Washington, liaising with the FBI and the Office of Strategic Services (OSS), under Colonel William J. Donovan and William Stephenson. He was awarded the Order of Merit by the US government 'for exceptionally meritorious achievement aiding US in prosecution of the war in Europe between December 1941 and May 1945'. Personal documents (BFA) and author's interview with Bell's widow, Tatti Bell, 9/4/2004.

p. 165 *Bristow recalled a conversation*: Desmond Bristow, *A Game of Moles* (London: 1993), p. 26.

p. 165 *the London rezidentura of the KGB (NKVD) officers*: The regularity with which British spies recruited by Russian intelligence saw their Russian 'controllers' during this time is not clear. As Anthony Boyle points out in *The Climate of Treason* (London: 1979), p. 202, the early months of the war 'was not the most auspicious season for Nazi or Soviet agents, however well hidden, to go about their business'. The official MI5 history reveals that, towards the end of 1939, John King, a Foreign Office cipher clerk, was convicted of working for the Soviets and sentenced to ten years' penal servitude.

During the summer of 1940 Churchill urged his cabinet that 'very considerable numbers' of British communists as well as fascists should be put in protective or preventive internment, including the leaders. 'It was hardly surprising that Philby, Burgess, Blunt . . . had little option but to lie low', ibid., p. 202.

On the other hand Blunt's biographer states that 'there is no doubt' he was passing MI5 documents to the Russian before June 1941, when Hitler broke the terms of the Nazi-Soviet Pact and invaded the Soviet Union. On 12 July 1941, two and half weeks after the invasion, the Soviet Union signed a Mutual Assistance Treaty with Britain. At Churchill's behest, the British intelligence services suspended intercepting Soviet intelligence and monitoring Soviet radio signals. See Carter, *Anthony Blunt*, pp. 274–6. What remained constant during this period was British intelligence's, and in particular MI5's, paranoia about German penetration of a Britain cut off from mainland Europe. Philby and his friends had little difficulty in persuading their masters of the necessity of focusing on Spain and Portugal as the main conduit for such agents.

p. 166 *Benton, the newly arrived Section V officer*: Benton, *The ISOS Years*, p. 388.

p. 167 *When Benton later asked Philby*: Ibid.

p. 167 *GW provided Calvo*: KV2/713 NA.

p. 168 *A personal file compiled by MI5*: Ibid.

p. 168 *Intercepts of telephone conversations*: KV2/2823 NA.

p. 168 *Days later, Burns*: Ibid.

p. 169 *As he reported to Philby*: Ibid.

p. 169 *Burns is anxious to keep his position*: Ibid.

p. 169 *not the slightest importance*: Ibid.

p. 169 *It is suspected*: Hand-written police report filed undated but numbered 54. Discovered by the author in Franco's Archive in Madrid.

p. 170 *One of them was Kemball Johnston*: Carter, *Anthony Blunt*, p. 290. Also West, *MI5*, p. 30.

p. 171 *Broomham-White admitted*: KV2/2823 NA.

p. 172 *drafted his latest case report*: Ibid.

p. 173 *Harris stoked the fires*: Ibid.

p. 174 *If Burns continued to cultivate*: The tracking of Velasco and Calvo's movements in Spain was consistent with the orders received by MI6 (SIS) counter-intelligence officers (Section V) based in the Madrid embassy. One of them, Kenneth Benton, recalled the importance his chief, Felix Cowgill, attached to catching German spies although the identification and apprehension of spies in the UK was the task of MI5. 'What Cowgill wanted was to identify spies *before* they came to Britain and pass the names and details to MI5 for action. His first objective was to assemble all information about the German intelligence services and how they operated abroad.' See Benton, *The ISOS Years*, p. 372.

p. 174 *Burns reported to London*: KV2/2823 NA.

p. 175 *Burns wrote to the Foreign Division*: Ibid.

p. 176 *Calvo was arrested*: KV2/712 and KV2/713 NA.

p. 176 *Camp 020 – a secret interrogation centre*: Some five hundred suspected enemy spies (twenty-five of them Spanish nationals) from dozens of countries passed through the camp. See introduction by Oliver Hoare and MI5 documents in *Camp 020* (London: Public Record Office, 2000).

p. 177 *Official MI5 historians*: The security service has in recent years publicised the phrase 'Violence is taboo' which 'Tin Eye' Stephens wrote in his in-house history, before adding, 'For not only does it produce answers to please, but it lowers the standards of information' (see MI5's website *www.MI5.gov.uk*).

In his introduction for interrogators Stephens wrote, 'Never strike a man. In the first place it is an act of cowardice. In the second place, it is not intelligent. A prisoner will lie to avoid further punishment and everything he says thereafter will be based on false premise.'

Other contemporary records released by MI5 show that on one occasion in September 1940 Stephens expelled a War Office interrogator from the camp for hitting a prisoner, the German double agent code-named Tate (Wulf Schmidt).

For a further defence of MI5's Second World War record, see Ben Macintyre, 'The Truth that Tin Eye Saw' (*The Times*, 10/2/2006) in which he concedes that Stephens 'did not eschew torture out of mercy . . . his motives were strictly practical'.

p. 177 *psychological torture of a most brutal kind*: The calculated use of intimidation to 'break' Calvo using 'evidence' drawn from a fraudulent diary is described by Philby in his memoir, *My Silent War*, p. 49. For Calvo's own views on his captivity, information provided to the author by Carlos Sentis.

p. 179 *Calvo was eventually released*: Calvo was among several Spanish detainees who were repatriated on 22 August 1945 via Gibraltar. KV2/714 NA.

p. 180 *the best and friendliest relations*: See Wigg, *Churchill and Spain*, pp. 6–7

p. 180 *Churchill paid several unpublicised social visits*: Anecdotal information provided to the author by Casilda Villaverde, Marquesa de Santa Cruz.

p. 180 *But how do you find time*: Ibid.

p. 180 *One evening Casilda found herself*: Ibid.

p. 181 *Such encounters*: See also Jane and Burt Boyar, *Hitler Stopped by Franco* (Marbella House, 2001), p. 181: 'Alba was not there on a mission to promote Spanish trade; the (Spanish) Embassy was intended to make friends and to influence them politically, so when luncheon was finished and he offered Churchill a cigar and cognac they would have labels the Prime Minister would recognise and enjoy before he had even tasted them'.

p. 181 *Alba, while aware that communications*: Spanish government document cited in Juarez, *Madrid, Londres, Berlin*, p. 71.

p. 181 *Personally, I think it is difficult*: West (ed.), *The Guy Liddell Diaries*, vol. 2, *1942–1945* (London: Routledge, 2005).

8: Hyacinth Days

p. 183 *Griffith first met Lazar*: Aline, Countess of Romanones, *The Spy Wore Red* (London: Bloomsbury, 1987), pp. 110–11.

p. 183 *an important figure in the Nazi world*: Lazar arrived in Spain in September 1938 as a representative of Transocean, the Nazi Party's overseas propaganda agency. A year later he had been appointed press attaché at the German embassy in Madrid, with a reported monthly budget of 200,000 pesetas. During the Second World War his attempts to influence the media in Spain proved more successful than those used by the Spanish official news agency EFE as a tool of Nazi propaganda in Latin America. EFE had pro-Allied journalists working for it, including its director Vicente Gallego. See Stanley G. Payne, *Franco and Hitler: Spain, Germany, and World War II* (London: Yale University Press, 2008), pp. 122–3.

p. 183 *His bedroom was decorated*: Hoare, *Ambassador on Special Mission*, p. 54.

p. 184 *Griffith's cover was nearly blown*: Aline, Countess of Romanones, *The Spy Wore Red*, pp. 144–5.

p. 184 *people like me had a busy nightlife*: Author's interview with Aline, Countess of Romanones.

p. 185 *The British had many more people*: Ibid.

p. 185 *From the moment of his arrival*: The challenge facing the British embassy in countering Nazi influence in Spain was laid out in a nine-page memorandum to Ambassador Hoare in

June 1940 by Captain Hillgarth urging a 'drastic re-organisation' of the embassy. Hillgarth wrote: 'Our press department is inefficient, not entirely through its own fault. Germans have bought (Spanish) editors and journalists . . . WE are much too inclined to accept every rebuff . . . WE make no attempt really to counteract German lies . . .' What was needed, Churchill's friend and adviser insisted, was to present the Spanish government with a 'decided policy, not a vague and hesitant one . . . the only thing the Spaniard respects is power, though he prefers it politely expressed', Templewood papers XIII.

p. 185 *'Programme for Film Propaganda'*: James Chapman, *The British at War: Cinema, State and Propaganda 1939–45* (I. B. Tauris, 1999). As Glen Newey has commented, 'films of this sort blurred generic boundaries between documentary and fiction – as, indeed, does propaganda itself', *New Statesman*, 12 July 1999.

p. 186 *The white rolls – nicknamed Churchills*: Author interview with Gómez-Beare.

p. 186 *Buckley was a devout Catholic*: According to his son, Patrick, Buckley temporarily lost his Catholic faith during the Spanish Civil War, regaining it during the Second World War. Patrick Buckley, interview with the author. Henry Buckley's journalism in Spain is examined in Preston, *We Saw Spain Die*, pp. 341–50. See Henry Buckley's book, *Life and Death of the Spanish Republic* (London: Hamish Hamilton, 1940).

p. 187 *I will write to thank Burns*: Letter from Buckley to his wife Maria Planas, Buckley Family Archive.

p. 187 *MI9 had developed a highly effective Spanish operation*: Author interview with Colin Creswell. See also Airey Neave, *MI9* (London: Hodder & Stoughton, 1969) and M. R. D. Foot and J. M. Langley, *MI9: Escape and Evasion* (London: Bodley Head, 1979). Juan Carlos Jimenez de Aberasturi had focused on the Basque involvement in the so-called Comet Line of escape and evasion of POWs. See his *El Camino de la Libertad* (Bilbao Ayuntamiento de Hernani, 2006). For Catalan escape routes, including US involvement bases on declassified US documents, see Martín de Pozuelo and Ellakuria, *La Guerra Ignorada*, pp. 169–87.

p. 188 *one of the founding players of FC Barcelona*: Author interview with Frederick Witty. See also Jimmy Burns, *Barça: A People's Passion* (London: Bloomsbury, 2000), pp. 131–2.

p. 188 *We now had working for us*: Mavis Bacca Dowden, *A Tale of Spain*, personal memoir, p. 48.

p. 189 *twenty spies identified directly by the embassy*: Benton, *The ISOS Years*.

p. 190 *For most of my time in Madrid*: Ibid.

p. 191 *If Burns enjoyed additional protection*: Franco knew who the spies were in the British and German embassies and let them 'run' as long as they did nothing that threatened his regime. It was a game he watched from the ringside. Problems came when pro-Axis elements in the Falangist party pursued the British. This happened in Huelva where the Germans had a big influence. William Cluett, manager of a British electricity company, and Joseph Pool Bueno, an Anglo-Spanish employee of Rio Tinto, were expelled from Spain for suspected spying activities. The British ambassador Samuel Hoare personally intervened on behalf of two others. Alexander Millan, an Anglo-Spanish shipping agent, was released from detention. However, Montagu W. Brown, the head of a railway company, was also expelled. See Jesus Ramiro Copeiro del Vilar, *Huelva en la Segunda Guerra Mundial* (Huelva: Imprenta Jimenez, 1996).

p. 191 *The agent in question was a Benedictine monk*: Based on research carried out by the Jesuit historian Fr Robert Graham BFA. During the Second World War several priests were drawn into espionage activities by the Allies and the Axis powers. Several ended up in concentration camps where they subsequently died.

Among those suspected by the Nazis of working for the Allies was an Austrian Marianist priest called Jakob Gapp who had been teaching in the Basque port of Lequeitio and in Cadiz after arriving in Spain in May 1939. In September 1941 Gapp moved to Valencia where he took the first steps in applying for a visa to Britain at the consulate. He visited the consulate several times, sharing information on the state of politics and the Church in Germany and collected copies of the pro-Churchill English Catholic weekly the *Tablet*.

The distribution of the *Tablet* in Spain had been organised by TB from the British embassy in Madrid. Although no record survives of Fr Gapp meeting TB before, he was suspected of being recruited as an agent by the British.

The *Tablet* provided Gapp with the text of the anti-Fascist Bishop of Calahorra on the dangers of Nazism and the persecution of Catholics in Germany and the Netherlands which the priest passed on to others. The *Tablet*, of which TB was one of the owner-directors, was also said to contain coded messages to pro-British factions and resistance groups.

Gapp was arrested by the Gestapo on the French-Spanish border at Hendaye after being persuaded to cross the Pyrenees for a meeting by a Nazi agent posing as Jewish refugee seeking conversion to the Catholic faith. At least three German intelligence services were well aware of the *Tablet*'s importance as a pro-Allied propaganda vehicle. Gapp was interrogated about his links with the magazine, having been kept under surveillance by the Gestapo since the Anschluss, when he had first spoken out against Nazism.

Gapp was taken to Berlin, found guilty of treason by the notorious Nazi Judge Roland Freisler and beheaded on 13 August 1943. Information provided for the author by John Cummings and Paul Burns. See also Gapp's entry in Cumming's revised *Butler's Lives of the Saints* (Collegeville: Burns & Oates, 1998), pp. 115–19.

p. 192 *on the same wavelength*: Anna Campbell Lyle, quoted by Pearce, *Bloomsbury and Beyond*, p. 199.

p. 193 *What Catholics realise*: Ibid.

p. 193 *on Hitler's side*: Ibid.

p. 193 *Campbell visited the British embassy*: Campbell's biographer Peter Alexander suggests that Burns hired the poet as an agent on his own initiative to 'act as a gatherer of background information on the mood of Spain'. Alexander adds: 'It is difficult to see what other information he can have expected, for Campbell had no access to men of influence in the country'.

p. 194 *Campbell kept his role secret*: Such was the claim made by Anna Campbell Lyle, *Poetic Justice*, p. 170. In fact, Roy Campbell, according to other accounts, seems to have been a most indiscreet agent. On 3 October 1941, Campbell wrote to his mother telling her that he had been on 'His Majesty's service' since 3 September 1939 and often on 'very dangerous work'. The letter is quoted by one of Campbell's biographers, Peter Alexander, in *Roy Campbell*, p. 186.

p. 194 *This way of drinking*: Campbell, *Light on a Dark Horse*, quoted by Jimmy Burns in *Spain: A Literary Companion*, p. 199.

p. 195 *I found him more than eager*: Burns, *Use of Memory*, p. 105. According to Campbell's biographer Peter Alexander the approach made by TB delighted Campbell, giving him a feeling of direct participation in the war, allowing him to 'hold up his head' when writing home to South Africa, where several of his brothers had signed up as soon as war had been declared. See Alexander, *Campbell*, p. 185. 'His method of gathering information was original: he would settle into a bar, have a few drinks, and tell a few jokes and tall stories at which he excelled. In this way he would soon collect a circle of acquaintances, for whom he would buy drinks while his money or credit lasted. When the evening had progressed to the stage where they were all lifelong friends, he would lower his voice and quieten the rowdy circle before sharing with them a great secret, which they were to keep under their hats: he was a British spy . . .'

p. 196 *the eccentric author*: Eleanor Smith, *Life's a Circus* (London: Longman, Green & Co., 1939).

p. 197 *An eternal high-spirited tomboy*: Burns, *Use of Memory*, p. 56.

p. 197 *naughty but never nasty*: *Time* magazine, 5 February 1940.

p. 198 *at least we have the gypsies on our side*: Burns, *Use of Memory*, p. 57.

p. 198 *war was erotic*: For an account of Mary Wesley's experience of wartime see Patrick Marnham, *Wild Mary* (London: Vintage, 2007).

p. 199 Coward's song: Burns, *Use of Memory*, p. 116.

p. 199 *I do feel for you*: David Jones's letters to TB, National Library of Wales (NLW), David Jones papers.

p. 200 *Ann seems to be working very hard*: Michael Richey's letters to his family, Richey papers, GEO.

p. 200 *Paul, a pilot with the RAF*: Paul Richey's heroic exploits are vividly captured in a personal record, *Fighter Pilot* (London: Cassell, 2001) and its sequel, co-written by Norman Franks, *Fighter Pilot's Summer* (London: Grub Street, 2004).

p. 200 *I remember the disposition of everything*: New York Times, 11 May 1941.

p. 202 *The MoI asked me to return*: Graham Greene to Mary Pritchett, letter published in *Graham Greene: A Life in Letters*, p. 107.

p. 202 *a form of dirty work*: Greene, *Ways of Escape*, p. 118.

p. 203 *Two Catholics*: Harman Grisewood papers, GEO.

p. 203 *realism in our own consciences*: Burns, *Use of Memory*, p. 166.

p. 203 *all this Ann thing*: David Jones's letters to TB, NLW.

9: Black Arts

p. 207 *I am installed at present*: Say Family Archive.

p. 208 *Poor Peter*: Ibid.

p. 208 *It seemed unreal*: Ibid.

p. 209 *Source says that Burns is madly in love*: MI5 file KV 2/2823 NA. The tracking of TB's personal relationships by his detractors in British intelligence extended to male friends. The suggestion was that some of them were homosexual, as if such proclivities were a treasonable offence. An MI5 officer in Wales and the police Special Branch were tasked with finding out what they could about Jim Ede, who had been communicating with TB over the case of a Bulgarian refugee who had asked the British embassy in Madrid to arrange for his brother's safe conduct out of Spain.

'We are rather interested in Tom Burns' friends, as some of them have turned out to be decidedly queer,' reported a member of MI5's Iberian section.

The investigation threw up nothing suspicious about Ede such as possible links with pro-Axis Welsh nationalists. 'So far as political leanings are concerned, Mr Ede has none . . . there is not the slightest reason to doubt that he is completely loyal to this country (Britain).' Ede was 'discovered' by the police to be a 'painter by profession' and a former secretary of the Tate Gallery. Ibid.

Not mentioned was the fact that Ede was a well-known and popular figure in London's artistic circles, a long-term friend and benefactor, together with TB, of the fellow Welsh painter and poet David Jones. See various references in the self-portrait of Jones in his letters, *Dai Greatcoat*.

p. 210 *M 12 confirmed*: Ibid.

p. 211 *Although Stordy is a strong Roman Catholic*: Ibid. MI5 appears to have overlooked the fact that TB and Stordy had known each other since school days. They had both been educated by the Jesuits at Stonyhurst College.

p. 213 *Each in his own way*: Author's interview with José Luis García.

p. 214 *In his report*: KV 2/2823 NA.

p. 215 *A mild form of wishful thinking*: Burns, *Use of Memory*, p. 98. The position of the pretender to the throne, Don Juan, was somewhat ambiguous until the final stages of the war when he and his supporters openly called for a democratic front to force Franco to give up power. The prince supported Franco during the civil war and, after his father King Alfonso XIII died in February 1941, praised the political and social values of the 'the Crusade', the Nationalists' term for the civil war. (See E. Vegas, *Memorias Politicas 1938–42* (Madrid: Acras, 1995), p. 242.) Then, in an interview with the *Journal de Genève* on 11 November 1942, he declared that 'my supreme ambition is to be King of a Spain in which all Spaniards, finally reconciled, might live together'. During 1943, Franco received two separate letters, one from a group of eight senior army officers, the other from a group of conservative politicians led by the Spanish ambassador in London, the Duke of Alba, urging him to agree to the restoration of a 'Catholic and traditional' monarchy, freed from any 'foreign influence', in other words turning its back on constitutional and liberal principles to the point of absolutism. See a book written by TB's eldest son, Tom Burns Marañón, *La Monarquia necesaria* (Barcelona: Planeta, 2005), pp. 105–7. Also Wigg, *Churchill and Spain*, pp. 29–33.

p. 216 *In Spain, the Knights of St George*: See Denis Smyth, *Diplomacy and Strategy of Survival: British Policy and Franco's Spain, 1940–41* (Cambridge: Cambridge University Press, 1986), pp. 222–5. Also David Messenger, *Against the Grain: Special Operations Executive in Spain, 1941–45* (*Intelligence & National Security*, vol. 20, no. 1 (March 2005)), pp. 173–90, and Mark Seaman (ed.), *Special Operations Executive: New Instrument of War* (Routledge, 2006), p. 65.

p. 216 *arrangements for Press Section*: FO 371 26834 NA.

p. 217 *merchants bankers*: Burns, *Use of Memory*, p. 88.

p. 217 *Guy Fawkes College*: See Boyle, *The Climate of Treason*, p. 205.

p. 217 *There had been very short visits*: Burns, *Use of Memory*, p. 115.

p. 218 *twin-tracked policy*: For background, see Messenger, *Against the Grain*, and Seaman, *Special Operations Executive*. Ambassador Hoare insisted on keeping a tight control both on SOE's operations in Gibraltar and in Spain. PREM 3 405/6, 4/21/2A, 3 405/6 NA.

p. 218 *quiet Peninsula*: For Ambassador Hoare's summary of the case for non-military intervention in Spain, see Hoare, *Ambassador on Special Mission*, p. 122.

p. 219 *Father D'Arcy flew*: Sire, *D'Arcy*, p. 121.

p. 219 *lower echelons of British intelligence*: Charles R. Gallagher, *Vatican Secret Diplomacy* (London: Yale University Press, 2008), pp. 5 and 142, who quotes the philosopher and historian Isaiah Berlin on his time serving in the British embassy in Washington during the Second World War. Berlin provided Churchill with a weekly summary of American opinion which was said to be the prime minister's favourite reading. According to Berlin, the British wanted to harness the power of the American Catholic political bloc, because American Catholics were 'better organised' than any other religious body in the US. Hurley liaised with, among others, Robert Wilberforce, chief religious propagandist for the British Information Services – the US arm of the MoI – and, through him, with MI6.

For its part, the US State Department, anxious to win over the Catholics in America, most of whom had Irish, Italian or German roots and were 'hardly sympathetic' to Britain, to Roosevelt's pro-war policy, fed him with anti-Axis propaganda material. 'The very basis of our faith is challenged by the orgies of extermination that are going on among the Jews of Europe.' Quoted by Michael Walsh in 'Bishop's Private War', *Tablet*, 20 December 2008.

p. 220 *The British have a large organisation*: Hayes, *Wartime Mission in Spain*, p. 74.

p. 221 *I doubted whether anyone*: Philby, *My Silent War*, p. 56.

p. 221 *Beevor was posted to Portugal*: The father of historian Antony Beevor described his recruitment thus in his overview of SOE wartime operations: 'I had no previous knowledge of secret activities, but had the advantage of legal training and practice, which at least develops discretion, analytical thinking and care in the use of words.' He had three weeks' training which included 'studying the chances of the Iberian Peninsula being invaded by the Germans' and being exposed to 'some of the latest techniques in demolitions and small arms'. Beevor had some involvement in Spain where the ambassador Sir Samuel Hoare 'was opposed to any secret activity which might provoke Franco to join the Axis' although not opposed to 'secret activities of which he knew and approved'. He was tasked with liaising closely with Captain Hillgarth and two Madrid-based SOE officers who handled the movement of special operations personnel going into or coming out of Gibraltar through Spain. In Portugal, his operations were infiltrated by the Portuguese secret police, as were those of MI6. See J. G. Beevor, *SOE* (London: Bodley Head, 1981), pp. 30–43. See also Neville Wylie, 'Special Operations' (*Journal of Contemporary History* vol. 56, no. 3, 2001), pp. 441–56.

Beevor's account is generally positive, suggesting that, despite challenging operational conditions, he succeeded in carving out a niche for SOE in Portugal and went some way to insuring Britain against a German invasion of Portugal. In the end he was let down by a combination of bad luck, the indiscretions of some of his agents and the Foreign Office's inability to show a united front in his defence against expulsion. Wyle nevertheless concludes that Beevor's unmasking in early 1942 was 'the worst incident of its kind to afflict SOE stations in neutral Europe', while judging the Foreign Office's reluctance to authorise SOE operations to have been in Britain's best interests.

p. 222 *the German was snatched by an SOE team*: author's correspondence with Anthony Beevor.

p. 222 *a British diplomatic bag*: CO 967/68 NA.

p. 223 *It is difficult to write nice things*: Philby, *My Silent War*, p. 57.

p. 223 *prescription for propaganda*: For an insider's account of US policy towards Spain during this period, see John Emmet Hughes, *Report from Spain* (New York: Henry Holt & Company, 1947).

p. 224 *The Spain that I had come into*: Burns, *Use of Memory*, p. 106.

p. 224 *Plans for an Allied occupation*: Smyth, *Diplomacy*, pp. 232–7.

p. 224 *Thunderbird november eight two am*: Hughes, *Report*, p. 263.

p. 225 *an attitude of unconcern*: Hoare, *Ambassador on Special Mission*, p. 177.

p. 225 *Hayes rung Jordana*: 'The ambassador (Hayes) was received by a Foreign Minister (Jordana) in bathrobe, pajamas, and a state of fear-worn nerves.' Franco could not be immediately reached because he was on a hunting trip so that for another half-hour Jordana 'pattered in his slippers up and down the floor, struggling with his worst fears of imminent disaster'. Finally the ambassador allowed Jordana to see Roosevelt's message. 'Poor Jordana smiled happily, sank bank in his chair, and sighed with relief, "Ah! Spain is not involved." ' Hughes, *Report*, p. 264.

In his published diaries, Jordana records simply that he went to see Franco in the country palace of El Pardo, outside Madrid, spent until four in the morning with the *Generalísimo* before returning to his office and 'giving orders'. A footnote by the sympathetic editor of the diary, Jordana's diplomat son Rafael, clarifies that the minister talked as a fellow soldier to the country's senior generals and impressed upon them the need to 'remain calm. Francisco Gomez-Jordana Souza, *Milicia y Diplomacia* (Burgos: Dossoles, 2002).

p. 226 *The role of the head of the Abwehr, Admiral Canaris*: According to documents in the Institute of Contemporary History in Munich cited by a recent Canaris biographer, the landings had been accurately predicted by the Abwehr. Indeed, it would have been surprising if the agency's station in Algeciras had failed to note the build-up of Allied vessels. However, the intelligence was overruled by Ribbentrop who relied on information provided by the rival Foreign Ministry Intelligence Department inside the German embassy in Madrid. The view from the embassy, presumably based on disinformation provided by the Allies, was that the Allied landing would not take place before the end of 1943. Richard Bassett, *Hitler's Spy Chief* (London: Weidenfeld & Nicolson, 2005), pp. 247–8.

Bassett makes an interesting case that British intelligence, through the MI6's Sir Stewart Menzies, was trying as early as December 1940 to exploit the possibilities raised by Canaris's growing opposition to Hitler. Separately, the Catholic writer John Cummings, a relation of whom worked closely with the German admiral, suggests that from 1938 onwards Canaris protected the 'respectable' – non-Communist – German resistance at the highest possible level. According to Cummings, the German spy chief was party to efforts at the Vatican from 1939 to obtain approval for an alternative German regime and 'later played a dangerous double game by negotiating with the British'. Correspondence with the author. See also Cummings, *Butler's Lives*, p. 118.

The view formed by the well-informed British military attaché in wartime Madrid, Brigadier Wyndham Torr, was that Canaris was a 'loyal German, opposed to Hitler and to his tyranny and methods of conducting the war, which he was convinced, from the outset, would result in German's ultimate defeat'.

In a revealing letter to Samuel Hoare, years after the war was over, Torr suggested that Canaris was used as a pawn by the British. 'We tapped C. [Canaris] without his knowing it and he never knowingly or willingly, worked for us directly, but often did so, knowingly indirectly, in order to further his beliefs.' A more severe judgement has been made by one of Hitler's best recent biographers, Ian Kershaw, who labels Canaris a 'professional obfuscator'. Quoted by Tony Barber, 'The Enemy Within', *Financial Times Magazine*, 16 April 2005.

p. 226 *Well, here we are*: Gilbert, *Churchill*, p. 733.

p. 227 *long road to tread*: Ibid., p. 734.

p. 228 *all eyes and ears*: Hayes, *Wartime Mission*, p. 95.

10: Deception

p. 229 *Only years later*: Detailed research of Operation Mincemeat, including interviews with some of the unwitting participants, and discovery of relevant documents, was carried out by local historian Jesus Ramirez Copeiro. British government documents include WO 106/5921, WO 208/3163. For the insider's classic account see Ewen Montagu, *The Man Who Never Was* (London: Evans, 1953). Mincemeat, wrote intelligence officer Hugh Trevor-Roper in his introduction to Montagu's *Beyond Top Secret* (London: Peter Davies, 1977), was the 'most spectacular single episode in the history of deception'.

p. 229 *the highly secretive interservice XX Committee*: Sir John Masterman's internal memorandum written in 1945 and first published as *The Double Cross System* (London: Yale University Press, 1992) described the basic idea of the deception policy during 1943 up to the beginning of the winter as 'containing the maximum enemy forces in Western Europe and the Mediterranean area and thus discourage their transfer to the Russian front', p. 133.

p. 230 *carefully vetted individuals*: Membership of the committee included representatives from the War Office, Naval Intelligence Division (NID), Air Ministry Intelligence, MI6 and MI5 which provided the chairman and the secretary. Masterman, *The Double Cross System*, p. 62.

p. 230 *most secret sources*: The Director of Naval Intelligence, John Godfrey, had acceded to a demand from Sir Stewart Menzies, the head of MI6, that the whole work of deciphering should be put under the control of MI6. Wireless signals, having been intercepted at various special receiving stations, were sent by teleprinter to Bletchley Park where they were deciphered and distributed on a very restricted 'need to know basis' to named persons. The 'product' was known as 'Special Intelligence' and deciphered messages or documents about the subject were marked 'Most Secret U', the letter U standing for Ultra. Later, when the Americans pointed out that the word 'most' could mean 'almost', this was altered to 'Top Secret U'. Montagu, *Beyond Top Secret*, p. 32.

p. 230 *Major Martin's identity*: The status of an officer in the Royal Marines allowed NID to exercise control over the communications involved in Mincemeat, although Martin wore a battledress 'as no normal uniform could be made to fit exactly'. The difficulty of obtaining underclothes, owing to the system of coupon rationing, was overcome by a gift of thick underwear from the wardrobe of the late Warden of New College, Oxford. Ibid., p. 137.

p. 230 *A colonel in the marines*: Author's interview with Patricia Davies.

p. 230 *Detailing the Allied plans*: The fictitious document included a cover letter from Admiral Mountbatten to Admiral Cunningham, the naval chief in the Mediterranean, to explain why Major Martin was travelling. The main deception letter was intended to give the impression that Sicily was *not* the next target of the Allies and that there were two other operations being mounted in the Mediterranean, indicating that landings were likely in Greece and Sardinia. Masterman, *The Double Cross System*, p. 138.

p. 230 *Ewan [Montagu] handed me the big brown envelope*: author's interview with Patricia Davies.

p. 231 *There we were in 1942*: Montagu, *The Man Who Never Was*, p. 25.

p. 232 *The Gibraltar-born Lieutenant Commander Gómez-Beare*: Information provided to the author by Gómez-Beare family.

p. 233 *a local German agent*: One of the most active Second World War spies in Huelva was Adolph Clauss, son of the German consul. He was briefly detained on behalf of the Allies by the Spanish at the end of the war but was subsequently released. Information provided to the author by the Clauss family. See also Ramilla, *España y los Enigmas Nazis*, p. 149, and Copeiro del Vilar, *Huelva*, pp. 307, 424.

p. 234 *The two cooperated on the basis of mutual trust*: Burns, *Use of Memory*, p.114

p. 234 *a young Spanish doctor*: Eduardo Fernández Contioso conducted the autopsy together with his father, Eduardo Fernández del Torno. The young Eduardo had only just returned to Huelva from his honeymoon. Information provided to the author by the Contioso family.

p. 234 *Franco wept*: Preston, *Franco*, p. 404.

p. 235 *Hayes pointed out*: Ibid.

p. 235 *secret meeting with a member of the Spanish royal family*: FO 954/27 NA.

p. 235 *German counter-moves*: Ibid.

p. 236 *On 27 July 1943 Hoare wrote to Eden*: FO 371/34788 NA.

p. 236 *reaction in Spain to Mussolini's fall*: Ibid.

p. 236 *I had cast a good bit of bread*: Hayes, *Wartime Mission*, p. 163.

p. 237 *lunch at the Garrick*: The Garrick Club has its roots 'deep in the need of actors, artists, and writers for a venue, a private place, for informal exchanges of view', writes its biographer Richard Hough, in *The Ace of Clubs* (London: André Deutsch, 1986). Since its first informal meeting of actors and nobles in 1831 the Garrick – named after the great eighteenth-century English actor David Garrick – had taken pride in the conviviality, intellectual calibre and informed gossip of its membership, which set it apart from the stuffiness, insularity and occasional prejudice of the other London gentlemen's clubs.

TB was proposed for membership by the actor and author Robert Speaight, part of his network of artistic friends who used to gather in his Chelsea house during the 1930s. Speaight was well connected with friends and relatives extending across government service. TB's candidacy was seconded by Rupert Hart-Davis, the influential and successful publisher, and approved by a committee chaired by the Catholic peer and Law Lord Lord Russell of Kilowen, and Daniel Macmillan, another leading publisher and brother of the Tory politician and future prime minister Harold Macmillan.

p. 237 *Burns had enticed the poverty-stricken Nadal*: Rafael Martinez Nadal, *Antonio Torres y la Politica Española del Foreign Office* (Madrid: Casariego, 1989), p. 97.

p. 239 *I couldn't believe what I was hearing*: Ibid., p. 98. Despite Nadal's shock and anger, the academic agreed to further meetings with Burns. They included lunch at Martinez, the popular Spanish restaurant in Swallow Street, off Piccadilly Circus, where TB urged Nadal to focus his broadcasts on what he claimed was a turning tide in the war, and the Allied fightback. Ibid., p. 124.

p. 240 *Nadal's circle of friends*: Ibid., pp. 22–3.

p. 240 *Enriqueta who introduced Blunt and Tomás to each other*: Author's interview with Enriqueta Harris. See also Carter, *Anthony Blunt*, p. 94.

p. 240 *an English translation of a book of Lorca verses*: Published as *Poems of Federico García Lorca* (London: The Dolphin Press, 1939).

p. 242 *It is not that we want Spain*: Quoted in Nadal, *Antonio Torres*, p. 36.

p. 242 *the notes of an out-of-tune flute*: Ibid., pp. 50–51.

p. 243 *I try and forget all that*: Author's interview with Enriqueta Harris.

p. 244 *the journalist John Marks was encouraged*: The Cambridge-educated Marks was the BBC's Spanish programme organiser until January 1942, after which he was posted to Madrid as the *Times* correspondent. Throughout the war Marks maintained close links with the Foreign Office and the Ministry of Information, who valued this fluent Spanish speaker as an astute observer of the local political scene. Marks was both fond of and knowledgeable about Spanish culture, enjoying eating, drinking, women and bulls. During the war Marks became a close friend of TB, and served him as an informal 'agent'.

p. 245 *During the summer of 1943*: FO371/34766, FO 371/34764, FO/34765 NA; Hayes, *Wartime Mission*, p. 149; Preston, *Franco*, p. 495. The pressures on Nadal built up throughout 1943, partly due to TB's personal intervention. See Nadal, *Antonio Torres*, p. 142. TB's enemies in MI5 saw his insistence on Nadal's eventual dismissal as one of the crowning episodes of Samuel Hoare's 'appeasement policy'. See MI5 file, KV 2/2823.

p. 245 *a new national state-run newsreel called No Do*: For a critical Spanish analysis of how Francoist propaganda focused on conveying a sense of political, social and cultural normality, see Pedro Montoliu, *Madrid en la Posguerra* (Madrid: Silex, 2005), pp. 284–9. For a UK perspective on how Spanish wartime propaganda was viewed within the Spanish film division at the Ministry of Information, see MoI files INF 1/572/; INF 1/574; INF 1/594; INF 1/596 NA.

p. 246 *One of the most interesting*: Ibid.

p. 246 *Fox, as you know*: Ibid.

p. 247 *The press attaché in Spain*: Ibid.

p. 247 *Under the guise of a national Spanish and neutral enterprise*: Ibid.

p. 247 *There was considerable contemporaneous*: Hayes, *Wartime Mission*, p. 149.

p. 248 *a growing discontent*: FO 954/27 NA.

p. 248 *information supplied to him by Burns*: The names of the informants listed by Hoare included Cardinal Pedro Segura, the Cardinal Archbishop of Seville, who maintained close relations with TB's assistant Bernard Malley. Other 'agents' of influence mentioned were General Manuel Matallana (an anti-communist Spanish Civil War officer who had fought for the Republic against Franco, before surrendering his troops), the writer José Martínez Ruiz Azorín and Gregorio Marañón, the prominent doctor and man of letters and TB's future father-in-law.

p. 248 *'I am glad', replied Roosevelt*: Quoted in Hayes, *Wartime Mission*, p. 163.

p. 249 *Hoare returned to the subject of Nadal*: FO 954/27 NA.

p. 249 *Churchill delivered a speech*: For the speech and the criticism it sparked see Wigg, *Churchill and Spain*, pp. 151–2. Also Preston, *Franco*, p. 513: 'Churchill's speech was a hostage to fortune from which Franco was to squeeze the last ounce of benefit both domestically and internationally.'

11: To Love in Madrid

p. 251 *a letter from Sir Malcolm Robertson*: Ronald Howard, *In Search of my Father* (London: William Kimber, 1981).

p. 251 *the Americans had been expanding their presence*: The possibility of a German occupation of Spain was viewed as a major strategic danger by the Allies, particularly in the months following the North African campaign of 1942 when supply lines were stretched. OSS agents began to arrive in Lisbon and Madrid in April 1942 under State Department cover. In the Spanish capital, the counter-intelligence section X-2 worked out of the offices of the US oil mission. Elizabeth P. McIntosh, *Sisterhood of Spies* (Annapolis: Naval Institute Press, 1998), pp. 168–9. See also Martín de Pozuelo and Ellakuria, *La Guerra Ignorada*, pp. 31–2. The US propaganda push, along similar lines to the British, is described in Hayes, *Wartime Mission*, p. 76.

p. 252 *At the time Starkie was a Catholic professor*: In the weeks preceding the outbreak of war, Starkie was visited in Dublin by Churchill's closest friend, the newspaper magnate and future Minister of Information Brendan Bracken. While in the Irish capital, Bracken stayed under an assumed name at the Jury's Hotel and had secret conversations with Starkie. See Charles Edward Lysaght, *Brendan Bracken* (London: Allen Lane, 1979). The contact was presumably not unconnected to the Anglophile professor's recruitment to government service. Bracken may also have been sounding out Starkie's views on Irish attitudes towards the imminent war with Germany.

p. 252 *For how could official Spain*: Burns, *Use of Memory*, p. 102.

p. 252 *Walter wanted to do anything to help the Allied cause*: Author's interview with Alma Starkie.

p. 252 *The horses belonged to the Spanish army*: Ibid.

p. 252 *The poor people of Madrid*: Ibid.

p. 253 *The Starkies allowed their own large flat*: Ibid. Starkie was part of a large Madrid-based organisation that the Allies used to help smuggle POWs and some 30,000 Jews through Spain and Portugal. The daughter of a Spanish doctor, who worked for the British and helped in the escape route, has written an account of this operation. See Patricia Martínez de Vicente, *Embassy y La Inteligencia de Mambru* (Velecio, 2003) and interview in *The Times*, 3/12/2003.

p. 254 *the crew crouched or suspended*: Burns, *Use of Memory*, p. 103.

p. 255 *Ought we to tell him*: Howard, *In Search of My Father*.

p. 256 *It proved, indeed, to be a gala affair*: Hayes, *Wartime Mission*, p. 97.

p. 256 *Brendan Bracken, the MoI chief, and Anthony Eden*: Howard, *In Search of My Father*.

p. 256 *Mr Leslie Howard is going to Spain*: FO NA.

p. 257 *It is very important just now*: Ibid.

p. 257 *He was very polite*: Author's interview with Olive Stock.

p. 257 *One of those he was scheduled*: In *El Vuelo de Ibis* (Madrid: Facta, 2009) the Spanish author José Rey Ximénez claims he was told the 'full story' of Howard's visit to Madrid when he interviewed Conchita Montenegro. Once dubbed the Spanish Greta Garbo because of her seductive sensuality, Montenegro, a one-time lover of the Spanish Hollywood director Edgar Neville, allegedly also had an affair with Howard whom she met, as a young actress, while filming *Never the Twain Shall Meet* in 1931. Montenegro later married Ricardo Giménez-Arnau, who was in charge of foreign relations for the Falange party.

Rey Ximénez claimed that Howard was sent to Madrid with a 'special message for Franco' which he delivered personally. 'Thanks to Howard, at least in theory, Spain was persuaded to stay out of the war,' the Spanish author alleged. *Guardian*, 6/10/2008.

p. 258 *he was keen to briefly rekindle an old flame in Montenegro*: Burns family archive

p. 258 *one of several German agents that tracked Howard*: The information about Gloria von Furstenberg was provided to the author during an interview with Aline Griffith, Countess of Romanones.

Such was Howard's reputation as a philanderer that his visit to Spain fuelled Madrid gossip about his alleged 'affairs'. Another German aristocratic agent he allegedly got involved with was the ravishing Colombian-born Countess Mechtild von Podewils. Rey Ximénez, *El Vuelo del Ibis*.

p. 258 *the pure white shoulderless tube of a dress*: Aline, Countess of Romanones, *The Spy Wore Red*, p. 234.

p. 259 *this charming English export*: Howard, *In Search of My Father*.

p. 260 *Long-term membership of the Garrick Club*: Howard was elected to the Garrick along with James Makepeace Thackeray, the grandson of the great nineteenth-century novelist W. M. Thackeray, in 1933. It was a controversial year for the club, with the Committee exercising its right of veto on a range of new applicants. Of the many portraits and sculptures of famous actors that adorn the club today, Howard's hangs in one of the club's most convivial locations – the members' bar. Hough, *The Ace of Clubs*, pp. 42 and 144.

p. 260 *the most unashamedly patriotic and propagandist*: On the importance of representations of nationhood and heroism in Second World War films, see review of *The Death of Colonel Blimp* by Sarah Knight in *Journal of Film Studies* (Institute of Film & TV Studies, University of Nottingham, Issue 6, 2006). For the collaboration between the government and the British film industry in propaganda, see also Chapman, *The British at War: Cinema, State and Propaganda 1939–45*.

p. 261 *There were no consequences*: Gilbert, *Churchill*, p. 747.

p. 261 *We have been rather anxious*: Ibid., p. 747.

p. 262 *it was not the prime minister but Howard*: British intelligence's suspicions about Kuno Weltzien, the German agent thought responsible for providing the information that led to the shooting down of Leslie Howard's plane, are in an MI5 KV2 file. NA.

p. 262 *the manifest*: Details collated by Howard's son, Ronald.

p. 263 *It is just possible*: Ibid.

p. 263 *Stow died*: Author's interview with Geoffrey's son, Michael Stow.

p. 263 *The Herrenvolk are not hard to recognise*: Quoted by Ronald Howard.

p. 263 *to some he apologised*: Ibid.

p. 264 *After the wild nightmare*: Letter from Howard to TB from Burns Family Archive.

p. 265 *Burns sent a message to the MOI*: INF file 1/572 NA.

p. 265 *how best to limit the sale of Spanish wolfram*: See Wigg, *Churchill and Spain* pp. 121–7.

p. 265 *I enjoyed meeting Marañón*: FO 370 NA.

p. 266 *intellectually, one of the best minds*: FO 954/27 NA.

p. 266 *Marañón became disillusioned*: For a detailed analysis of how developments in the Civil War impacted on Marañón, see 'La Guerra de Marañón', research paper by Antonio Lopez Vega (Madrid: Fundación Marañón, 2006). On the restrictions Marañón initially found on returning from exile, see the elliptical account – written when Franco was still in power – of his first authorised biographer, Marino Gomez-Santos, *Vida de Marañón* (Madrid: I. B. Tauris, 1971), p. 382.

p. 266 *one of the public men mainly responsible for King Alfonso's downfall*: FO 954/27 NA.

p. 267 *Marañón is back*: Burns, *Use of Memory*, p. 107.

p. 269 *empty apart for her presence*: Ibid., p. 108.

p. 269 *Mabel's early memories*: Based on Mabel Burns's conversations with the author.

p. 271 *If I am not out of here in one hour*: Ibid.

12: Marriage

p. 273 *Mabel found Warrington-Strong*: Author's conversations with Mabel Burns.

p. 274 *Steadfastly he gazed*: BFA.

p. 275 *contact with Franco's representative*: Gomez-Santos, *Vida de Marañón*, p. 350.

p. 275 *Mabel dressed up as a gypsy*: Source material held in BFA.

p. 275 *amiable businessman named Oscar Schindler*: Ibid.

p. 276 *I have always been at the service of my country*: Gregorio Marañón, *Obras Completas*, vol. 2 (Madrid: Espasa Calpe, 1966), pp. 353–5.

p. 276 *I never tire of saying*: Ibid., pp. 351–2.

p. 276 *well-drilled exhibition of Nazi loyalty*: BFA. The *Cap Arcona* was built and conceived in the mid-1920s for service between North America and Argentina, a route 'every bit as prestigious as the better remembered North American run' (quoted in www.garemaritime. com). She sunk on 3 May 1945 in the Baltic Sea, four days after Hitler's suicide and four days before Germany's unconditional surrender after being attacked by the RAF. British pilots were targeting fleeing Nazis who were believed to be on their way to Norway. The ship was transporting thousands of inmates from the Neuengamme concentration camp along with their SS guards. About five thousand of those on board perished, of which the majority were prisoners. For a detailed account see Benjamin Jacobs and Eugene Pool, *The 100 Years Secret* (Connecticut, US: The Lyons Press, 2002).

p. 277 *The only thing that matters*: Author's conversations with Mabel Burns.

p. 277 *She dreamed of becoming a Cambridge undergraduate*: Ibid. Mabel Burns left no record of which college she applied to. In subsequent correspondence with the author, her suggestion of anti-Franco bias in the university has been questioned by one Cambridge historian, Dr Peter Martland: 'In 1938, there were certainly communists like Maurice Dobb (the Marxian economics lecturer) but the place still reeked of the old Tory right.'

p. 278 *I like England and I like English men*: Mabel Burns's diary, BFA.

p. 278 *As the years passed*: Extensive enquiries made by the author failed to shed light on Nelly Hess's fate.

p. 279 *People are beginning to make contact with the soldiers*: Paris diary entries quoted in Gomez-Santos, *Vida de Marañón*, p. 374.

p. 280 *The years I lived in Paris*: Ibid., p. 375.

p. 280 *the summons Maranon received one day*: Ibid., p. 375. Marañón refers, without identifying him by name, to a 'German governor, a well-known Gestapo chief'. Hans Josef Keiffer was the Nazi counter-intelligence chief in Paris at the time. His seemingly civilised treatment of Marañón was deceptive, the behaviour of a ruthless senior Gestapo officer who used his charm to befriend his victims and extract information. British agents held at the Paris Gestapo headquarters in Avenue Foch were 'fed and nurtured and generally encouraged to feel "at home" ', writes Sarah Helm in *A Life in Secrets* (London: Abacus, 2007), p. 331. Kieffer's employees, with his approval, took charge of torture at a Gestapo detention centre in the Place des Etas-Unis, and subsequent executions. When the war ended, Kieffer tried to exonerate himself by claiming he never 'knew' about the torture of those he had befriended – but he was directly implicated in the execution of British soldiers and hanged for crimes against humanity at Wuppertal. Ibid. See also war crimes case file WO 235 NA.

p. 281 *It was only long after the war*: Author's conversations with Mabel Burns.

p. 281 *The only German she befriended*: Ibid. p. 282 *His name was Clemente Pelaez*: Ibid. While Mabel was not short of suitors among the young Francoist civil war veterans her brother Gregorio had fought alongside, it was Pelaez who most persistently courted her.

p. 283 *Miranda told Burns to stop the car*: Burns, *Use of Memory*, p. 109.

p. 283 *dressed in the traditional Andalusian country clothes*: Burns family archive.

p. 284 *We were going to be married*: Ibid., p. 109.

p. 285 *there was the wildest possible gambling in this commodity*: Templewood papers XIII.

p. 285 *It is well, therefore, to reconsider our position*: Hoare, *Ambassador on Special Mission*, p. 248. The ambassador's policy towards Spain remained pragmatic. Hoare considered the absence of an effective opposition to the Franco regime alongside his perception that Franco could not be trusted as an ally. He argued against a total economic embargo because of the risk of social upheaval and the ensuing 'general confusion' being exploited by the Nazis. Policy, he concluded, should remain focused on non-intervention and countering any non-neutral pro-Axis acts by the regime.

p. 286 *Spain, however much she may need it, is not ready*: FO 954/27 NA.

p. 287 *the whole of Madrid*: Unidentified journalist's diary, BFA.

p. 289 *her face hidden beneath a veil*: Author's conversations with Mabel Burns.

p. 291 *shutting down the spy networks*: Hoare, *Ambassador on Special Mission*, p. 268.

p. 292 *SD officers with the haziest notions*: Bassett, *Hitler's Spy Chief*, p. 282.

p. 293 *the links between the Abwehr in Madrid and their agents in Britain*: Benton, *The ISOS Years*, p. 407. According to its chief architect, 'the basic idea of the deception policy during 1943 and up to the beginning of the winter was to contain the maximum enemy forces in Western Europe and the Mediterranean area and thus discourage their transfer to the Russian front', Masterman, *The Double Cross System*, p. 133.

p. 293 *a Spaniard called Juan Pujol*: As one of its more objective chroniclers warns readers, a 'miasma of falsehood, deception and deceit' surrounds the case of Juan Pujol, alias Garbo. Mark Seaman's introduction to MI5's official summary prepared by Pujol's case officer Tomás Harris (London: Public Record Office, 2000), p. 2. The summary conflicts on several points with Pujol's own memoirs written decades earlier: Juan Pujol and Nigel West, *Garbo* (London: Weidenfeld & Nicolson, 1985). Other material relevant to the Garbo case is MI5 files KV2 series numbers 39, 40, 42, 63, 64, 66 and 69. NA. A recent biographer concludes that Pujol may have initially entered the spy game for purely mercenary reasons – he approached the Germans first. His subsequent activities suggest he was motivated by a mixture of idealism, adventurousness and opportunism but contributed to the defeat of Nazism although the full facts of his story are likely for ever to remain a mystery. Javier Juarez, *Juan Pujol, el espia que derroto a Hitler* (Madrid: Temas de Hoy, 2004), p. 413.

p. 294 *a network of bogus sub-agents*: Pujol and his handler Harris expanded a network across the UK military and government machinery from the RAF to the BBC. 'Agents' included a drunken RAF officer in Glasgow, an anti-Communist War Office linguist and a Gibraltarian waiter whom Garbo claimed had been working for him for some time and was 'one hundred per cent loyal to the German cause'. KV2/41 NA.

According to one UK intelligence estimate, by the end of the war Garbo had registered at least fourteen 'agents' and eleven official 'contacts', all notional. Benton, *The ISOS Years*, p. 375.

p. 294 *deceiving Germans about Operation Torch*: As part of the deception, Pujol removed one of his 'agents' from Liverpool before the Germans could deploy him, and reported on Allied convoys *after* the landings had taken place. KV2/41 NA.

p. 294 *main contribution to the Allied victory*: Pujol's role in the success of Operation Overlord was widely celebrated on the sixtieth anniversary of D-Day in June 2004. Garbo was described as the Allies' 'top double agent' by the BBC which also acknowledged that the story surrounding the Spaniard was 'almost beyond belief' (press pack issued by BBC, 14/5/2004). The deception included the fictitious First US Army Group (FUSAG), the 'existence' of which led the Germans to hold back seven of their divisions in the Pas de Calais, pointlessly, for two weeks after D-Day.

p. 294 *the VI and V2 bombs*: For an account of the damage wrought by the bombs and the mishandled information provided to the public by the government, see Maureen Waller, *London, 1945* (London: John Murray, 2005).

p. 295 *arrested on suspicion*: Juarez, *Juan Pujol*, pp. 349–50.

p. 295 *struggle between MI6 and MI5*: The rivalry within Whitehall over who should control Pujol and in what way appears to have been most marked in the early stages. It has been noted by official historians of British intelligence in the Second World War – see Michael Howard, British Intelligence in the Second World War, vol. 4 (London: HMSO, 1990), p. 16, and F. H. Himsley and C. A. G. Simkins, p. 113, both cited by Mark Seaman in his introduction to the Harris 'summary'.

The most fluid intelligence cooperation on the Garbo case appears to have passed through the personal friendship between Harris at MI5 and Kim Philby at MI6. 'As far as our department was concerned, Philby made all the major decisions (on Garbo)', Desmond Bristow of MI6's Section V's Iberian section told the spy catcher Peter Wright. See Bristow, *A Game of Moles*, p. 264.

p. 295 *the Ministry of Information's Spanish section*: One of the notional 'agents' Pujol claimed as a friend was given the code symbol J (3). The alleged 'high-ranking official' was never named. However, Harris claims that a careful examination of the information provided by J (3) and a check on the movements of Billy McCann, the head of the section, while in Spain, would have led the Germans to the conclusion that J (3) and McCann were one and the same. Harris describes the character as 'certainly the most important of all Garbo's contacts'. J (3) was represented as increasingly indiscreet, with Pujol telling his German handler that he had first befriended him while working as a part-time employee at the MoI. Harris claimed that McCann was told 'in confidence' about Garbo's deception although there is no separate verification of this. Pujol also created a fictitious agent at the MoI, primarily with the aim of using him as a source of deception material. The 'agent' was an unnamed employee at the MoI in charge of censorship. KV2/41 NA.

13: Liberation

p. 297 *José Felix Lequerica*: Elsewhere described as 'intensely ambitious, quite unprincipled, and a highly skilled operator in high places'. His mother was from the Urquijo family, one of the Spanish banking dynasties, aiding his status as one of the prominent members of the Basque financial and industrial establishment which had helped finance Franco during the Spanish Civil War. Wigg, *Churchill and Spain*, p. 160.

p. 298 *expand and let his indiscretions roll*: Burns, *Use of Memory*, p. 112. The Lequerica dinner was also noted in a private guest book diary Mabel Burns kept during her and TB's stay in Calle del Prado. BFA.

p. 298 *If history were conclusive*: FO 954/127 NA.

p. 299 *an eccentric prone to indiscipline*: Laing was reprimanded for dressing up in full regimental regalia on one of his wartime outings to a London nightclub. Regimental notes seen by the author.

p. 299 *Laing was introduced to the eighteen-year-old Cayetana*: Author's interview with Peter Laing.

p. 300 *one of the most beautiful women in Spain*: Quoted in essay on Goya by John F. Moffitt in *Journal of Art History*, vol. 50, issue 3 (1981), pp. 119–35. Robert Hughes, in *Goya* (London: Harvill Press, 2003), questions whether the painter became Alba's lover. He suggests instead as more likely that the duchess represented for Goya an erotic 'type' who stirred his fantasies of 'dark *maja*-hood and lithe proletarian sex'.

p. 300 *Of Cayetana at first sight*: Unpublished memoirs of Peter Laing and his interview with the author.

p. 300 *her outings from the embassy*: Among her regular chaperones was Casilda Villaverde, the Marquesa de Santa Cruz, the young wife of her father's deputy in the Spanish embassy in Madrid. Author's interview with Casilda Santa Cruz.

p. 301 *He's a Red Catalan!*: Peter Laing diary note.

p. 302 *Burns was assigned to work on a propaganda operation*: FO 371/41886 NA and Templewood papers XIII.

p. 302 *An armed guard of* maquisards: Templewood papers XIII.

p. 302 *days of great joy*: Burns, *Use of Memory*, p.115.

p. 302 *The road was lined with cheering crowds*: Hayes, *Wartime Mission in Spain*, p. 257.

p. 304 *This is the most appalling news*: BFA.

p. 304 *I'm writing just to let you know*: Grisewood papers, GEO.

p. 305 *The effect [of your speech] has been frankly bad*: Templewood papers XIII.

p. 305 *an uncompromising attitude towards Franco's Spain*: For a sympathetic account of Hoare's belated attempt to force a U-turn in Churchill's benevolent attitude towards Franco, which the ambassador himself had backed for most of the war, see Wigg, *Churchill and Spain*.

p. 307 *Sentis had worked as Franco spy in Paris*: Personal information collated by MI5. KV2/2823 NA.

p. 308 *He [Sentis] has been pretty coy with me*: Ibid.

p. 308 *no gibes at England of any kind*: Ibid.

p. 309 *Marañón showed Burns a telegram*: Ibid.

p. 309 *This communication from Brugada*: Ibid.

p. 310 *main [Spanish] source of information to the [Spanish] embassy is under our control*: Ibid.

p. 310 *Burns got positive vindication*: Author's interview with Carlos Sentís. Details of the trip to Dachau were noted by MI5. KV2/2824 NA.

p. 311 *The reports filed by Sentis*: 'The horrors of the Dachau concentration camp', *La Vanguardia*, 15/5/1945. 'Witness of the end of the War', *La Vanguardia*, 29/11/1945. The journalist's style – cynical and verging on the flippant at times – and anti-communist views during and after the Spanish Civil War have drawn criticism in recent years from the Catalan left. Writing in *El País* (14/1/2006 'Franquistas en Barcelona') Jordi Gracia questions Sentis's professed Anglophilia and describes Spain's political neutrality, which Sentis supported, as 'false because it had its political heart with the Axis powers'. See Francesc Vilanova I Vila Abadal, *La Barcelona franquista i l'Europa totalitaria* (Barcelona: Empuries, 2005). Nevertheless, Sentis's articles have survived the test of time as unique eyewitness accounts in the Spanish language of one of the great human horrors of the twentieth century. Sentis arguably did for Spanish readers what the BBC's Richard Dimbleby did with his broadcasts for the British, providing an 'unforgettable, definitive statement about human atrocity' (see Jonathan Dimbleby, *Richard Dimbleby* (London: Coronet, 1977), p. 180).

p. 311 *John Amery was interned in northern Italy*: David Faber, *Speaking for England* (Pocket Books, 2007), pp. 478–80.

p. 311 *he had been granted Spanish citizenship*: Ibid.

p. 311 *parcel of warm things*: Templewood papers XIII.

p. 312 *apocalyptic horror*: Julian Amery, *Approach March: A Venture in Autobiography* (London: Hutchinson, 1973), p. 89.

p. 314 *I wonder if I might trouble you*: Templewood papers XIII.

p. 314 *We'll squash those dwarfs flats*: Burns, *Use of Memory*, p. 81.

p. 315 *Laing and Burns*: Author's interview with Peter Laing.

p. 316 *the resident SOE officer in Madrid*: Faber, *Speaking for England*, p. 493.

p. 317 *conspiracy to manufacture evidence*: Ibid., p. 497.

p. 318 *It was a bleak day*: Author's interview with Helen Rolfe. She was married to a British intelligence officer. Her sister was an SOE agent who was captured and executed by the

Germans.

p. 318 *Part of me was furious*. Author's interview with Enriqueta Harris.

p. 319 *A dossier prepared by the OSS's*: Donald P. Steury, *The OSS and Project Safehaven* (CIA Government Library), p. 8.

Aftermath

p. 321 '*Call-me-God*': Burns, *Use of Memory*, p. 117. Brigadier Wyndham Torr, together with the naval attaché Captain Hillgarth – whom Hoare had recommended earlier for a CMG – maintained key informants at the highest level of the Spanish military. They complemented much of the political intelligence gathered on the civilian members of the Franco regime (including the Falange) and the Catholic Church by TB and his team, most notably Bernard Malley. When the former Grenadier officer Peter Laing became an assistant press attaché in Madrid, he worked closely with Torr and TB.

p. 321 *He [Burns] has done most remarkable work*: Templewood papers XIII: 7.

p. 322 *a former evangelical lay missionary*: Prior to the Second World War, 'Grubb had spent a good deal of his early life in Latin America, mostly in Brazil, where as a missionary he had lived for several years in the backwaters of the Amazon, working among the Indians', Sir Robert Marett, *Through the Back Door* (Oxford: Pergamon Press, 1969), p. 5. TB claimed that it was in Latin America that Grubb developed an 'evangelical zeal' and 'hatred of Rome'.

p. 322 *Grubb, for his part, despised Burns*: In his autobiography, Grubb criticises TB's wartime mission without naming him, recalling Madrid as the 'the only case I can remember of a violent clash of interests' between the Ministry of Information and the ambassador over the duties of the press attaché. Grubb, *The Crypts of Power*, p. 110.

p. 322 *I am sorry I had to knock you off*: Burns, *Use of Memory*, p. 117.

p. 323 *This might of course be considered a minor sin*: KV2/2824 NA.

p. 323 *He is an Anglo-Chilean*: Ibid.

p. 324 *information provided by Blunt*: According to his biographer, the great mass of British secret intelligence Blunt passed on to the Soviets dates from 1942, although there is no doubt he was giving documents to his controller Anatoli Gorsky in the months before June 1941, when Hitler broke the terms of the Nazi-Soviet Pact and invaded the Soviet Union. See Carter, *Anthony Blunt*, p. 274.

p. 325 *Spaniards must be really puzzled*: A cutting of the *Tribune* diary piece is to be found in MI5's personal file on TB – KV2/2824 NA.

p. 325 *The new Labour foreign secretary, Ernest Bevin*: See Preston, *Franco*, p. 542.

p. 325 *he ordered that any further honours*: Author interview with Peter Laing.

p. 326 *politically gunpowder*: Author's copy of unpublished memoirs of Sir Victor Mallet – courtesy of Mallet family.

p. 326 *A series of suggestions kept reaching me*: Ibid.

p. 327 *outside the official diplomatic protocol*: Burns, *Use of Memory*, pp. 112–13.

p. 327 *Gousev, who wished, like his boss Stalin, to have the Allies break off relations*: Preston, *Franco*, p. 542.

p. 327 *Mallet wrote to the Foreign Office*: FO 371/46835? NA.

p. 328 *A violent or provocative act*: Ibid.

p. 329 *someone who would be loyal to higher ideals*: Preston, *Franco*, p. 544.

p. 329 *German officials and agents considered a security and political risk*: Copies of list in Spanish Foreign Ministry archive (AMAE) R/2160/3.

p. 329 *Those repatriated*: The post-war fate of Leissner (alias Lenz), Meyer-Doyer and Mosig are noted in Collado Seidel, *España: Refugio Nazi*, pp. 169 and 311. Also in archive files (AMAE) R/5651/29 and (AMAE) R/5651/17.

p. 330 *German military and economic aid*: Bernhardt oversaw the running of Sofindus, a consortium that straddled mining and shipping interests, using 'front companies' ostensibly managed by Spaniards. See Collado Seidel, *España: Refugio Nazi*, pp. 147–9, 185–8.

p. 330 *short period in a detention camp in Caldas del Rey*: During the final stages of researching this book, the author discovered a surviving member of the Clauss family – Klaus Clauss, grandson of Ludwig, living in Huelva. Growing up and working in post-war Spain, Klaus had earned a reputation for his hedonistic lifestyle, throwing lavish parties for his business partners and clients either in town or out in La Luz, a large country estate his family brought from the Pérez de Guzmán, an old established Andalusian family.

There was never a shortage of women and drink in Klaus's wild *fiestas*. But in 2006 he was in retirement, suffering from throat cancer. He was living in a large semi-colonial town house, obscured from the outside world by tropical trees and a perimeter gate and wall. Klaus agreed to speak through his lawyer and interpreter in a dimly lit room decorated with antiques. He described his wartime childhood in Huelva as being a relatively happy and uneventful one until the day the local authorities, under pressure, detained his grandfather, father and uncle. He attended a local school and had German and Spanish friends, although German was spoken at home. He claimed to have been unaware at the time of the wartime activities of the elders in his family. He described them as 'loyal Germans' – his father was a veteran of the First World War – who he remembered had spent much of their time listening to Nazi broadcasts on the radio

p. 330 *Lazar eluded an order for his arrest*: Lazar's personal file at the Spanish Foreign Ministry archives contains photographs and letters surrounding his 'escape'. Separately, the Franco archive contains the copy of an undated and previously undiscovered letter from Lazar to the *Generalísimo* pleading for Spanish residence. In it, Lazar argues that his reputation as a 'notorious anti-communist' means that he would be 'sacrificed' by the Soviets were he to be repatriated to his native Austria. He also claims that his wife is too ill to leave Spain (Franco archive document 618/19). British information on Lazar is recorded in FO 371/60439.

p. 331 *Lazar lashed out at the evils of communism: Hamburger Anzeiger*, 10/12/1953

p. 331 *the Cold War was under way*: In 1946 a report was placed before the UN Security Council estimating that between 2000 and 3000 Nazi officials, agents and war criminals were living in Spain in addition to tens of thousands of ex-members of the Vichy government (mentioned by Preston, *Franco*, p. 550). This may have been an inflated figure, and several of the more prominent Nazis subsequently left for South America. Allied pressure on Franco's Spain neutralised the feared attempt of a resurgent Nazi state in southern Europe (see Collado Seidel, *España: Refugio Nazi*, p. 313).

In 1947 the UN body CROWCASS (Central Registry of War Criminals and Security Suspects) drew up a list of more than 60,000 names of individuals worldwide wanted for war crimes committed between September 1939 and May 1945. Over the next fifty years an estimated 6500 were caught. Many of the more notorious criminals were in Allied custody for a while but were released for lack of evidence and uncertainty over their true identities. In recent years evidence of the US, Britain and the Soviet Union's complicity in allowing some Nazis to escape justice has emerged. CIA documents reveal that some 118 German scientists helped develop the US space programme, while in the UK Clement Attlee's post-war Labour government favoured East Europeans, among them former Nazis, over non-whites and Jews in its immigration policy. British intelligence recruited many as agents and sent them into the Eastern Bloc, where some also worked for the Russians, a subject dealt with by David Cesarani in his book *Justice Delayed* (London: Phoenix, 2001) and John Le Carré, in *The Spy Who Came in from the Cold* (London: Coronet Books, 2005). See also 'The Nazi most wanted list' in *The Week*, 14/2/2009.

p. 331 *spiteful and exaggerated tone*: Victor Mallet memoirs.

p. 332 *Bristow kept track of Nazis, communist agents*: Bristow, *A Game of Moles*, p. 196. In retirement, Bristow owned up to a long-standing friendship with a Spaniard who had a house in Antequera, near Málaga, but only partly identifying him as 'José Muñoz'. He was José Antonio Muñoz Rojas, one of TB's wartime contacts. Several wartime agents of influence in Spain were maintained during the Cold War period by the British. (Author's interview with Munoz Rojas.)

p. 322 *political trials and visiting prisons*: Bristow found that, despite the 'apparent viciousness' of some court sentences, the general atmosphere within Francoist prisons was 'very informal'. He dismissed the outraged reporting in the US and British media as the product of left-wing propaganda. Ibid., pp. 196–7.

While several historians have focused on the repressive power of the Francoist state, a detailed examination of court documents shows that prosecutors relied on Franco's grassroots support at local level to identify and provide evidence against, and convict, Republicans. Peter Anderson, *In the Interests of Justice*? (CUP: Contemporary European History, 2009), 18: pp. 25–44.

p. 333 *Those who had venerated Philby*: In *The Climate of Treason* Boyle describes the 'ever loyal' Broomham-White as one of Philby's friends and advocates, 'perhaps the most ardent believer of the traitor's innocence'. When the Soviets announced on 30 July 1963 that they had not only granted Philby's request for political asylum, but had also conferred on him the privileges of Russian citizenship, Broomham-White went into decline and died five months later.

p. 334 *Surveyor of the Queen's Pictures*: On 15 November 1979, Margaret Thatcher announced that in 1964 Blunt had admitted to being a Russian spy in return for immunity from persecution. He died on 26 March 1983 and his ashes were scattered on Martinsell Hill overlooking the town of Marlborough where he had walked as schoolboy. Carter, *Anthony Blunt*, p. 497.

p. 334 *The doubts as to whether or not Tomás Harris was a Soviet agent*: In an interview with the author, Enriqueta Harris defended her reputation as a wartime employee of the Ministry of Information and an art historian. She insisted her brother had never betrayed his country.

p. 334 *post-war anonymity and self-exile*: At the end of the war, Pujol was paid a gratuity of £15,000 by MI5 to 'help him on his way'. He was later located in Venezuela by the spy writer Rupert Allason (Nigel West) and persuaded to make a 'sentimental' return to London. There he met some of his former MI5 colleagues and was granted an audience at Buckingham Palace with the Duke of Edinburgh. He receded into relative obscurity as several books on his life appeared. He died in 1988. Seaman, Introduction to *The Spy Who Saved D-Day*, p. 29.

p. 334 *'ideal situation' to further Soviet infiltration*: Bristow, *A Game of Moles*, p. 274.

p. 334 *fake paintings scam*: Ibid., p. 275.

p. 335 *The greatest mystery of all*: While the police report into the crash suggested an accident, the suspicion that the car was tampered with and that the Russians were involved endured. Spy writer Chapman Pincher suggested that several MI5 officers were convinced that Harris was murdered by the Russians. The theory revolved round Blunt's arrest three months later and the anticipation that Harris was about to be brought in for questioning by British intelligence. See Pincher, *Too Secret Too Long*, p. 390. Also one of Pincher's alleged sources MI5's Peter Wright and his book *Spy Catcher* (London: Viking, 1987), p. 260. Pincher claimed that Harris's wife, Hilda, who survived the crash, could not understand why the car crashed because her husband was 'not driving fast and no other car was involved'. But the MI6 Madrid officer, Desmond Bristow, who was at the scene the day after the crash, reported that Hilda had told him that Harris was 'driving like hell' after consuming a 'couple of drinks', had got into an argument with his wife, and then lost control of the car after crossing a humpback bridge (Bristow, p. 279).

More than forty years after the crash, Harris's sister Enriqueta carried whatever doubts she may have had to the grave. In her final interview she told the author that her brother had been 'driving too fast and hit a tree'. The Mallorcan authorities believed that because they 'exhibited the case as if warning people of the dangers of speeding'.

p. 335 *Oblique suggestions from SIS (MI6)*: Burns, *Use of Memory*, p. 116.

p. 335 *A source code-named Poodle*: KV 2/ 2824.

p. 337 *Every thinking Englishman*: TB's lecture to the Ateneo is in the Burns Family Archive.

p. 338 *Dr Marañón was a true sage*: Archie Roosevelt, *For Lust of Knowing*, Little, Brown, 1988), p. 414. According to Roosevelt's wife Lucky, the American spy maintained close personal ties with TB during his subsequent posting in London in the early 1960s, during which the political sex scandal known as the Profumo affair fuelled CIA concerns about

Soviet-inspired honeytraps. Roosevelt was tasked by his director, John McCone, with filing detailed daily reports on the case. In his memoirs, he wrote: 'McCone was a man who took his Catholic religion very seriously indeed, and I am sure he must have been shocked by some of the spicy items I served him.' Ibid., p. 470.

p. 339 *Franco burst into tears*: The anecdote was shared by Mabel with her family and subsequently related by her son, the author and journalist Tom Burns Marañón, during his eulogy at her remembrance service in London in September 2008.

p. 340 *swarthy, squat, Japanese appearance*: Waugh, *Diaries*, p. 643.

p. 341 *Mabel felt it a terrible abuse of her hospitality*: Mabel Burns in conversation with the author.

p. 341 *Dr Hyde, so to call the better side of Evelyn*: Burns, *Use of Memory*, p. 65.

p. 341 *I am sorry that you have come down in the world*: Ibid., p. 65.

p. 342 *These masks cracked*: Ibid., p. 65.

p. 342 *Tom Burns gave me enthralling task*: Waugh, *Diaries*, p. 700.

p. 343 *He [Greene] almost turns things upside down*: Copy of letter from TB to Waugh in Burns Family Archive.

p. 343 *the idea of willing my own damnation*: Quoted in Hastings, *Evelyn Waugh*, p. 546.

p. 343 *Graham seemed to have a spotlight on him*: Burns, *Use of Memory*, p. 58.

Select Bibliography

Archives

National Archives, Kew, London
London Library
Garrick Club archive
Ministerio de Asuntos Exteriores (Madrid)
Hemeroteca Municipal del Ayuntamiento de Madrid
Museo de Historia de Madrid
Fundación Sabino Arana
Fundación Francisco Franco
Archivo EFE
Georgetown University Library, Washington DC
John Burns Library, Boston, Mass.
National Archives, Washington DC
Fundación Marañón

Private collections

T. F. Burns papers
Mabel Marañón papers
Templewood papers, University Library, Cambridge
Conde de Fontanar papers
Sir Victor Mallet papers
Churchill Archives, Cambridge
Rosemary Say papers
Peter Laing papers
Gabriel Herbert papers
Gómez-Beare papers
Walter Bell papers

Newspapers, periodicals, academic papers

The Times
Financial Times
Hamburger Anzieger
Guardian
New York Times
Time magazine
Tablet
The Week
ABC
Journal of Art History
Historical Journal, Cambridge University Press
Studies in Intelligence, Washington, DC
Andersen, P., *In the Interests of Justice* (CUP: Contemporary European History, 2009)
Heath, D., *SIS & British Foreign Policy during the Great War* (University of Cambridge, 2002)
Benton, K., *The ISOS years* (Journal of Contemporary History, 1995)
Messenger, D., *Against the Grain: Special Operations Executive in Spain, 1941–45* (Intelligence & National Security, 2005)
Ryan, Eoin, *The Anglo-Spanish Shadow War: 1939–45* (Cambridge University draft thesis)
Smyth, D., *Diplomacy & Strategy of Survival: British Policy & Franco's Spain 1940–41* (Cambridge University Press, 1986)
Steury, D. P, *The OSS and Project Safehaven* (CIA government library)
Viswanathan, Vivek, *Final Turn: Sir Samuel Hoare in Spain* (Cambridge University draft thesis)
Wylie, N., *Special Operations* (Journal of Contemporary History, 2001)

Printed sources

Alcázar de Velasco, *Memorias de un agente secreto* (Barcelona, 1979)
Alexander, Peter, *Roy Campbell* (Oxford, 1982)
Amery, Julian, *Approach March: A Venture in Autobiography* (London, 1973)
Bacca Dowden, Mavis, *Spy-Jacked* (Frome, 1991)
Bassett, Richard, *Hitler's Spy Chief* (London, 2005)
Beesley, Patrick, *Very Special Admiral: The Life of J. H. Godfrey* (London, 1980)
Beevor, Antony, *The Battle for Spain* (London, 2006)
Beevor, J. G., *SOE* (London, 1981)
Belloc, Hilaire, *Many Cities* (London, 1920)
Bloch, Michael, *Operation Willi* (New York, 1984)
Bolín, Luis, *Spain: The Vital Years* (Philadelphia, 1967)
Bower, Tom, *The Perfect English Spy* (London, 1995)
Boyar, Jane and Burt, *Hitler Stopped by Franco* (Marbella House, 2001)
Boyle, Anthony, *The Climate of Treason* (London, 1979)
Bristow, Desmond, *A Game of Moles* (London, 1993)
Bryan, J. and Murphy, J. V., *The Windsor Story* (London, 1979)
Buchanan, Tom, *Britain and the Spanish Civil War* (Cambridge, 1997)
Buckley, Henry, *Life and Death of the Spanish Republic* (London, 1940)
Burns, Jimmy, *A Literary Companion to Spain* (London, 1994; Málaga, 2006)
— *Barça: A People's Passion* (London, 2000)
Burns Marañón, Tom, *La Monarquia necesaria* (Barcelona, 2005)
Burns, T. F., *The Use of Memory* (London, 1993)
Campbell Lyle, Anna, *Poetic Justice* (Francestown, 1986)
Campbell, Roy, *Light on a Dark Horse* (London, 1971)

Carter, Miranda, *Anthony Blunt: His Lives* (London, 2001)

Cave Brown, Anthony, *The Secret Servant* (London, 1988)

Cesarani, David, *Justice Delayed* (London, 2001)

Chapman, James, *The British at War: Cinema, State and Propaganda 1939–45* (London, 1999)

Chaves Nogales, Manuel, *Juan Belmonte, Matador de Toros* (Madrid, 1969)

Chitty, Susan, *Gwen John* (London, 1981)

Collado Seidel, Carlos, *España: Refugio Nazi* (Madrid, 2005)

Copeiro del Vilar, Jesus Ramiro, *Huelva en la Segunda Guerra Mundial* (Huelva, 1996)

Cornwell, John, *Hitler's Pope* (London, 2000)

Craig, Mary (ed.), *Woodruff at Random* (London, 1978)

Curry, John, *The Security Service 1908–1945* (London, 1999)

Dimbleby, Jonathan, *Richard Dimbleby* (London, 1977)

Dorril, Stephen, *MI6 – Fifty Years of Special Operations* (London, 2000)

— *Black Shirt* (London, 2006)

Eccles, David, *By Safe Hands* (London, 1983)

Faber, David, *Speaking for England* (London, 2007)

Finlayson, Iain, *City of the Dream* (Canada, 1992)

Foot, M. R. D., and Langley, J. M., *MI9: Escape and Evasion* (London, 1979)

Gallagher, Charles, R., *Vatican Secret Diplomacy* (London, 2008)

Gellhorn, Martha, *The View from the Ground* (London, 1989)

Gilbert, Martin, *Churchill* (London, 2000)

Gómez-Jordana, Francisco, *Milicia y Diplomacia* (Burgos, 2002)

Gómez-Santos, Marino, *Vida de Marañón* (Madrid, 1971)

Greene, Graham, *Ways of Escape* (London, 1980)

— *The Confidential Agent* (London, 2001)

Greene, Richard (ed.), *Graham Greene: A Life in Letters* (London, 2007)

Grubb, Kenneth, *The Crypts of Power* (London, 1971)

Gutierrez Rueda, Laura and Carmen, *El Hambre en el Madrid de la Guerra Civil* (Madrid, 2003)

Hastings, Adrian, *A History of English Christianity* (London, 2005)

Hastings, Selina, *Evelyn Waugh* (London, 1995)

Hayes, Carlton, *Wartime Mission in Spain* (New York, 1945)

— *The United States and Spain* (New York, 1951)

Helm, Sarah, *A Life in Secrets* (London, 2007)

Hemingway, Ernest, *Fiesta, the Sun Also Rises* (London, 1982)

— *For Whom the Bell Tolls* (London, 2005)

— *Death in the Afternoon* (London, 2007)

Hillgarth, Mary, *A Private Life* (Mallorca, 1984)

Himsley, F. H., and Simkins, C. A. G., *British Intelligence in the Second World War* (London, 1990)

Hoare, Sir Samuel, *Ambassador on Special Mission* (London, 1946)

Hooper, Walter, *C. S. Lewis: A Companion and Guide* (London, 1996)

Hough, Richard, *The Ace of Clubs* (London, 1986)

Howard, Michael, *British Intelligence in the Second World War* (London, 1990)

Howard, Ronald, *In Search of My Father* (London, 1981)

Hughes, John Emmet, *Report from Spain* (New York, 1947)

Hughes, Robert, *Goya* (London, 2003)

Irwin, Francis, *Stonyhurst War Record* (Stonyhurst, 1927)

Jacobs, Benjamin, and Pool, Eugene, *The 100 Years Secret* (Connecticut, 2002)

Jiménez de Aberasturi, Juan Carlos, *El Camino de la Libertad* (Hernani, 2006)

Jones, David (ed.), René Hague, *Dai Greatcoat* (London, 1980)

Juarez, Javier, *Juan Pujol, el espia que dermoto a Hitler* (Madrid, 2004)

— *Madrid, Londres, Berlin* (Madrid, 2005)

Kemp, Peter, *Mine Were of Trouble* (London, 1957)

Kennedy, A. L., *On Bullfighting* (London, 1999)
Le Carré, John, *The Spy Who Came in from the Cold* (London, 2005)
Lloyd-Morgan, Ceridwen (ed.), *Gwen John: Letters and Notebooks* (London, 2004)
Lorca, Federico García, *Poems* (London, 1939)
Luca de Tena, J. I., *Mis Amigos Muertos* (Barcelona, 1971)
Lysaght, Charles Edward, *Brendan Bracken* (London, 1979)
McCarthy, Fiona, *Eric Gill* (London, 1989)
Marañón, Gregorio, *Obras Completas*, vol. 2 (Madrid, 1966)
Marett, Robert, *Through the Back Door* (London, 1969)
Marnham, Patrick, *Wild Mary* (London, 2007)
Martín de Pozuelo, Eduardo, and Ellakuria, Iñaki, *La Guerra Ignorada* (Barcelona, 2008)
Martínez Nadal, Rafael, *Antonio Torres y la politica española del Foreign Office* (Madrid, 1989)
Martínez de Vicente, Patricia, *Embassy y la inteligencia de Mambru* (London, 2003)
Masterman, John, *The Double Cross System* (London, 1992)
Montagu, Ewen, *The Man Who Never Was* (London, 1953)
— *Beyond Top Secret* (London, 1977)
Montoliu, Pedro, *Madrid en la Posguerra* (Madrid, 2005)
Muir, T. E., *Stonyhurst College* (London, 1992)
Nash, Elizabeth, *Madrid* (Oxford, 2001)
Neave, Airey, *MI9* (London, 1969)
Noel, Gerard, *Pius XII, the Hound of Hitler* (London, 2008)
Ortega y Gasset, José, *Viajes y Países* (Madrid, 1957)
Orwell, George, *1984* (London, 1959)
Payne, Stanley, G, *Hitler and Franco: Spain, Germany, and World War II* (London, 2008)
Pearce, Joseph, *Bloomsbury and Beyond* (London, 2002)
— *Old Thunderer: A Life of Hilaire Belloc* (London, 2002)
Peterson, Maurice, *Both Sides of the Curtain* (London, 1950)
Philby, Kim, *My Silent War* (New York, 2003)
Pincher, Chapman, *Too Secret Too Long* (London, 1984)
Powell Fox, Rosalind, *The Grass and the Asphalt* (Cadiz, 1997)
Preston, Paul, *Doves of War* (Boston, 2002
— *Franco* (London, 1993)
— *We Saw Spain Die* (London, 2008)
Ramilla, Ivan, *Espana y los Enigmas Nazi* (Madrid, 2006)
Rankin, Nicholas, *Telegram from Guernica* (London, 2003)
Richey, Paul, *Fighter Pilot* (London, 2001)
— with Norman Franks, *Fighter Pilot's Summer* (London, 2004)
Romanones, Aline, Countess of, *The Spy Wore Red* (London, 1987)
Roosevelt, Archie, *For Lust of Knowing* (Boston, 1988)
Sánchez Soler, Mariano, *Los Banqueros de Franco* (Madrid, 2005)
— *Ricos por la guerra de España* (Madrid, 2007)
Scott-Ellis, Priscilla, *The Changes of Death* (London, 1995)
Seaman, Mark (ed.), *Garbo: The Spy Who Saved D-Day* (London, 2000)
— *Special Operations Executive: New Instrument of War* (London, 2006)
Shelden, Michael, *Graham Greene: The Man Within* (London, 1995)
Sherry, Norman, *The Life of Graham Greene* (London, 1990)
Sire, H. J. A., *Father Martin D'Arcy* (Leominster, 1997)
Smith, Eleanor, *Life's a Circus* (London, 1939)
Stafford, David, *Churchill and Secret Service* (London, 1887)
Stonor, Julia, *Sherman's Wife* (London, 2006)
Sykes, Christopher, *Evelyn Waugh* (London, 1982)
Taylor, A. J. P., *English History: 1914–1945* (London, 1981)
Taylor, D. J., *Orwell, A Life* (London, 2003)
— *Bright Young People* (London, 2008)

Thomas, Hugh, *The Spanish Civil War* (London, 1977)

Thomson, Ian, *Articles of Faith* (Oxford, 2006)

Vegas, E., *Memorias Politicas 1938–42* (Madrid, 1995)

Vicente, Ana, *Arcadia* (Lisbon, 2006)

Vickers, Hugo, *Elizabeth, The Queen Mother* (London, 2005)

Vilanova, Francesc, *La Barcelona franquista i l'Europa totalitaria* (Barcelona, 2005)

Wall, Bernard, *Headlong into Change* (London, 1969)

Waller, Maureen, *London, 1945* (London, 2005)

Walsh, Michael, *The Tablet* (London, 1990)

Waugh, Evelyn, *Diaries* (London, 1979)

— *Put Out More Flags* (London, 2000)

West, Nigel, *MI5, British Secret Service Operations 1909–1945* (London, 1981)

— *MI6, British Secret Service Operations 1909–19* (London, 1983)

— (ed.), *The Guy Liddell Diaries*, vol. 1, *1939–42* (London, 2005)

— (ed.), *The Guy Liddell Diaries*, vol. 2, *1942–45* (London, 2005)

— with Juan Pujol, *Garbo* (London, 1985)

West, W. J, *The Quest for Graham Greene* (London, 1988)

Wigg, Richard., *Churchill and Spain* (Eastbourne, 2008)

Williams, Michael E., *St Alban's College, Vallodolid* (London, 1986)

Wilson, A. N., *Hilaire Belloc* (London, 1984)

Wright, Peter, *Spy Catcher* (London, 1987)

Ximenez, José Rey, *El Vuelo de Ibis* (Madrid, 2009)

Index